JN069801

はじめて受ける人のための
TOEIC® L&R テスト
全パート対策
スピードマスター

山根　和明
Yamane Kazuaki

Jリサーチ出版

TOEIC is a registered trademark of Educational Testing Service (ETS).
This publication is not endorsed or approved by ETS.
*L&R means LISTENING and READING.

　TOEIC® テストは合格、不合格という試験でなく、初級者なら300〜500点、中級者なら600〜700点、上級者なら800点以上を狙うという分かりやすい基準で、非英語圏、特に日本や韓国を中心としたアジア圏、東欧圏で人気が高まってきました。特に韓国では、大学卒業生の大企業への就職が狭き門のため、高度な英語力が求められており、そのためには TOEIC® が格好の判断基準となり学生たちは競って予備校にまで通って TOEIC® を受験するようになり、サムスンなどの財閥企業をねらう学生たちは、900点以上は当たり前という現状です。日本ではまだそこまで過熱してはいませんが、欧米への輸出を増やしている企業や、東南アジアに生産拠点を構える企業は、英語が使えて IT に明るい学生を確保することにやっきとなっています。そんな企業は履歴書に TOEIC® の点数を要求するようになり、その**標準点**として**600点**を要求してきています。

　これはある一流企業の国際戦略部長の職にある友人の言葉ですが、「600点あれば一応 "英語は捨てていないな" というレベルだと判断する。あとはうちでネイティブ講師の英語特訓クラスで鍛えればものにな

る。だから、成績を含めて他の条件が見劣りしなければ採りますよ」と言っていました。ですから、**まず600点を確保することを目標にすること**が大切なのです（もちろん、500点や550点を基準にしている企業もありますが）。そしてこれこそが、私が600点レベルの人を育てる問題集を刊行し続けている理由の一つです。

　そしてこれまで**英語の苦手な受験生**に、私が提唱する各種戦略 "山根メソッド" を駆使して何とか600点を取らせてきました。でもそこで終わりではありません。本書で学ぶ学習法をその後も徹底練習していけば、**600点の次は700点そして800点…と取れるようになるはず**なのです。これも私が600点レベル育成の問題集を書き続ける理由の1つです。

　さあみなさん、迷いを捨てて、本書を使って、私の "聴く勉TOEIC® 講座" ワールドへ飛び込んでいらっしゃい！　こんなに分かりやすく、楽しく TOEIC® 対策の学習ではきるのですよ!!

山根 和明

CONTENTS

Chapter1　山根メソッドで ゼロから始めるパート別攻略!

英語はスポーツと同じ。ルールが分かってこそおもしろい!

リスニングセクション

Chapter1 山根メソッドで ゼロから始めるパート別攻略!

　そもそも TOEIC® L&R TEST とはどういうテストなのか、各パートの出題内容や試験本番で受験者がとるべき行動からはじまり、山根先生独自のメソッドによるパート別の戦略を習得。その直後に練習問題を解きまくることで、超効率的に実力アップ!

> この Part で使用する音声のトラック番号です。リスニングの問題音声と、山根先生の解説[聴く勉 TOEIC 講座!]が含まれます。

> そのパートの試験本番の流れと、受験者がその際に取るべき行動を解説! 特にリスニングセクションでは非常に重要!

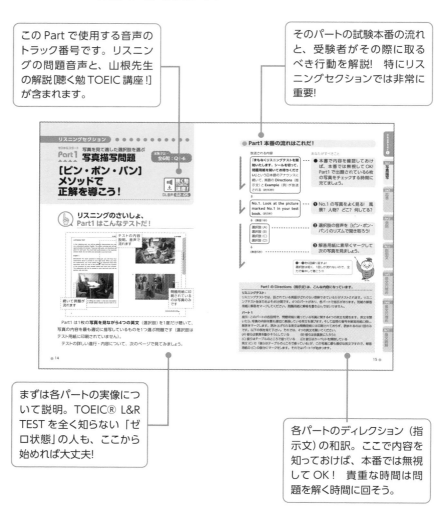

> まずは各パートの実像について説明。TOEIC® L&R TEST を全く知らない「ゼロ状態」の人も、ここから始めれば大丈夫!

> 各パートのディレクション（指示文）の和訳。ここで内容を知っておけば、本番では無視して OK! 貴重な時間は問題を解く時間に回そう。

各パートを攻略するための [山根メソッド] の解説。ゲーム感覚で楽しみながらできるものばかりなので、TOEIC 初級者にも取り組みやすい！

[山根メソッド] のまとめ。試験本番直前に見返すのもオススメ！

ここからが本番！ [山根メソッド] を学んだ直後、すぐに TOEIC 形式の練習問題に取り組むことで、実力アップに直結！

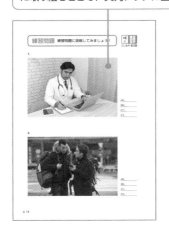

本書最大の特長のひとつ、山根先生の音声講座！ 本を見ながらしっかり聞いて復習することで、超効率的に実力が上がる！

Chapter2 完全模試にチャレンジ！ 解答・解説（本冊） 問題（別冊）

　本番と同様の完全模試1回分にチャレンジ！ 問題は別冊仕様で使いやすい！ リーディングテストは「山根メソッド」にのっとって、制限時間を設けて解いていきます（マークシートは別冊の巻末にあります）。解き終わったら必ず、本冊の解説部分を見ながら音声講座を「聴く勉」しましょう！

音声ダウンロードについて

STEP 1 商品ページにアクセス！ 方法は次の3通り！

● QRコードを読み取ってアクセス。

● https://www.jresearch.co.jp/book/b561122.html を入力してアクセス。

● Jリサーチ出版のホームページ（https://www.jresearch.co.jp/）にアクセスして、「キーワード」に書籍名を入れて検索。

STEP 2 ページ内にある「音声ダウンロード」ボタンをクリック！

STEP 3 ユーザー名「1001」、パスワード「25113」を入力！

STEP 4 音声の利用方法は2通り！ 学習スタイルに合わせた方法でお聴きください！

● 「音声ファイル一括ダウンロード」より、ファイルをダウンロードして聴く。

● ▶ボタンを押して、その場で再生して聴く。

※ダウンロードした音声ファイルは、パソコン・スマートフォンなどでお聴きいただくことができます。一括ダウンロードの音声ファイルは.zip形式で圧縮してあります。解凍してご利用ください。ファイルの解凍が上手く出来ない場合は、直接の音声再生も可能です。

音声ダウンロードについてのお問合せ先：**toiawase@jresearch.co.jp**（受付時間：平日9時〜18時）

Chapter 1

●●●●●●●●●●

山根メソッドで
ゼロから始めるパート別攻略!

まずはL=300点、R=200点 ⇒スコア500を狙う!

　手ぶらで!　ゼロから!　TOEIC 学習を始めるための、はじめの一歩となる章です。

　まずは INTRODUCTION で英語に関する最重要事項をチェック!

　次に、TOEIC® L&R TEST のそれぞれのパートについて、テストがどのように行われるのか、その進行や、その時に受験者がとるべき行動などについて学びます。

　それから、目標の600点を獲得し、その後にも英語力を伸ばせるようになるための攻略法=“山根メソッド”を知るとともに、その直後に頻出パターンの練習問題に取り組みます。答え合わせをしたら、解説ページを見ながら山根先生による音声講座 [聴く勉 TOEIC 講座!] を聞いて、しっかり復習・練習することで、まずはスコア500を狙える力をつけましょう!

INTRODUCTION　英語の基本ルール

聴く勉
TOEIC
講座！
DL音声 01

　例えばラグビーというスポーツを例に考えてみましょう。

　試合を見るにしてもルールが分かるからこそ面白く感じるわけで、ただがむしゃらに「走って、ぶつかって」を見ているだけでは、それほどの興奮はしませんよね？ **言葉だって同じです。** 基本のルール（＝文法）が分かってこそおもしろいのです。ですが、スポーツをやったり、見たりするのに、ルールから入る人はあまりいませんよね。**まずは実地体験し、その中でルールを身につけて**いきますよね。本来ならば、語学も同じでなければならないのですが、日本の英語教育はどうしても文法中心となってしまっていて、その結果、英語嫌いを量産してきているわけです。ですからこの INTRODUCTION では、ややこしい受験文法はいったん置いておいて、**本当に基本的なものだけ**を身につけていきましょう。

最重要ルール

「英語は『2つの木』でできている」とイメージする！

［A＝B］の木　　［is, am, are などの be 動詞が実る木］

現在　　I am happy now.
今幸せである

過去　　I was happy last year.
去年幸せだった

未来　　I will be happy next year.
来年幸せになるだろう

現在完了　I have been happy since last year.
去年からずっと幸せである

[A が〜する] の木　[go, want, like などの動詞が実る木]

現在	I study English every day. 毎日英語を勉強**する**
過去	I studied English last year. 去年英語を勉強**した**
未来	I'll study English next year. 来年英語を勉強**するつもりだ** [だろう]
現在完了	I've studied English for 3 years. 3年間英語を勉強**している** I've just [already] studied English. すでに英語を勉強**している** I've never studied English. 今まで英語を勉強**したことがない**

ポイント❶

重要なのは、[**進行形**(〜している;〜しようとしている)]と[**受け身**(〜される;〜されている)]になると、**すべて[Aが〜する]の木に実る**ということ。これは覚えておこう!

[進行形]

I'm studying English now.

I was studying English then.

I will be studying English tomorrow.

I've been studying English for 3 hours.

[受け身]

English is spoken in Canada.

English was spoken in Okinawa....

English will be spoken in.......

English has been spoken in.....

ポイント❷

> しかし、**進行形や受け身にできない2種類の動詞がある!**

1　動きのない動詞（like, want, know, have, see, hear など）

⇒見た目で進行してるかどうかがわからないから**進行形にできない!**
× I **am knowing** his name. ⇒〇 I **know** his name. 私は彼の名前を知っている。

2　自分が動くだけで他に働きかけない動詞
（go, come, live, sit, stand など）

⇒目的語がないから受け身にできない!
× Tokyo **is lived.**

あとはこれに will 以外の助動詞（can, may, must, shall, should）と to 不定詞（こと;べき;して;ため）と on, in, by, with などの前置詞、そして現在分詞（-ing）と過去分詞（-ed）による後ろから修飾の使い方などを知っておけば OK ですが、思い出しも兼ねて、ちょっと例文を見ておきましょう!　なお、この文法事項については、Chapter1 のPart5 攻略のところでまた出てきますので、ここではサラッと流すだけで OK!

ポイント❸

> **[助動詞]** は、動詞にさまざまなニュアンスをくっつける!

Can you stay here?　　　ここに**いられ**ますか?
Can [May] I stay here? ここに滞在**できます**か?
Must I stay here?　　　私はここにい**なければなりません**か?
Shall I stay here?　　　ここに**いよう**か?
You should stay here.　ここにいる**べき**です。

ポイント❹

[to 不定詞] は、こと・べき・して・ための4つの用法!

I like **to play** soccer. サッカー**することが**好き ⇒こと
This is a good book **to read**. これは**読むのに**良い本だ ⇒べき
I'm glad **to see** you. あなたに**お会いできて**うれしいです ⇒して
I went to the park **to see** Ken. ケンに**会うために**公園に行った ⇒ため

ポイント❺

[分詞] は、後ろから名詞を修飾する!

Look at the boy standing near the fence. 柵の近くに立っている少年
Look at the fence broken by the boy. 少年が壊した柵
Have you seen a bird singing songs? さえずっている鳥

🦉 ただし、単独の分詞なら前から修飾できる。
 例 Look at the **dancing** girl.（dancing を強く言わない）This is a **broken** glass.

ポイント❻

[前置詞] のニュアンスと [接続詞] に注目!　接続詞は、超基本の and, but, or に加えて、that, when, if, because, though の役割をつかめれば OK。あとは単語力アップに励もう!

The train is running **through** the tunnel. その列車はトンネルを走っています。
The river **between** A city **and** B city is called Tone.
A 市と B 市の間の川は利根川と呼ばれている。

I think **that** your presentation went well.
あなたのプレゼンはうまくいくと思う。

If you order in bulk, you can get a discount.
大量注文すれば、値引きしてもらえる。

ゼロからスタート
Part1
写真を見て適した選択肢を選ぶ
写真描写問題

本番では…
全6問：Q1-6

[ピン・ポン・パン]メソッドで正解を導こう！

聴く勉
TOEIC
講座！

DL音声 **02-05**

リスニングのさいしょ、Part1 はこんなテストだ！

テストの内容説明。音声で流れます

続いて例題が流れます

問題用紙に印刷されているのは写真のみです

　Part1 は1枚の**写真を見ながら4つの英文**（選択肢）を1度だけ聴いて、写真の内容を最も適切に描写しているものを1つ選ぶ問題です（選択肢はテスト用紙に印刷されていません）。

　テストの詳しい進行・内容について、次のページで見てみましょう。

Chapter ❶

Part 1 写真描写

Part 2 応答

Part 3 会話

Part 4 説明文

Part 5 短文穴埋め

Part 6 長文穴埋め

Part 7 長文読解

● Part1 本番の流れはこれだ！

放送される内容 　　　　　　　　　あなたがすべきこと

「まもなくリスニングテストを開始いたします。シールを切って、問題用紙を開いてお待ちください」という日本語のアナウンスに続いて、英語の **Directions**（指示文）と **Example**（例）が放送される《約90秒》　- - -

● 本書で内容を確認しておけば、本番では無視して OK! Part1 で出題されている6枚の写真をチェックする時間に充てましょう。

No.1. Look at the picture marked No.1 in your test book.《約5秒》　- - -

❶ No.1 の写真をよく見る！ 風景？ 人物？ どこ？ 何してる？

《無音1秒》

選択肢 (A)
選択肢 (B) - - - - - - - - - - - - - - -
選択肢 (C)
選択肢 (D)

❷ 選択肢の音声を［ピン・ポン・パン］のリズムで聞き取ろう！

《無音5秒》 - - - - - - - - - - - - - - -

❸ 解答用紙に素早くマークして次の写真を見ましょう。

❶～❸を6回繰り返すよ!
選択肢は短く、1回しか流れないので、全力で集中して聴こう !!!

Part1 の Directions（指示文）は、こんな内容になっています。

リスニングテスト：
リスニングテストでは、話されている英語がどれぐらい理解できているかがテストされます。リスニングテスト全体でおよそ45分間です。4つのパートがあり、各パートで指示があります。別紙の解答用紙に解答をマークしてください。問題用紙に解答を書き込んではいけません。

パート 1
指示：このパートの各設問で、問題用紙に載っている写真に関する4つの英文を聞きます。英文を聞いたら、写真の内容を最も適切に表現している英文を選びます。そして設問の番号を解答用紙に探し、解答をマークします。読み上げられる英文は問題用紙には印刷されておらず、読まれるのは1回のみです。以下の例を見て下さい。それでは、4つの英文を聞いてください。
(A) 彼らは家具を動かそうとしている 　　　(B) 彼らは会議室に入ろうと
(C) 彼らはテーブルのところで座っている 　(D) 彼らはカーペットを掃除している
英文 (C) の「彼らはテーブルのところで座っている」が、この写真に最も適切な英文ですので、解答用紙の (C) の部分にマークをします。それではパート1が始まります。

これが
[ピン・ポン・パン] メソッドだ！

●英語の耳を開くために知っておくべきこと

英語の聞き取りで非常に大事なことは **「リズム」をつかむこと**。音の強弱や速さなどのリズムに反応することがとても大切なのです。

まず、代名詞（they / he / she など）以外の**主語は必ず強く発音されます**。

そして、いつ、どこで、誰と、何をして…などといった、**「相手に伝えたい部分」も強く発音されます**。

たとえば、A man is holding a mobile phone.（男性が携帯電話を持っています）という英文について考えてみましょう。

A man is holding a mobile phone.

ピン	ポン	パン
誰が	～する	何を

極端に表現するとこんな感じで、「大きい単語＝強く読まれるところ」と「小さい単語＝弱く読まれるところ」が発生します（音声を聞くと、**流れるようなリズム**になっていることがよくわかります）。

これが、**「ピン・ポン・パン」**（もっと長い場合はさらに続けて「ピン・ポン・パン」）**のリズムで続く**と心得て、リズムに乗って、ゲーム感覚で、強い部分を聞きとる練習をするのが大事なのです。

●本番でも「ピン・ポン・パン」で〇×△！

試験本番でも、強いところ＝「ピン・ポン・パン」をしっかり聞いて、**写真と合っているかどうか**、判断する**だけ**です。特に動詞と名詞に注意して聞き取りの練習をすれば、初級者でも**4問**は正解できます！

ただし、**出題者はできるだけ答えを見つけにくく**しようとします。ですの

で、最後まで聞いても分からない場合も多々あります。その場合は即座に「△」として、すぐ次の選択肢に進み、「×」を出す作業に没頭！ これが戦略です。ちなみに、本試験の6問中5問目と6問目は少し長い文になります。

●特に注意すべきポイントはこれだ！

現在完了と受け身の進行形の聞き取りも、重要ポイントです。

> Dishes **have been set** on the table.
> （皿がテーブルに並べられている）
>
> Dishes **are being set** on the table.
> （皿がテーブルに並べられているところだ）

　前者は写真の中に、皿がテーブルに置かれた状態が写っていれば OK ですが、後者の場合は、**テーブルセッティングをしている人が写っていなければダメ**です。これを聞き分けて判断できるように練習を重ねましょう。

最強！解答テクニック

❶　[ピン・ポン・パン] で強く読まれる部分に集中！

❷　強く読まれる部分に１ヵ所でも間違いがあったら [×]

❸　すごく自信がある＆完全に正解だと思ったら [○]

❹　聞き取れない・わからない場合は×ではなく [△]

❺　[○] もしくは [△] の選択肢のどれかをマークする

❻　現在完了と受け身の進行形、場所を表す前置詞には特に注意！

✏本番の TOEIC L&R TEST では、問題用紙にメモを取ることは禁止されていますので、○や×を書き込むのは練習するときだけにしましょう！

Chapter ❶

Part 1 写真描写

Part 2 応答

Part 3 会話

Part 4 説明文

Part 5 短文穴埋め

Part 6 長文穴埋め

Part 7 長文読解

1.

(A)＿＿＿＿＿
(B)＿＿＿＿＿
(C)＿＿＿＿＿
(D)＿＿＿＿＿

2.

(A)＿＿＿＿＿
(B)＿＿＿＿＿
(C)＿＿＿＿＿
(D)＿＿＿＿＿

Chapter 1

Part 1
写真描写

Part 2
応答

Part 3
会話

Part 4
説明文

Part 5
短文穴埋め

Part 6
長文穴埋め

Part 7
長文読解

3.

(A)＿＿＿＿＿
(B)＿＿＿＿＿
(C)＿＿＿＿＿
(D)＿＿＿＿＿

4.

(A)＿＿＿＿＿
(B)＿＿＿＿＿
(C)＿＿＿＿＿
(D)＿＿＿＿＿

5.

(A)_____
(B)_____
(C)_____
(D)_____

6.

(A)_____
(B)_____
(C)_____
(D)_____

解答・解説

1. 正解：(D)

(A) He's **taking out** a **stethoscope.**

彼は聴診器を取り出そうとしている。　　　　　➡️✕

(B) He's **pointing** at the **writing pad.**

彼は筆記パッドを指さしている。　　　　　➡️✕

(C) He's **looking** at the **picture** on the **table.**

彼はテーブルの写真を見ている。　　　　　➡️✕

(D) He's **wearing** a **lab coat.**

彼は白衣（研究室着）を着ている。　　　　　➡️◯

> **ポイント** 4文とも「人」が主語⇒すべて動作に注目！

2. 正解：(A)

(A) One **man** is **holding** a **mobile phone.**

一人の男性が携帯電話を握っている。　　　　➡️◯

(B) They're **talking** on the **phone.**

彼らは電話で話している。　　　　　➡️✕

(C) A **mobile phone** is **being polished.**

携帯電話が磨かれているところだ。　　　　➡️✕

(D) A **tall guy** is **putting** on a **fur scarf.**

背の高い男性が毛皮の襟巻きを巻こうとしている。　➡️✕

> **ポイント** 人物写真は行動＝現在進行形と身構えよう。

 語句 ❑**beverage** =drink　❑**put on**　〜を身につける（動作）
❑**wear**　　〜を身につける（状態）

Chapter ❶

Part 1 写真描写

Part 2 応答

Part 3 会話

Part 4 説明文

Part 5 短文穴埋め

Part 6 長文穴埋め

Part 7 長文読解

3. 正解：(B)

(A) The **man** is **hugging** a little **girl**.
男性は小さな女の子を抱きしめている。　➡×

(B) There's a **picture hanging** on the **wall** behind them.
彼らの背後に写真が掛かっている。　➡○

(C) The **woman** is **sharing** a **laptop** with the man.
女性は男性とノートブックパソコンを共有 (シェア) している。➡×

(D) They're **smiling** in a **conference room**.
彼らは会議室でほほ笑んでいる。　➡×

ポイント ちょっとひっかけ問題。人にだけ注目してしまうとキケン！

語句 □hold 掴む　□fold 畳む

4. 正解：(C)

(A) **Pedestrians** are **walking** up and down the **street**.
歩行者たちが通りを上がったり下がったりしている。　➡×

(B) The **bus** has been **caught** in a **traffic jam**.
バスが渋滞にはまっている。　➡×

(C) **All** the **vehicles** are in the **same direction**.
すべての車輌は同じ方角に向いている。　➡○

(D) A number of **people** are **waiting** for **taxis**.
数多くの人々がタクシーを待っている。　➡×

ポイント 「〜の方角に」は to でなく in なので注意。be caught[stuck] in a traffic jam

5. 正解 : (D)

(A) A **bench** is being **cleaned.**
ベンチが清掃されているところだ。 →×

(B) A **woman** is **proceeding** to the **departure gate.**
女性が出発ゲートに進んでいる。 →×

(C) A **jet plane** is **ready** to **take** off.
ジェット機が離陸しようとしている。 →×

(D) A **suitcase** has been **placed** on the **floor.**
スーツケースが床に置かれている。 →○

ポイント be + -ing に注意！ また、has been + 過去分詞の聞き取りにも注意！

6. 正解 : (B)

(A) They're **exiting** the **meeting room.**
彼らは会議室を出ようとしている。 →×

(B) **One man** is **using** a **computer** while **talking.**
一人の男性が話しながらパソコンを使っている。 →○

(C) They're **lifting glasses** with **water.**
彼ら水の入ったコップを掲げている。 →×

(D) They're **facing** the **computer** on the **table.**
彼らはテーブルのパソコンの方を向いている。 →×

ポイント 進行形の動詞が聞きとれていれば正解が導き出せる問題

語句 ❑**exit** 出口；出る ❑**hold** 保持している ❑**face** ～の方を向く

● ● ● ● ● ● ● ● ● ● ● ● ●

ゼロからスタート Part2

設問を聞いて適した答えを選ぶ
応答問題

本番では…
全25問：Q7-31

出題パターンは6パターン！
[○×△ゲーム]で
5W1Hは絶対取ろう！

聴く勉
TOEIC
講座！
DL音声 **04-15**

Q⇒Aのシンプル構造、
Part2 はこんなテストだ！

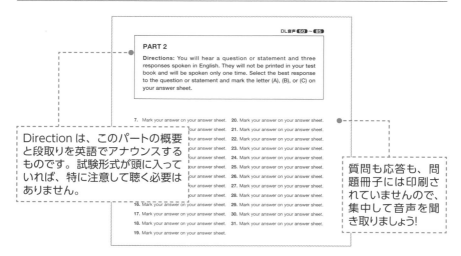

DL音声 60 ~ 85

PART 2

Directions: You will hear a question or statement and three responses spoken in English. They will not be printed in your test book and will be spoken only one time. Select the best response to the question or statement and mark the letter (A), (B), or (C) on your answer sheet.

7. Mark your on your answer sheet. 20. Mark your answer on your answer sheet.
   our answer sheet. 21. Mark your answer on your answer sheet.
   our answer sheet. 22. Mark your answer on your answer sheet.
   our answer sheet. 23. Mark your answer on your answer sheet.
   our answer sheet. 24. Mark your answer on your answer sheet.
   our answer sheet. 25. Mark your answer on your answer sheet.
   our answer sheet. 26. Mark your answer on your answer sheet.
   our answer sheet. 27. Mark your answer on your answer sheet.
   our answer sheet. 28. Mark your answer on your answer sheet.
16. Mark your answer on your answer sheet. 29. Mark your answer on your answer sheet.
17. Mark your answer on your answer sheet. 30. Mark your answer on your answer sheet.
18. Mark your answer on your answer sheet. 31. Mark your answer on your answer sheet.
19. Mark your answer on your answer sheet.

Direction は、このパートの概要と段取りを英語でアナウンスするものです。試験形式が頭に入っていれば、特に注意して聴く必要はありません。

質問も応答も、問題冊子には印刷されていませんので、集中して音声を聞き取りましょう！

　Part2 は、**1つの質問（または発言）と、3つの応答がそれぞれ1度だけ**放送されます。問題冊子には、**質問も応答も印刷されていません。** 音声を聞いて、質問（発言）に対して最も適切な応答を選びます。

Chapter❶

Part 1 写真描写

Part 2 応答

Part 3 会話

Part 4 説明文

Part 5 短文穴埋め

Part 6 長文穴埋め

Part 7 長文読解

● Part2 本番の流れはこれだ!

放送される内容　　　　　　　　　　あなたがすべきこと

英語の **Directions**（指示文）が
放送される《約30秒》

- - -

● Part1 とは違い、特にすることはありません。25 問立て続けにこなさなくてはなりませんので、まずはリラックスして、Part1 で働かせた頭をクールダウン。

↓

No.7 の質問文《約5秒》

- - - - - - - - -

● 質問文の最初の1語を確実に聞き取れるように集中しましょう!　どの出題パターンかな?

↓《無音1秒》

応答 (A)
応答 (B)
応答 (C)

- - - - - - - - - - -

● [○×△ゲーム] 感覚で聞き取ろう!

↓《無音5秒》

- - - - - - - - - -

● 解答用紙に素早くマーク

No.8 の質問文が始まる…

全部で25問だよ!
放送は1回しか流れないので、
全力で集中して聴こう!!!

Part2 の Directions（指示文）は、こんな内容になっています。

パート2

指示：英語で話される質問もしくは発言と、それに対する3つの応答文を聞きます。問題用紙には印刷されておらず、放送は1回のみ流れます。質問や発言に対する最も適切な応答文を選び、解答用紙（A）、(B)または（C）の文字にマークしてください。

[パターン見抜き] &
[○×△ゲーム] で攻略せよ!

全25問（設問7〜31）のこのパートは、1つの質問もしくは発言に対して応答（選択肢）が3つ、それぞれ一度だけ聞き、最も適切な応答を1つ選びます。質問も応答も印刷されていません。集中して耳を澄まして、**質問 [発言] のパターンを見抜き、[○×△ゲーム感覚] で攻略**するのが基本です。

●まずは6つのパターンを知り、見抜こう!

そして、このパートで出される質問 [発言] は、**6つのパターン**に分類できます。これをしっかり**把握**することが、Part2 攻略の**第一歩**です。

設問を聞いてどのパターンなのかを見抜き、続いて放送される応答 (選択肢) を聞いて、その質問や発言への応答として**ふさわしくない**内容を含む選択肢に「×」を、**わからないものに「△」**をつけましょう。すると、**合っている&残っているもの**が正解となります!

リスニングテストにおいて、質問 [発言] の英文に含まれる単語と同じ発音、もしくは似た発音に聞こえる単語が選択肢に出てきたら要注意です!
これはミスを誘うために仕組まれた、別の意味の単語である可能性があるのです。これを distractor と言いますが、山根メソッドでは double sound trick、略して「ダブトリ」と呼びます。頼りすぎるのは危険ですが、答えがわからないときの " 奥の手 " として覚えておき、解答の根拠にするといいでしょう。

Chapter 1

Part 1 写真描写

Part 2 応答

Part 3 会話

Part 4 説明文

Part 5 短文穴埋め

Part 6 長文穴埋め

Part 7 長文読解

パターン 1 絶対取りたい！ 5W1H 問題！

これは **When**（いつ）／ **Where**（どこ）／ **Who**（だれ）／ **What**（なに）／ **Why**（なぜ）／ **How**（どう）で始まる疑問文です。**Yes/ No で答えられない**質問文ですね。

Part2 ではこのパターンが**最も多く**出題され、また、**最もやさしい**ので、落とさないように頑張りましょう!

特に When ／ Where ／ Who ／ How の **"3W1H"** の設問は**超狙い目**ですよ!

最強！解答テクニック

❶ 「いつ」「どこで」「だれ」「なに」「なぜ」「どのように」を表す最初の疑問詞に注目！

❷ Yes/No の答えはない！

練習問題 練習問題に挑戦してみましょう！

練習問題音声

DL音声 05

1. (A) ＿＿＿ (B) ＿＿＿ (C) ＿＿＿
2. (A) ＿＿＿ (B) ＿＿＿ (C) ＿＿＿
3. (A) ＿＿＿ (B) ＿＿＿ (C) ＿＿＿
4. (A) ＿＿＿ (B) ＿＿＿ (C) ＿＿＿
5. (A) ＿＿＿ (B) ＿＿＿ (C) ＿＿＿
6. (A) ＿＿＿ (B) ＿＿＿ (C) ＿＿＿
7. (A) ＿＿＿ (B) ＿＿＿ (C) ＿＿＿

....

✎本番の TOEIC L&R TEST では、問題用紙にメモを取ることは禁止されていますので、○や×を書き込むのは練習するときだけにしましょう!

解答・解説

DL音声 06

1. 正解：(A)

🇺🇸 W → 🇬🇧 M

Where is the best place to park near your office?
貴方の事務所の近くで駐車するベストな場所はどこですか？

(A) At a vacant lot behind the library.
図書館の裏手の空き地です。

(B) Yes, we can see the park from my office.
はい、私の事務所からその公園は見えます。

(C) Usually on Sundays.　普通日曜日です。

ポイント Where の質問なので場所で答える。Yes/No では答えられない。時 ((C) の Sunday) では答えられない。

2. 正解：(B)

🇬🇧 W → 🇨🇦 M

How many masks will be delivered to the hospital?
病院に何枚のマスクが配達されますか？

(A) I don't think that's enough.
それが十分だとは思いません。

(B) More than 100,000, I hope.
10万枚以上だと良いですね。

(C) We delivered them last week.
先週それらを配達しました。

ポイント How many と数を尋ねている。(A) は意見を述べている。(C) は When..? の答えなので不正解。

3. 正解：(B)

🇦🇺 M → 🇺🇸 W

How can I tell when the Shinkansen will start running again?
新幹線が運行をいつ再開するのかどうやってわかりますか？

(A) I know it runs very fast.
それはとても速く走ります。

(B) Just take a look at their website.
そのウエブサイト（ホームページ）をただ見てください。

(C) Yes, it's punctual to the minute.
はい、それは1分もたがえません。

ポイント 問題分の tell は「告げる」でなく「分かる / 判断する」だからその方法を答えている。5W1H 型だから (C) の Yes/No は×！

● 28

4. 正解：(C) ⸻⸻⸻ 🇺🇸 M → 🇦🇺 M

When **does the September issue come out?** 　9月号はいつ出ますか？

(A) October comes next. 　次は10月が来ます。

(B) Sorry, we're completely sold out.
申し訳ございません。すべて売り切れました。

(C) At the end of August, I think.
8月の終わりだと思います。

⸻⸻⸻⸻

🔖ポイント When のなので時だ。issue は「発行物」のこと。他にも話し合いなどの「問題」の意味がある重要語。

5. 正解：(B) ⸻⸻⸻ 🇬🇧 M → 🇺🇸 W

Which **of these photos do you prefer?** 　この写真のどれを (より) 好みますか？

(A) Yes, they are great. 　はい、それらはすばらしい。

(B) The one I took on the beach. 　私が浜辺で撮ったやつです。

(C) In front of the station. 　駅の前に。

⸻⸻⸻⸻

🔖ポイント Which? (どれ) と尋ねているから (A) の Yes/No は×。(C) の in front of (前に) とは Where? の答えだ。

6. 正解：(B) ⸻⸻⸻ 🇨🇦 M → 🇬🇧 W

Who**'s making a speech at the luncheon?** 　昼食会ではだれがスピーチをしますか？

(A) Ms. Ohara is making salad for lunch.
Ms. Ohara が昼食にサラダを作ります。

(B) It's the founder of our organization.
うちの協会の創設者です。

(C) By practicing it in English.
英語でそれを練習することによって。

⸻⸻⸻⸻

🔖ポイント Who...? と尋ねられているが、(A) と早とちりしないこと(Ms. Ohara is. なら〇)。(C) は How...? の定番の答え方。

7. 正解：(C) ⸻⸻⸻ 🇺🇸 W → 🇬🇧 W

Why **did the delivery person come so late?** 　配達員はなぜこんなに遅く来たの？

(A) Because he wanted to be on time.
なぜなら、彼は時間通りに来たかった。

(B) No, he wasn't late.
いいえ、彼は遅れなかった。

(C) He said he was stuck in traffic.
彼は交通渋滞に巻き込まれたと言った。

⸻⸻⸻⸻

🔖ポイント why は理由を尋ねる疑問視。しかし、because (なぜなら) があるからといっていつも正解とは限らない！

Chapter ❶

Part 1 写真描写

Part 2 応答

Part 3 会話

Part 4 説明文

Part 5 短文穴埋め

Part 6 長文穴埋め

Part 7 長文読解

次に点を狙えるのがこのパターン。A なのか B なのか、**どちらかを選択する**ことが要求される問題です。

例えば Tea or coffee? とたずねられたら、Tea. ／ Coffee. ／ Both. ／ Either. ／ Neither. ／ Milk... など、**複数の回答候補**が瞬時に考えられます。なお、**Yes/No では答えられない**ので、万が一選択肢に入っていたら即「×」です。

最強！解答テクニック

❶ A か B かのどちらかだけでなく、「両方」「どっちでも」「どっちもなし」など、複数の答えを想定すべし！

❷ Yes/No の答えだけは絶対にない！

練習問題 練習問題に挑戦してみましょう！

DL音声 **07**

1. (A) _____ (B) _____ (C) _____
2. (A) _____ (B) _____ (C) _____
3. (A) _____ (B) _____ (C) _____
4. (A) _____ (B) _____ (C) _____

....

🖐本番の TOEIC L&R TEST では、問題用紙にメモを取ることは禁止されていますので、○や×を書き込むのは練習するときだけにしましょう！

解答・解説

1. 正解：(A)　🇬🇧 M → 🇨🇦 M

Are you going to Hokkaido by train or by plane?
北海道へは電車でそれとも飛行機で行かれますか？

(A) You know I don't like flying.　私飛ぶのは好きじゃないのよね。

(B) It costs a lot of money.　多くのお金がかかります。

(C) Yes, the best season there is summer.
　　はい、そちらの最高の季節は夏です。

> **ポイント** 正解の (A) では「飛行機」＝「空を飛ぶ」と言い換えている。A or B の質問に Yes/No は×なので (C) は即座に不正解とわかる。

2. 正解：(C)　🇺🇸 M → 🇺🇸 W

Do you want me to fix lunch for you or cater a box lunch?
あなたにお昼ご飯作りましょうか、それともお弁当を取りましょうか？

(A) I'm certain it can be fixed.　それは修理できると確信しています。

(B) By sending an e-mail.　E-メールを送信することで。

(C) Do you know a good caterer around here?
　　この近くに良い仕出し屋さんを知っている？

> **ポイント** (C) はお弁当を取りたい気持ちが出ている。(B) は How...? の答えの定番！

3. 正解：(A)　🇦🇺 M → 🇬🇧 W

Would you like to reserve a room with a queen-size bed or with a king-size one?
セミダブルベッドの部屋を予約なさりたいですか、それともダブルベッドの部屋を？

(A) I prefer a larger one.　大きい方がいいですね。

(B) I'd like to pay a visit to their castle.　彼らのお城に訪れたいですね。

(C) Yes, that would be fine.　はい、それはすてきでしょうね。

> **ポイント** queen-size bed = semi-double bed です。また、king-size bed = double bed です。

4. 正解：(B)　🇬🇧 M → 🇨🇦 M

Is the road being repaired in June or in July?
道路は6月に修復されるのですか、それとも7月ですか？

(A) It rains a lot more in June.　6月にはもっと雨が降ります。

(B) Actually, it's in August.　実は、8月なのですよ。

(C) Sorry, it is not.　申し訳ない、それは違います。

> **ポイント** A or B の答え方には、複数のパターンが考えられます。必ずしも質問文に入っている A や B であるとは限りません。

Chapter ❶

Part 1 写真描写

Part 2 応答

Part 3 会話

Part 4 説明文

Part 5 短文穴埋め

Part 6 長文穴埋め

Part 7 長文読解

パターン 3　実はクセ者！　Yes/No 疑問文！

　例えば Do you like baseball?（野球は好きですか）のような、通常、Yes/No で答えることができる疑問文です。「単純疑問文型」とも呼ばれます。

　中学英語でもまず最初に習う形の疑問文ですので、一見簡単そうに見えますが、TOEIC® で出される選択肢では、**わざと Yes/No が省かれることが多く、練習が必要**となってきますので、パターン2よりもむしろ少しハードルが高いかもしれません。

最強！解答テクニック

❶　簡単そうに見えて、実はクセ者！

❷　Yes/No の応答文が正解とは限らない。

❸　Yes/No を補って答えるイメージと心得よう！

練習問題 練習問題に挑戦してみましょう！

DL音声 09

1.　(A) _____ (B) _____ (C) _____
2.　(A) _____ (B) _____ (C) _____
3.　(A) _____ (B) _____ (C) _____
4.　(A) _____ (B) _____ (C) _____
5.　(A) _____ (B) _____ (C) _____
6.　(A) _____ (B) _____ (C) _____

🖊本番の TOEIC L&R TEST では、問題用紙にメモを取ることは禁止されていますので、〇や×を書き込むのは練習するときだけにしましょう！

Chapter ①

Part 1 写真描写

Part 2 応答

Part 3 会話

Part 4 説明文

Part 5 短文穴埋め

Part 6 長文穴埋め

Part 7 長文読解

解答・解説

聴く勉 TOEIC 講座！
DL音声 10

1. 正解：(B)

🇺🇸 M → 🇦🇺 M

Do you have time to review these figures?
これらの数値を検討する時間はありますか。

(A) This hotel commands a fine view.
このホテルは素晴らしい景色を見晴らせます。

(B) No problem.
大丈夫です［お安い御用ですよ］。

(C) I forgot to bring my watch with me.
時計を持って来ることを忘れました。

> **ポイント** Yes, I do. を、好意を込めて言う表現。(A) は review と view のダブトリですね。

2. 正解：(C)

🇺🇸 W → 🇬🇧 M

Did you hear Melissa was recognized for her work with an award?
Melissa が仕事に対して賞を持って表彰されたのを知ってる？

(A) Yes, she walks very very fast.
はい、彼女はとても速く歩きます。

(B) At the conference.
会議において。

(C) For her outstanding leadership?
彼女の並外れたリーダーシップで？

> **ポイント** Did you ～？つまり Yes/No で答えるタイプの疑問文だからといって、(A) の Yes に飛びつかないこと！

🇬🇧 W → 🇨🇦 M

3. 正解：(A)

Is George going to pick up the clients this time?
George は今回顧客を迎えに行きますか？

(A) No, it's my turn.
いいえ、私の番です。

(B) He already picked up his air ticket.
彼は既に自分の切符を受け取りました。

(C) When are you going there?
あなたはいつそこへ行きますか？

> **ポイント** ていねいに言うと、No, he isn't. I'm going to pick up... という意味だから正解。

4. 正解：(B) ▓▓ W → ▨▨ M

Do you **know if Bob is going to submit a proposal for funding?**
あなたは Bob が資金調達の提言書を提出するかどうか知っていますか？

(A) Yes, it was refunded yesterday.
　　　はい、それは昨日返金されました。

(B) I haven't heard the announcement yet.
　　　私はまだアナウンスを聞いていません。

(C) No, he isn't going by subway.
　　　いいえ、彼は地下鉄では行きません。

> **ポイント** I don't know. に代表される、「無責任アンサー」シリーズのひとつ。

5. 正解：(C) ▓▓ M → ▨▨ M

Is there **a manual for this photo copier around here?**
この辺りにこのコピー機の使用説明書がありますか？

(A) Yes, it requires some manual labor.
　　　はい、それは少しの手作業が必要です。

(B) You need some more copy paper for it.
　　　それにはもう少しコピー用紙が必要です。

(C) Oh, I saw it on that shelf.
　　　ええ、あの棚の上に見ましたよ。

> **ポイント** 説明書のある場所を知りたがっているので、(C) が正解。

6. 正解：(B) ▓▓ M → ▨▨ W

Have many customers **responded to our survey?**
我々の調査に何人の客が応答してくれましたか？

(A) We sell custom-built cars to young people.
　　　私共は若者へカスタムカーを売っています。

> **語句** ❑ **custom-built** 注文に応じて作られた

(B) Quite a few did it.
　　　かなりの者がそうしました。

(C) No, not too many people.
　　　いいえ、それほど多くの人々ではありません。

> **ポイント** quite a few は「全く少し」ではなく「かなりの数の」という意味 (a few が肯定だから)。

Chapter ❶

Part 1 写真描写

Part 2 応答

Part 3 会話

Part 4 説明文

Part 5 短文穴埋め

Part 6 長文穴埋め

Part 7 長文読解

パターン 4 **依頼、誘い、提案、許可の特殊疑問文！**

Would you...? ／ **Could you...?** ／ **Can you...?** ／ **Can I...?** ／ **Shall I...?** ／ **How about...?** ／ **Why don't you [we]...?** ／ **Do you want me to...?** などの表現で、誘いや依頼、提案、許可などを表す疑問文です。このパターンの疑問文の場合、答えが Yes の場合は、「**喜んで**」という気持ちを表す言葉が続く応答文が、断る場合は No ではなく、**Sorry** から始めて相手に対して**申し訳ない**という気持ちを表す応答文が多く出てきます。

最強！解答テクニック

❶ [A or B] パターンと組み合わさった質問文もある。

❷ Yes の場合は「喜んで」、No の場合は「申し訳ない」の気持ちで表現することもある。

練習問題 練習問題に挑戦してみましょう！

DL音声 **11**

1. (A) _____ (B) _____ (C) _____
2. (A) _____ (B) _____ (C) _____
3. (A) _____ (B) _____ (C) _____
4. (A) _____ (B) _____ (C) _____
5. (A) _____ (B) _____ (C) _____
6. (A) _____ (B) _____ (C) _____
7. (A) _____ (B) _____ (C) _____

....
🖊本番の TOEIC L&R TEST では、問題用紙にメモを取ることは禁止されていますので、〇や×を書き込むのは練習するときだけにしましょう！

解答・解説

1. 正解：(C)

Can I see your passport?
パスポートを拝見してもいいですか?

(A) Yes, you can.
はい、できます。

(B) None of your business.
大きなお世話です。

(C) Sure.
もちろんです。

> **ポイント** 空港などの係官の決まり文句。(A) も文法的には正しいが、この疑問文では能力を聞いているわけではないのでおかしい。

2. 正解：(A)

Would you help me arrange a company retreat?
会社の慰安旅行の手配 [準備] を手伝っていただけますか?

(A) With pleasure.
喜んで。

(B) No, I wouldn't visit the office.
いいえ、私はそのオフィスをどうしても訪問しませんでした。

(C) From our supplier
我が社の業者さんから

> **ポイント** Would you...? は、丁寧なお願い、提案、誘いを表します。

3. 正解：(C)

Could you measure the room before we order the furniture?
その家具を注文する前に部屋の寸法を計っていただけますか?

(A) Yes, please go ahead.
ええ、どうぞお先に。

(B) Why don't you major in finance?
財務を専攻したらどうですか?

(C) Sure, I can take care of that.
もちろん、私が面倒見ましょう。

> **ポイント** Could you...? は「~していただけますか?」とていねいに依頼する表現。(B) は measure と major のダブトリ。

Chapter ❶

Part 1 写真描写

Part 2 応答

Part 3 会話

Part 4 説明文

Part 5 短文穴埋め

Part 6 長文穴埋め

Part 7 長文読解

4. 正解：(B)

Would you like me to book a single room for you?

シングルのお部屋お取り致しましょうか？

(A) Yes, I want to get some books.

はい、少し本を手に入れたいです。

(B) If you don't mind.　もし、差し支えなければ。

(C) Whatever you like.　お好きなもの何でも。

ポイント Would you like me to...? は米語表現で Shall I...? で提案を表す。

5. 正解：(B)

How can I tell if the heater is running out of kerosene?

ヒーターの灯油が切れかかっているかどうかどうやって分かりますか？

(A) Eighteen liters, I think.

18リットルだと思います。

(B) This light here will turn red.

ここにあるこのライトが赤くなります。

(C) You can tell me to do it.

あなたは私にそれをするよう言えますよ。

ポイント やり方を知りたがっている。tell は「判断する」という意味。

6. 正解：(A)

How about strolling along the beach after dinner?

夕食後浜辺を散策するのはいかがですか？

(A) That's what I wanted to say.

それって私が言いたかったことです。

(B) No, I didn't go to the beach.

いいえ、私は浜辺には行きませんでした。

(C) By using a long board　長い板を使うことで

ポイント How about ... ?（〜はいかがですか）と、提案・誘いを受けている。

7. 正解：(C)

Why don't you outsource this outdoor gear to a Chinese company?

このアウトドア用品を中国の会社に外注したらどうですか？

(A) Because I've been there many times.

なぜなら、私はそこへ何度も行ったことがあります。

(B) We've set up a new manufacturing outfit in China.

我々は中国に新しい製造チームを立ち上げた。

(C) That's a great idea.　それはよい考えですね。

ポイント Why don't you...? も How about -ing? も What do you say to〜? も大体同じ。

Aren't you...?/ Didn't you...?/ Haven't you...? のような**否定疑問文**や、例えば It's a beautiful day, **isn't it**? のような**付加疑問文**やで質問されるパターンで、多くの日本人が苦手とするパターンです。この例文の場合、「いい天気ですね、そうではありませんか?」のように和訳するのではなく、「**〜だよね?**」つまり「いい天気**だよね?**」ととらえると、わかりやすくなります。否定疑問文でも同様です。

　質問文で述べられている内容（上記の例文だと It's a beautiful day, の部分）=**事実をよく聞きとって**、それに対して正しく反応している応答文を選ぶ必要があります。

最強！解答テクニック

❶ すべて「〜だよね?」だととらえよう!

❷ 質問文内の事実をしっかり聞き取って応答を選ぼう!

練習問題 練習問題に挑戦してみましょう!

DL音声 **13**

1. (A) _____ (B) _____ (C) _____
2. (A) _____ (B) _____ (C) _____
3. (A) _____ (B) _____ (C) _____
4. (A) _____ (B) _____ (C) _____
5. (A) _____ (B) _____ (C) _____

....

✎本番の TOEIC L&R TEST では、問題用紙にメモを取ることは禁止されていますので、○や×を書き込むのは練習するときだけにしましょう!

解答・解説

Chapter ❶

Part 1 写真描写

Part 2 応答

Part 3 会話

Part 4 説明文

Part 5 短文穴埋め

Part 6 長文穴埋め

Part 7 長文読解

聴く勉 TOEIC 講座！ DL音声 **14**

1 正解：(C) ▇▇ W → ▨▨ M

You've operated this machine before, haven't you?
以前にこの機械を操作したことあるんだよね？

(A) No, it's not so easy. いいえ、それはそんなに簡単ではありません。
(B) How long have you worked on it? あなたはそれにどのくらい取り組んでいますか？
(C) Yes, but a long time ago. ええ、でもずっと以前です。

ポイント 「〜はありませんね？」としないで、「〜だよね？」と反応すること。

2 正解：(B) ▨▨ W → I◆I M

It's a beautiful day, isn't it? 良い天気ですよね？

(A) Yes, it's unstable weather. ええ、一定しない天候です。
(B) Yes, it really is. ええ、本当にそうですね。
(C) Only weekdays. 平日にのみです。

ポイント 挨拶の決まり文句。「…ですよね？」と反応すること！

3 正解：(C) ▇▇ M → ▨▨ M

Don't you **think we should take an umbrella?** 傘持って行った方が良いと思いますよね？

(A) I prefer a folding umbrella. 私は折り畳み傘の方が好きです。
(B) Let's buy take-out food here. ここでテイクアウトの食べ物を買いましょう。
(C) Is it supposed to rain? 雨が降りそうですか？

ポイント 「傘を持って行く方がよい」とは、「雨が降るかも知れないから…」と符合する。

4 正解：(C) ▨▨ M → ▇▇ W

Wasn't the meeting **supposed to last only one hour?**
会合は 1 時間しか続かないことになっていたんだよね？

(A) No way! だめだよ！
(B) Yes, we were supposed to be here. ええ、私たちはここに来ることになっています。
(C) I thought it was. そうだと思っていました。

ポイント (C) の冒頭は、Yes が省略されている。

5 正解：(A) I◆I M → ▨▨ W

Haven't you **put forward the budget yet?** もう、予算提示したんだよね？

(A) I'm already done. 私はすでにしましたよ。
(B) You'd better reduce expenditures. 支出を減らした方が良い。
(C) Yes, I look forward to seeing you soon. ええ、まもなくお会いできるのが楽しみです。

ポイント 「〜したのではありませんか？」と反応したらだめ！ (A) は Yes. I'm... のこと。

質問文ではなく、話し手が**意見や感想**を述べる文。

質問されているわけではないので、疑問詞などのヒントがあるわけではなく、**聞き取れないと正解がわからない**。つまりこのパートでいちばんの**難問**になります。

聞き取れないと答えがわからないパターンではありますが、以下のテクニックで点が取れる可能性もありますので、頭の隅に入れておきましょう。

最強！解答テクニック

❶ **最難関**のパターン。聞き取れなかったら答えられない。

❷ ただし次のテクニックで正解が取れるかも！

　　▼ Yes/No の答えは捨てる！

　　▼ 5W1H の答えは捨てる！

　　▼「ダブトリ」があったらそれを捨てる！！

練習問題 練習問題に挑戦してみましょう！

DL音声 **15**

1. (A) _____ (B) _____ (C) _____
2. (A) _____ (B) _____ (C) _____
3. (A) _____ (B) _____ (C) _____
4. (A) _____ (B) _____ (C) _____
5. (A) _____ (B) _____ (C) _____
6. (A) _____ (B) _____ (C) _____

✎本番の TOEIC L&R TEST では、問題用紙にメモを取ることは禁止されていますので、○や×を書き込むのは練習するときだけにしましょう！

解答・解説

Part 1 写真描写

Part 2 応答

Part 3 会話

Part 4 説明文

Part 5 短文穴埋め

Part 6 長文穴埋め

Part 7 長文読解

1. 正解：(C) ·· 🇦🇺 M ➡ 🇺🇸 M

The zoo offers a free parking ticket to a family.

その動物園は家族客に無料の駐車券を提供している。

(A) Yes, they are.

ええ、彼らはそうです。

(B) I'm afraid there isn't a park there.

そこには公園はないと思います。

(C) That's really convenient for us.

それって私たちには本当に好都合ですね。

....

ポイント (B) は parking（駐車場）と park（公園）のダブトリ。(C) は、駐車が無料だと、子供を連れて気楽に行けるなど話し手の都合が見える。

2. 正解：(C) ·· 🇺🇸 W ➡ 🇬🇧 W

There's a charge for two digital cameras on this invoice.

この請求書には2つのデジカメの請求料金がある。

(A) Did you get my voicemail message?

私のボイスメールの伝言届いていますか？

(B) I don't have small change.

小銭がありません。

(C) That must be incorrect.

それは間違っているに違いないです。

....

ポイント (A) は invoice（請求書）と voicemail（ボイスメール）のダブトリ。(C) は請求書に自分の知らない charge（課金）がなされているという背景が見える。

3. 正解：(B) ·· 🇨🇦 M ➡ 🇬🇧 M

The paint I want to buy is out of stock now.

私の買いたい塗料がいま在庫切れだ。

(A) Just put it on the shelf.

ただ棚の上に置いてください。

(B) Would you like a rain check?

購入予約券が要りますか？

(C) You bought some stocks, didn't you?

あなたは株を少し買いましたよね。

....

ポイント (B) は在庫切れの場合、再入荷したら購入したいという場合に予約をするから正解とわかる。(C) は stock（在庫）と stocks（株）のダブトリ。

4. 正解：(C)

I think we should increase public investment in education n 🇺🇸 M → 🇦🇺 M
今は教育に公共投資を増やすべきだと思う。

(A) Yes, educational expenses are increasing.
えぇ、教育費は増加しています。

(B) At a famous private high school
有名な私立高校で

(C) I couldn't agree more.
大賛成です。

ポイント (C) は「これ以上の同意はできないでしょう」という仮定法の表現。

5. 正解：(A)

I need to buy a new mobile phone. 🇺🇸 M → 🇬🇧 M
新しい携帯電話を買いたいな。

(A) You are buying one again?
また1つ買うの?

(B) He is very old.
彼はとても年老いている。

(C) That's my extension number.
それは私の内線番号です。

ポイント 「1つ持っているのに、また?」という気持ちが込められています。

6. 正解：(A)

I have to call the building manager about a leak in the roof. 🇦🇺 M → 🇬🇧 W
屋根の雨漏りについて建物管理者に電話しなくっちゃ。

(A) Are you still having problems?
まだ問題があるの?

(B) Are they raising the rent?
彼らは家賃を値上げするの?

(C) They've built a lot of houses here.
彼らはここに多くの家を建てた。

ポイント leak（漏れ）はやっかいなこと。多分その部屋には他にも問題があったのだろうと推察できる。

Chapter❶

Part 1 写真描写

Part 2 応答

Part 3 会話

Part 4 説明文

Part 5 短文穴埋め

Part 6 長文穴埋め

Part 7 長文読解

リスニングセクション

ゼロからスタート
Part3 ▲▲▲▲

会話文を聞いて内容についての質問に答える

会話問題

本番では…
全39問：Q32-70

[24秒先読み攻撃＆
待ち伏せ作戦]で
正解へたどり着け！

聴く勉
TOEIC
講座！

DL音声 **17-24**

図表を見る問題もあり、
Part3 はこんなテストだ！

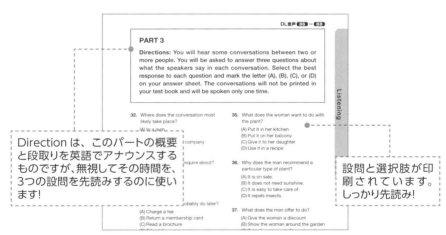

DL音声 **86** ～ **88**

PART 3

Directions: You will hear some conversations between two or more people. You will be asked to answer three questions about what the speakers say in each conversation. Select the best response to each question and mark the letter (A), (B), (C), or (D) on your answer sheet. The conversations will not be printed in your test book and will be spoken only one time.

Listening

32. Where does the conversation most likely take place?

    (A) ...

...company

...inquire about?

...probably do later?

(A) Charge a fee
(B) Return a membership card
(C) Read a brochure

35. What does the woman want to do with the plant?

    (A) Put it in her kitchen
    (B) Put on her balcony
    (C) Give it to her daughter
    (D) Use it in a recipe

36. Why does the man recommend a particular type of plant?

    (A) It is on sale.
    (B) It does not need sunshine.
    (C) It is easy to take care of.
    (D) It repels insects.

37. What does the man offer to do?

    (A) Give the woman a discount
    (B) Show the woman around the garden

Direction は、このパートの概要と段取りを英語でアナウンスするものですが、無視してその時間を、3つの設問を先読みするのに使います！

設問と選択肢が印刷されています。しっかり先読み！

　2人もしくは3人の会話英文を聞き、それに続いて流れる3つの設問に答えます。

　会話は問題用紙に印刷されていませんが、**設問（英語）と4つの選択肢（A～D・英語）は印刷されています。** 図表などを見ながら聞いて答える問題もあり!

● Part3 本番の流れはこれだ！

放送される内容　　　　　　　　　　あなたがすべきこと

英語の **Directions**（指示文）が
放送される《約30秒》 - - - ● 設問と選択肢（4つ）は問題用
紙に印刷されていますので、
最初の会話の設問3つ（Q32
〜34）を先読みしましょう！

↓

**Questions32 through 34
refer to the following
conversation.**《約3秒》 - - - ● 次に放送される英語の会話
音声を聞き取る態勢に入りま
しょう！

↓《無音1秒》

会話文《30〜50秒程度》 - - - - - - - ● 先読み＋推理で待ち伏せリス
ニングし、「これだ!」という語
が聞こえたら、どんどんマー
クしていくこと！

↓《無音1秒》

設問32《5秒程度》
《無音8秒》
設問33《5秒程度》 - - - - - - - - - - ● マークが終わり次第、次の3
つの設問を先読み&推理する！
《無音8秒》
設問34《5秒程度》

↓《無音8秒》

Questions35 through 37 refer ...（次の問題が始まる）

1つの会話に3つの質問！　全部で13セット！
放送は1回しか流れないので、
確実に先読みし、待ち伏せよう !!!

Part3 の Directions（指示文）は、こんな内容になっています。

パート3
指示：2人または3人の会話をいくつか聞いていきます。それぞれの会話で3問ずつ、会話の内容に
関する質問に答えます。それぞれの質問に対して最適な応答を1つ選んで、解答用紙の (A)(B)(C)(D)
から1つマークしてください。会話は問題用紙に印刷されていませんし、放送されるのは1度だけです。

[24秒先読み攻撃＆待ち伏せ作戦]で ガッチリ得点！

Part3 の攻略法は簡単に言うと、**会話文の前半で2つ、後半で1つのキーワードをあらかじめ待ち伏せる**というものです。

●試験本番ではこう動こう！

テストの最初に流れる Direction の時間を使って、最初の問題の3つの設問を**「先読み」**し、誰のセリフを待ち伏せたらいいのかを**推理**しておきます。その推理をもとに、会話文の放送を**「待ち伏せ」**態勢で聞きます。

会話文の放送を聞きながら、「待ち伏せ」ている語が出てきたらすぐに解答をマークしていきます。そして、会話文の放送が終わると「Questions 32... などと、設問が読まれる時間＋無音時間（8秒×3問＝24秒）が始まります。この時間を利用して、次の3つの設問（と選択肢）を先読みし、キーワードを「待ち伏せ」します。

初級者には最初は少し難しいかもしれませんが、**このタイミングで突っ走るのが、Part 3 の基本戦略**です。

ポイント 1 3W1H 設問は選択肢もざっと見る！

3つの設問を先読みする際に1つ、頭に入れておきたいことがあります。

それは、（Part2 でも出てきましたが）ここでも**ねらい目は3W1H**——つまり **Who** と **When** と **Where** と **How**——だということです！ なぜなら、3W1H の設問では、**選択肢が短い**単語の場合が多いので、「待ち伏せ」しやすい＝**正解をつかむ可能性が高い**のです。ですので、これらの設問に関しては、選択肢にも目を通しておきましょう。

ポイント 2 長い選択肢は「キーワード」を探そう！

先読みの際、長い選択肢は全部読んでいると**時間が足りない**ので、本文

Chapter❶

Part 1 写真描写

Part 2 応答

Part 3 会話

Part 4 説明文

Part 5 短文穴埋め

Part 6 長文穴埋め

Part 7 長文読解

のキーワードを言い換えているようなポイントとなる語を探そう。特に、**動詞や目的語が重要!** この練習を積んで、6割以上の正解率を狙おう!

ポイント 3 捨てる勇気を持つべし!

　とにかく一刻も早く解答を終えて次の設問3つを先読みしていかないと、得点できるはずの設問を落としてしまうことにつながりかねません。つまり大切なのは、**捨てる勇気を持つ**ことです。すべてに正解できるわけではないと心得て、まずは、**各問題で2問正解**することを目指しましょう!

　※なお、この Part3 からは演習の都合上、本番と同じ番号で入ります。

最強! 解答テクニック

❶ 冒頭 Direction の時間に最初の設問3つを先読み!
❷ 会話文を待ち伏せ態勢で聞き、答えがわかり次第どんどんマーク!
❸ 「捨てる勇気」を持ち、まずは各問題で2問正解を目指そう!

練習問題　練習問題に挑戦してみましょう！

DL音声 **17**

Part 1 写真描写

Part 2 応答

Part 3 会話

Part 4 説明文

Part 5 短文穴埋め

Part 6 長文穴埋め

Part 7 長文読解

32. When is the woman's original appointment?

(A) This Friday at 3pm.　　(B) This Friday at 2pm.

(C) Next Friday at 3pm.　　(D) Next Friday at 2pm.

33. Why can't the woman see Dr. Siegel next Wednesday?

(A) Because Dr. Siegel is not available.

(B) Because the woman needs to take her daughter to hospital.

(C) Because the women will be out of town.

(D) Because the woman has a business meeting.

34. What does the man ask the woman to bring?

(A) Her insurance card

(B) Her social security card

(C) Her temperature records

(D) Her medical records

---

35. What is the man asking the woman to do?

(A) To correct his bills

(B) To give him an invoice

(C) To give him a discount on his bill

(D) To remove the tax on this bill

36. Which of the following will the hotel do?

(A) Change 2 nights to 3 nights

(B) Change the tax charges

(C) Remove the minibar charges

(D) Remove the service charges

37. What is the new consumption tax on hotels?

(A) 10.15%　　(B) 10.7%

(C) 10.75%　　(D) 10.1%

解答・解説

聴く勉 TOEIC 講座！ DL音声 18

32. 正解：(B)

When is the woman's original appointment?
女性の元々の診察予約はいつですか？

(A) **This Friday 3pm.** 今週金曜の午後3時
(B) This Friday 2pm. 今週金曜の午後2時
(C) **Next Friday 3pm.** 来週金曜の午後3時
(D) **Next Friday 2pm.** 来週金曜の午後2時

ポイント 男性のセリフに 2pm this Friday とベタで出ている。だれでもできないといけない！
⇒ **Level 1**

33. 正解：(C)

Why can't the woman see Dr. Siegel next Wednesday?
女性はどうして Dr. Siegel に診てもらえないのか？

(A) **Because Dr. Siegel is not available.** なぜなら Dr. Siegel の都合がつかない。
(B) **Because the woman needs to take her daughter to hospital.**
なぜなら女性は娘を病院へ連れて行く必要があるから。
(C) Because the women will be out of town. なぜなら女性は町を出るから。
(D) **Because the woman has a business meeting.**
なぜなら女性は仕事の会合があるから。

ポイント 女性のセリフで next Friday を待ち伏せすれば abroad（海外）が聞こえる。be abroad を be out of town で言い換え (paraphrase) している。 ⇒ **Level 2**

34. 正解：(C)

What does the man ask the woman to bring?
男性は女性に何を持って来るように頼んでいるか？

(A) **Her insurance card** 保険証
(B) **Her social security card** 社会保障証
(C) Her temperature records 体温記録
(D) **Her medicine records** 投薬記録

ポイント 最後の問題で男性の頼む (ask...to〜) セリフなので男性の最後のセリフの中に Please つまり命令形風のものを聞き取る気持ちで待ち伏せる。ベタで出ている。コツはだれのセリフの何を「待ち伏せるか」を瞬時に判断すること。練習すれば初級者でも6割はすぐに取れます！ ⇒ **Level 1**

35. 正解：(A)

What is the man asking the woman to do?
男性は女性に何をするよう頼んでいるか？

(A) To correct his bills　　　　　　請求書を訂正するように

(B) To give him an invoice　　　　　送り状 (請求書つづり) をくれるように

(C) To give him a discount on his bill　請求書への割引をするように

(D) To remove the tax on this bill　　請求書から税金を除くように

> **ポイント** 男性のセリフは不満たらたらでマイナスイメージだ。それはなぜか？　過重請求されたから。コツは bill, invoice, discount, tax をキーワードとしてこれを聞き取ること　⇒ **Level 3** !

36. 正解：(C)

Which of the following will the hotel do?
ホテルは次のどれをするだろうか？

(A) Change 2 nights to 3 nights　　2泊から3泊に変更

(B) Change the tax charges　　　　税金を変更する

(C) Remove the minibar charges　　ミニバーの料金を無しにする

(D) Remove the service charges　　サービス料を無しにする

> **ポイント** これも直接女性 (＝ホテル側) のセリフにないので難しい。男性の3つの不満が聞き取れれば簡単に (C) だと分かる　⇒ **Level 3** !

37. 正解：(C)

What is the new consumption tax on hotels?
ホテル利用にかかる新しい消費税はいくらか？

(A) 10.15%

(B) 10.7%

(C) 10.75%

(D) 10.1%

> **ポイント** これは簡単。ただ、最初の男性のセリフで「この 10.75% の税は何だ？」を聞いていないとできないが…　⇒ **Level 1'** !

Part 1 写真描写
Part 2 応答
Part 3 会話
Part 4 説明文
Part 5 短文穴埋め
Part 6 長文穴埋め
Part 7 長文読解

Questions 32-34 refer to the following conversation

W: Hello, my name is Anne Smith. I am calling to reschedule my appointment with Dr. Siegel. I can't make it this Friday because I need to take my daughter to hospital.

M: OK, let me check. You do have an appointment at 2pm this Friday. Now Dr. Siegel's openings within this month are only next Wednesday's 5 to 6pm and next Friday's 3-4pm. Which slot would you like?

W: I can't do next Wednesday because I will still be abroad that day. I'll take Friday 3-4pm.

M: OK, I'll put you down for next Friday 3-4pm. Don't forget to bring your temperature record with you then.

女性：もしもし、Anne Smith と申します。Siegel 先生との診察予約の変更の為、お電話しています。この金曜日都合がつかないのです、娘を病院へ連れて行く必要がありますので。

男性：分かりました。確認させてください。確かに、この金曜2時に予約が入ってますね。現在、Siegel 先生の今月の診察は来週の水曜午後5時から6時と来週の金曜午後3時から4時のみですね。どの時間枠がよろしいでしょうか？

女性：来週の水曜日はだめなんです、その日は多分まだ国外にいますので。金曜の3時から4時のにします。

男性：分かりました。来週の金曜の3時から4時に入れておきましょう。その際、体温の記録をお持ちになることをお忘れなく！

語句

- ❏ **appointment** 　[名]　会う日時を決める約束　※医者との場合は「診察予約」
- ❏ **reschedule** 　[動]　予定を変える
- ❏ **slot** 　[名]　（時間などの）空き枠
- ❏ **can make it** 　何かをうまくクリアする　※it は状況の it
- ❏ **do** 　（強めで）なるほど；確かに
- ❏ **opening** 　[名]　開店；開業
- ❏ **put down** 　書き留める (=write down)
- ❏ **temperature** 　[名]　温度　※発音注意 [テムプリチュア]

Chapter ①

Part 1 写真描写

Part 2 応答

Part 3 会話

Part 4 説明文

Part 5 短文穴埋め

Part 6 長文穴埋め

Part 7 長文読解

会話文スクリプト

Questions 35-37 refer to the following conversation

M: Hi, I think there is something wrong on my bill. First, I only stayed for 2 nights, but your bill says 3. Second, I didn't eat anything in the mini bar. And last what is this 10.75% tax? Isn't it normally 10.1%?

W: Sorry Sir, let me check. Was your room 1506 and your surname Green?

M: Yes, if you go to that room now, you'll find that your minibar still has everything in it.

W: Sorry Sir, I think there was some mistake with our computer system and we mixed you up with another Mr. Green. We will correct your bill right away. But the tax is fine. It is the new consumption tax on hotels.

男性：ヤァ、僕の請求書何か間違っていると思うんだが。まず2日しか泊まってないのに、お宅の請求書には3泊となっているよ。次に、ミニバーでは何も食べなかったよ。それから最後にこの10.75%の消費税って何？　それって、普通10.1%じゃない？

女性：申し訳ございません、お客様。確認させてください。お部屋は1506でお名前はGreen様でございましたね？

男性：そうだよ、もしその部屋に今行ってみれば、お宅のミニバーがまだ何もかもそこにあるはずだよ。

女性：申し訳ございません、お客様。コンピューターのシステムにミスがあってあなた様をもう一人のMr. Greenと一緒にしてしまったのだと思います。直ぐさま、お客様の請求書を訂正させていただきます。でも税金は異常ありません。それはホテル利用への新しい消費税なのです。

語句

□ **something wrong**	なにか変だ；おかしい
□ **bill**	名 請求書　動 請求する
□ **mix up**	混ぜる
□ **correct**	動 訂正する　※ collect(集める) と混同しないこと
□ **right away**	即座に　=immediately　※頻出
□ **consume**	動 消費する
□ **consumer**	名 消費者
□ **consumption**	名 消費

38. What is the woman requesting?
(A) To change the return policy of the store
(B) To return the shoes she bought
(C) To discuss with the store manager on the compensation for her injury.
(D) To exchange a pair of shoes.

39. What does "look" mean when the man said "OK look, how about this?"
(A) Take a look at another pair of shoes
(B) Take a look at the return policy
(C) Listen to what I am about to say
(D) Drop the unreasonable request.

40. If the woman accepts the man's proposal, how much would she get as a refund?
(A) 85% of what she paid
(B) 100% of what she paid
(C) 90% of what she paid
(D) She'll get no refund.

---

41. Why does the man want to sell his camera?
(A) To correct his bills
(B) Its battery doesn't work well.
(C) He wants to use new lenses.
(D) He wants to have a waterproof camera.

42. What does the man say about the camera?
(A) Its batteries do not last long.
(B) Its lens needs to be replaced.
(C) He bought it six years ago.
(D) Its shutter works fine.

43. What does the woman say about the camera?
(A) The man cannot get a refund.
(B) The man cannot enjoy a discount.
(C) The camera is beyond repair.
(D) The camera has certain problem that would reduce its value.

解答・解説

Part 1 写真描写

Part 2 応答

Part 3 会話

Part 4 説明文

Part 5 短文穴埋め

Part 6 長文穴埋め

Part 7 長文読解

38. 正解：(B)

What is the woman requesting?
女性は何を要求しているか？

(A) To change the return policy of the store　その店の返品方針を変えること

(B) To return the shoes she bought　買った靴を戻すこと

(C) To discuss with the store manager on the compensation for her injury.
彼女の怪我への補償について店長と話し合うこと

(D) To exchange a pair of shoes.　別の一足へ変更すること

> **ポイント** request（要求）だから女性の望み（want, would like, hope など）を待ち伏せる！　冒頭に「返品したい」とベタで出てくる。boots が shoes に言い換えられている　⇒ **Level 1'**！　簡単ですよ！

39. 正解：(C)

What does "look" mean when the man said "OK look, how about this?"
男性が OK, look, how about this? と言ったが、look はどんな意味か？

(A) Take a look at another pair of shoes　別の一足を見て下さい。

(B) Take a look at the return policy　返品方針を見て下さい。

(C) Listen to what I am about to say　私が言おうとしていることを聞いて

(D) Drop the unreasonable request.　法外な要求を打ち切る

> **ポイント** 訳を見て！　be about to~ は「まさに〜しようとしている」という意味。unreasonable は「納得行かない；法外な」　⇒ **Level 3**

40. 正解：(D)

If the woman accepts the man's proposal, how much would she get as a refund?
もし女性が男性の提案を受け入れるならば彼女は返金としていくらを手にするか？

(A) 85% of what she paid　支払った金額の 85%

(B) 100% of what she paid　支払った金額の 100%

(C) 90% of what she paid　支払った金額の 90%

(D) She'll get no refund.　返金は全く受けない。

> **ポイント** 男性のセリフ You can switch to another for free. で分かる　⇒ **Level 2**！

41. 正解：(C)

Why does the man want to sell his camera?
男性はどうして自分のカメラを売りたいのか？

(A) To correct his bills　　　　　　　　　シャッターが良く作動しないから。

(B) Its battery doesn't work well.　　　　バッテリーが良く作動しないから。

(C) He wants to use new lenses.　　　　彼は新しいレンズを使いたがっているから。

(D) He wants to have a waterproof camera.　彼は防水カメラを持ちたがっているから。

> 🖊ポイント　男性の最初のセリフには出てこない。後半のセリフに出てくる　⇒ **Level 1'**

42. 正解：(C)

What does the man say about the camera?
男性はそのカメラについてどう言っているか？

(A) Its lens needs to be replaced.　　　バッテリーが長くもたない。

(B) Its lens needs to be replaced.　　　レンズ交換が必要。

(C) He bought it six years ago.　　　　彼はそれを6年前に買った。

(D) Its shutter works fine.　　　　　　シャッターはうまく作動する。

> 🖊ポイント　これは簡単、ほとんどベタで出ている。I've had it for six years.（6年間所有している）とは He bought it six years ago.（6年前に買った）ということ　⇒ **Level 2**！

43. 正解：(D)

What does the woman say about the camera?
女性はそのカメラについてどう言っているか？

(A) The man cannot get a refund.　　　男性は返金を手にすることができない。

(B) The man cannot enjoy a discount.　男性は減額を受けられない。

(C) The camera is beyond repair.　　　そのカメラは修理できない。

(D) The camera has certain problem that would reduce its value.
　　そのカメラにはその価値を減ずるある問題がある。

> 🖊ポイント　速く読めれば簡単な問題。シャッターが問題で、高値で引き取れないことが分かれば簡単。beyond は「〜を越えている」、certain は「ある」だが「確かな」という意味もある。　⇒ **Level 2**！

Chapter ❶

Part 1 写真描写

Part 2 応答

Part 3 会話

Part 4 説明文

Part 5 短文穴埋め

Part 6 長文穴埋め

Part 7 長文読解

会話文スクリプト

Questions 38-40 refer to the following conversation

■ **W:** Hey, I want to return these boots. I bought them from you last Friday. They hurt a lot.

M: I'm sorry to hear that, Ma'am. Can I see your receipt? Oh, this item was on sale. Sale items cannot be returned.

■ **W:** This doesn't work. Sale items may not be perfect but they shouldn't be allowed to cause injuries. Can I speak to your manager?

M: OK, look, how about this? You can exchange them with another pair for free. That pair should be no more expensive than this pair, of course. In addition, I will give you a 15% coupon on our new spring items.

女：ねえ、このブーツ返したいんだけど。先週の金曜にお宅から買ったの。(靴で)足がすごく痛いのよ。

男：それは申し訳ございません、お客様。領収証見せてもらえますか？　ああ、これは売り出しの品物でしたね。売り出しの品は返品できないのです。

女：これはそうはいかないんじゃない？　売り出し商品は完璧ではないかも知れないけど、怪我をさせるものであってはならないはずよ。店長と話せる？

男：わかりました。ほら、これなどどうですか？　無料で別の一足と交換できますよ。それはもちろんこれと同じくらい値段は張るはずです。加えてこの春の新製品への15%引きのクーポン券をさしあげます。

語句

❏ **hurt** 動　傷つける
　　※「〜が痛い！」と訳すことが多い。例:These boots hurt a lot.(このブーツはすごく痛い)
❏ **item** 名　品目
❏ **work** 動　作用する；ことがうまく運ぶ
❏ **look** 人を引き付ける時の表現
　　※必ずしも「見て！」とは限らない。ここでは「まあまあ、私の言うことを聞いてくださいよ」くらいのニュアンス
❏ **no more expensive than...**
　　…よりも高価であることは決してない⇒「〜と変わらず高価ですよ」という強調表現

Questions 41-43 refer to the following conversation

■ **M:** Hi, my friend told me that you take used cameras? I've brought one today, and I'd like to know its price. Should I speak with you or someone else?

▒ **W:** I can help you. Do you mind if I take a look at your camera?

■ **M:** Sure. It's a Photoshot X01. I've had it for six years. Now I am upgrading my lens and need a new one to go with the new lens. The camera is still in perfect working condition including its batteries. Its shutter is bit slow but that seems to be normal wear and tear.

▒ **W:** Sorry, the shutter has a problem. We will have to lower the offer because of this problem.

男性：コンニチワ。友人が言ってたんだけど、中古のカメラ取ってくれるの？　今日、一台持って来たので、値段が知りたいんだ。君と話していい？　それとも他の人と？
女性：私が承ります。お客様のカメラを見せていただいてもよろしいでしょうか？
男性：もちろんだよ。Photoshot X01だよ。それを手にして6年になるね。今ね、僕のレンズをグレードアップしようとしてるんだ、それでその新しいレンズに合うやつが必要なのさ。カメラはまだ完璧に作動するよ、バッテリーも含めてね。シャッターがちょっと遅いけど、それって通常の摩耗とほころびのようだよ。
女性：申し訳ありませんが、シャッターが問題ですね。お値段を差し引かなければならないでしょうね、この問題で。

語句

❏ **used**	形　中古の　※発音は [ユーズド]。used to~（~したものだった）とは発音が違うので注意
❏ **Do you mind if~?**	~して構いませんか？　※会話の定番。Part2で頻出
❏ **to go with~**	~と合う；釣り合う
❏ **wear**	名　摩耗
❏ **tear**	名　ほころび；裂け目　※発音は [テア]
❏ **be perfect working conditions**	完全な作動環境にある　※ conditions はいつも複数

練習問題 練習問題に挑戦してみましょう！

DL音声 21

Part 1 写真描写

Part 2 応答

Part 3 会話

Part 4 説明文

Part 5 短文穴埋め

Part 6 長文穴埋め

Part 7 長文読解

44. What type of event is being held?
   (A) A training session
   (B) A school festival
   (C) An education fair
   (D) A job interview

45. How can the woman get the event brochure?
   (A) She can get it at the registration desk.
   (B) She can get it at the entrance.
   (C) The man will get it for her.
   (D) She can download it from the online registration.

46. What is NOT true about the woman's friend?
   (A) She needs to pay $10.
   (B) She has registered online for this event.
   (C) She is interested in overseas education.
   (D) She wants to attend this event.

---

47. Why is the woman calling the man?
   (A) To confirm the date when he borrowed the book
   (B) To confirm the name of the book he borrowed
   (C) To request for the return of the book
   (D) To inform the late penalty.

48. When did the man ask George to return the book for him?
   (A) April 2
   (B) April 12
   (C) April 16
   (D) April 22

49. When will a late return penalty come about?
   (A) When a book is not returned for more than 14 days.
   (B) When a book is returned late for a second time.
   (C) When a book is not returned for more than 30 days.
   (D) When a book is returned late for a third time.

※ 50-64 はここでは省きます。

44. 正解：(C)

What type of event is being held?
どのようなタイプのイベントが開催されているか？

(A) A training session　研修会

(B) A school festival　学園祭

(C) An education fair　教育フェア

(D) A job interview　就職面接

ポイント　簡単。冒頭でずばり言っているので。各選択肢の名詞だけにらんで聞けばすぐ！
⇒ **Level 1**

45. 正解：(C)

How can the woman get the event brochure?
女性はどうやってイベントのパンフを手に入れられるか？

(A) She can get it at the registration desk.　登録受付デスクで手に入れられる。

(B) She can get it at the entrance.　入り口で手に入れられる。

(C) The man will get it for her.　男性が彼女の代わりに取ってあげる。

(D) She can download it from the online registration.
オンライン登録からダウンロードできる。

ポイント　男性の Let me get it for you ＝ I'll get it for you. のこと　⇒ **Level 2**！

46. 正解：(B)

What is NOT true about the woman's friend?
女性の友人について当てはまらないものはどれか？

(A) She needs to pay $10.
彼女は10ドル払う必要がある。

(B) She has registered online for this event.
彼女はこのイベントにオンライン登録をした。

(C) She is interested in overseas education.
彼女は海外の教育に興味がある。

(D) She wants to attend this event.
彼女は首尾よくその会合に参加できる。

ポイント　正しいものを除いていけば OK　⇒ **Level 2**！

Chapter ❶

Part 1 写真描写

Part 2 応答

Part 3 会話

Part 4 説明文

Part 5 短文穴埋め

Part 6 長文穴埋め

Part 7 長文読解

47. 正解：(C)

Why is the woman calling the man?

女性はその男性に電話しているのか？

(A) To confirm the date when he borrowed the book

彼がその本を借りた日を確認するため

(B) To confirm the name of the book he borrowed

彼が借りた本の名前を確認するため

(C) To request for the return of the book 本の返却を要求するため

(D) To inform the late penalty. 延滞罰則金を知らせるため

> ポイント 女性の最初のセリフの最後に We haven't received your book. (まだ、返却されてませんよ) とある ⇒ **Level 2**！

48. 正解：(C)

When did the man ask George to return the book for him

男性はいつ George に彼に代わって返してくれるよう頼んだか？

(A) April 2

(B) April 12

(C) April 16

(D) April 22

> ポイント When, Where, Who, How の問題は初級者用なので取ること！ George を待ち伏せすれば簡単 ⇒ **Level 1**！

49. 正解：(A)

When will a late return penalty come about?

延滞罰則金はいつ生じるだろうか？

(A) When a book is not returned for more than 14 days

本が14日以上の間戻らない時

(B) When a book is returned late for a second time

本が2度目に対して遅れて返却の時

(C) When a book is not returned for more than 30 days

本が30日以上の間戻らない時

(D) When a book is returned late for a third time

本が3度目に対して遅れて返却の時

> ポイント come about は「生ずる」。このイディオムが分からなくても女性の最後のセリフを待って penalty を待ち伏せしておけば more than 14 days (14日以上) は絶対聞こえるはず ⇒ **Level 2**！

Questions 44-46 refer to the following conversation.

M: Welcome to our Education Fair. This year we have invited 17 overseas universities to join our fair so that you can get information not only on domestic schools but also on overseas schools.

W: Sounds good. Where can I get an event brochure?

M: You can get it from our information desk, which is right beside the registration desk. Let me get it for you to save you a trip.

W: Thanks a lot. Actually, my friend didn't register for this fair in advance, but she is with me. Can she register now on the spot?

M: Yes, she can, but there is a $10 processing fee for admissions without prior registration.

男性：ようこそ私どもの教育フェアへ！　今年度は17大学を私共のフェアにお誘いしています、皆様が国内の学校に限らず海外の学校に関しての情報を得ることができますようにとね。

女性：いいですね。どちらでイベントのパンフいただけますか？

男性：案内カウンターで手に入りますよ、登録受付デスクのすぐ側の。あなたが移動する手間を省けるように私が取って上げましょう。

女性：ありがとうございます。実は、友人がこのフェアへのオンライン登録を前以てしなかったのですが、今一緒に来ているのです。彼女、今その場で登録受付できます？

男性：ええ、できますよ。でも10ドルの処理費用があります、前もっての登録なしの入会には。

語句		
❏ **fair**	名	ここでは「合同説明会」のこと　※他に「見本市；品評会；博覧会」などの意味もある。また、形容詞として「フェアな；公正な；きれいな」などの意味もあるので注意。
❏ **overseas**	形	海外の　副　海外に　※副詞の場合だけ =abroad なので注意！
❏ **domestic**	形	国内の；家庭内の
❏ **so that~ can**		～できるようにと　※目的構文
❏ **not only A but also B**		A だけでなく B も　※ also がない場合もある
❏ **brochure**	名	折り畳んだだけのパンフレット　※発音は [ブロウシュア]
❏ **save your trip**		移動の手間を省く　※この trip は「旅」でなく「移動」
❏ **in advance = beforehand**		前もって
❏ **on the spot**		その場で　❏ **processing fee**　処理費
❏ **prior**	形	前の；先の

Chapter ①

Part 1 写真描写

Part 2 応答

Part 3 会話

Part 4 説明文

Part 5 短文穴埋め

Part 6 長文穴埋め

Part 7 長文読解

会話文スクリプト

Questions 47-49 refer to the following conversation.

W: I am calling about a book you have borrowed from us. Our records show that you checked out the "Revolution" on April 2. You were supposed to return it by April 22. We haven't received your book.

M: I think I have returned this book. I asked my classmate George to drop it in the library book drop box. Wait a minute. Let me check my chat history with George. OK, it was April 16. He should have returned this book for me on that day.

W: OK. We will double check. But note that for any late returns, a late penalty of $0.50 will be charged for each day of delay when a book is not returned for more than 14 days.

M: OK. I will also check with George and call you back.

女性：あなたが当方（私共）からお借りになっている本についてお電話差し上げています。当方の記録では貴方は「革命」という本を4月2日にお借りになっています。あなたは4月22日までに返却することになっています。当方ではまだ貴方の本を受け取ってはいません。

男性：返却したと思いますけど。僕は級友のGeorgeに図書館の返却箱へ投函してくれるように頼みました。ちょっと待ってください。Georgeとのチャットの履歴を確かめてみます。間違いないです。4月16日でした。彼はその日に僕の代わりにこの本を返却したはずです。

女性：わかりました。二重確認をしてみましょう。しかし、どんな返却遅れに対しても50セントの延滞罰則金が1日、1日の遅れに課されます、14日以上もの間返却されない時にね。

男性：わかりました。僕もまたGeorgeに確認取ってみます、そしてこちらからお電話します。

語句

❑ **be supposed to~**		～することになっている
❑ **drop**	動	投函する
❑ **history**	名	履歴
❑ **should have+p.p.**		～したはずだ　※「～すべきだったのに…」という後悔を表す時もあるので注意！
❑ **note that...**		～に留意する
❑ **charge**	動	課金する

65. What type of event is being organized by the speaker's company?

(A) A travel seminar

(B) An award ceremony

(C) A trip for employees

(D) A school interview.

66. What does the man want the woman to do?

(A) To email the man the package details

(B) To fax the man the package details

(C) To book the hotel.

(D) To pay a 20% deposit.

67. Look at the graphic.What travel package will the man most likely select?

(A) Korea Wonderland

(B) China Gourmet Trip

(C) Meet the Kangaroo in Australia

(D) Romantic Weekend in Paris.

Price List	
Korea Wonderland	$500 /person
China Gourmet Trip	$760 /person
Meet the Kangaroo in Australia	$530 /person
Romantic Weekend in Paris	$600 /person

68. What most likely is the woman's job?

    (A) Event organizer

    (B) Photographer

    (C) Animal trainer

    (D) Shooter

69. Look at the graphic. Which booth does the woman want?

    (A) Nature A

    (B) Nature B

    (C) Nature C

    (D) Animal B

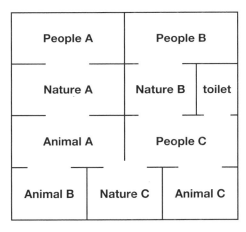

70. What does the man ask the woman for?

    (A) Registration forms

    (B) Name card

    (C) Booth map

    (D) Exhibition certificate

Part 1 写真描写
Part 2 応答
Part 3 会話
Part 4 説明文
Part 5 短文穴埋め
Part 6 長文穴埋め
Part 7 長文読解

解答・解説

65. 正解：(C)

What type of event is being organized by the speaker's company?
話し手の会社ではどのようなタイプの催しが準備されているか？

(A) A travel seminar　　　　　出張／旅行研修会
(B) An award ceremony　　　　受賞式典
(C) A trip for employees　　　社員のための旅行
(D) A school interview　　　　学校の面接

ポイント 最初の男性のセリフにもろにある　⇒ **Level 1'**

66. 正解：(B)

What does the man want the woman to do?
男性は女性に何をしてもらいたいのか？

(A) To email the man the package details　パックの詳細を email すること
(B) To fax the man the package details　　パックの詳細をファクスすること
(C) To book the hotel.　　　　　　　　　ホテルを予約すること
(D) To pay a 20% deposit.　　　　　　　20% の頭金を払うこと

ポイント 男性の最後のセリフにズバリ。だれでもできる問題　⇒ **Level 1**

67. 正解：(A)

Look at the graphic. What travel package will the man most likely select?
図をみなさい。男性はどのような旅行パックを多分選びそうですか？

(A) Korea Wonderland　　　　　　　韓国ワンダーランド
(B) China Gourmet Trip　　　　　　中国グルメツアー
(C) Meet the Kangaroo in Australia　オーストラリアでカンガルーとご体面
(D) Romantic Weekend in Paris.　　パリでのロマンチックな週末

ポイント 図表の定番問題。値段の方だけを見て会話をしっかり聞くとすぐにできる。550ドル未満でないといけないし、アジアでないといけないことを忘れないで！　⇒ **Level 1**

価格表	
コリアワンダーランド	500 ドル（1名）
チャイナグルメトリップ	760 ドル（1名）
オーストラリアでカンガルーに会う	530 ドル（1名）
パリでのロマンチックな週末	600 ドル（1名）

Chapter ①

Part 1 写真描写

Part 2 応答

Part 3 会話

Part 4 説明文

Part 5 短文穴埋め

Part 6 長文穴埋め

Part 7 長文読解

68. 正解：(B)

What most likely is the woman's job?
女性の仕事は多分何だろうか？

(A) Event organizer　イベント主催者
(B) Photographer　　写真家
(C) Animal trainer　動物調教師
(D) Shooter　　　　狩猟家、射撃手

ポイント 超簡単な問題。すぐに photo と聞こえる　⇒ **Level 1'**

69. 正解：(C)

Look at the graphic. Which booth does the woman want?
図を見なさい。女性はどのブースを選ぶでしょうか？

(A) Nature A
(B) Nature B
(C) Nature C
(D) Animal B

ポイント 女性のセリフをしっかり聞き、want, like, prefer, choose などを待ち伏せる
　⇒ **Level2**

70. 正解：(B)

What does the man ask the woman for?
男性は女性に何を求めていますか？

(A) Registration forms　登録申し込み書
(B) Name card　　　　名票
(C) Booth map　　　　ブースの地図
(D) Exhibition certificate　展示会証明書

ポイント もちろん最後の問題なので、男性の最後の頼みのセリフを待ち伏せれば、OK.
　　Would/Do you mind -ing? は人にていねいに頼む時のお決まり文！　⇒ **Level 1**

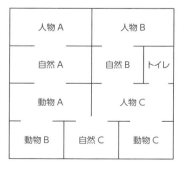

Questions 65-67 refer to the following conversation and price list.

M: I'm calling to get some information about your travel packages. My company is organizing a company trip as an award for 10 employees.

W: Sure. What price range and days are you looking at? And any particular country you would like to visit?

M: We are on a budget of no more than $550 per person. We are thinking of 2 or 3 days anywhere in Asia.

W: We do have a few packages that fit your requirements. Please note that we require a 20% deposit if you book any package. Now how do you want me to send you the package details?

M: Can you fax them?

男性：ようこそ私共男性：おたくの旅行パックについての情報を手に入れたくて電話しているんだ。うちの会社が10名の賞をもらった社員のために社員旅行を準備してるんだけどね。

女性：おまかせ下さい。どんなお値段幅と日数をお考えでしょう？ そして何か訪れたい特定の国でも？

男性：一人につき550ドルまでの予算なんだけどね。アジアのどこでもいいんだけど、2～3日を考えているんだ。

女性：お客様のご要件にぴったりのパックが2、3ございますとも。どのようなパックに予約なさいましても20%の頭金を申し受けますことご留意ください。それではパックの詳細をどのようにお送りいたしましょうか？

男性：ファックスできる？

語句

❑ **package**	名	一括のセット（パック旅行）
❑ **award**	名 賞 動 賞を与える ※発音は［アウォード］	
❑ **range**	名 幅；帯	
❑ **look at~**	~を考慮する（目を向けるから）	
❑ **particular**	形 特定の	
❑ **budget**	名 予算	
❑ **no more than~**	~以上ではあり得ない ※ = only	
❑ **requirement**	名 要件	
❑ **deposit**	名 頭金；内入金；保証金	
❑ **do you want me to~**	= Shall I~?	
❑ **details**	名 詳細点	

Chapter ❶

Part 1
写真描写

Part 2
応答

Part 3
会話

Part 4
説明文

Part 5
短文穴埋め

Part 6
長文穴埋め

Part 7
長文読解

会話文スクリプト

Questions 68-70 refer to the following conversation and the chart.

🏴 **W:** I'd like to register for this year's Coup Photo Exhibition. I think it'll be a good way to help my photo business.

🏴 **M:** Sure, Ma'am. Our exhibition has been very popular among photo buyers. This year we have three types of booths and their locations are shown on this map. Which booth would you like?

🏴 **W:** I basically shoot mountains. So I'll take the nature booth. Among the three you have, I prefer the one beside the animal booth. The one next to the restroom is no good.

🏴 **M:** Sure, let me register for you. Do you mind giving me your name card? I'll fill out these forms based on that.

🏴 **W:** Oh, will you? Thanks a lot.

女性：今年の Coup 写真展に登録したいのだけれど。私の写真ビジネスに役立つよい方法だと思うんだけど。

男性：もちろんでございます、お客様。私共の展示会は写真のバイヤーさんにとってとても人気がございます。今年は3タイプのブースをご用意してございまして、その場所はこの地図に示して御座います。どちらをお好みで？

女性：私は基本的に山を撮るのよね、そこで、自然ブースにしたいわね。お持ちの3つのブースの中で動物ブースの隣のがいいわね。トイレの隣のはだめよ。

男性：かしこまりました。お客様に代わり登録させていただきます。お客様の名票をいただけないでしょうか？ おっしゃったことに基づきまして、これらの書式に書き込みましょう。

女性：まぁ、やってくれるの？ 本当にありがとう。

語句

❏ **register**	動	登録する
❏ **exhibition**	名	展示会
❏ **booth**	名	ブース
❏ **location**	名	場所
❏ **basically**	副	基本的に
❏ **shoot**	動	写真を撮る
❏ **restroom**	名	トイレ
❏ **name card**		名票　※名刺は business card

ゼロからスタート

Part4 説明文を聞いて内容についての質問に答える

説明文問題

本番では…
全30問：Q71-100

[24秒先読み攻撃＆待ち伏せ作戦]で6割正解を目指せ！

聴く勉
TOEIC
講座！
DL音声 **25-32**

トークを聞いて答える、Part4 はこんなテストだ！

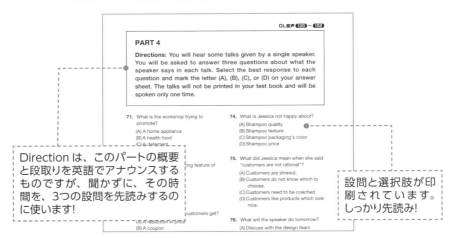

DL音声 **100** ～ **102**

PART 4

Directions: You will hear some talks given by a single speaker. You will be asked to answer three questions about what the speaker says in each talk. Select the best response to each question and mark the letter (A), (B), (C), or (D) on your answer sheet. The talks will not be printed in your test book and will be spoken only one time.

71. What is the workshop trying to promote?

(A) A home appliance
(B) A health food
(C) A detergent

Direction は、このパートの概要と段取りを英語でアナウンスするものですが、聞かずに、その時間を、3つの設問を先読みするのに使います！

...ing feature of

...customers get?

(A) A reduction in price
(B) A coupon

74. What is Jessica not happy about?

(A) Shampoo quality
(B) Shampoo texture
(C) Shampoo packaging's color
(D) Shampoo price

75. What did Jessica mean when she said "customers are not rational"?

(A) Customers are shrewd.
(B) Customers do not know which to choose.
(C) Customers need to be coached.
(D) Customers like products which look nice.

76. What will the speaker do tomorrow?

(A) Discuss with the design team

設問と選択肢が印刷されています。しっかり先読み！

　1人の音声による短いトークを聞き、それに続いて流れる3つの設問に答えます。

　説明文は問題用紙に印刷されていませんが、**設問（英語）と4つの選択肢（A ～ D・英語）は印刷されています。**

Chapter ①

Part 1 写真描写

Part 2 応答

Part 3 会話

Part 4 説明文

Part 5 短文穴埋め

Part 6 長文穴埋め

Part 7 長文読解

● Part4 本番の流れはこれだ！

放送される内容　　　　　　　　　　あなたがすべきこと

> 英語の **Directions**（指示文）が
> 放送される《約30秒》

- - - ● 設問と選択肢（4つ）は問題用紙に印刷されていますので、最初のトークの設問3つ（Q71〜73）を先読みしましょう！

> **Questions71 through 73**
> **refer to the following talk.**
> 《約3秒》

- - - ● 次に放送される英語のトーク音声を聞き取る態勢に入りましょう！

《無音1秒》

> パッセージ《30〜40秒程度》

- - - - - - ● 音声を聞きながら、「答え」と思うものをどんどんマークしていきます！

《無音1秒》

> 設問71《5秒程度》
> 《無音8秒》
> 設問72《5秒程度》
> 《無音8秒》
> 設問73《5秒程度》

- - - - - - ● マークが終わり次第、次の3つの設問を先読み&推理する！

《無音8秒》

Questions74 through 76 refer ...（次の問題が始まる）

> 1つのパッセージに3つの質問！　全部で10セット！
> 放送は1回しか流れない。確実に先読みし、待ち伏せよう!!!

Part4 の Directions（指示文）は、こんな内容になっています。

パート4

指示：1人の話者によって話されるいくつかのトークを聞いていきます。それぞれのトークで3問ずつ、内容に関する質問がなされます。それぞれの質問に対して最適な応答を1つ選んで、解答用紙の (A)(B)(C)(D) から1つマークしてください。トークは問題用紙に印刷されていませんし、放送されるのは1度だけです。

[先読み攻撃＆待ち伏せ作戦] で ガッチリ得点！

●試験本番ではこう動こう！

　アナウンスや**スピーチ**、**ナレーション**などさまざまなトークを聞いて設問に答えるわけですが、ここでも Part3 と同様に、**先読みと待ち伏せ**が重要になってきます。試験本番では、トークの放送が終わり、1問目の設問**が聞こえ始めたと同時に3問ぶんの答えを選択**できている必要があります。

　このパートで高得点を出すために最も大切なことは、次の問題の設問の**先読みに費やす時間をいかに多く確保するか**ということですから、ぜひとも練習を重ねて、理想の速さに届くよう頑張りましょう！

ポイント 1　3つの設問先読みの鉄則はこれだ！

　先読みする設問のうち、**3W1H**（= Who と When と Where と How）の設問は選択肢が短いものが多く、初級者向けです。**短い選択肢**にざっと目を通せるようになっておくと、**高得点**につながります！

　逆に設問と選択肢が長いものは、**上級者用**の問題なので、設問だけ読んで「待ち伏せ」準備はしますが、狙いが外れたら速やかに**捨てましょう**。

　Part4 では3つの設問を先読みする際に、トークの内容を**予測**することも大切です。**広告**や**スピーチ**、**案内文**や**ニュース**、**天気予報**などがよく出題されます。

ポイント 2　トークを聞く時の注意点

　1〜2語で構成された短い選択肢は見ながら聞いても OK です。逆に、長いものを見ながらトークを聞いてしまうと、選択肢に気を取られて**何も聞き取れなく**なるので、見ながら聞いてはいけません！

Chapter①

Part 1 写真描写

Part 2 応答

Part 3 会話

Part 4 説明文

Part 5 短文穴埋め

Part 6 長文穴埋め

Part 7 長文読解

ポイント 3　まずは1＆3問目を取る気持ちで！

　1問目と3問目は必ず取る!という決意が大切です。1問目で特によく聞かれる「**主題**は何か」「**目的**は何か」「**話し手**は誰か」「**聞き手**は誰か」という問題を解くカギは**最初の2〜3文**にあります。しかし、もしその部分を聞いても1問目の答えがわからない場合は、**即座に捨てて2&3問目に集中！**

ポイント 4　後半の図表問題は難し……くない！

　後半の図表を見て答える問題は、**一見難しそうに思われるかもしれません**が、必ずしもそんなことはありません。これも同様に先読みして、図からトーク内容を予測し、何を読み取ればよいかを**推測**する練習をすれば、**実はこの手の問題のほうが簡単だったりします！**

ポイント 5　問題終了前に、次の3つの設問先読みは絶対！

　1問目の設問が読み上げられるのが聞こえた時点で、3問目までの**答えを選んでマーク**します。そして即座に次の問題の**3つの設問を読み始められる**ようになりましょう！　2問目の設問が読み上げられるタイミングで移ることができれば**16秒以上**ありますから、次の3つの設問を**しっかり先読み**できます。

最強！解答テクニック

❶　Directions の時間に最初の設問3つを先読み！

❷　初級者は設問と選択肢が短めのもの中心に待ち伏せ！

❸　1＆3問目を必ず取ると決意せよ！

❹　「主題・目的・話し手・聞き手」は冒頭2〜3文にあり！

❺　1問目の放送時間内に解答⇒次の3設問を先読み！

71. What document does the speaker request the attendants read at the meeting?

(A) A memo from the lawyer   (B) An investigation report

(C) Car sales report   (D) An interview report

72. How many of the customer complaints relate to the overheating of engines?

(A) 93%   (B) 95%

(C) 96%   (D) 92%

73. According to the speaker, what is the challenge?

(A) There are a lot of customer complaints.

(B) Local law is strict on product liabilities from cars.

(C) The company's lawyer found a problem.

(D) Customer complaints were not properly handled.

---

74. Why is the speaker unhappy about Jimmy?

(A) Jimmy went to the wrong airport.

(B) Jimmy's car broke down when picking up a guest.

(C) Jimmy called the wrong taxi.

(D) Jimmy was mistaken about the flight arrival time.

75. Why does the speaker ask his colleagues not to wear jeans?

(A) Because it is a company policy.

(B) Because Jeff is visiting the office.

(C) Because the speaker doesn't like jeans.

(D) Because it is not a Friday when Jeff visits.

76. What business is the speaker's company in?

(A) Hotel   (B) Apparel

(C) Car   (D) Research

解答・解説

71. 正解：(B)

What document does the speaker request the attendants read at the meeting?

話し手は会議で何の書類を読むよう要求されているか？

(A) A memo from the lawyer　弁護士からのメモ

(B) An investigation report　調査報告書

(C) Car sales report　車輌販売報告書

(D) An interview report　面接報告書

> **ポイント** 少し難。(C) にしたくなるが、これは、「受け取ったでしょ？」と言っているだけで、「調査報告書を私が話をするときに見てほしい」と言っている　⇒ **Level 3**

72. 正解：(A)

How many of the customer complaints relate to the overheating of engines?

顧客のクレームのどのくらい多くがエンジンのオーバーヒートに関するものか？

(A) 93%

(B) 95%

(C) 96%

(D) 92%

> **ポイント** overheat.. がキーワードと見抜き、ここを聞き取れば「93%」と直前にある　⇒ **Level 1**

73. 正解：(B)

According to the speaker, what is the challenge?

話し手によれば課題とは何か？

(A) There are a lot of customer complaints.　多くの顧客からのクレームがある。

(B) Local law is strict on product liabilities from cars.
現地法が車の製造責任に関して厳しい。

(C) The company's lawyer found a problem.　会社弁護士が問題を見つけた。

(D) Customer complaints were not properly handled.
顧客からのクレームが適切に処理されなかった

> **ポイント** challenge を待てば「ベトナムの法律が厳しい…」と聞きとれるはず　⇒ **Level 2**

> **語句** □ **liability** 名 （課されている）責任　※複数なし。liabilitiesha は「負債」

74. 正解：(B)

Why is the speaker unhappy about Jimmy?
話し手はどうして Jimmy に不満なのか？

(A) Jimmy went to the wrong airport.
　　Jimmy が間違った空港へ行った。

(B) Jimmy's car broke down when picking up a guest.
　　Jimmy の車が顧客を乗せているときに壊れた。

(C) Jimmy called the wrong taxi.
　　Jimmy が間違ったタクシーを呼んだ／に電話した。

(D) Jimmy was mistaken about the flight arrival time.
　　Jimmy が飛行便の到着時間についてミスをした。

> **ポイント** unhappy とはマイナスイメージだ。Jimmy... と聞こえてきたら集中して聞くと、必ず車が run out of gas と聞こえる。run out of gas が分からなくても car に関するものは (B) しかない！　⇒ Level 2

75. 正解：(A)

Why does the speaker ask his colleagues not to wear jeans?
話し手はなぜ同僚たちへジーンズを着用しないよう求めているのか？

(A) Because it is a company policy.
　　Because it is a company policy. なぜなら会社の方針だから

(B) Because Jeff is visiting the office.
　　なぜなら Jeff はその会社を訪問しようとしているから。

(C) Because the speaker doesn't like jeans.
　　なぜなら話し手はジーンズが好きでないから。

(D) Because it is not a Friday when Jeff visits.
　　なぜなら Jeff が訪れるのは金曜日ではないから。

> **ポイント** jeans がキーワードであるのは当然なので、ここをしっかり聞く。最後に会社のポリシーと聞こえれば OK　⇒ Level 1

76. 正解：(B)

What business is the speaker's company in?
話し手の会社はどんな商売なのか？

(A) Hotel　　ホテル

(B) Apparel　　服飾

(C) Car　　車

(D) Research　　研究；調査

> **ポイント** 最後の2行に we make jeans と出てくる　⇒ Level 2

スクリプト

Questions 71-73 refer to the following talk.

🇺🇸 **M:** The purpose of this meeting is to find out the best way to handle the customer complaints / about our new cars sold in Vietnam. / You should have received over the weekend a sales report of our new model Rose X96, / launched last February. / During the past 12 months, / we have received 195 customer complaints. / 93% of these complaints relate to the overheating of the engines. Our quality team has done an investigation report / so that you can take a look as I speak. / The challenge is that Vietnam law seems to impose a very strict standard on car defects and recalls. / Our lawyer is preparing a memo on this. / I will send this memo to you tomorrow.

　この会合の目的は顧客のクレームに対処するベストな方法を見いだすことです、ベトナムで売られている我が社の新しい車に関してのね。皆さんは週末に亘って我が社の新しい車 RoseX96 についての売上報告書を受け取られたはずです、この2月に発売されたやつのね。過去12カ月中、195通の顧客クレームを受け取りました。これらの93%はエンジンのオーバーヒートに関するものです。我が社の品質管理チームは調査報告書を作成しました、私がお話する時にご覧になれるようにと。難題はベトナムの法律が車の欠陥やリコールにとても厳しい基準を課しているようだということです。我が社の弁護士はこれに関してメモを用意しています。明日このメモを皆さんにお送り致します。

語句

❏ **purpose** 　名　目的
❏ **find out** 　（調べて）知る；分かる
　　　　　　　　※文法的には to find out とすべきところ特に米語では to が省かれる傾向がある
❏ **handle** 　動　対処する = address、deal with~
❏ **launch** 　動　発売する（元来は「発射する」）
❏ **complaint** 　名　不平；不満；文句　※日本でいう「クレーム」のこと
❏ **relate to~** 　~に関する
❏ **challenge** 　名　難題；課題
❏ **seem to~** 　~するようだ　　❏ **impose** 　動　課す
❏ **strict** 　形　厳しい　　❏ **standard** 　名　基準；標準
❏ **defects** 　名　欠陥　　❏ **recall** 　名　リコール；不良品回収
❏ **memo** 　メモ　※日本語のメモより意味が深く「覚書」のような感じで A-4 用紙 3~4 枚あることもある

Questions 74-76 refer to the following instructions.

🇦🇺 **M:** The first topic of today's meeting is Jeff's visit next week. / He has changed his flight time and arrival airport. / Kathy, make sure you speak with Jimmy about these changes. / Jimmy needs to do a better job. / Last time his car ran out of gas half way / and our guest had to call a taxi. / Next, I want to emphasize / that we don't have "Casual Friday". / So when Jeff comes in next Friday, / make sure he doesn't wear jeans. / The fact that we make jeans / doesn't mean we can wear them at work. / This has been our policy for three years / and we are not changing it for Jeff. /

　本日の会合の最初の話題は来週の Jeff の訪問についてだ。彼は飛行機の便と到着空港を変更した。Kathy、Jimmy とこれらの変更についてちゃんと話してくれ。Jimmy はもっとよい仕事をする必要があるんだ。前回、彼の車が途中でガス欠になっちゃって、うちのお客さんがタクシーを呼ばなければいけなかったんだ。次に、強調したいね、「普段着着用金曜日」は我が社には無いってことをね。そこで、Jeff が次の金曜にやってきたら、必ずジーンズを履かないよう念を押して。うちがジーンズを作っているという事実は、仕事中にジーンズを履いてよいと言う意味じゃないんだ。これは3年前からの我が社の方針であって、Jeff のために変えることはしない。

 語句

□ **make sure (that)~**	かならず~してほしい
□ **run out of~**	~が不足する
□ **emphasize**	動　強調する
□ **Casual Friday**	金曜普段着制

練習問題 練習問題に挑戦してみましょう！

77. What is the most amazing feature of THINEX?
   (A) It improves the heart rate.
   (B) It manages weight by increasing metabolism
   (C) It does not affect general appetite.
   (D) It has extra vitamins and minerals.

78. How can you get a 20% discount?
   (A) By ordering more than $400
   (B) By ordering at the end of the seminar
   (C) By ordering through a special hotline.
   (D) By joining a campaign program

79. How can you join the "money-back" program?
   (A) By ordering more than $400
   (B) By ordering more than $400 in six months
   (C) By referring a friend to attend the seminar
   (D)By referring a friend to buy THINEX

---

80. What company does the speaker work for?
   (A) Hospital   (B) Research lab
   (C) Cinema   (D) Construction company

81. About how many beds does the hospital want after the expansion?
   (A) 1,500   (B) 3,000
   (C) 4,500   (D) 5,000

82. According to the speaker, what does the hospital's lab do?
   (A) Research on emergency operations
   (B) Research on cancer
   (C) Research on new medicine
   (D) Research on diabetes

77. 正解：(C)

What is the most amazing feature of THINEX?
THINEX のもっとも驚嘆すべき特徴は何か？

(A) It improves the heart rate. 心拍数を改善する。

(B) It manages weight by increasing metabolism
代謝作用を増加させることで体重を管理する。

(C) It does not affect general appetite. 一般的な食欲に影響を与えない。

(D) It has extra vitamins and minerals. 特別なビタミンとミネラルが含まれている。

ポイント THINEX という語句を集中すれば、すぐにベタで聞こえる ⇒ **Level 1**

78. 正解：(B)

How can you get a 20% discount?
どうやれば20%の割引を得られるか？

(A) By ordering more than $400 400ドル以上注文することで

(B) By ordering at the end of the seminar セミナーの終わりに注文することで

(C) By ordering through a special hotline. 特別の直通電話で注文することで

(D) By joining a campaign program キャンペーン企画に参加することで

ポイント 20% discount を待ち伏せれば、その直前に聞こえる ⇒ **Level 1'**

79. 正解：(A)

How can you join the "money-back" program?
どうすれば money-back プログラムに参加できるか？

(A) By ordering more than $400 1回注文で400ドル以上注文することで

(B) By ordering more than $400 in six months 6カ月で400ドル以上注文することで

(C) By referring a friend to attend the seminar
友達にセミナーに出るように言うことで

(D) By referring a friend to buy THINEX 友達に THINEX を買うように言うことで

ポイント money-back program を待ち伏せれば、「ミニマムで 400 ドル」と聞こえるはず ⇒ **Level 1'**

Chapter ❶

Part 1 写真描写

Part 2 応答

Part 3 会話

Part 4 説明文

Part 5 短文穴埋め

Part 6 長文穴埋め

Part 7 長文読解

80. 正解：(D)

What company does the speaker work for?

話し手は何の会社で働いているか？

(A) Hospital　　　　　　　病院

(B) Research lab　　　　　研究所

(C) Cinema　　　　　　　映画館

(D) Construction company　建設会社

📝ポイント キーワードの construction は最後の2文まで出ない。bidding opportunity（入札機会）でピンと来るとよいが、初級者では難しいかも。ざっと流して聞いて分かる問題 ⇒ **Level 1'**

81. 正解：(C)

About how many beds does the hospital want after the expansion?

約どのくらいのベッドを病院は望んでいるか、拡張の後に。

(A) 1,500

(B) 3,000

(C) 4,500

(D) 5,000

📝ポイント bed がキーワード。このあとに triple にしたいと言っている。つまり 1,500 × 3＝4,500

82. 正解：(B)

According to the speaker, what does the hospital's lab do?

話し手によれば病院の研究室 [所] は何をするのか？

(A) Research on emergency operations　緊急手術の研究

(B) Research on cancer　　　　　　　　癌の研究

(C) Research on new medicine　　　　　新薬の研究

(D) Research on diabetes　　　　　　　糖尿病の研究

📝ポイント lab をしっかり聞き取れば次に cancer が出てくる。lab と love を間違えないように！　前者は強く a と e の中間の音を出して lab、後者はラと鼻にぬいて下唇を軽くかんで v の音を！

Questions 77-79 refer to the following advertisement.

🏴 **W:** Thank you for joining our health seminar today / on new weight management product THINEX. / The most amazing feature of this product is that / it suppresses your craving for sugar but does not affect your general appetite. / Also, / unlike many other weight management products on the market, / it doesn't make your heart rate faster. / If you order at the end of this seminar, / you will get an early bird discount of 20%. / In addition, / if you order a minimum of $400 in one order, / you will be eligible for our "money-back program", / where we will refund you if your BMI doesn't come down six months from the date of your purchase. / Recommend THINEX to your friends / and you may get more discount!/

　本日は私共の健康セミナーへ参加くださりありがとうございます——新しい体重管理製品 THINEX に関しての。この製品のもっとも驚嘆すべき特徴は、糖への渇望を押さえるが一般的な食欲には差し障りないというものです。また、市場にある他の多くの体重管理製品とは違って、心臓の鼓動を速くすることはありません。もしこのセミナー終了時にお申し込みになれば、早く来る人勝ちの20%割引きを得られます。加えて、1回の注文で最低でも400ドルをご注文くだされば、当社の「現金お返しプログラム」の資格が得られます、そのプログラムではご購入の日から6カ月で BMI が下がらなかったら払い戻しいたします。THINEX をお友達へお勧め下さい、そうすればさらに割引が得られるでしょう。

語句

☐ **weigh**	動	～の重さがある；重さをはかる
☐ **weight**	名	重さ
		※ weigh と way, weight と wait は発音が同じなので Part1,2 では繰り返し出題されている。注意！
☐ **amazing**	形	驚くほどの
☐ **feature**	名	特色
☐ **crave for~**		～をすごく求める
☐ **appetite**	名	食欲　※発音は [アピタイト]
☐ **early bird**		早起き鳥
		※早く起きる鳥はミミズなどえさをより多くとれることから。早い者勝ちの意味で使う。
☐ **be eligible for~**		～に対して資格がある；～に適っている

☐ **suppress**	動	押さえる；止める
☐ **affect**	動	(悪い) 影響を及ぼす
☐ **unlike**		～とは違って

Chapter ❶

Part 1 写真描写

Part 2 応答

Part 3 会話

Part 4 説明文

Part 5 短文穴埋め

Part 6 長文穴埋め

Part 7 長文読解

スクリプト

Questions 80-82 refer to the following speech.

🇺🇸 **W:** We've just got a new bidding opportunity from the Kingston General Hospital, / the largest hospital in the state. / They want to expand their existing patients' facilities / so that they can take in more patients. / Currently they have about 1,500 beds. / They want to triple this capacity through the expansion. / In addition, / they want to build a new building for operation rooms. / They also want to expand their lab facilities. / Last year they hired 15 researchers for their cancer research lab. / I really want us to get this project. / This would be the largest construction project for us in three years. / The contract value will be much bigger / than that of the cinema project we did last year.

　私共はこの度 Kingston 総合病院から新しい入札の機会を得ました——州最大の病院ですが。病院では既存の患者施設を拡張したがっておられます、さらに多くの患者さんを受け入れられるようにと。現在1500のベッドがあります。この収容能力を拡張により3倍にしたく思っておられます。加えて、手術室のため新しいビルの建設を望んでおられます。また、その研究室施設の拡張も望んでおられます。昨年ガン研究室に15名の研究員を雇用されました。私は本当にこのプロジェクトを得たいと思います。これは私共にとって3年で最大の建設プロジェクトでありましょう。その契約価値はうんと大きくなるでしょう、昨年我が社が行った映画館プロジェクトの建設より。

語句

❏ **bid** 動 入札する
❏ **expand** 動 拡張する
❏ **expansion** 名 拡張
❏ **existing** 形 既存の
❏ **patient** 名 患者　※発音は[ペイシャント]。形容詞で「我慢強い」という意味もあるので注意。
❏ **facility** 名 施設
❏ **currently** 副 今現在に
❏ **triple** 3倍
❏ **capacity** 名 キャパ；収容能力
❏ **in addition** 加えて
❏ **lab** 名 =laboratory 実験室、研究室（所）
❏ **contract** 名 契約
❏ **cinema** [英] =movie [米]

83. What company does the speaker work for?

(A) A restaurant　　　　　　(B) A bakery

(C) A soup store　　　　　　(D) A broadcasting company

84. What is the most well-known product being sold?

(A) cinnamon rolls　　　　　(B) chocolate donuts

(C) bagels　　　　　　　　　(D) butter rolls

85. What makes the new branch different from all the other branches?

(A) You can have soup in it.

(B) You can buy cinnamon rolls in it.

(C) You can pay with smart phones in it.

(D) You can charge your smart phones in it.

---

86. When will Sally give birth to her baby?

(A) May　　　　　　　　　　(B) June

(C) July　　　　　　　　　　(D) August

87. Which of the following does the company NOT cover in its relocation program?

(A) Rent in Berlin　　　　　(B) Home-visiting trip

(C) Kid's school fees　　　　(D) Relocation costs

88. What is suggested about Wendy?

(A) She will be in Berlin for 2 years if she joins the relocation program.

(B) She is also going to have a baby.

(C) She has no children.

(D) She has never been to Berlin before.

※ 89-94 はここでは省きます。

Chapter ①

Part 1 写真描写

Part 2 応答

Part 3 会話

Part 4 説明文

Part 5 短文穴埋め

Part 6 長文穴埋め

Part 7 長文読解

解答・解説

83. 正解：(B)

What company does the speaker work for?
話し手は何の会社で働いているか？

(A) A restaurant　　　　　　　　レストラン

(B) A bakery　　　　　　　　　　パン屋

(C) A soup store　　　　　　　スープの店

(D) A broadcasting company　放送会社

ポイント 注意していればすぐに bakery と聞こえる　⇒ **Level 1**

84. 正解：(A)

What is the most well-known product being sold?
売られている最も有名な製品は何か？

(A) cinnamon rolls　　　　シナモン・ロール

(B) chocolate donuts　　チョコ・ドーナツ

(C) bagels　　　　　　　　ベイゲル

(D) butter rolls　　　　　　バター・ロール

ポイント これも簡単。famous=well-known だから　⇒ **Level 2**

85. 正解：(A)

What makes the new branch different from all the other branches?
新支店が他のすべての支店と違うものは何か？

(A) You can have soup in it.　　　　　　　そこではスープが飲める。

(B) You can buy cinnamon rolls in it.　　そこではシナモン・ロールが買える。

(C) You can pay with smart phones in it.　そこではスマホで払える。

(D) You can charge your smart phones in it.　そこではスマホに充電できる。

ポイント 当然後半に来ると読む。special ということは different ということ！　⇒ **Level 2**

86. 正解：(B)

When will Sally give birth to her baby?

Saslly はいつ出産するか？

(A) May 5月

(B) June 6月

(C) July 7月

(D) August 8月

> **ポイント** 冒頭の一節を注意して聞くだけ。expect は「期待する；予期する」 ⇒ **Level 1**
> ちなみに pregrant（妊娠している）という語は日本語でもそうであるように、直接
> すぎるのであまり使わない方が良い。

87. 正解：(C)

Which of the following does the company NOT cover in its relocation program?

再配置計画で会社が持たないものは次のどれか？

(A) Rent in Berlin ベルリンでの家賃

(B) Home visiting trip 国にかえる旅費

(C) Kid's school fees 子供の学費

(D) Relocation costs 移転費

> **ポイント** これも簡単。最後に子供の教育はカバーできない、とある ⇒ **Level 2**

88. 正解：(C)

What is suggested about Wendy?

Wendy について何が分かるか?

(A) She will be in Berlin for 2 years if she joins the relocation program.
彼女はもしこの再配置計画に加わればベルリンに2年いることになろう。

(B) She is also going to have a baby. 彼女にもまた赤ちゃんが生まれる予定だ。

(C) She has no children. 彼女には子供はいない。

(D) She has never been to Berlin before. 彼女は以前ベルリンに行ったことがない。

> **ポイント** 答えは最後にある。「子供の教育費はカバーしないが、あなたに対しての問題点では
> ない」とは子供がいないということ。Level 2 の paraphrase とするには、話し手
> の意見(気持ち)が入っているので ⇒ **Level 3**

スクリプト

Questions 83-85 refer to the following announcement.

M: We are happy to announce the opening of our third branch on Sommer Street next Monday. / As with all of our current bakery stores, / this new branch will bring you all kinds of fresh bread / including our famous cinnamon rolls. / It will also offer fruit cakes, bagels, donuts and butter rolls. / What makes this new branch special is that / it will have its own eat-in restaurant / where hot sandwiches, coffee and soups are served. / In this new branch, / you will also be able to use your mobile phones to pay for your orders / just like our flagship store on Dane Street.

　来週の月曜に Sommer Street に私共の3番目の支店の開店することをお知らせできてうれしく思います。現在の私共のすべてのベーカリー同様に、この新支店は皆様にあらゆる種類のフレッシュなパンをお届け致します、私共の有名なシナモン・ロールを含みましてね。またこの支店ではフルーツケーキ、ベイグル（ドーナツ状の堅ロールパン）、ドーナツ、そしてバター・ロールも提供させていただきます。この支店を特別なものにしていることは、固有のイートインレストランを持つことです、そこではホット・サンド やコーヒー、そしてスープが出されますよ。この新支店では、注文したものの支払いに携帯電話がお使いになれます、Dane Street にあるうちの旗艦店と全く同様に。

語句

❑ **including~**	～を含んで
❑ **what makes A B**	A を B にしている物
	※ what は「～のこと」「～のもの」という関係代名詞 ）。関係副詞の where は「そしてそこでは…」と頭から訳して行くと良い
❑ **flagshop**	图 「旗の店」とは「一番中心の店」のこと

Questions 86-88 refer to the following talk.

🇺🇸 **W:** Wendy, I want to talk to you about our relocation program. / Sally is going to have a baby / and her expected date is in June. / After that, she will go on maternity leave until next May. / So she can no longer be relocated to our Berlin office, / which was originally the plan. / Would you like to apply for this program? / It is a one-year assignment in our Berlin headquarters / starting from this August. / The company will cover relocation costs, / housing and one home-visiting trip. / We won't cover kids education / but I don't think that will be an issue for you. /

　Wendy、我が社の再配置計画についてお話ししたいです。Sally に赤ちゃんが生まれます、それで出産予定は6月なのです。その後彼女は出産休暇に来年の5月まで入ります。それでもはやうちのベルリン事務所へは移れなくなりました、もともとはそういう計画だったのですが。この計画に申し込んでみませんか？　それはうちのベルリン本社での1年の任務です、この8月から始まります。会社が移転費用は補填します、住居費そして1回の里帰りも。子供の教育費は補填できません、でもそれはあなたへの問題点ではないすよね。

 語句

❏ **relocate**	動　移転する　※ re+locate
❏ **maternity**	母であること　※ mother から
❏ **leave**	名　休暇；許可　※頻出！
❏ **no longer**	もはや〜でない
❏ **apply for〜**	〜へ申し込む
❏ **assignment**	名　任務；割り当てられた仕事
❏ **headquarters**	名　本社
❏ **cover**	動　カバーする；補填する；持つ
❏ **housing**	名　住居 (集合的に)
❏ **home**	名　母国

練習問題 練習問題に挑戦してみましょう！

Part 1 写真描写

Part 2 応答

Part 3 会話

Part 4 説明文

Part 5 短文穴埋め

Part 6 長文穴埋め

Part 7 長文読解

95. What products does the speaker's company make?

(A) toys

(B) tablets

(C) cellphones

(D) books

96. Look at the graphic. Which country does the chart refer to?

(A) Thailand

(B) Vietnam

(C) China

(D) Japan

Sales & Amount	
100,000	75,000
the first six months	**the last six months**

97. What is the speaker's suggestion?

(A) Develop new products with digital features

(B) Re-train the sales team

(C) Spend more on marketing

(D) Be more creative in the commercials.

98. What is suggested about Serena?

    (A) She will have a baby soon.

    (B) She likes socks.

    (C) She doesn't like boots.

    (D) She likes books.

99. Look at the graphic. How much is the gift?

    (A) $28.9

    (B) $25

    (C) $27

    (D) $29

A pair of boots	$ 28.90
Two pairs of baby socks	$ 25.00
A massage coupon	$ 27.00
A book on children games	$ 29.00

100. Who is the speaker probably calling?

    (A) Her boyfriend

    (B) Her boss

    (C) Serena's cousin

    (D) Serena's husband

解答・解説

95. 正解：(A)

What products does the speaker's company make?

話しての会社はどんな製品を作っているか？

(A) toys おもちゃ

(B) tablets タブレット

(C) cellphones 携帯電話

(D) books 本

> **ポイント** 最初聞いていると「自動車かな？」と思う人も多いだろう。子供たちのことが出てきて初めておもちゃだと分かるという仕組みだ　⇒ **Level 1**

96. 正解：(D)

Look at the graphic. Which country does the chart refer to?

図を見なさい。チャートはどの国のことに言及していますか？

(A) Thailand タイ

(B) Vietnam ベトナム

(C) China 中国

(D) Japan 日本

> **ポイント** 日本はまあまあで、25％減少なら75％になっているはずだから　⇒ **Level 2**

97. 正解：(A)

What is the speaker's suggestion?

話し手の提案は何か？

(A) evelop new products with digital features デジタル機能をもつ新製品を開発する

(B) Re-train the sales team 営業チームを再訓練する

(C) Spend more on marketing マーケティングにもっとお金を使う

(D) Be more creative in the commercials. コマーシャルにもっと創造的になる

> **ポイント** digital が聞き取れれば、だれでもできる問題　⇒ **Level 1'**

売上げと金額	
100,000	75,000
最初の6ヶ月	過去6ヶ月

98. 正解：(A)

What is suggested about Serena?
Serina について何が分かるか？

(A) She will have a baby soon.　彼女にまもなく赤ちゃんが生まれる。

(B) She likes socks.　　　彼女はソックスが好きだ。

(C) She doesn't like boots.　　彼女はブーツが嫌いだ。

(D) She likes books.　　　彼女は本が好きだ。

> 🔖ポイント baby shower や present を買うと聞こえれればだれでも (A) が正解だと分かる
> ⇒ **Level 2**

99. 正解：(C)

Look at the graphic. How much is the gift?
図を見なさい。話しての選ぶ贈り物はいくらだろうか？

(A) $28.9　28.9 ドル

(B) $25　25 ドル

(C) $27　27 ドル

(D) $29　29 ドル

> 🔖ポイント トーク最後で「足のマッサージが好きだからこれに決めた！」とある。

ブーツ 1 足	28.9 ドル
赤ちゃん用くつ下 2 足	25 ドル
マッサージのクーポン	27 ドル
子供のゲームの本	29 ドル

100. 正解：(A)

Who is the speaker probably calling?
話し手はだれに電話しているのか？

(A) Her boyfriend　　彼女の恋人

(B) Her boss　　　彼女の上役

(C) Serena's cousin　Serina のいとこ

(D) Serena's husband　Serina の夫

> 🔖ポイント あわてると (D) にしてしまう人がいるかも。Serina は祝いを受ける人。だとすれば
> 話し手の夫か恋人ということになる　⇒ **Level 2**

スクリプト

Questions 95-97 refer to the following announcement.

🇬🇧 **M:** I called this meeting / because our board meeting is on next Wednesday / and one of the items on the agenda for this board meeting is the decreased sales in our Asia market in the last six months. / I want to first go over the monthly sales report with you. / As you can see from the report, / our sales in Thailand dropped 30% / and those in Vietnam dropped 40%. / Japan is slightly better with a 25% drop. / The worst country is China / where our sales dropped 45%. / One of the challenges we are facing is that / more and more children are turning to digital devices and online games. / Teddy bears are no longer their favorites. / I think we should develop new toys with digital features / to respond to the market in this digital era./ Otherwise / our sales will continue to suffer / and commercials won't help. /

　この会合を招集しました、なぜなら私共の役員会が来週開催され、そしてこの役員会の議題の一つがこの過去6カ月におけるアジア市場での販売の落ち込みだからです。私はまず皆様と月ごとの売れ上げ報告書をよく検討したいと思います。報告書から分かりますように、我が社のタイでの売上は30%落ちており、そしてベトナムでは40%落ちています。日本は25%の落ちでまあまあです。最悪なのは中国です、そこでは当社の売上は45%落ちました。私共が直面している難題の一つは、次第に多くの子供たちがデジタルの装置やオンラインゲームの方へ向きを変えつつあることです。テディーベア(熊さんの縫いぐるみ人形)はもはや彼らのお気に入りではないのです。私共もデジタルの特徴を持った新しいおもちゃを開発すべきだと思います、このデジタル時代の市場に応ずるために。さもなければ、我が社の売上は損害を受け続け、コマーシャルは手助けにならないでしょう。

📝 語句

❏ call	動 招集する	❏ board meeting	役員会；重役会
❏ because...	～なので	❏ decrease	⇔ increase
❏ go over	詳しく調べる；検討する		
❏ face	動 ～に直面する	❏ turn to~	～へと向きを変える
❏ device	名 装置；仕掛け	❏ respond to~	～に応える
❏ otherwise	さもないと	❏ suffer	動 苦しむ；被害を受ける

Questions 98-100 refer to the following telephone conversation.

🏴 **W:** Serena will have a baby shower next Friday. / All of us are going. / I'm now on Emezon to find her a present. / It seems there are a lot to choose / with in a budget of $30. / Serena has made it clear to us / that she doesn't want for anything for the baby's use as she has enough already. / She wants something for herself. / So I guess all baby stuff is out. / Also her cousin is bringing her a pair of boots, / so I think we should avoid shoes. / What do you think, / honey? / Any advice? / What? / Books? / Serena is not a fan of books... / Ah, I found something. / I'm sure she will like it / because she loves foot massage! / OK thanks honey /. It's solved! / Call you later... /

来週の金曜日は Serena が baby shower を受ける日です。私たちみんな行きます。私は今彼女へのプレゼントを見つけるため Emezon にいます。たくさん選ぶものがありそうです、30ドル以内の予算で。Serina は私たちにはっきりさせていました、子供が使うものはもう十分にあるので何も欲しくはないと。彼女は自分が使うものが欲しいと。それで私が思うのは、すべての赤ちゃん用品はずれてます。また、彼女の従姉妹がブーツを持って来るそうです、それで靴は避けないと。あなた、どう思う？なにかアドバイスある？なに？本？Serina は本のファンじゃないです。あぁ、一つ見つけたよ。彼女きっとそれを気に入るよ、彼女、足のマッサージが大好きだから。OK ありがとう、あなた。解決です。あとで電話するね。

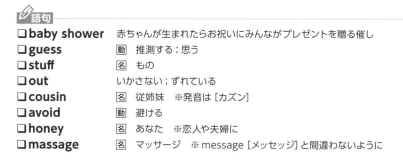

語句

❏ **baby shower**		赤ちゃんが生まれたらお祝いにみんながプレゼントを贈る催し
❏ **guess**	動	推測する；思う
❏ **stuff**	名	もの
❏ **out**		いかさない；ずれている
❏ **cousin**	名	従姉妹 ※発音は [カズン]
❏ **avoid**	動	避ける
❏ **honey**	名	あなた ※恋人や夫婦に
❏ **massage**	名	マッサージ ※ message [メッセッジ] と間違わないように

Chapter ❶

Part 1 写真描写

Part 2 応答

Part 3 会話

Part 4 説明文

Part 5 短文穴埋め

Part 6 長文穴埋め

Part 7 長文読解

COLUMN

英語力上達に TOEIC® を生かす方法〜 Part1 編〜

　近年、TOEIC® に対しての実業界の依存度はどんどん高まっています。大手企業の 85% が入社時に同テストを参考にしているとデータに現れています。大学の教員をしていますとこの風潮、確かに実感しますね。一流と言われている会社の人事に教え子が何人かいるのですが、皆口を揃えて「まずは 600 点は最低ラインで…800 点あれば十分ですね」と言います。でもこれは入社時の英語力査定の目安で、実際には聞けて、話せないと話になりません。特に海外と取引のある会社に入社した場合、痛感することになります。600 点レベルでも下手でも堂々と外国人と話せる学生もいれば、800 点あってもほとんどしゃべれない学生もいます。しかしこの差は、TOEIC 勉強の仕方次第で、かなり改善できると思います。

　まず、発音です。日本人の英語発音はほとんどがカタカナ発音です。これは中学、高校でテスト中心、すなわち読めて訳せて穴埋めができれば良いという受験英語学習をしてきたからです。点さえ取れれば、正しい発音やイントネーションに気をつける必要はないわけです。でも、これでは英語でのコミュニケーションには役に立ちません。大学生や社会人は、発音を良くすることをまず考えるべきです。

　そのためにまずは TOEIC® の Part1 を利用しましょう。6 つの写真を見ながら、例えば一匹の犬が男性に吠えかかっている写真で、正解文がA dog is barking at the man. だとします。これを、dog と barkingと man を強く発音し、声優のマネをして何度も何度も口に出して言うことです。この時、文字を見てだめです。あくまでも耳で聞いて、口を動かします。

　特に F と V（下唇を軽く噛む）、L（舌先を上の歯の裏に当ててラリルレロと言う）と R（舌を下に沈めてラリルレロとあいまいな発音で言う）の音、s と sh の違い（例：see は [スィー] で she は [シー]）、舌先を軽く噛む th の音、そして bad の d や but の t など語尾の t と d のあとに「オ」の音を残さないことを意識して声に出す練習をすれば、Part1 の 6 題だけでも結構効果があります。ここでしっかり発音のコツをつかんで自信を持ちましょう！

短い英文の穴を埋める！
ゼロからスタート Part5 短文穴埋め問題

本番では… 全30問：Q101-130

[中学レベル 英文法探し]で 速攻解答しよう！

聴く勉 TOEIC 講座！ DL音声 33-36

30問を12分で！ Part5 はこんなテストだ！

entire Reading test will last 75 minutes. There are three parts, and directions are given for each part. You are encouraged to a as many questions as possible within the time allowed. You must mark your answers on the separate answer she not write your answers in your test book.

PART 5

Directions: A word or phrase is missing in each of the sent below. Four answer choices are given below each sen Select the best answer to complete the sentence. Then ma letter (A), (B), (C), or (D) on your answer sheet.

> Direction（指示文）は 読まなくても OK！

> 4つの選択肢の中から、 空欄に入るのにふさわし いものを選びます。

101. Ms. Wada has run a small shop with ------- own savings since last year.
(A) she
(B) her
(C) hers
(D) herself

> 空欄は点線で表されています。

new school pe completed in two months.
(A) highly

104. ------- manufacturing costs have not significantly decreased, Takeda Co. has experienced a sharp fall in its yearly expenditure.
(A) Although
(B) Despite
(C) Because
(D) Owing to

105. When this afternoon's business seminar ends, Dr. Hewitt will have his staff

　リーディングセクションの最初のパート。**短い英文の空欄**になっている部分に入る語句を、(A) 〜 (D) の選択肢の中から選びます。

　大切なのはスピード！ **1問20秒めやす、30問12分で通過**できるように練習しましょう！ コツは **「これは中学レベルの問題だ!」と判断したものだけ**を解き、難しい単語・知らない単語が並ぶ「語彙問題」を捨てる（=どれでもいいからマークする）勇気を持つことです！

Chapter①

Part 1 写真描写

Part 2 応答

Part 3 会話

Part 4 説明文

Part 5 短文穴埋め

Part 6 長文穴埋め

Part 7 長文読解

● **Part5 本番の流れはこれだ!**

テストの開始

Part4 の放送が終わって、This is the end of the listening test. Turn to Part 5 in your test book. End of recording. と流れたら、**そのまますぐにリーディングテスト (Part5) を開始しましょう。**

出題パターン

Part5 で出題されるのは以下の3パターンです。 選択肢に注目!

1 品詞選択問題　ヒントは空所の前後にあり!

例 Adam was able to make an immediate -------to the date because the flyer was still in the top drawer.

(A) correct

(B) correct**ion**

(C) correct**ly**

(D) correct**ed**

> 選択肢を見てみると、correct とその派生語、**つまりいろんな品詞の単語がずらり!**　空欄にどの品詞の単語が入るべきかを見抜く問題だ!　**空所の前後**を見てヒントを探そう!

2 文法問題　中学レベル文法の見極めがポイント!

例 Most companies used to prefer ------- staff from within rather than externally, especially for senior-level positions.

(A) **to be** recruit**ed**

(B) **to** recruit

(C) recruit

(D) recruit**s**

> recruit という動詞がどの形で空欄に入るべきか=**文法ルール**から解答を導く問題。この後解説する**「中学レベル英文法」**かどうかを素早く見極めよう!

3 語彙選択問題　単語を知らなかったらとりあえずどれかにマーク!

例 Few members of the staff ------- in the company retreat, so it has been cancelled.

(A) enroll**ed**

(B) defeat**ed**

(C) reliev**ed**

(D) except**ed**

> 選択肢が全て動詞の過去形になっている=この空欄に動詞の過去形が入ることは**確定**しているのだから、あとはどの単語が**意味的に適切か**判断しなくてはならない…それが語彙問題!　単語の意味を知らなかったら考えても**時間の無駄**!　捨てる勇気を持とう!

※ Part5 の Directions の内容は、P107 にあります。

4つの設問パターンを知って攻略せよ！

パターン 1 出題率最多の[品詞選択]は絶対取ろう！

本書で学習しているみなさんは、Part5 において、何をおいてもこの**「品詞選択問題」を絶対に取る**ことです！ **毎回10問近く出題**されるので、50点近く稼げる計算。何としても理解しておきたいところ！

1 名詞 数えられる・数えられない（可算・不可算）に注目！

数えられる名詞＝可算名詞という。1つの場合（例：a pen）／複数の場合（例：pens）／限定的な場合（例：the pen / this pen / my pen）がある

数えられない名詞＝不可算名詞といい、いくつかの種類がある。

● 物質名詞（例：wood / iron / metal / water など）

● 抽象名詞（例：love / truth / honesty など）

● **抽象名詞ではないが形がはっきりしないもの⇒ TOEIC® で頻出 !!**

とくに **information**（情報）／ **advice**（忠告）／ **equipment**（備品;機器）／ **baggage [luggage]**（荷物）／ **furniture**（家具）などは出題頻度が高い！

> なお、「数えられない名詞」を数えるには、**a piece of ~** や two pieces of ~ などを用いるよ！
> 不可算名詞がたくさんある場合は、**much[a lot of]** water と言うよ！(pen など可算名詞の場合は many を使う)。
> 逆に少ない場合は、**a few** coins（少しのコイン）や **few** coins（少ししかないコイン）、**a little** water（少しの水）や **little** water（少ししかない水）と表現するよ！

2 動詞 形の変化に注意！

動詞は主語の後に置かれ、その形が変化する場合があります。特に、**主語と遠く離れているときは要注意!** また、助動詞の後にくる場合は、受け身でないかどうか、特に注意を払いましょう。

The professor who gave the lecture on patriotism **had** an
[主語] [動詞]
energetic attitude while standing on the platform.（愛国主義について講義をしたその教授は演壇に立っている間エネルギッシュな姿勢だった）

3 形容詞 連体詞と補語に注意!

　形容詞は、**名詞を修飾している連体詞**になる場合と、主語・目的語と**イコール関係の補語**になる場合があります。

　また、形容詞は **-ful** や **-ous** や **ial** や **-tive** などの語尾が多いということも頭に入れておきましょう。例えば、wonder**ful**（素晴らしい）、fam**ous**（有名な）、industr**ial**（産業の）、competi**tive**（競争の）などがありますね。なお、イコール関係でのみ使える形容詞は、ほとんど「a...」の形です。例えば、afraid、awake、asleep、aware、alike、ashamed などですね。

4 副詞 形容詞との違いに注意!

　副詞は、名詞以外のもの、おもに**動詞・形容詞を修飾**します。**形容詞と副詞を区別する問題は非常によく出題されます**。例えば、happy と happily、beautiful と beautifully、interesting と interestingly などのように、副詞は、**語尾に -ly の形**がよく見られます。つまり、-ly が付いていたら**「副詞じゃないか?」**と疑ってみることです。

　ただし! **名詞に -ly が付いたものは形容詞**なので混同しないように! **friendly**（きさくな）、**timely**（時を得た）、**costly**（費用がかさむ）などがそれにあたります。

最強!解答テクニック

❶ 名詞：「数えられる or 数えられない」に注目!

❷ 動詞：形の変化に注意。特に主語と離れているとき!

❸ 形容詞：名詞を修飾している場合と、主語［目的語］と「＝」になる場合がある!

❹ 副詞：形容詞と区別する問題が頻出! 語尾が -ly は副詞の可能性が大!

---

1. Adam was able to make an immediate -------to the date because the flyer was still in the top drawer.

   (A) correct   (B) correction   (C) correctly   (D) corrected

   ヒント☞ immediate は「即座の」

---

2. Most companies here outsource production overseas, but Okada Corp.is one ------- exception.

   (A) notice   (B) noted   (C) note   (D) notable

---

3. It seems like Ms. Ferguson is glad to find a ------- spot to build a house on.

   (A) likeness   (B) like   (C) likelier   (D) likely

---

4. To handle office work accurately, even a part-time worker must fill out this form -------.

   (A) careful   (B) carefulness   (C) most careful   (D) carefully

---

5. This shape memory T-shirt is ------- designed for business people travelling abroad.

   (A) specified   (B) specifically   (C) specific   (D) specify

---

6. The matter is still in ------- even after they had a long discussion.

   (A) disputes   (B) disputable   (C) disputed   (D) dispute

---

解答・解説

1. 正解：(B) correction

ポイント make an ------- となっているので、空所は必ず名詞が入るはず。

[訳]アダムは日付を即座に訂正することが出来た、そのチラシがまだ一番上の引き出しにあったので。

2. 正解：(D) notable

ポイント exception（例外）が名詞なので、直前には形容詞が来るので noted（著名な）か notable（注目に値する）の選択となる。

[訳]当地のほとんどの会社は海外に生産を外注している、しかし岡田社は注目に値する例外だ。

 語句 ❑**notice** 通知 ❑**note** メモ

3. 正解：(D) likely

ポイント a ------- spot となっているので、空所には形容詞（like, likely）が入る。likelier は比較級なので不適。like+ 名詞または節がくる。likely（見込みのありそうな）が正解。なお、be likely to〜（〜しがちな；ありえる）は頻出。

[訳]Ms. Ferguson は家を建てるのに見込みありそうな場所をみつけて喜んでいる。

4. 正解：(D) carefully

ポイント fill out this form（この書式に書き込む）で文として成立しているので、修飾語句しかいらない→副詞 carefully が正解。

[訳]オフィス作業を処理するためには、パートの従業員でもこの書式に注意深く記入しなければならない。

5. 正解：(B) specifically

ポイント is designed で受け身の文が完成しているので designed を修飾する⇒副詞だ！

[訳]この形状記憶 T シャツは特にデザインされている、海外へ出張するビジネスマンのために。

 語句 ❑**specify** 動 特定する；明確にする ❑**specific** 形 特定の；特有の；明確な

6. 正解：(D) dispute

ポイント in の後なので名詞！

[訳]その問題は依然として論争中だ、長い話し合いがあった後ですらも、だ。

 語句 ❑**dispute** 名 論争 動 論争する ❑**in dispute** 論争中 ※複数ではない

7. The professor who gave a lecture on patriotism had an ------- attitude while standing on the platform.

(A) energetic (B) energy (C) energies (D) energetically

8. It is ------- that global warming will affect various fields, such as agriculture.

(A) expectant (B) expected (C) expecting (D) expectation

9. Toyoda Cars promises to give a fair trade-in price on any vehicle, ------- of the condition it is in.

(A) regards (B) regarding (C) regarded (D) regardless

10. It is ------- that young people tend to ignore the ordinance prohibiting using a cell phone while driving.

(A) disappoint　　　　(B) disappointing
(C) disappointment　　(D) disappointed

11. Most schools and offices are closed today in ------- of a national holiday.

(A) observe (B) observation (C) observing (D) observance

12. MX-5 fountain pen can be purchased ------- at Queen Department Store.

(A) exclude (B) exclusive (C) excluding (D) exclusively

Chapter❶

Part 1 写真描写

Part 2 応答

Part 3 会話

Part 4 説明文

Part 5 短文穴埋め

Part 6 長文穴埋め

Part 7 長文読解

7. 正解：(A) energetic

ポイント an ------- attitude（姿勢；態度）なので、------- には形容詞が入る。had の主語が the professor であることをつかもう！

[訳] 愛国主義について講義をしたその教授は演壇に立っている間エネルギッシュな姿勢だった。

語句 ❑ **energetic** 精力的な；エネルギッシュな

8. 正解：(B) expected

ポイント is の後なので形容詞か名詞だが、ここは it ~ that 構文になっている。すなわち「that 以下が予測される」となるのが普通。人が主語なら I am expecting that …（~を予測している）と、-ing は OK。expectant は形容詞で、We are expectant of ~（又は that …）などと使って「~を期待している」を表す。expectation は名詞。expect は動詞で予測する；期待する」。

[訳] 地球温暖化が農業のような種々の分野に影響をおよぼすだろうことが予測される。

9. 正解：(D) regardless

ポイント これは (being) regardless of~（~にもかかわらず）という分詞構文が成句として独立したものなので、知らなければ 100% できない。regarding~（~に関して）は前置詞。regard A as B は「A を B と見なす」で、regards（敬意；心遣い）は手紙の最後に書く言葉。

[訳] Toyoda Cars 社はどんな車にも公正な下取り価格を出すことを約束している、それがどんな状態であるかを問わず。

10. 正解：(B) disappointing

ポイント disappoint（がっかりさせる）は他動詞。disappointing（がっかりさせるような）、disappointed（がっかりさせられている）という意味になる。it ~ that 構文なので、that 以下がどちらの意味になるかを考えれば簡単。喜怒哀楽を表す動詞（please, excite, surprise, delight など）は、常にこのスタイルをとることに注意。

[訳] 若者が、運転中に携帯電話を使うことを禁じている条例を無視する傾向にあるのはがっかりだ。

11. 正解：(D) observance

ポイント in ------- of となっているので、空所には名詞が来る。したがって obeservation（観察）か observance（順守）。obeserving は of があるのでだめ！ observe に「観察する」「(所見として) 述べる」と「順守する」「(祝日を) 祝う」の 4 つの意味があることを記憶しましょう。

[訳] 大抵の学校や会社は本日閉まっている、国民の祝日を順守して [祝って]。

12. 正解：(D) exclusively

ポイント be purchased at~（~で購入される）で文が完成されることに注目。ならば at（前置詞）の前には副詞だ！

[訳] MX-5 という万年筆は、クイーン百貨店で独占的に購入することができる。

語句 ❑ **exclude** 動 除外する　❑ **exclusive** 形 独占的な

パターン 2 [動詞をふさわしい形にする問題] 6つの重要ポイントはこれだ！

1 時制・規則動詞・不規則動詞

中学で学習する動詞のルール：**時制**（現在・過去・未来・現在完了など）、**規則動詞** (-ed)、**不規則動詞**についてひととおり頭に入れておきましょう。

2 be 動詞が必要なケース＝進行形と受け身

例えば A mobile phone is **being** polish**ed**.（携帯電話が磨かれている）などのような、進行形と受け身を合わせた「〜されているところ」を意味する**受け身の進行形**には注意!

3 現在完了：継続・完了・経験を表す

例えば The store has **been** closed for five days.（その店は5日間ずっと閉まっている）は「ずっと〜だ」という**継続**を表す完了形です。現在完了には「継続」のほか、「**完了**」と「**経験**」も表現します。

4 助動詞の用法を覚えよう!

can、**may**、**must**、**will**、**shall**、**might**、**would**、**should** などは必須!助動詞の後には通常動詞の**原形か現在完了形**のどちらかが置かれます。

例 She **may be** a dancer.（彼女はダンサー**かもしれない**）

She **may have been** a dancer.（彼女はダンサー**だったかもしれない**）

このように、原形を置くか完了形を置くかで**時制の違い**を表現できます。

5 準動詞＝ to 不定詞・分詞・動名詞をチェック!

不定詞＝「こと」「べき」「して」「ため」が基本!

例えば I want **to master** English.（私は英語をマスターしたい）という文の場合、「〜する" **こと** "」を欲していることになります。また、This is a good book to read.（これは読むのによい本だ）であれば「読む" **べき** "」と

Chapter ❶

Part 1 写真描写

Part 2 応答

Part 3 会話

Part 4 説明文

Part 5 短文穴埋め

Part 6 長文穴埋め

Part 7 長文読解

なり I'm glad **to see** you. なら「会えて」つまり「**" ～して "** うれしい」ということを意味します。さらに I went to the States **to master** English.（英語をマスターするために米国へ行った）は、～する**" ために "** を表します。ただし、「（人）に～させる」を表す**使役動詞**（make、have、let、help）や see、hear、feel などの**知覚動詞**では、to が脱落した**原形不定詞**を取ります。

例 I **made** her **go** there.（私は彼女をそこへ行かせた）

I **saw** him **cross** the street.（私は彼が通りを横切るのを見た）

☞ 分詞 (-ing / -ed) は直前、直後の名詞を修飾する!

the **broken** window（割れた［割られた］窓）のように、修飾する対象が**1語**であれば**前から修飾**できますが、the window **broken last night**（昨夜割られた窓）のように、**2語以上**になると**後ろからしか修飾**できません。

☞ 動名詞= -ing は「～すること」を表す!

I like **dancing**.（踊ることが好き）のような文で「～すること」という意味を表します。また、He is proud **of being** a TV newscaster.（彼はテレビキャスターであることを誇りに思っている）のように、前置詞の後に動詞を置く場合は動名詞にする必要があります。

---

6 主語 (S) と動詞 (V) を常に意識しよう!

常に主語 (S) と動詞 (V) を意識して見つけるクセをつけましょう。これは**全パートにわたって重要**なことです。コツは、「英文の中で、**まず動詞 (V) を見つけて前に戻れば、主語 (S) が見えてくる!**」ということです。

最強！解答テクニック

❶ **動詞の時制・規則動詞・不規則動詞を再チェック!**

❷ **進行形・受け身は** be **動詞必須。受け身の進行形に注意**

❸ **過去とのかかわりを伝えるのが現在完了**

❹ **助動詞の用法を覚えるべし!**

❺ to **不定詞・分詞・動名詞をチェックすべし!**

---

1. Most companies used to prefer ------- staff from within rather than externally, especially for senior-level positions.

   (A) to be recruited   (B) to recruit   (C) recruit   (D) recruits

---

2. Over the next three years, the government ------- to hold a world-wide event in Tokyo.

   (A) planning   (B) having planned   (C) plans   (D) to plan

---

3. Javis Technology is pleased to ------- that it will open a new branch in Singapore.

   (A) announce   (B) announcing   (C) announced   (D) announces

---

4. Mr. Cooper fixed the computer problem that ------- down transactions all last weekend.

   (A) slows   (B) has slowed   (C) had slowed   (D) will slow

   ヒント transactions は「処理」

---

5. A world-famous expert on the corona virus gave a shocking speech at the fundraiser ------- by NPO.

   (A) organizer   (B) organizing   (C) was organized   (D) organized)

---

6. A great deal of excitement ------- in the news of Japan's victory as soon as it was reported on TV.

   (A) generated   (B) was generated

   (C) will generate   (D) to be generated)

Chapter ①

Part 1 写真描写
Part 2 応答
Part 3 会話
Part 4 説明文
Part 5 短文穴埋め
Part 6 長文穴埋め
Part 7 長文読解

解答・解説

聴く勉 TOEIC 講座！
DL音声 **34**

---

1. 正解：(B) to recruit

ポイント prefer to ~（~する方を好む）を、prefer A to B（B より A の方を好む）と混同しないこと！ used to~ は「~したものだった」。

[訳]大抵の会社は外部より内部から職員を置く方を好んだものだった、特に幹部クラスのポストには。

---

2. 正解：(C) plans

ポイント 計画表に書き込むような予定は現在形で表す。もちろん is planning や will plan も OK.

[訳]今後3年にわたって、政府は東京で世界規模のイベントを行う計画だ。

---

3. 正解：(A) announce

ポイント be pleased to~ は「~してうれしい」。to は前置詞でなく不定詞。

[訳] Javis Tecnology 社は Singapore に新支社をオープンできてうれしく思っている。

---

4. 正解：(C) had slowed

ポイント 修理した時（過去）と処理が遅くなった時（それより古い過去）が明らかに違う。ただし、会話では分かり切っているとして過去形 slowed down でも通用する。

[訳] Mr. Cooper はパソコンの問題を解決した、先週末ずっと処理を遅くしていた問題を。

 語句 ❏**transactions** 图 処理

---

5. 正解：(D) organized

ポイント NPO によって準備・主催された fundraiser（募金活動）なので organized と ed 形にする。

[訳]世界的に有名なコロナウイルスの専門家が衝撃的なスピーチをした、NPO 主催の募金活動パーティーで。

---

6. 正解：(B) was generated

ポイント generate が「発生させる；起こす」という他動詞だと知らないとできない。

[訳]日本の勝利のニュースに大きな興奮が巻き起こった、テレビでそれが報じられるやいなや。

---

7. Most stores here ------- at 5:00 p.m. tomorrow due to a road repair on Troy Boulevard.

(A) close　(B) will be close　(C) to close　(D) has been closed

8. The first 50 visitors to Queen's Bakery on May 1 will ------- a complimentary ticket for a puppet play.

(A) receive　(B) be received　(C) to receive　(D) receiving

9. Dr. Yamagata showed a ------- look in order to make no mention of the fact.

(A) determined　　　　　(B) determining

(C) determination　　　 (D) determinative

10. For the purpose of providing better insulation, single-pane glass ------- with a double-pane version in next year's models.

(A) will replace　　　　 (B) has replaced

(C) will be replaced　　 (D) has been replaced

11. Kansai Electronics hopes ------- a hike in new clients after the outsourcing of their production facilities to overseas.

(A) seen　(B) sees　(C) to see　(D) seeing

ヒント☞ hike は「急上昇」

Part5 の Directions（指示文）は、こんな内容になっています。

リーディングテスト

リーディングテストでは、様々な種類の文書を読んで、いくつかのタイプの質問に答えます。リーディングテスト全体で 75 分間です。3つのパートがあり、各パートで指示があります。制限時間内にできるだけ多くの質問に答えることをお勧めします。別紙の解答用紙に解答をマークしてください。問題用紙に解答を書き込んではいけません。

7. 正解：(A) close

ポイント 2番と同じ。現在形でよい。もちろん will close や will be closed も OK。

[訳]こちらのほとんどの店は午後5時に閉店する、Troy Boulevard（大通り）の道路修復のせいで[のために]。

8. 正解：(A) receive

ポイント receive は「〜を受け取る」という意味の他動詞（＝目的語を取る動詞）。

[訳] 5月1日に Qween's Bakery への最初の50人のお客さんは受け取る事になります、無料の人形劇のチケットを。

9. 正解：(A)determined

ポイント これは難問。look が「表情」という名詞であるため、その前なので形容詞が来る。determined（毅然とした）、determinative（限定的な）のどちらか。an interested look なども同じで -ing 形にしないように。

[訳]山形博士は毅然とした表情をした[示した]、その事実に対して何も言及しないようにと。

10. 正解：(C) will be replaced

ポイント replace A with B は「A を B と交換する（他動詞）」。re ＝再び、place ＝置くで覚える。

[訳]より良い断熱を提供する目的で、一枚ガラスの窓は二重窓に取り替えられます、来年の機種において。

11. 正解：(C) to see

ポイント want to〜 や wish to〜 などと同じで、hope to〜 は「〜するのを希望する」。hope that〜 節も。

[訳]関西電子は新規顧客の急上昇を望んでいる、自社の生産設備を海外に外注した後で。

 語句 ❏ **hike** 図 急上昇

Part 1 写真描写

Part 2 応答

Part 3 会話

Part 4 説明文

Part 5 短文穴埋め

Part 6 長文穴埋め

Part 7 長文読解

パート5

指示：以下の文は、それぞれ単語かフレーズが抜けています。それぞれの文の下に 4 つの選択肢があります。文を完成させるために最も適切な語句を選んでください。そして解答用紙の (A)(B)(C)(D) の文字にマークしてください。

パターン 3 ［接続詞］か［前置詞］は書き換え練習が有効！

まずは基本の前置詞を見て、その意味をおさらいしましょう。

- ☐ **in** the river　　　　　　中に
- ☐ **on** the bridge　　　　　　上に
- ☐ **under** the bridge　　　　下に
- ☐ **by** the river　　　　　　そばに
- ☐ **across** the river　　　　よぎって；横断して
- ☐ **between** the houses　　2つのものの間に
- ☐ **among** the trees　　　　～の間に
- ☐ **at** the bus stop　　　　　～の地点に
- ☐ **around** the park　　　　～の回りに
- ☐ **through** the park　　　　～を通り抜けて
- ☐ **into** the river　　　　　　～の中へ
- ☐ **onto** the stage　　　　　～の上へ
- ☐ **toward** the park　　　　～の方へ
- ☐ **in front of** the park　　～の前に
- ☐ **behind** the door　　　　～の背後に
- ☐ **above** he table　　　　　～の上方に
- ☐ **below** the river　　　　～の下流・下方に

　ここでは「前置詞＋名詞」と「接続詞＋センテンス」の違いに注目しましょう。特に、**while と during**、**though と despite と in spite of ～**、**because と because of ＝ owing to** など、よく出題されるものを、まずは**セットで覚えておきましょう**。

Chapter ❶

Part 1 写真描写

Part 2 応答

Part 3 会話

Part 4 説明文

Part 5 短文穴埋め

Part 6 長文穴埋め

Part 7 長文読解

例 **During** my stay in Paris, I met Dr. Harry.
　　　　　名詞

⇒ **While** I was staying in Paris, I met Dr. Harry.
　　　　　主語　　動詞

（私はパリ滞在中に Harry 博士に会った）

　during は前置詞なので次に**名詞**が来ます。接続詞 while に書き換える場合は「**主語 ＋ 動詞**」の形をとります。

　次に、and、or、but という**等位接続詞**に注目しましょう。等位接続詞とは、前後の**節・句・単語**が等位、つまり**同じレベル**の状態でつないでいる接続詞ということです。ですので、and、or、but が文中に出てきたら、**何と何をつないでいるのかをしっかり見極める**ことが重要となります。中でも **and は最重要**と考えましょう。「節 +and ＋ 節」「句 +and ＋ 句」「名詞 +and ＋ 名詞」「動詞 ＋ and ＋ 動詞」「形容詞 ＋ and ＋ 形容詞」「副詞 ＋ and ＋ 副詞」などのいずれなのか、神経を集中して読み取ることが重要です。

最強！解答テクニック

❶ [前置詞＋名詞] と [接続詞＋文] の違いに注目！

❷ 特によく出る言い換え表現①：while と during

❸ 特によく出る言い換え表現②：though と despite と in spite of

❹ 特によく出る言い換え表現③：because と because of ＝ owing to

❺ and, but, or が出てきたら、何と何をつないでいるかしっかり見極めよう！

1. The facilitator didn't make any comments ------- the break between the two sessions.

   (A) because　(B) during　(C) while　(D) than

2. ------- the snow had been cleared from our neighbourhood, the roads were still very slippery.

   (A) So that　(B) Because　(C) Although　(D) In case

3. Since Mr. Linde was away on business when the assembly line suddenly halted, no one on the production floor knew ------- component had malfunctioned.

   (A) there　(B) when　(C) whether　(D) which

   ヒント☞ component は「部品」、malfunction は「誤作動する」

4. All vegetables in this section ------- those marked in red, should be placed on the shelf on the aisle.

   (A) except　(B) apart　(C) over　(D) unlike

5. It may take time as to ------- we should revise the budget now or postpone its decision.

   (A) even　(B) despite　(C) since　(D) whether

6. The development of housing lots is booming now in this area ------- the effort of the city-planning experts to create more public park space.

   (A) as soon as　(B) in case　(C) even still　(D) despite

解答・解説

DL音声 35

Part 1 写真描写

Part 2 応答

Part 3 会話

Part 4 説明文

Part 5 短文穴埋め

Part 6 長文穴埋め

Part 7 長文読解

---

1. 正解：(B) during

ポイント the break（休憩）の間となるはずなので during（「~ の間に」という前置詞）。while は主語、動詞を取る接続詞なのでだめ。

[訳]進行役はなにもコメントを出さなかった、2 つの会合の中休み中に。

---

2. 正解：(C) Although

ポイント 順接か逆接かを考える。ここでは clear（＋）、slippery（－）なので逆接 ⇒ Although が正解とわかる。

[訳]雪は近辺から取り除かれていたが、道路はまだとても滑りやすかった。

---

3. 正解 (D) which

ポイント knew に注目し、その主語が no one だと気が付けば簡単。「どの部品が誤作動したのかを」と knew の目的語になることに気づくべき。ただ、難問。

[訳] Mr. Linde が出張で留守だったので、組み立てラインが突然止まった時に、製造フロアのだれも判らなかった、どの部品が誤作動だったのか。

 語句 ❑ **component** 名 部品 ❑ **malfunction** 動 誤作動する

---

4. 正解：(A)except

ポイント except（〜を除いて（前置詞））と unlike（〜と違って（前置詞））は頻出！

[訳]このコーナーのすべての野菜で、赤い札をつけてあるもの以外のものは、通路のところの棚に置いてください。

---

5. 正解：(D) whether

ポイント as to+ 名詞 [名詞句、節も OK] は「〜に関しては」。ただし文頭では As for~ となることに注意。

[訳]時間がかかるかも知れない、今予算を改定すべきか、この決定を先送りするかどうかに。

---

6. 正解：(D) despite

ポイント 空欄の後を見ると主語＋動詞になっていない、ならば前置詞だとわかる。

[訳]この地域において宅地開発が今ブームになっている、もっと多く公共の公園スペースを作り出そうとする都市計画専門家の努力にもかかわらずだ。

---

7. Please be sure to check under your seat ------- in the overhead compartment for any belongings you may have forgotten.

(A) and　(B) but　(C) because　(D) so

ヒント☞ belongings は「持ち物」

---

8. Ms. Corman will not be able to attend the managers' meeting on Thursday ------- a medical appointment.

(A) if　(B) because　(C) due to　(D) since

---

9. ------- returning the merchandise, do not forget to bring your receipt, please.

(A) When　(B) Upon　(C) Whether　(D) Then

---

10. ------- the company is out of the red, we can invest more in Research and Development.

(A) Because of　(B) Though　(C) Now that　(D) Even if

---

11. We will increase our order, ------- you give us a better discount.

(A) even if　(B) though　(C) providing　(D) despite

---

12. We are reminded to treat those exchange students with a warm welcome ------- that a friendly environment can be maintained.

(A) as　(B) then　(C) so　(D) if

Chapter①

Part 1
写真描写

Part 2
応答

Part 3
会話

Part 4
説明文

Part 5
短文穴埋め

Part 6
長文穴埋め

Part 7
長文読解

7. 正解 : (A) and

ポイント A and B になることに気が付くこと。

[訳] あなたの座席下と頭上戸棚の中を必ずチェックしてください、あなたが忘れているかもしれないどんな持ち物に対してもね。

 語句 ☐ **belongings** 名 持ち物

8. 正解 : (C) due to

ポイント due to ~ = because of ~ = owing to ~ = on account of ~ (~ために ; ~のせいで)。頻出！

[訳] Mr. Corman は木曜日部長会議には出席できないでしょう、内科予約のせいで。

9. 正解 : (A) When

ポイント -ing があるからと言ってすぐに動名詞 (~すること) と思ってはだめ。when や while の場合は主語 +be 動詞が省略された進行形だ。

[訳] 商品を返品しようとする場合、レシートをお忘れにならないでください。

10. 正解 : (C) Now that

ポイント now that は接続詞で「今や~なのだから」。これも頻出！

[訳] 今や会社は赤字から脱しているので、我々は研究開発にもっと多く投資できる。

11. 正解 : (C) providing

ポイント providing that~ や provided that~ という分詞構文で「if~」と考えたらよい。

[訳] 注文を増やしましょう、ただし、もっと値引きしてくださればね。

12. 正解 : (C) so

ポイント so that 構文 (so that 以下できるように、という目的構文) に気づくことができれば正解できる。

[訳] 我々はあたたかい歓迎でそれら交換留学生に接するよう念を押されている、親しみある環境が維持されることができるようにとね。

パターン 4 [代名詞][関係詞]の問題!

1 代名詞の注意点はこれだ!

英語では、最初に登場した人や物について**繰り返し言う際**、he、she、they、it などに**置き換えます**。格の変化に注意して復習しましょう。

例 **Ken** loves **his** family.（Ken は Ken の⇒彼の家族を愛している）

例 **The doctor** killed **himself [herself]**.（その医者は自殺した）
　　 主語　　　　　動詞　　　　目的語

2つ目の例文のように、主語と目的語が同じ場合のみ -self となります。

2 関係詞で要注意は "whose" と "コンマ which" だ!

まずは関係詞に関するポイントを、さらっとおさらいしておきましょう。

- 「**人**」を表す関係詞：**who** - **whose** - **whom**（アメリカでは **who**）
- 「**もの・動物**」を表す関係詞：**which** - **whose** - **which**
- **共通**の関係詞：**that** - **ナシ** - **that**
- 目的格の who(m)、which、that は**ほとんどの場合省略される**。
- 「**場所**」：**where**　「時」：**when**　「理由」：**why**　「方法」：**how**

この中で、TOEIC® L&R テストで気をつけたいのは、"**whose**" と "**コンマ which**" です。

まずは whose について。例えば This is a new word **whose** meaning everybody knows.（これは誰もがその意味を知っている新語だ）という文の場合、**whose = its** なので、「これは新語だ」⇒「そしてそれの意味を誰もが知っている」のように、頭から意味をとっていくのがコツです。しかし、だからといって This is a new word, its meaning everybody knows. は誤りで、コンマの後に and か but を付けるか、its を whose に替えて関係代名詞として接続詞の代用をさせる必要があります。そして、このパターンは**非常によく出題される**のでしっかり記憶しておきましょう!

Chapter ❶

Part 1
写真描写

Part 2
応答

Part 3
会話

Part 4
説明文

Part 5
短文穴埋め

Part 6
長文穴埋め

Part 7
長文読解

　続いては"コンマ which"について。例えば He said he didn't say yes, **which** was a lie.（彼はイエスと言わなかったと言ったが、それは嘘だった）という文の which は**前文の内容**を指しています。コンマの前にある先行詞が「人」の場合は who、「もの・ことがら」の場合は which ですが、例文のように前文の内容を引き継ぐ場合も which が使われます。

最強！解答テクニック

❶ 英語では、人や物について繰り返し言及するとき、代名詞で置き換える！

❷ 代名詞(he, she, they, it など)は、格の変化に注意！

❸ whose の正しい理解が重要！　よく出題される！

❹ コンマ +which は前文の内容を表す！

❺ 関係代名詞の which と関係副詞の where・when を混同しないように！

この Chapter で取り組む練習問題（48問）は、Part5 の基本文法問題を**ほとんどカバー**してあります。リーディング300点レベルなら**4割の19問以上**、400点レベルなら**5割の24問**を20分で取れるように頑張りましょう！

---

1. Employees shouldn't fail to log out of ------- work e-mail accounts when leaving for the day.

(A) that (B) who (C) their (D) its

---

2. To apply for the position of sales manager, send us an e-mail ------- the appropriate job vacancy code on the subject line.

(A) with (B) from (C) where (D) in

ヒント☞ job vacancy code は「求人コード」、the subject line は「件名（の線）」

---

3. Restaurants and hotels in this area can benefit ------- the city's investment in the tourism industry.

(A) in (B) from (C) on (D) to

---

4. The popularity of this sports magazine is declining even though ------- writers are talented.

(A) we (B) ours (C) our (D) ourselves

---

5. The specimens to be analyzed were taken ------- random from the laboratory.

(A) of (B) at (C) on (D) to

---

6. Tickets can only be refundable if ------- are returned one hour before boarding.

(A) you (B) we (C) they (D) theirs

---

7. The store you are looking for is just ------- from the bank over there.

(A) inside (B) above (C) beside (D) across

解答・解説

---

1 正解：(C) their

ポイント 自分たちの仕事上の E メールのアカウントだから。fail to~ は「～するのを怠る」。

[訳] 社員は仕事上の E メールのアカウントをログアウトすることを怠ってはいけない、1 日の仕事を終えて退社するときには。

---

2 正解：(A) with

ポイント 「～を伴った；～の付いた」となることが判れば with が導き出せる。

[訳] 営業責任者の職責に応募するには、件名のところにある適切な求人コードを付けてメール下さい。

 語句 ❏ **job vacancy code** 求人コード ❏ **the subject line** 件名(の線)

---

3 正解：(B) from

ポイント benefit は「利益を得る」という動詞で、from(~ から)、by(~ によって) となる。頻出！

[訳] この区域のレストランやホテルは利益を得ることができる、観光産業への市の投資から。

---

4 正解：(C) our

ポイント こんな中学一年最初レベルの問題も、実際多く出題されたことがある。

[訳] このスポーツ雑誌の人気は衰えつつある、たとえ我が社の書く人たちが有能であってもだ。

---

5 正解：(B) at

ポイント これは知らなければできない。at random は「無作為に；でたらめに」の意味。

[訳] 分析されることになっている見本は、実験室で無作為に抽出された。

 語句 ❏ **specimen** 图 見本

---

6 正解：(C) they

ポイント 何が払いもどされるのか？ チケットだ！ only は強めで「初めて」のニュアンス。

[訳] チケットは (初めて) 払い戻され得る、もし搭乗 1 時間前に返却されれば。

---

7 正解：(D) across

ポイント across from~ は「～からよぎったところに」＝ 向かいに ＝ opposite です。

[訳] お探しのお店はあちらの銀行の向かい側にありますよ。

---

8. The cafeteria, ------- provides reasonable meals for college students, is located on the first corner.

(A) who (B) when (C) where (D) which

9. DH Finance Solutions is used to ------- with overseas suppliers because they have hired international staff.

(A) deal (B) be dealed (C) dealing (D) dealers

10. Mr. Shipley has already been to the Grand Hartwell Theater -------, but this will be his first time seeing its back stage.

(A) ago (B) then (C) ever (D) once

11. Queen's Department Store is having a clearance sale to make ------- for the new spring line.

(A) room (B) a room (C) the room (D) rooms

12. As all our locations are individually owned and operated, prices will vary ------- location to location.

(A) in (B) by (C) from (D) on

13. Ms. Costeau believes that she owes her promotion ------- good luck.

(A) to (B) for (C) of (D) with

Chapter❶

Part 1
写真描写

Part 2
応答

Part 3
会話

Part 4
説明文

Part 5
短文穴埋め

Part 6
長文穴埋め

Part 7
長文読解

8　正解：(D) which

ポイント 主語は the cafeteria で動詞は is だ。まずはこれを見抜くこと。

[訳]大学生のためにお手頃価格の食事を提供するそのカフェテリアは最初の角にあります。

9　正解：(C) dealing

ポイント be used to+ 名詞は「～に慣れている」＝be accustomed to。used to～ （～したものだった）との違いに注意。頻出！　必ず覚えておくこと！

[訳]DH Finace Solutions 社は海外の業者の扱いには慣れている、色んな国の職員を雇っているからね。

10　正解：(D) once

ポイント have been to ～（～へ行ったことがある(＝現在完了の経験)）だから once しかない！

[訳] Mr. Shipley はすでに Grand Hartwell Theater に一度行ったことがある、しかし今回、その楽屋をみるのは初めてだろう。

11　正解：(A) room

ポイント いつも出題される。room が無冠詞の場合「部屋」ではなく「スペース」のこと。

[訳] Queen's デパートは在庫一掃セールをしようとしている、新しい春物へスペースを空けるために。

12　正解：(C) from

ポイント 成句。from A to B （A から B へ）は、例えば from door to door （一件一件）など。a や the は不要！　location は「位置；場所；所在地」の意味からある事業の拠点をさすのでここでは「店舗」。

[訳]私共のすべての店舗は個々に所有され運営されていますので、価格は店ごとに異なります。

13　正解：(A) to

ポイント owe （負う）は使い方が難しい。I owe you 300 yen. ＝ I owe 300 yen to you. (私は君に３００円借りがある)。だから借用書のことを I.O.U. (I owe you.) と言うよ。

[訳] Ms. Costeau は、昇進は運が良かった （＝幸運に負う）のだと思っている。

ゼロからスタート Part6

4つの大問 ＆ 4つの設問！

長文穴埋め問題

本番では…
全16問：Q131-146

[中学文法探し]で計16問を8分で駆け抜けろ！

聴く勉
TOEIC
講座！

DL音声 37-40

Part5 の発展形！
Part6 はこんなテストだ！

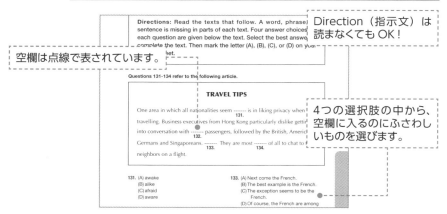

Direction（指示文）は読まなくても OK！

空欄は点線で表されています。

4つの選択肢の中から、空欄に入るのにふさわしいものを選びます。

　Part6 は長文なので難しそうに感じるかもしれませんが、**Part5 の発展形**だと考え、中学レベルの英文法を駆使して駆け抜けましょう！

　大切なのはスピード！　4つの大問があり、それぞれに設問が4問ですので、**合計16問を8分で駆け抜ける**練習が必要です！　コツは「これは中学レベルの問題だ！」と判断したものだけを解き、難しい単語・知らない単語が並ぶ「語彙問題」を捨てる勇気を持つことです！

Chapter❶

Part 1 写真描写

Part 2 応答

Part 3 会話

Part 4 説明文

Part 5 短文穴埋め

Part 6 長文穴埋め

Part 7 長文読解

● Part6 本番の流れとポイントはこれだ！

テストの開始

Part5 を解き終わったら、間髪を入れずに Part6 に取り掛かります。（理想としては）12分で Part5 を解き終わっているはずなので、続く**8分で 16問を駆け抜けましょう!**

出題パターン

Part6 で出題されるのは Part5 と同様に、以下の3パターンです。

1 品詞選択問題

⇒4つの選択肢の中から、最適な品詞の単語を選ぶ問題

2 文法問題

⇒文法ルールから解答を導く問題。「中学レベル英文法」かどうかを素早く見極めよう!

3 語彙選択問題

⇒語彙力が足りない＝単語の意味を知らなかったら答えられない。捨てる勇気を持とう!

基本的には Part5 と同じなのですが、長文の**文脈**から正解を導く必要がある問題が出題されることがあります。ですが**まずは設問となっている文のみで解答できるもの**に取り組んでいきましょう。

Part6 の Directions（指示文）は、こんな内容になっています。

パート6
指示：次の文書を読んでください。いくつかの文で、単語やフレーズが空欄になっています。それぞれの文に4つの選択肢があります。文書を完成させるのに最適な選択肢を選んでください。そして、解答用紙の (A)(B)(C)(D) のどれか1つをマークしてください。

時間を計って8分で駆け抜け練習
⇒解説をチェック！

● Part6 は Part5 の発展形！

　Part6 の問題文の内容は、**実務書式**や**ビジネスレター**、**メール**などが中心です。

　Part6 は基本的に "**Part5 を発展させた長文編**" と考えて取り組んでいってください。ですので、こちらも Part5 で出てきた4つのパターンを中心に習得しておくことが大切です。

1　出題率最多の［品詞選択］
2　［動詞］をふさわしい形にする問題
3　［接続詞］か［前置詞］か問題
4　［代名詞］［関係詞］の問題

　そしてこのあと取り組む練習問題の設問のうち、中学英文法レベルの問題には 中 、そして語彙問題には V のマークをつけました。

●制限時間8分でトレーニング！

　初級者レベル（300〜400点）では、いきなり8分で16問解答することは**できません**ので、Part6 でも V **問題を捨てる勇気**を持つことです。そして英文はめ込み問題は、直後の文にスムーズにつながる（整合性がある）ものを選ぶことで、**4問中2問**は取れます。

　まずはストップウォッチを8分にセットして、中 の問題を中心に、**できてもできなくても**（分からない設問は4つの選択肢のどれかをマークする）とにかく最後まで通り抜けましょう。8分たったら手を止めて、[解答・解説]ページを開いて [聴く勉 TOEIC 講義！] を聴いて下さい！

Chapter ❶

Part 1
写真描写

Part 2
応答

Part 3
会話

Part 4
説明文

Part 5
短文穴埋め

Part 6
長文穴埋め

Part 7
長文読解

最強！解答テクニック

❶ [品詞選択] は絶対取ろう！！

❷ 語彙問題を捨てる勇気を持とう！

❸ 中学英語を再チェック！ 動詞の時制・規則動詞・不規則動詞

❹ 進行形・受け身は be 動詞必須！ 受け身の進行形に注意！

❺ 過去とのかかわりを伝えたいときに使われるのが現在完了

❻ 助動詞 (can, may, must, will, shall, might, would, should など) の用法を覚えるべし！

❼ to 不定詞・分詞・動名詞をチェックすべし！

❽ 関係詞は whose とコンマ which に注意！

❾ [前置詞＋名詞] と [接続詞＋文] の違いに注目！

❿ 英文はめ込み問題は直後の文にスムーズにつながるものを選ぶ！

Questions 1-4 refer to the following e-mail

To:	Alice Ruzinski
From:	Elen Alvis
Date:	March 23
Subject:	Position at Gartera's Real Estate

Dear Ms. Ruzinski,

I would like to schedule an individual interview at our office on April 2 at 10 a.m. It will ---1--- for approximately forty-five minutes. ---2---. You should e-mail me your résumé including images of your past projects ---3--- this Friday. ---4--- you be offered the position, you will have to provide evidence that you have a valid state license.

I look forward to hearing from you!

Elen Alvis
Gartera's Real Estate

1. V

(A) go

(B) last

(C) take

(D) have

2.

(A) I'm afraid it won't work for you.

(B) Let me wait for you in the waiting room then.

(C) Please let me know if this appointment time works for you.

(D) I hope it will be enough time for you to express yourself.

3. 中

(A) by

(B) for

(C) until

(D) on

4. V

(A) If

(B) Could

(C) Would

(D) Should

Chapter ①

Part 1 写真描写

Part 2 応答

Part 3 会話

Part 4 説明文

Part 5 短文穴埋め

Part 6 長文穴埋め

Part 7 長文読解

1-4 番は次のメールに関するものです。

To:	Alice Ruzinski
From:	Elen Alvis
Date:	March 23
Subject:	Position at Gartera's Real Estate

Dear Ms. Ruzinski,

I would like to schedule an individual interview / at our office on April 2 at 10 a.m. / It will **1(B) last** for approximately forty-five minutes. / **2(C) Please let me know** / if this appointment time works for you. / You should e-mail me your résumé / including images of your past projects **3(A) by** this Friday. **4(D) Should** you be offered the position, / you will have to provide evidence / that you have a valid state license.

I look forward to hearing from you!

Elen Alvis
Gartera's Real Estate

メール本文の訳

我が社で個人面談を予定したいと思います、4月2日午前10時に。およそ45分間続くでしょう。[2-C] この待ち合わせ時間が都合よいかどうかお知らせください。履歴書をお送りください、あなたの過去の企画の画像を含んで、この金曜までに。万一職位（ポスト）を提示されましたら、有効な州のライセンスがある証拠を提供しなければなりません。ご連絡お待ち申し上げております。

語句

❏ schedule	動	予定する	❏ individua	形	個人の
❏ approximately	副	およそ	❏ appointment	名	アポ
❏ resume	名	履歴書	❏ images	名	画像
❏ evidence	名	証拠	❏ valid	形	有効な
❏ license	名	許可証；免許証			

1. 正解：(B)

(A) go 　　行く
(B) last 　続く
(C) take 　〜がかかる
(D) have 　もつ

2. 正解：(C)

(A) I'm afraid it won't work for you.
それはあなたにとってうまくいかないのでは。

(B) Let me wait for you in the waiting room then.
待合室で待たせていただきます。

(C) Please let me know if this appointment time works for you.
この待ち合わせ時間が都合よいかどうかお知らせください。

(D) I hope it will be enough time for you to express yourself.
お気持ちを述べられるのに十分な時間だとよいですね。

ポイント 直前に面接時間を指定してきているから。this appointment time がカギ。

3. 正解：(A)

(A) by
(B) for
(C) until
(D) on

ポイント 空所に適した前置詞を入れる問題。by は「〜までに」、for は「〜の間」、until は「〜までずっと」、on は「〜に接して」。

4. 正解：(D)

(A) If
(B) Could
(C) Would
(D) Should

ポイント If はあとに主語＋動詞がくる。Could と Would は「〜？」となるので不正解。If S should の倒置である (D) Should が正解。

Part 1 写真描写

Part 2 応答

Part 3 会話

Part 4 説明文

Part 5 短文穴埋め

Part 6 長文穴埋め

Part 7 長文読解

Questions 5-8 refer to the following memo.

MEMO

To: Department Managers
From: Maurice Tolliver
Subject: Annual Trip

Date: 10 March
For Stellar Auto's annual hiking trip, we ------- to Oroana Mountain on
                                          5
13 April. ------- Although it's an optional activity, please encourage
          6
everyone to join us for this event. If we have more than twenty hikers
------- up, we will qualify ------- a special group hike with two private
   7   8
guides.
Please send me a list of participants by 31 March.

5. 中
(A) will head   (B) have headed   (C) headed   (D) heading

6.
(A) I'm sure you know a better activity than this.
(B) I will e-mail everyone a detailed description of the event tonight.
(C) You might want to e-mail me whether you'd like to join the even or not.
(D) Every employee has to take part in this event because it's an annual one.

7. 中
(A) to sign   (B) signed   (C) sign   (D) signing

8. V
(A) of   (B) to   (C) with   (D) for

解答・解説

5-8 番は次のメモに関するものです。

MEMO

To: Department Managers
From: Maurice Tolliver
Subject: Annual Trip

Date: 10 March
For Stellar Auto's annual hiking trip, / we **5(A) will head** to Oroana
Mountain on 13 April. / **6(B) I will e-mail everyone a detailed description
of the event tonight.** / Although it's an optional activity, / please
encourage everyone to join us / for this event. / If we have more than
twenty hikers **7(C) sign** up, / we will qualify **8(D) for** a special group hike
/ with two private guides.
Please send me a list of participants/ by 31 March. /

メモ本文の訳

Stellar Auto 社の恒例のハイキングについては、4月13日に Oroana Mountain に向います。[6-B] 私
は今夜イベントの詳細をみんなにメールしましょう。これは任意の活動ですが、どうぞみんなに参加するよ
う勧めて下さい、この行事に。もし、20人以上のハイカーに申し込んでもらえれば、2人の個人的なガイ
ドさん付きの特別団体ハイキングの資格がもらえます。3月31日までに参加者のリストをお送り下さい。

語句

❑ **hiking**	名	徒歩旅行
❑ **annual**	形	毎年恒例の
❑ **optional**	形	選択の；任意の
❑ **encourage A to〜**		A に〜するよう励ます
❑ **participant**	名	参加者　派 **participate** 動 参加する

5. 正解：(A)

(A) will head
(B) have headed
(C) headed
(D) heading

> **ポイント** 4月13日は未来なの (A) が正解。head to[for] 〜で「〜へ向かう」という意味を表す。(B) は現在完了形で「〜したところだ」。(C) は過去形、(D) は現在分詞形。

6. 正解：(B)

(A) I'm sure you know a better activity than this.
あなたはきっとこれよりよい活動をご存じでしょう。

(B) I will e-mail everyone a detailed description of the event tonight.
私は今夜イベントの詳細をみんなにメールしましょう。

(C) You might want to e-mail me whether you'd like to join the even or not.
あなたがイベントに参加したいかどうかを私にメールされたらいかがですか。

(D) Every employee has to take part in this event because it's an annual one.
年中行事ですから全従業員はこの行事に参加しなければいけません。

> **ポイント** 直前に「4月13日にハイキングをやる」と言っているので。「その詳細を送る」とつながる。

7. 正解：(C)

(A) to sign
(B) signed
(C) sign
(D) signing

> **ポイント** 使役動詞 have＋目的語＋原形だから (C) が正解。

8. 正解：(D)

(A) of
(B) to
(C) with
(D) for

> **ポイント** qualify for〜で「〜の資格がある」

練習問題 制限時間2分で挑戦してみましょう!

Questions 9-12 refer to the following letter.

Dear Ms. Martinez,

I am very pleased to hear about the ------- relocation of the Smith
9
family to Georgia. They informed us they are very much pleased
with the apartment provided, especially the fully ------- apartment.
10
-------. Your services have been invaluable to the Smith family and
11
their company as well. Also, I want to express my gratitude for the
------- I received.
12
Thank you for your assistance.

With best regards,

Landon Beaumont

9. 中

(A) succeed   (B) success   (C) successful   (D) succeeding

10. V

(A) supplied   (B) prepared   (C) geared   (D) furnished

11.

(A) Following your advice, I looked for a better apartment, but in vain.

(B) Also, like you mentioned, they are happy with the apartment location.

(C) In case of relocation, summer is the busiest season for moving
companies.

(D) In addition, I hope more volunteers will join us to find good apartments.

12. V

(A) compensation   (B) dedication   (C) contribution   (D) reputation

9-12番は次のメモに関するものです。

Dear Ms. Martinez,

I am very pleased to hear about the **9(C)** <u>successful</u> relocation of the Smith family to Georgia. / They informed us / they are very much pleased / with the apartment provided, / especially the fully **10(D)** <u>furnished</u> apartment. / **11(B)** <u>Also, / like you mentioned, / they are happy with the apartment location.</u> / Your services have been invaluable / to the Smith family and their company as well. / Also, / I want to express my gratitude / for the **12(A)** <u>compensation</u> I received.

Thank you for your assistance.

With best regards,

Landon Beaumont

手紙本文の訳

　スミスご夫妻のジョージアへの移転について聞きとても喜んでいます。ご夫妻は用意されたアパートにとても満足していますと知らせて下さいました、特に家具の十分に備わったアパートにです。[11-B] また、あなたが言ったように、彼らはアパートの場所に満足しています。あなたのご奉仕は大変価値のあるものでした、スミスご夫妻とその会社にも。また、感謝の気持ちを表したいと思います、私がいただきましたお心遣いに対しても。ご助力感謝します。

語句

❑ **relocation**	名	移転	❑ **provided**	形	用意された
❑ **furnished**	形	家具調度の備わった	❑ **mention**	動	（言葉で）触れる
❑ **location**	名	位置；場所			
❑ **invaluable**	形	価値をつけられないほどの	❑ **express**	動	表明する
❑ **gratitude**	名	感謝	❑ **compensation**	名	報酬；報い
❑ **regards**		よろしく；敬具　※元来は「尊敬」「敬意」の意味			

9. 正解：(C)

(A) succeed 　動 成功する
(B) success 　名 成功
(C) successful 　形 成功している（＋名詞だから）
(D) succeeding

10. 正解：(D)

(A) supplied 　供給する（過去形）
(B) prepared 　用意する
(C) geared 　適合させる（〜to）
(D) furnished 　家具を備える

11. 正解：(B)

(A) Following your advice, I looked for a better apartment, but in vain.
あなたの忠告に従って、私はより良いアパートを探しましたが、無駄でした。

(B) Also, like you mentioned, they are happy with the apartment location.
また、あなたが言ったように、彼らはアパートの場所に満足しています。

(C) In case of relocation, summer is the busiest season for moving companies.
移転の場合、夏は引っ越し会社にとって一番忙しい季節です。

(D) In addition, I hope more volunteers will join us to find good apartments.
加えて、よいアパートを見つけるのにより多くのボランティアが参加してくれるでしょう。

ポイント 直後の文に、「貴方の奉仕がとても貴重（invaluable）」とあるので (B) が正解。

12. 正解：(A)

(A) compensation 　報酬
(B) dedication 　献身；専念
(C) contribution 　貢献
(D) reputation 　名声

Chapter ❶

Part 1 写真描写

Part 2 応答

Part 3 会話

Part 4 説明文

Part 5 短文穴埋め

Part 6 長文穴埋め

Part 7 長文読解

Questions 13-16 refer to the following article.

New Energy Conservation Efforts Underway

Sternberg Manufacturing is seeking to reduce its energy usage both to cut overhead expenses and ------- awareness of environmental protection.
13

Based on recommendations made by the Ministry of the Environment last month, the company will ------- three major improvement projects.
14
The first among them is scheduled to be carried out by Urban Energy Services in May. ------- . In addition, HR director has chosen Derek Kent
15
to carry out employee training ------- conservation techniques.
16

13. 中

(A) heighten   (B) to heighten   (C) heightening   (D) heightened

14. V

(A) undergo   (B) abandon   (C) ignore   (D) endure

15

(A) Eco-friendly products are what all the staff have long wanted.

(B) The schedule for the training has not been set yet.

(C) The distruction of nature in this country is very serious.

(D) The others will follow next year, as funding allows.

16

(A) regard   (B) regards   (C) regardful   (D) regarding

解答・解説

13-16 番は次の記事に関するものです。

New Energy Conservation Efforts Underway

Sternberg Manufacturing is seeking to reduce its energy usage/ both to cut overhead expenses / and **13(B)** to heighten awareness of environmental protection. /

Based on recommendations made by the Ministry of the Environment last month, / the company will **14(A)** undergo three major improvement projects. / The first among them is scheduled to be carried out / by Urban Energy Services in May. / **15(D)** The others will follow next year, / as funding allows. / In addition, / HR director has chosen Derek Kent/ to carry out employee training / **16(D)** regarding conservation techniques.

訳

新しいエネルギー保全努力が進行中
Sternberg Manufacturing はエネルギー使用を減らす事を求めている、双方のために、間接経費をカットし、環境保護の意識を高める。
先月環境省からなされた勧告に基づいて、会社は3つの主要な改善計画を受け入れる。それらの中で最初のものは実行される予定だ、Urban Energy Services により5月に。[15-D] その他のものは来年に続く、財源が許すにつれて。加えて、人事部長は Derek Kent を選んだ、保全技術に関して社員研修を実行するため。

語句

❏ seek	動	求める	❏ reduce	動	減らす
❏ usage	名	使用	❏ overhead expenses		間接経費
❏ awareness	名	意識	❏ recommendation	名	勧告
❏ carry out		実行する	❏ funding	名	財源
❏ conservation	名	保全			

13. 正解：(B)

(A) heighten 　動 高める
(B) to heighten
(C) heightening
(D) heightend

<samp>ポイント</samp> A and B 形に注目する

14. 正解：(A)

(A) undergo 　受ける；経験する
(B) abandon 　断念する；放棄する
(C) ignore 　無視する
(D) endure 　耐える

15. 正解：(D)

(A) Eco-friendly products are what all the staff have long wanted.
環境に優しい製品がすべての職員が長いこと望んでいたものだ。

(B) The schedule for the training has not been set yet.
研修の予定はまだ決まっていない。

(C) The distruction of nature in this country is very serious.
この国の自然破壊は非常に深刻だ。

(D) The others will follow next year, as funding allows.
その他のものは来年に続く、財源が許すにつれて。

<samp>ポイント</samp> 直前の文の the first among them に注目。すると残りは2つあることになるから、(D) が最適とわかる。

16. 正解：(D)

(A) regard 　動 見なす
(B) regards 　名 敬意
(C) regardful 　形 注意深い
(D) regarding 　前 ～に関して

<samp>ポイント</samp> regard A as B は「A を B と見なす」

COLUMN

英語力上達に TOEIC® を生かす方法〜 Part2-4 編〜

　93 ページのコラムでは、Part1 を使って発音をカッコ良くする方法について述べましたが、ここでも引き続き、TOEIC® を使って英会話力をアップさせるトレーニングを紹介いたします。

　Part2 では、正解のセンテンスを覚えてナレーション音声をマネしまくって、そのシチュエーションを想像しながら一人芝居をして言いまくることです。

　Part3 と 4 は、ただ聞き流して答えが分かる程度で満足していては、実際の場面で役に立つ英語力は身に付きません。ネイティブスピーカーの質問に対して、自分流で英文を考えて答える一人芝居をすることです。これは案外楽しいものです。例えば会話文を聞いた後、Where are the speakers working now? と尋ねる設問の場合、黙っていてはだめです。即座に Well, at a restaurant. や They are working at a restaurant. などと、あたかも応答するように答えていくのです。

　1 セットの TOEIC® テストで Part3 は 39 問、Part4 は 30 問あります。これらをすべて一人芝居気分で応答を作って言えるようにしてごらんなさい。外国人と話をしていて、すぐ反応のできる自分に「いける！」と自信が持てるようになりますよ！

　そして繰り返しになりますが、こういったトレーニングを行う際には、R と L、V と F の音や、英語独特の th の出し方、s と sh の区別などについて、絶えず意識することです。そして語尾の d や t の音に母音「オ」を残さないということを、いつも念仏のように唱え、意識させるのです。あとは強弱のリズムを意識すれば、間違いなく「あなたは発音がきれいですね！」と言われるようになります。そうすると英語学習にはずみがつき、相乗効果でどんどん英語を話す力が上がっていきますよ！

Part 1 写真描写
Part 2 応答
Part 3 会話
Part 4 説明文
Part 5 短文穴埋め
Part 6 長文穴埋め
Part 7 長文読解

Part 7 長文読解問題

ゼロからスタート

リーディングパート最難関!

本番では…
全54問:Q147-200

試験本番は
[探し物は何ですか?ゲーム]
感覚で進めるべし!

聴く勉 TOEIC 講座!
DL音声 **41-55**

👆 **リーディングパート最難関!**
Part7 はこんなテストだ!

短いメモや広告、手紙や記事、
e-mail など、文書の種類は実
にさまざま!

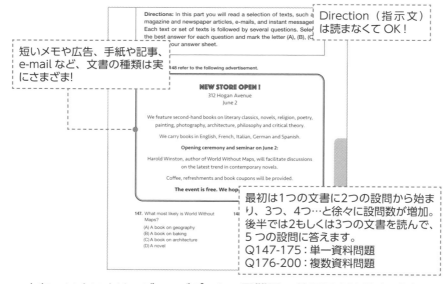

Directions: In this part you will read a selection of texts, such a magazine and newspaper articles, e-mails, and instant message Each text or set of texts is followed by several questions. Selec the best answer for each question and mark the letter (A), (B), (C your answer sheet.

Direction(指示文)
は読まなくて OK!

...48 refer to the following advertisement.

NEW STORE OPEN !
312 Hogan Avenue
June 2

We feature second-hand books on literary classics, novels, religion, poetry, painting, photography, architecture, philosophy and critical theory.

We carry books in English, French, Italian, German and Spanish.

Opening ceremony and seminar on June 2:

Harold Winston, author of World Without Maps, will facilitate discussions on the latest trend in contemporary novels.

Coffee, refreshments and book coupons will be provided.

The event is free. We hop...

147. What most likely is World Without Maps?
(A) A book on geography
(B) A book on baking
(C) A book on architecture
(D) A novel

最初は1つの文書に2つの設問から始ま
り、3つ、4つ…と徐々に設問数が増加。
後半では2もしくは3つの文書を読んで、
5 つの設問に答えます。
Q147-175:単一資料問題
Q176-200:複数資料問題

　さあ、いよいよリーディングパートで**最難関**の英語長文速読力が試され
る Part7 です。さまざまな種類の文書を読んで、それに関する設問に答え
るもので、いずれも4つの選択肢の中から最も適切な答えを選びます。設
問176以降は**複数(2ないしは3)の文書**を読んで答える問題です。

Chapter❶

Part 1 写真描写

Part 2 応答

Part 3 会話

Part 4 説明文

Part 5 短文穴埋め

Part 6 長文穴埋め

Part 7 長文読解

● Part7 本番の流れとポイントはこれだ！

テストの開始

Part6 を解き終わったら、即座に Part7 に取り掛かります。（理想としては）12分で Part5 ⇒8分で Part6 を解き終わっているはずなので、**残り時間は55分**です。

出題内容

Part7 で出題されるのは以下の3パターンです。

①シングルパッセージ問題　10セット29問

⇒文書が1つの問題。1セットの設問数が2〜4問と幅がある。

②マルティプルパッセージ問題　5セット25問

⇒文書が2つのダブルパッセージ問題は、2セットで設問数は10問、文書が3つのトリプルパッセージ問題は、3セットで設問数は15問。

Part7 の設問は、大きく分けて以下の6パターンに分けられます。

1 「これは何に関する新聞記事でしょうか」などのような、文書全体で**話題**となっていることや文書の**目的**を問う問題

2 「〇月×日には何が予定されていますか」などのような、本文内で述べられている、**具体的な内容**について問う問題

3 「〇〇さんとは誰だと推察されますか」のように、本文の内容から**推測**して答えを導き出す問題

4 設問内に **NOT** と大文字で表記される、本文とは**内容が合わない**選択肢を選ぶ問題　⇒ 上級者向け

5 設問内で示された 1 文を、文書の中の適切な場所に**挿入**する問題

6 **複数**の文書の情報をピックアップして、正解を導き出す問題

Part7 の Directions（指示文）は、こんな内容になっています。

パート7

指示：このパートでは、あなたは雑誌や新聞の記事やメール、ショートメッセージなどの文書を読みます。それぞれのテキストにはいくつかの質問がついています。各設問に最適な答えを選び、解答用紙の (A)(B)(C)(D) のどれか1つをマークしてください。

450点、500点…と、近い目標をクリアしていこう！

　このパートでは、時間管理を徹底し、**できるものだけを一瞬で判断**してやっていくという手段を取ります。この本を選んでくれた受験生諸君は、まずは600点が目標でしょう。そのためには**450点、500点…と、近い目標をクリア**していくことが大切です。

　そこでまず、この章では、**1問1分**で通過する練習をします。それには問題文を**いかに速く読むか**というのが非常に重要になってきます。600点以上のレベルを目指すなら、**英語の語順のまま意味を取れる**ようになることが必要条件です。いちいち日本語に訳しながら読んでいては時間が足りなくなります。以下の2つの英文と日本語訳のセットを比べてみてください。

---

[1] **I am asking because I may have a candidate for your current open role.**

そちらの現在のオープンになっている職務に対して候補者があるかも知れませんので、お尋ねする次第です。

[2] **I am asking / because I may have a candidate / for your current open role.**

私はお尋ねしています / 候補者があるかも知れませんので / そちらの現在のオープンになっている職務に対して。

　両方とも同じ英文ですが、訳し方が違います。[1] のほうは日本語の語順に置き換えながら和訳しており、[2] は、英文の**意味の区切り**ごとにスラッシュを入れ、それに合わせて**頭から読み下す**ように訳したもの。みなさんは普段からこの [2] のようにして英文を読むクセをつけましょう。

Chapter❶

Part 1 写真描写

Part 2 応答

Part 3 会話

Part 4 説明文

Part 5 短文穴埋め

Part 6 長文穴埋め

Part 7 長文読解

●[探し物は何ですか?ゲーム]&ねらい目問題を取る!

　普段から「語順通り読み＝速読」の訓練を積んだら、試験本番では、以下のような手順＝［探し物は何ですか?ゲーム］感覚で進めましょう。

> ①まずは設問をチェックし、その中に**キーワードを探す**
> ②問題文の**必要箇所を探し**（スキャニング）、解答する

　そしてここでも、リスニングセクションと同様に、**3W1H**（= Who, When, Where, How）の疑問文は、**初級者にとってねらい目**の設問となりますので、目を光らせて点を稼ぎましょう!

　それからもう1つ、実はねらい目なのは**後半 Q176 以降のマルティプルパッセージ問題**!　英語読解力をあまり必要としない「図表」などの資料が含まれている場合があり、比較的読み解きやすい可能性がありますので、Q165 くらいから Q175 までの難しいと感じる問題は飛ばして、Q176 以降を先にやってみるのがベターです!

　さらにもう1つは、**チャット形式**で複数の人間がやり取りする文書の問題。これはほかの文書と比べて非常に簡単ですので、真っ先に解きにいきましょう。**得点源です**!

{ 最強!解答テクニック }

❶ 問題文を読む際には、語順どおりに意味をつかむ読み方をすること!

❷ まずは設問を見てキーワードになりそうな語句を探す⇒問題文の中の重要箇所を探す、[探し物は何ですか?ゲーム] で攻略せよ!

❸ ねらい目は…① 3W1H　② Q176 以降　③チャット形式と心得よ!

Questions 147-148 refer to the following advertisement.

Born Feb 21 2020, 8 weeks old Pom pups available today(Clair and Chao) First shots completed on April 4. Records will be provided to new owners.

Clair is 10 lbs and Chao is 13 lbs. Full registration. Great temperament and puppy pad trained.

Accepting non-refundable $300 deposits now. Reservation will be in the order of deposits. Sorry no farm visit due to the virus. Please email for further info. More pics available.

> **ヒント☞** Pom は「ポメラニアン犬」、pups は puppy の複数形略語。puppy pad は「子犬トイレ台」、shot はこの場合「注射」。lbs は pounds という単位を表す言葉。temperament は「気質」

147. What is suggested about the puppies?

(A) They have received vaccination.

(B) They are being sold at $300.

(C) They are of different colors.

(D) They were born in registered vet clinic.

> **ヒント☞** vaccination は「ワクチン接種」、vet は「獣医」

148. What will the puppies' owner provide?

(A) Second shots

(B) Farm visit

(C) Photos

(D) Puppy pad

解答・解説

147-148番は次の広告に関するものです。

Born Feb 21 2020, / 8 weeks old Pom pups available today(Clair and Chao). / First shots completed on Apri1 4. / Records will be provided to new owners. /

Clair is 10 lbs and Chao is 13 lbs. / Full registration. / Great temperament and puppy pad trained. /

Accepting non-refundable $300 deposits now. / Reservation will be in the order of deposits. / Sorry no farm visit due to the virus. / Please email for further info. / More pics available.

訳

2020年2月21日生まれ、生後8カ月のポメラニアン犬の子犬、本日御立て可能。(Clair, Chao)
第1回予防接種2020年4月終了。記録は新飼い主に提供される。
Clair 10ポンド、Chao 13ポンド。完全登録済み。すばらしい気性、そして子犬パッド訓練済み。
返金なしの300ドル保証金ただ今受付中。予約は保証金の順番による。ウイルスのため農場への連れ出しはしていません。更なる詳細はEメールを。さらに多くの写真ご用意あり。

....

ポイント 広告なので無駄を一切省いていることに注意。

 語句

❑ **pup**	名	子犬 (= puppy)
❑ **available**	形	手に入る
❑ **shot**	名	注射 (= injection)
❑ **provide**	動	準備する；提供する
❑ **lbs**		pounds のこと(ラテン語のポンドを表す libra の複数で lbs だが pounds と読む)
❑ **registration**	名	登録；登記
❑ **temperament**	名	気性
❑ **info.**		= information
❑ **pics**		= pictures
❑ **further**		さらなる (far-further-furthest)

147. 正解：(A)

What is suggested about the puppies? 子犬たちについて何が分かるか？

(A) They have received vaccination. ワクチン接種済み
(B) They are being sold at $300. 300ドルで売られている
(C) They are of different colors. 色が種々だ
(D) They were born in registered vet clinic. 登録されている獣医院で生まれた

ポイント shot（注射）がわかれば簡単だが… ⇒ **Level 2**

148 正解：(C)

What will the puppies' owner provide? 子犬たちの所有者は何を用意するだろう？

(A) Second shots 2度目の注射
(B) Farm visit 農場への訪問
(C) Photos 写真
(D) Puppy pad 子犬用パッド

ポイント new owner ではないことに注意 ⇒ **Level 1**

Chapter ❶

Part 1 写真描写

Part 2 応答

Part 3 会話

Part 4 説明文

Part 5 短文穴埋め

Part 6 長文穴埋め

Part 7 長文読解

練習問題 めやすは「1問1分」です！

Questions 149-150 refer to the following email

Date:	Feb 25 2019
From:	Lindsay Smith
To:	David Chow
Subject:	RE: Apt378 Jones St.

David,

I'd like to terminate my lease with you on Apt3,785 Jones Street
San Francisco, CA. Per our lease agreement dated Aug 8, 2018,
e-mail constitutes a written notice. So I am sending you this
written notice that I will terminate the above lease agreement on
March 31, 2019, and I will vacate the premise on or before date.
I expect to receive the return of my lease deposit according to the
terms of the lease.

Lindsay

ヒント☞ terminate は「打ち切る」、constitute は「構成する」、premise は「土地建物」、
terms は「(契約)条件」

149. What is the purpose of this email?

(A) To put an end to a lease　　(B) To lease a property

(C) To renew a lease　　(D) To notify a lease deposit

150. Which of the following is closest in meaning to "vacate the premise"?

(A) Clean the apartment

(B) Move out of the place

(C) Restore the property

(D) Check the rooms for damages

解答・解説

聴く勉
TOEIC
講座！
DL音声 **42**

149-150 番は次のメールに関するものです。

Date:	Feb 25 2019
From:	Lindsay Smith
To:	David Chow
Subject:	RE: Apt378 Jones St.

David,

I'd like to terminate my lease with you / on Apt3,785 Jones Street San Francisco, CA. / Per our lease agreement dated Aug 8, 2018, / e-mail constitutes a written notice. So I am sending you this written notice / that I will terminate the above lease agreement on March 31, 2019, / and I will vacate the premise on or before date.

I expect to receive the return of my lease deposit / according to the terms of the lease.

Lindsay

メール本文の訳

御社との賃貸借契約を打ち切りたいと思います、カリフォルニア州、サンフランシスコの Jones Street785 のアパート3号室に関しての。2018年、8月付けの私共の賃貸借契約によれば、Eメールで書面による通知を構成できるとあります。そこで、私はこの書面による通知をお送りしています、私が上記の賃貸借契約を2019年3月31日に打ち切り、その日またはそれ以前に土地建物を明け渡すという書面による通知を。賃貸借契約の保証金をお返しいただけることを期待しております、賃貸契約の条件に従って。

語句

☐ **terminate**	動	打ち切る	☐ **lease**	名	リース (賃貸借契約)
☐ **agreement**	名	同意；契約	☐ **constitute**	動	構成する
☐ **notice**	名	通告	☐ **above**	前	上記の
☐ **vacate**	動	空にする	☐ **vacant**	形	空の
☐ **Premise**	名	土地建物	☐ **deposit**	名	証金；頭金；内金
☐ **terms**	名	(契約の) 条件			

149. 正解：(A)

What is the purpose of this email? このEメールの目的は何か？

(A) To put an end to a lease　リースを取りやめる
(B) To lease a property　物件をリースする
(C) To renew a lease　リースを更新する
(D) To notify a lease deposit　リースの保証金を知らせる

ポイント メールの場合、あいさつ、お礼などを除いて目的はまず最初に来る。わざと terminate などという難しい語が出てくるが、プラスイメージかマイナスイメージかで素早く判断すれば簡単な問題　⇒ **Level 2**

150. 正解：(B)

Which of the following is closest in meaning to "vacate the premise"?
次のどれが "vacate the premise" の意味に最も近いか？

(A) Clean the apartment　アパートを清掃する
(B) Move out of the place　その場を立ち退く
(C) Restore the propery　物件を修復する
(D) Check the rooms for damages　部屋の損害をチェックする

ポイント vacate も premise も知らなくても on or before date などから「出て行く」と推測できる　⇒ **Level 2**

賃貸借契約でよく使う語彙をわざと出題して皆さんに覚えさせようと仕組んでいる！

Questions 151-153 refer to following flyer.

SUPPORT OUR STUDIES!

Heaflex Clinic is currently looking for female smokers who meet the following requirements for a subsidized clinical trial:

(a) Aged under 65
(b) Using tabacco,nicotine or e-cigerette regularly
(c) Not having high blood pressure or heart diseases.

You would receive $5,000 if you are qualified for and complete our clinical trial.
You would get $100 for each friend you refer to us who are qualified for and complete our clinical trial(with a cap of $500).

Email us at info@heaflexclinic.com for more information.

Heaflex Clinic   51 Montain Drive,20185 LA   972-2857-295

ヒント subsidized は「助成金を受けている」、clinical trial は「臨床試験」

151. What does "subsidized" mean in the first sentence?
(A) Participants of the clinical trial will be paid.
(B) The clinical trial is reported in press.
(C) The clinical trial receives grant from the government or organizations.
(D) The clinical trial is done secretly.

152. Who would most likely qualify for the clinical trial?

(A) Sandy, female, 64, heavy smoker for 20 years, backache.

(B) Richard, male, 62, heavy smoker for 20 years, hard of hearing.

(C) Mary, female, 46, heavy smoker for 15 years, heart disease.

(D) Cindy, female, 68, heavy smoker for 20 years, backache.

153. If a man makes 10 referrals for the clinical trial and six of them are qualified for and complete the clinical trial, how much will he be paid?

(A) $500

(B) $600

(C) $1,000

(D) $3,000

解答・解説

151-153番は次のチラシに関するものです。

SUPPORT OUR STUDIES!

Heaflex Clinic is currently looking for female smokers / who meet the following

requirements for a subsidized clinical trial:

    (a) Aged under 65

    (b) Using tabacco, nicotine or e-cigerette regularly

    (c) Not having high blood pressure or heart diseases.

You would receive $5,000 / if you are qualified for and complete our clinical trial. / You would get $100 for each friend you refer to us / who are qualified for / and complete our clinical trial (with a cap of $500). /

Email us at info@heaflexclinic.com for more information.

Heaflex Clinic　51 Montain Drive,20185 LA　972-2857-295

本文の訳

私共の研究を支援下さい。

Heaflex Clinic は現在女性の喫煙者をさがしています、助成金の出る臨床試験への次の要件を満たされる女性の喫煙者を。

    (a) 65歳未満

    (b) タバコ、ニコチン、電子タバコを定期的に使用している

    (c) 高血圧または心臓疾患がないこと

5000ドルお受取になるでしょう、もし資格があり、当院の臨床試験を終えられれば。

当方へご紹介下さるお友達で資格にあてはまり、臨床試験を終えられるなら一人につき100ドル差し上げます（上限は500ドルです）。更なる情報をお求めなら info@heaflexclinic.com へメール下さい。

Part 1 写真描写

Part 2 応答

Part 3 会話

Part 4 説明文

Part 5 短文穴埋め

Part 6 長文穴埋め

Part 7 長文読解

151. 正解：(C)

What does "subsidized" mean in the first sentence?
第1文の "subsidized" の意味は？

(A) **Participants of the clinical trial will be paid.**
臨床試験の参加者はお金を支給される。

(B) **The clinical trial is reported in press.** 臨床試験は報道される。

(C) **The clinical trial receives grant from the government or organizations.**
臨床試験は政府か団体から助成金を受ける。

(D) **The clinical trial is done secretly.** 臨床試験は秘密裏に行われる。

ポイント sub は「サブリーダー」の sub、side は sit。「補助的に置かれる」という意味から「助成金・補助金を出す」という意味だが、当然、知らないので、勘でやって次を取る
⇒ **Level 1'**

152. 正解：(A)

Who would most likely qualify for the clinical trial?
この臨床試験にだれが多分資格を有するだろうか

(A) **Sandy, female, 64, heavy smoker for 20 years, backache.**
Sandy、女性、64歳、20年の常習喫煙者、腰痛

(B) **Richard, male, 62, heavy smoker for 20 years, hard of hearing.**
Richard、男性、62歳、20年の常習喫煙者、難聴

(C) **Mary, female, 46, heavy smoker for 15 years, heart disease.**
Mary、女性、46歳、15年の常習喫煙者、心臓疾患

(D) **Cindy, female, 68, heavy smoker for 20 years, backache.**
Cindy、女性、68歳、20年の常習喫煙者、腰痛

ポイント 初級者はこれを取ること。64歳女性、68歳女性、46歳女性の中で65歳未満で心臓に欠陥があってはいけないとなれば答えは (A)。名探偵になりましょう
⇒ **Level 2**

153. 正解：(A)

If a man makes 10 referrals for the clinical trial and six of them are qualified for and complete the clinical trial, how much will he be paid?
もしある人が10通の臨床試験への紹介をして、その内6名が適確とされ、そして臨床試験を終えれば彼はいくら支払われるだろうか？

(A) $500

(B) $600

(C) $1,000

(D) $3,000

ポイント 普通なら 100 × 6=600 ですが、本文内に "with a cap..." とあるのがミソ。cap は帽子＝頭なので「上限」という意味。よって500ドル以上にはならない
⇒ **Level 2**

Questions 154-156 refer to the following letter.

Dear. Lee,

I really enjoyed meeting with you yesterday. It is my pleasure to be considered for the auditing services for your company, Maple, Inc. The purpose of this letter is to set forth the terms and conditions that will govern our relationship.

A. Scope of Services

The services that we will provide include the following:
--reviewing the company's board resolutions, board meeting minutes, executive compensation schemes and other relevant documents.

--Interview members of the board and senior management; and preparing the audit report.

B. Fees & Billing

Fees for the audit work will be billed by the hour. The hourly rates of the associates who will work on this audit range from $100 to $800. We will normally send you monthly invoices for our fees and costs. We appreciate your payment within 30 days of the invoice.

We sincerely hope that the arrangement set forth in this letter is acceptable to you. We look forward to establishing a mutually beneficial relationship with you.

Very truly yours,

Ven Schiller LLP

Chapter ①

Part 1
写真描写

Part 2
応答

Part 3
会話

Part 4
説明文

Part 5
短文穴埋め

Part 6
長文穴埋め

Part 7
長文読解

📝 語句

❏ **auditing service** 監査業務
❏ **minutes** 名 議事録
❏ **compensation schemes** 報酬の仕組み

154. What is the purpose of this letter?

    (A) To ask for information

    (B) To explain a policy

    (C) To set out service terms

    (D) To request a service

155. Which of the following is closest in meaning to "range" in paragraph B?

    (A) spread

    (B) increase

    (C) charge

    (D) recover

156. What will Ven Schiller LLP do if it is engaged by Maple, Inc?

    (A) Hire a manager for the company

    (B) Organize a company trip

    (C) Replace a director for the company

    (D) Interview a director

153 ●

解答・解説

154-156 番は次の手紙に関するものです。

Dear. Lee,

I really enjoyed meeting with you yesterday. / It is my pleasure / to be considered for the auditing services for your company, Maple, Inc. The purpose of this letter is / to set forth the terms and conditions / that will govern our relationship. /

A. Scope of Services

The services that we will provide / include the following: /
– reviewing the company's board resolutions, / board meeting minutes, / executive compensation schemes / and other relevant documents.
– Interview members of the board and senior management; / and preparing the audit report. /

B. Fees & Billing

Fees for the audit work / will be billed by the hour. / The hourly rates of the associates / who will work on this audit range from $100 to $800. / We will normally send you monthly invoices / for our fees and costs. / We appreciate your payment / within 30 days of the invoice.

We sincerely hope / that the arrangement set forth in this letter / is acceptable to you. / We look forward to establishing a mutually beneficial relationship with you. /

Very truly yours,

Ven Schiller LLP

手紙本文の訳

昨日はお会いできて実に楽しかったです。光栄です、御社の監査業務へ考慮いただけて。この書簡の目的は、私共の関係を制する契約諸条件を述べさせていただくことです。

A. 業務範囲

当方がご提供する業務は次のとおりです：
– 御社の役員決議事項、役員会議事録、役員報酬の体系と、他の関連書類
– 役員および上級管理職の皆様への面接；そして監査報告書の準備

B. 料金と請求業務

監査業務にたいする料金は、時給で請求されます。この監査業務に携わる職員の時給のレートは100ドルから800ドルにわたります。当方では月ごとの請求書をお送りします、通常料金と費用に関して。仕送り状発行の30日以内にお支払いいただけるとありがたいです。この書状に述べました取り決めを受諾頂けること、心より希望したします。御社と互恵的関係が築けますよう期待しております。

Chapter①

Part 1 写真描写

Part 2 応答

Part 3 会話

Part 4 説明文

Part 5 短文穴埋め

Part 6 長文穴埋め

Part 7 長文読解

語句

- ❏ **audit** 動 監査する
- ❏ **terms and conditions** 契約諸条件 ※頻出！
- ❏ **govern** 動 治める；制する
- ❏ **resolve** 決定[決議]する
- ❏ **executive** 名 執行役員
- ❏ **scheme** 名 体系；仕組み
- ❏ **bill** 動 請求する
- ❏ **associates** 名 同僚；社員 ※弁護士の場合はヒラの弁護士
- ❏ **invoice** 名 仕送り状；請求書
- ❏ **arrangement** 名 取り決め；協議
- ❏ **mutually** 副 相互に

- ❏ **set forth** (意見などを)述べる；出発する
- ❏ **scope** 名 範囲
- ❏ **minutes** 名 議事録
- ❏ **compensation** 名 報酬
- ❏ **relevant** 形 関連した
- ❏ **appreciate** 動 感謝[評価]する
- ❏ **mutual** 形 相互の
- ❏ **beneficial** 形 利益をもたらす；恩恵的な

154　正解：(C)

What is the purpose of this letter?　この手紙の目的は何か？

(A) To ask for information　情報を求める
(B) To explain a policy　方針の説明
(C) To set out service terms　業務の（契約）条件を企画する
(D) To request a service　業務を要求する

ポイント ビジネス文だから不慣れだと思うが、余計なことは一切書かれないものだから、慣れれば以外と読みやすい。目的は必ず最初に来る。しかし、手紙、メールの場合最初に時候のあいさつ、感謝などの導入文が来ることに注意。ここでは本文2行目のpurpose がキーワード ⇒ **Level2**

155.　正解：(A)

Which of the following is closest in meaning to "range" in paragraph B?
段落 B の中の "range" の意味にもっとも近いのはどれか？

(A) spread　広がる
(B) increase　増加する
(C) charge　課金する
(D) recover　回復する；取り戻す

ポイント range は「幅」。100ドルから800ドルの広がりがあるということ。

156.　正解：(D)

What will Ven Schiller LLP do if it is engaged by Maple, Inc?
Ven Schiller LLP はもし Maple 社に雇用されたら何をするだろうか？

(A) Hire a manager for the company　会社の経営者を雇う
(B) Organize a company trip　社内旅行を準備する
(C) Replace a director for the company　取締役を替える
(D) Interview a director　取締役にインタビューする

ポイント 監査 (audit) 業務として雇用される (be engaged by~) 人がやることは？　A 段落の最後にある ⇒ **Level 1**

Questions 157-158 refer to the following e-mail.

Date:	Feb 25 2016
From:	seltzer@ alumni.wsw.edu
To:	e.walworth@gladmail.com

Dear Emily,

We hope you and your family are staying safe and healthy.

We note that you are a user of our alumni directory WSW Community. Our records show that you have chosen to serve as a source of advice and guidance for current students.
We are migrating WSW Community to WSW Amicus, an upgraded new online alumni directory. Would you be willing to continue to be a valuable resource for current students in the new directory?

If so, please click here and select "yes" in the "Link" tab to make your professional information visible to our students. You may also want to update your professional information if they are out of date. No personal information will be shared.
We appreciate as always your professional help to our students. If you have any questions about WSW Amicus, please contact us at amicus@wsw.edu.

Helen Selzer
Dean of Alumni Association

ヒント☞ migrate は「移す」、directory は「名簿」

157. What is the purpose of this email?

    (A) To organize an alumni gathering

    (B) To sell online directory to alumni

    (C) To request for alumni donation

    (D) To request alumni to log into a new directory

158. What is true about WSW Amicus?

    (A) All information in it is up-to-date.

    (B) It is an online job search engine.

    (C) It displays personal information of alumni.

    (D) It is upgraded from WSW Community.

Chapter ①

Part 1 写真描写

Part 2 応答

Part 3 会話

Part 4 説明文

Part 5 短文穴埋め

Part 6 長文穴埋め

Part 7 長文読解

解答・解説

157-158 番は次のメールに関するものです。

Date:	Feb 25 2016
From:	seltzer@ alumni.wsw.edu
To:	e.walworth@gladmail.com

Dear Emily,

We hope / you and your family are staying safe and healthy. /

We note / that you are a user of our alumni directory WSW Community. / Our records show / that you have chosen to serve/ as a source of advice and guidance/ for current students. / We are migrating WSW Community to WSW Amicus, / an upgraded new online alumni directory. / Would you be willing to continue/ to be a valuable resource for current students in the ne directory? / If so, / please click here / and select "yes" in the "Link" tab / to make your professional information/ visible to our students. / You may also want to update your professional information / if they are out of date. / No personal information will be shared. / We appreciate as always / your professional help to our students. / If you have any questions about WSW Amicus, / please contact us at amicus@wsw.edu. /

Helen Selzer
Dean of Alumni Association

メール本文の訳

　我々は思います、あなたとご家族が安寧で健康にお過ごしだと。我々は留意しております、貴方が私共の同窓生住所録 WSW Community のご利用者だと。私どもの記録によりますと貴方は現在校生へのアドバイスそしてガイダンスの発信源として奉仕することを選ばれております。私共は WSW Community を WSW Amicus へ移行いたします、グレードアップされた新しいオンライン同窓生住所録です。次の名簿におきましても現在校生のため貴重なる発信源となることをお続けになっていただけるでしょうか？

　もし、そうであれば、ここをクリックされ Link のタブの Yes を選んでください、貴方の専門職情報を当校の学生たちが目にすることができるように。また、あなたの専門職情報を更新なさりたいかも知れません、もし古くなっていれば。個人情報は共有することはありません。貴方様の学生たちへの専門家としてのご援助いつも感謝しております。もし何か WSW Amicus についてご質問がございましたら、amicus@wsw.edu の私共へご連絡ください。

Helen Selzer
同窓会会長

Chapter ❶

Part 1 写真描写

Part 2 応答

Part 3 会話

Part 4 説明文

Part 5 短文穴埋め

Part 6 長文穴埋め

Part 7 長文読解

語句

❏ note	動	心に留めている	❏ alumni	名	同窓生 [アラムナイ]	
❏ directory	名	名簿；リスト	❏ serve	動	仕える	
❏ source	名	源	❏ migrate	動	移行する	
❏ be willing to~		~しても差し支えない	❏ resource	名	源	
❏ make...visible		見えるようにする。				

157. 正解：(D)

What is the purpose of this email?　このEメールの目的は何か？

(A) To organize an alumni gathering　　同窓生の集い

(B) To sell online directory to alumni　　オンライン名簿を同窓生に売る

(C) To request for alumni donation　　同窓生寄付への要求をする

(D) To request alumni to log into a new directory
　　同窓生へ新しい名簿へのログインを要求する

ポイント 「~していただけるでしょうか？」という依頼を見抜く　⇒ Level 2

158. 正解：(D)

What is true about WSW Amicus?　WSW Amicus に当てはまるものは何か？

(A) All information in it is up-to-date.
その中のすべての情報は更新されている。

(B) It is an online job search engine.
オンラインの就職検索エンジンだ。

(C) It displays personal information of alumni.
同窓生の個人情報を載せている。

(D) It is upgraded from WSW Community.
WSW Community から更新されている。

ポイント 難題。ざっと skimming できないと厳しい。時間がないときは捨てるべし！

Questions 159-160 refer to the following text message chain.

9:05a.m. Sam: We've won the bid! The contract value is $87M!

9:06a.m. Liz: Great! Have you told Mark? He will be thrilled. He has been under performance pressure recently. This would save him.

9:15a.m. Sam: Not yet. I am still waiting for Kathy's e-mail confirmation. I want something in writing before I tell Mark. You know clients sometimes change their minds.

9:20a.m. Liz: Months of overtime finally paid off! Guess we can take a break?

9:21a.m. Sam: I don't think so, Liz. After we get the contract, we probably have more work to do. But at least our bonus this year won't be as ugly as last year.

159. Who is Kathy?

(A) Sam's client

(B) Sam's wife

(C) Sam's colleague

(D) Sam's boss

160. What is suggested of the winning of the contract?

(A) It will increase pressure on Mark.

(B) It will make Mark lose temper.

(C) It is a result of months of hard work.

(D) It will save Sam and Liz from more overtime work.

解答・解説

159-160 番は次のテキストメッセージのやりとりに関するものです。

9:05a.m. Sam: We've won the bid! / The contract value is $87M! /

9:06a.m. Liz: Great! / Have you told Mark? / He will be thrilled. / He has been under performance pressure recently. / This would save him.

9:15a.m. Sam: Not yet. / I am still waiting for Kathy's e-mail confirmation. I want something in writing / before I tell Mark. / You know / clients sometimes change their minds. /

9:20a.m. Liz: Months of overtime finally paid off! / Guess we can take a break? /

9:21a.m. Sam: I don't think so, Liz. / After we get the contract, / we probably have more work to do. / But at least / our bonus this year won't be as ugly as last year. /

Chapter ①

Part 1 写真描写

Part 2 応答

Part 3 会話

Part 4 説明文

Part 5 短文穴埋め

Part 6 長文穴埋め

Part 7 長文読解

訳

サム：入札勝ち取ったぞ！契約値は8700万ドルだ!

リズ：すごいわね。Markに話した？ 喜びに震えるわよ。彼は最近業績(を上げる)プレッシャーに迫られてたからね。彼の救いになるわね。

サム：まだだよ。 Kathyの確認のメールをまだ待ってるんだ。何か書面でのものが欲しいんだよね、Markに言う前に。顧客って時々心変わりするだろ？

リズ：何カ月もの残業がついに成果を上げたわね。一休みできると思う？

サム：そうは思わないな、Liz。契約が取れたら、多分仕事がさらに増えるよ。でもさ、少なくとも今年のボーナスは昨年ほど酷くはないだろうよ。

語句

❏ **bid** 图 入札　　❏ **be trilled** 震える　　❏ **at least** 少なくとも

159. 正解：(A)

Who is Kathy?	Kathyとはだれか？
(A) Sam's client	Samの顧客
(B) Sam's wife	Samの妻
(C) Sam's colleague	Samの同僚
(D) Sam's boss	Samの上司

ポイント 簡単な問題。Kathyの所を読めばすぐに顧客とわかる。このようにアメリカ人は、特に上司でも、顧客でも、名前の呼び捨てが当たり前なので私たち日本人（アジアの人達もそう）は戸惑う。だからMarkも責任者つまり、上司だろう ⇒ **Level 1**

160. 正解：(C)

What is suggested of the winning of the contract?
契約を勝ち得たことについて何が分かるか？

(A) It will increase pressure on Mark.
　　それはMarkのプレッシャーを増加させるだろう。

(B) It will make Mark lose temper.
　　それはMarkを立腹させるだろう。

(C) It is a result of months of hard work.
　　それは何カ月もの努力の結果である

(D) It will save Sam and Liz from more overtime work.
　　それはSamとLizをさらなる残業から救うだろう。

ポイント この手のスマホのtext messageは一気に最後まで読んでやると良い。その際に、プラスイメージで進行しているかマイナスイメージで進行しているかを考えて読むのがコツ。知らない単語は「多分良い意味だろう」又は「悪い意味だろう」と推測してどんどん飛ばすことだ ⇒ **Level 2**

Questions 161-164 refer to the following post.

If you are a Winston College student, you are eligible to join any of Peninsula's seven boards: News, Business, Arts, Editorial, Design, Sports and Technology. Applicants accepted both spring and fall. Visit our website for more information.

Peninsula publishes every morning. Monday through Friday except on university and federal holidays. In addition, we publish an Opinions Section on Wednesday, covering social and political events and commentaries. Contributions are welcome. We are proud of our alumni currently active in business, journalism and politics. Over 17 Peninsula alumni have won the Pulitzer Prize.

---

161. Which of the following most accurately describes "Peninsula"?

(A) a university club

(B) a university newspaper

(C) a federal magazine

(D) a charity organization

162. What does "contributions" mean in "Contributions are welcome"?

(A) articles

(B) donations

(C) applications

(D) comments

163. In the above paragraph, what does "alumni" means?

    (A) Persons who were in the same class

    (B) Persons who went to the same college

    (C) Persons who were on Peninsula

    (D) Persons who contributed to Peninsula.

164. Which of the following would be the most likely accepted as topic in the Opinions Section?

    (A) How to apply for Winston College

    (B) The impact of affirmative action on college enrollment

    (C) The life of a famous alumni

    (D) Food choices in students' cafe

Chapter ❶

Part 1 写真描写

Part 2 応答

Part 3 会話

Part 4 説明文

Part 5 短文穴埋め

Part 6 長文穴埋め

Part 7 長文読解

161-164 番は次の投稿に関するものです。

If you are a Winston College student, / you're eligible to join any of Peninsula's seven boards: / News, Business, Arts, Editorial, Design, Sports and Technology. / Applicants accepted / both spring and fall. / Visit our website for more information. /

Peninsula publishes every morning. / Monday through Friday / except on university and federal holidays. / In addition, / we publish an Opinions Section on Wednesday, / covering social and political events and commentaries. / Contributions are welcome. / We are proud of our alumni currently active / in business, journalism and politics. / Over 17 Peninsula alumni / have won the Pulitzer Prize. /

訳

　もし貴方が Winston 大学の学生なら、あなたは Peninsula の7つの部局のどれにでも参加する資格があります、すなわち、ニュース、ビジネス、芸術、編集、デザイン、スポーツそして科学技術です。応募は春、秋両方で受け付けます。さらなる情報は私共のウェブをご覧ください。

　Peninsula は毎朝発行されます。大学や連邦の祝日を除いて月曜から金曜まで。加えて、水曜日には Opinion コーナーを出します、それは社会的、政治的行事と論評を扱います。寄稿は歓迎致します。私共は現在ビジネス、ジャーナリズムそして政治で活躍している私共の同窓生を誇りにしています。17名以上の Peninsula 同窓生がこれまでピューリッツア賞を獲得しています。

語句

❏ **be eligible to do**	～する資格がある		❏ **board**	名 （ここでは）部局
❏ **application**	名 応募		❏ **publish**	動 発行[出版]する
❏ **except**	～を除いて		❏ **federal**	米 連邦の
❏ **section**	名 （ここでは）コーナー		❏ **cover**	動 報道する；扱う
❏ **commentary**	名 論評		❏ **contribution**	名 寄稿；寄付
❏ **alumni**	名 同窓生[アラムナイ]			

Chapter ①

Part 1 写真描写

Part 2 応答

Part 3 会話

Part 4 説明文

Part 5 短文穴埋め

Part 6 長文穴埋め

Part 7 長文読解

161 正解：(B)

Which of the following most accurately describes "Peninsula"?

次のどれがもっとも Peninsula を正確に記述しているか？

(A) a university club　　　大学のクラブ

(B) a university newspaper　大学の新聞

(C) a federal magazine　　連邦の雑誌

(D) a charity organization　慈善の団体

ポイント　2段落目の最初にズバリ「毎朝発行する」とある　⇒ Level 1

162 正解：(A)

What does "contributions" mean in "Contributions are welcome"?

"Contributions are welcome." の中の contributions の意味は？

(A) articles　　　（寄稿）記事

(B) donations　　寄付

(C) applications　応募

(D) comments　　意見

ポイント　これは単語力がある人でもあわてて (B) にしそう。文意からコラムなどに記事を寄稿することを指す。単語力の問題。

163 正解：(C)

In the above paragraph, what does "alumni" means?

上記の文中 "alumni" は何を意味するか？

(A) Persons who were in the same class　　　同じクラスだった人達

(B) Persons who went to the same college　　同じ大学に行った人達

(C) Persons who were on Peninsula　　　　　Peninsula に携わった人達

(D) Persons who contributed to Peninsula　　Peninsula に寄稿した人達

ポイント　普通は同じ学校を出た人達のことを言うが、ここでは (C)。最後の文で分かる

164 正解：(B)

Which of the following would be the most likely accepted as topic in the Opinions section?

Opinion コーナーでの話題としてもっとも取り上げられそうなのは次のどれか？

(A) How to apply for Winston College　Winston 大学への申し込み方法

(B) The impact of affirmative action on college enrollment
　　大学への入学に関しての 肯定的な活動の影響

(C) The life of a famous alumni　　有名な同窓生の人生

(D) Food choices in students' café　学生食堂での食べ物のチョイス

ポイント　Opinions のところを読むと social, political, commentaries とあるので「意見・論評」だ！　⇒ Level 3

Questions 165-167 refer to the following article

Wireless communications company WireCom, Inc. said its net earnings rose in it's latest quarter but warned that economic conditions might hold back profits in the future.

The Chicago-based company said its net income rose to $26 million, or 36 cents a share in the fiscal first quarter. That compares with $17 million,23 cents, a year earlier.

The company warned in February that canceled orders from South Korea would cause its second quarter profits to fall short of first-quarter levels. It also said it was cutting 700 temporary jobs.

"These conditions may continue and could impact earnings in the future," the company said on Tuesday.

WireCom also cited lower demand for its single-mode personal communication services Q phones in the United States and South Korea, as well as a delay in the introduction of its dual-mode cellular Q phone.

165. What is the best heading for this article?

(A) "WireCom Cuts Jobs"

(B) "Demand Lower for WireCom Q Phones"

(C) "WireCom Net Income Rises but Outlook Clouded"

(D) "WireCom Stocks Gain After Hours"

166. Which of the followings would NOT reduce future revenues?

(A) less demand for Q phones

(B) canceled orders

(C) increased shipping costs to South Korea

(D) introducing the dual-mode Q phones behind schedule.

167. How much did stocks rise in the first quarter?

(A) 23 cents a share   (B) 36 cents a share

(C) 59 cents a share   (D) 87.5 cents a share

Part 2

解答・解説

165-167 番は次の記事に関するものです。

> Wireless communications company WireCom, Inc. said / its net earnings rose in it's latest quarter / but warned / that economic conditions might hold back profits in the future. / The Chicago-based company said / its net income rose to $26 million, / or 36 cents a share / in the fiscal first quarter. / That compares with $17 million,23 cents, / a year earlier. / The company warned in February / that canceled orders from South Korea / would cause its second quarter profits / to fall short of first-quarter levels. / It also said / it was cutting 700 temporary jobs. /
>
> "These conditions may continue / and could impact earnings in the future," / the company said on Tuesday. / WireCom also cited lower demand / for its single-mode personal communication services Q phones / in the United States and South Korea, / as well as a delay in the introduction of its dual-mode cellular Q phone. /

訳

無線通信会社の WireCom 社は言った、この前の四半期で純収益が上昇したと、しかし警告した、経済状況は将来において利潤を抑えるであろうと。シカゴに本拠を置くこの会社は言った、純益は2600万ドル、すなわち1株あたり36セント上昇したと、最初の財政年度において。それは1年前の1700万ドル、23セントと比較してである。会社は2月に警告した、韓国からの注文キャンセルのせいで第2四半期の利益は第1四半期のレベルには及ばないであろうと。また言った、700人の一時的な仕事を切ることになろうと。「これらの状況は引き続くであろうし、将来の収益に影響を及ぼすであろう」と火曜日に会社は述べた。WireCom はより低い需要を引き合いに出した、その単一モードの個人コミュニケーションサービスの Q フォンに対しての、合衆国と韓国における、そのデュアルモードの携帯 Q フォンの導入の遅れについてはもちろんのことだが。

Chapter 1

Part 1 写真描写

Part 2 応答

Part 3 会話

Part 4 説明文

Part 5 短文穴埋め

Part 6 長文穴埋め

Part 7 長文読解

❏ **latest**	形 一番最近の	❏ **quarter**	名 四半期
❏ **warn**	動 警告 [注意] する	❏ **hold back**	抑える
❏ **profit**	名 利益		
❏ **cause A to...**	A に〜引きおこさせる（A が原因で〜となる）		
❏ **fall short of〜**	〜に及ばない		
❏ **temporary**	形 一時的な ※いわゆる派遣の仕事を temporary job という		
❏ **impact**	動 影響を与える		
❏ **cite**	動 引き合いにだす ※見積もるという意味もある		
❏ **as well as...**	〜はもちろんのこと	❏ **dual**	形 二元性の；二重の

165. 正解：(C)

What is the best heading for this article?　この記事のベストな見出しは？

(A) "WireCom Cuts Jobs"　WireCom 従業員カット

(B) "Demand Lower for WireCom Q Phones"
WireCom の Q フォンの需要は減る

(C) "WireCom Net Income Rises but Outlook Clouded"
WireCom の純収益は上がるが見通しは曇る

(D) "WireCom Stocks Gain After Hours"
終業後 WireCom 株上昇

ポイント 記事の大切なことは最初に来る！

166. 正解：(C)

Which of the followings would NOT reduce future revenues?
次のどれが将来の歳入を減らさないだろうか？

(A) less demand for Q phones　Q フォンの需要減

(B) canceled orders　　　　　　注文のキャンセル

(C) increased shipping costs to South Korea
韓国への運送費高騰

(D) introducing the dual-mode Q phones behind schedule.
二元モード Q フォンの予定より遅れての導入

ポイント NOT だから記事に出ていないものだ！

167. 正解：(B)

How much did stocks rise in the first quarter?
第1四半期において株価はどれだけ上がったか？

(A) 23 cents a share　　　(B) 36 cents a share
(C) 59 cents a share　　　(D) 87.5 cents a share

ポイント 第1四半期を見たらよいだけ。簡単！

Chapter ①

Part 1 写真描写

Part 2 応答

Part 3 会話

Part 4 説明文

Part 5 短文穴埋め

Part 6 長文穴埋め

Part 7 長文読解

練習問題 めやすは「1問1分」です！

Questions 168-171 refer to the following letter.

THE QUINCEY STREET BAKERY

Dear Friend:

This Christmas, why don't you delight your friends and relatives with our famous Luxury Fruitcake? Here is what we offer:

QUALITY- An automatic refund or a replacement cake if there is even the slightest doubt about freshness or safe delivery.

CONVENIENCE- Just mail your gift list to us in the pre-addressed envelope. We will send all packages prepaid and deal with the customs documentation necessary for the arrival of your gifts.

ECONOMY- Prices include delivery to the United States and Puerto Rico. For surface mail shipments to other countries, add $5,$5.50 and $6.00 respectively for regular, medium and large cakes.

Christmas will be here before you know it, so send us your order today. We promise that you, your friends and your relatives will be delighted with our world-famous cake and our personal attention to your requests.

Sincerely,

Arnold H. Bohm.

President

168. What does the letter encourage people to do?

    (A) Buy a cake for themselves

    (B) Send cakes as a gift

    (C) Order a special kind of cake

    (D) Buy a cake and enter a competition

169. How should people contact the Quincey Street Bakery?

    (A) By phone

    (B) By fax

    (C) By e-mail

    (D) By mail

170. What additional service does the company provide?

    (A) Dealing with customs procedures

    (B) Providing gift-wrapping

    (C) A discount for multiple orders

    (D) Different types of cake

171. Where will the company deliver its products?

    (A) USA only

    (B) USA and US possessions

    (C) USA and Europe

    (D) Worldwide

解答・解説

Part 1 写真描写

Part 2 応答

Part 3 会話

Part 4 説明文

Part 5 短文穴埋め

Part 6 長文穴埋め

Part 7 長文読解

168-171 番は次の手紙に関するものです。

THE QUINCEY STREET BAKERY

Dear Friend:

This Christmas, / why don't you delight your friends and relatives / with our famous Luxury Fruitcake? / Here is what we offer: /

QUALITY-An automatic refund or a replacement cake / if there is even the slightest doubt / about freshness or safe delivery. /

CONVENIENCE-Just mail your gift list to us / in the pre-addressed envelope. / We will send all packages prepaid / and deal with the customs documentation / necessary for the arrival of your gifts. /

ECONOMY-Prices include delivery to the United States and Puerto Rico. / For surface mail shipments to other countries, / add $5, $5.50 and $6.00 respectively / for regular, medium and large cakes. /

Christmas will be here / before you know it, / so send us your order today. / We promise / that you, your friends and your relatives will be delighted with our world-famous cake / and our personal attention to your requests.

Sincerely,
Arnold H.Bohm.
President

手紙本文の訳

親愛なる皆様へ、

今年のクリスマス、皆様のご友人、親戚を喜ばせるのはいかがでしょう、弊社の有名な Luxury Fruitcake で？　私共が提供しますものは…。

品質——自動的に返金またはケーキのお取り替え致します、もし少しでもその新鮮さまたは安全配達にご疑念でもございますれば。

便利さ——皆様の贈り物リストをただ私共へ送付ください、あらかじめ宛て名書きした封筒に入れて。私共はすべての小包を前払いでお送りし、貴方様のギフトの到着に必要な税関書類を処理いたします。

経済性——価格には合衆国とプエルト・リコへの配達費を含んでいます。他の国々への海陸郵便配達へは5ドル、5．5ドル、6ドルを普通、中、大のケーキそれぞれに追加となります。

クリスマスは気が付く前にやってきます。ですから本日注文ください。我々は約束します、あなた、貴方のご友人、ご親戚のかたがたが私共の世界的に有名なケーキに、また私共が皆様のご要望に個人的な注意をはらっていることにお喜びになることを。

168. 正解：(B)

What does the letter encourage people to do?
手紙は人々へ何を勧めているか？

(A) Buy a cake for themselves　　　　　自身のためにケーキを買う
(B) Send cakes as a gift　　　　　　　　贈り物としてケーキを送る
(C) Order a special kind of cake　　　　特別な種類のケーキを注文する
(D) Buy a cake and enter a competition　ケーキを買ってコンペに参加する

> **ポイント** 最初の1〜2行を読むだけで、「クリスマスの贈り物にいかが？」という主旨が感じられる。その後の CONVENIENCE のところを読めばはっきりする。

169. 正解：(D)

How should people contact the Quincy Street Bakery?
人は Quincy Street Bakery にどうやって連絡をとったらよいか？

(A) By phone　　電話で
(B) By fax　　　ファクスで
(C) By e-mail　　e-mail で
(D) By mail　　　郵便で

> **ポイント** CONVENIENCE の欄に Just mail... とあるので簡単！

170. 正解：(A)

What additional service does the company provide?
会社はどんな追加のサービスを提供するか？

(A) Dealing with customs procedures　税関手続きを扱う
(B) Providing gift-wrapping　　　　　　贈り物のラッピングを提供する
(C) A discount for multiple orders　　　複数注文へ値引きする
(D) Different types of cake　　　　　　　違ったタイプのケーキ

> **ポイント** CONVENIENCE のところに deal with the custom documentation（税関の書類を処理する）とある。設問にある additional service の言い換え表現だ。

171. 正解：(D)

Where will the company deliver its products?　会社はどこへその製品を配達するか？

(A) USA only　　　　　　　　　合衆国だけ
(B) USA and US possessions　合衆国とその占有地
(C) USA and Europe　　　　　合衆国とヨーロッパ
(D) Worldwide　　　　　　　　全世界に

> **ポイント** 税関の手続きでも分かるが、ECONOMY の欄に to other countries がある。なお surface mail は、陸上便・海上便の双方を指す表現。

Chapter ①

Part 1 写真描写

Part 2 応答

Part 3 会話

Part 4 説明文

Part 5 短文穴埋め

Part 6 長文穴埋め

Part 7 長文読解

練習問題 めやすは「1問1分」です！

Question 172-175 refer to the following notice

Dear customers,

We are happy to announce the introduction of automatic cashier machines to our store. [1] You can pay for your purchase by scanning the barcode printed on the package of each commodity at those lanes. [2] The machines accept credit cards only. A camera is installed on the premise to discourage any potential thefts or other inappropriate behaviors. Please note that we will not be able to give you cash back at lanes 1-8. [3] If you need cash back, please use the regular lanes from 9-15. For customers who want the express check-out, please use lane 1, which is reserved for express check-out and can scan up to five items. [4] Separately, our entire 2nd floor will be closed for renovation from Sep 2. Our seafood and fruits sections will temporarily be moved to the 3rd floor. Our restaurant bar and the elevator to the 2nd floor will be closed during that period.

172. When should a customer use lanes 9-15?

    (A) When he or she needs to return a product

    (B) When he or she needs a receipt

    (C) When he or she wants more cash on hand

    (D) When he or she wants to express check-out

173. In which of the positions marked [1],[2],[3], and [4] does the following sentence best belong?

"They are installed in lanes 1-8."

(A) [1]

(B) [2]

(C) [3]

(D) [4]

174. Cindy is shopping at the store. She should use lane 1 if she--

(A) has four items in her cart

(B) doesn't have a credit card

(C) needs cash back

(D) is concerned about thefts

175. Which of the following will happen during the renovation period?

(A) Customers should buy fruits on the 2nd floor.

(B) Customers should buy fish on the 2nd floor.

(C) The restaurant bar will be moved to the 3rd floor.

(D) Customers cannot use the elevator to the 2nd floor.

Chapter ①

Part 1
写真描写

Part 2
応答

Part 3
会話

Part 4
説明文

Part 5
短文穴埋め

Part 6
長文穴埋め

Part 7
長文読解

解答・解説

172-175 番は次の通知に関するものです。

Dear customers,

We are happy to announce / the introduction of automatic cashier machines to our store. / [1] They are installed in lanes 1-8. / You can pay for your purchase / by scanning the barcode / printed on the package of each commodity / at those lanes. / The machines accept credit cards only. / A camera is installed on the premise / to deter any potential thefts / or other inappropriate behaviors. / Please note / that we will not be able to give you cash back / at lanes 1-8. / If you need cash back, / please use the regular lanes from 9-15. / For customers / who want the express check-out, / please use lane 1, / which is reserved for express check-out/ and can scan up to five items. / Separately, / our entire 2nd floor / will be closed for renovation / from Sep. 2 2021. / Our seafood and fruits sections / will temporarily be moved to the 3rd floor. / Our restaurant bar and the elevator to the 2nd floor / will be closed / during that period. /

本文の訳

　当店に自動レジを導入した事をお知らせできることをうれしく思います。[1]それらは1-8レーンに設置されています。皆様はご購入品に対しお支払いいただけます、それらのレーンでそれぞれの商品のパッケージに印刷されているバーコードをスキャンすることで。機械はクレジットカードのみしか受け付けません。店内にはどんな窃盗になりそうな行為、または他の不適切な行為をも思いとどまらせるカメラが設置されております。レーン1-8では現金を払い戻すことはできませんことご留意下さい。もし、現金を払い戻す必要があれば、9-15の通常のレーンをご使用下さい。お急ぎで勘定を済ませたいお客様には1レーンをお使い下さい、そこは急ぎの勘定扱いのため取ってあり、5品目までスキャン可能です。

　別件ですが、当店の2階全フロアは改装のため2021年9月2日からクローズいたします。当店の海産物と果物のコーナーは一時的に3階へ移されます。レストランバーと2階へのエレベーターはその間クローズです。

172. 正解：(C)
When should a customer use lanes 9-15?
顧客はいつ9- 15レーンを使うべきか

(A) When he or she needs to return a product 商品を戻す必要がある時

(B) When he or she needs a receipt 領収証が必要な時に

(C) When he or she wants more cash on hand 手元にもっと現金がほしいときに

(D) When he or she wants to express check-out 急ぎの勘定をしたいとき

ポイント 9-15 レーンの所を読むだけ！ ズバリ出ている！ ⇒ Level 1

173. 正解：(A)
In which of the positions marked [1], [2], [3], and [4] does the following sentence best belong?
[1]、[2]、[3]、または [4] のマークのある位置のどこに次の文が入るか？

"They are installed in lanes 1-8."

(A) [1]   (B) [2]

(C) [3]   (D) [4]

ポイント 簡単だが、あわてると直前の1- 8につられて [3] にしてしまう。後ろの文の at those lanes の those に注目すること。代名詞を重視するくせをつけよう！

174. 正解：(A)
Cindy is shopping at the store. She should use lane 1 if she...
Cindy は店で買い物をしている。彼女はもし…なら1レーンを使うべきだ。

(A) has four items in her cart カートに4品目載せていれば

(B) doesn't have a credit card クレジットカードがなければ

(C) needs cash back 現金の返金を必要とするなら

(D) is concerned about thefts 窃盗を心配するなら

ポイント 5品目までだったら1レーンですぐに勘定を済ませられるから ⇒ Level 2

175. 正解：(D)
Which of the following will happen during the renovation period?
改装期間中には次のどれが生じるだろう？

(A) Customers should buy fruits on the 2nd floor. 客は2階で果物を買うはずだ。

(B) Customers should buy fish on the 2nd floor. 客は2階で魚を買うはずだ。

(C) The restaurant bar will be moved to the 3rd floor.
レストランバーは3階へ移されるだろう

(D) Customers cannot use the elevator to the 2nd floor.
客は2階へ上るエレベーターは使えない。

ポイント 後半の改装の部分を読めばすぐにエレベーターがクローズと分かるはず ⇒ Level 1

Chapter ①

Part 1 写真描写

Part 2 応答

Part 3 会話

Part 4 説明文

Part 5 短文穴埋め

Part 6 長文穴埋め

Part 7 長文読解

練習問題 Stage3 (Q176-200) は30分で通過しましょう！

Questions 176-180 refer to the following letter and manuscript

Dear, Patrick,

I know you've been busy these days, but I'd like to ask you something.
We've been receiving a lot of letters from readers concerning the new recycling law that went into effect on April 1. Would you please write up a short article (200 words or so) that we can insert into Friday's environmental page?
Be sure to (1) tell how the law works, (2) mention who it affects, (3) point out its aimes and goals, and (4) have it on my desk by 9:00 tomorrow morning.
Sorry for the rush.

Marine

The new Municipal Recycling Law calls for three-way cooperation among consumers, government, and business and industry. Consumers get the process started by separating their trash into four different categories:(1) burnable (excluding newspapers, which are recycled separately); (2) glass bottles; (3) PET bottles; and (4) metal cans. City and local governments are then in charge of collecting the trash and transporting it to designated public and private recycling sites. Various industries and businesses, including packaging and container makers as well as food producers and sellers (supermarkets, convenience stores, and restaurants), must arrange for the actual recycling and disposal.
The new law aims to help solve the twin problems of decreasing landfill space. The new system ensures that recycling responsibilities are shared equally by everyone.

176. Who is Marine?

(A) A newspaper editor

(B) A consumer adviser

(C) A radio station host

(D) An environmental expert

177. What can we say about Patrick's article?

(A) It's too long.

(B) It answers all the readers' questions about the new law.

(C) Marine will probably be pleased with it.

(D) Patrick is too busy to reply to Marine's letter.

178. Which of these is NOT covered by the new recycling law?

(A) Newspapers

(B) Metal cans

(C) PET bottles

(D) Burnable garbage

179. Which of these statements does NOT answer Marine's third request?

(A) The new law will help save natural resources.

(B) The new system will save space.

(C) The new law aims to be fair for everyone involved.

(D) The new law designates various recycling sites.

180. What is the correct order for the recycling process?

(A) Separate, transport, recycle

(B) Consumer, industry, business

(C) Consumer, business, government

(D) How it works, who it affects, what its purpose is

解答・解説

聴く勉 TOEIC 講座！ DL音声 51

176-180 番は次の手紙と原稿に関するものです。

Dear, Patrick,
I know you've been busy these days, / but I'd like to ask you something. /
We've been receiving a lot of letters from readers / concerning the new recycling law / that went into effect on April 1. / Would you please write up a short article (200 words or so) / that we can insert into Friday's environmental page? / Be sure to (1) tell how the law works, / (2) mention who it affects, / (3) point out its aims and goals, / and (4) have it on my desk / by 9:00 tomorrow morning. / Sorry for the rush. /

Marine

語句

- ❏ **concerning** 前 〜に関して
- ❏ **write up** 詳しく書く
- ❏ **affect** 〜に影響を及ぼす
- ❏ **go into effect** 発効する
- ❏ **insert** 動 挿入する
- ❏ **point out** 指摘する
- ❏ **aim** 名 目的

The new Municipal Recycling Law calls for three-way cooperation / among consumers, government, and business and industry. / Consumers get the process started / by separating their trash into four different categories: / (1) burnable (excluding newspapers, which are recycled separately); / (2) glass bottles; / (3) PET bottles; / and (4) metal cans. / City and local governments are / then in charge of collecting the trash / and transporting it to designated public / and private recycling sites. / Various industries and businesses, / including packaging and container makers / as well as food producers and sellers / (supermarkets, convenience stores, and restaurants) /, must arrange for the actual recycling and disposal. / The new law aims / to help solve the twin problems / of decreasing landfill space. / The new system ensures / that recycling responsibilities are shared equally / by everyone. /

181

最近、とてもお忙しいのは分かっていますが、お願いがあるのです。読者の皆さんから多くのお手紙をいただいているのです、新しいリサイクル法に関しての、4月1日に発行された。短い記事を書いていただけますか（200語がその辺りで）、金曜日の環境ページに挿入できるものを。必ず (1) その法律はどのように機能するのか言っていただき、(2) だれに影響があるのか名を挙げていただき、(3) その目的と目標を指摘いただき、そして (4) 私のデスクへ明朝9時までに届けていただきますようお願いします。慌ただしくさせて申し訳ありません。

新しい自治体のリサイクル法は3方向の協力を求めています、消費者、政府、そしてビジネス、産業の。消費者はそのゴミを4つの部門分けることでその工程を始めます。すなわち (1) 燃えるもの（新聞は除きます、これは別途にリサイクルされるので）、(2) ガラス瓶、(3) ペットボトル、そして (4) 金属の缶です。それで、市と地方自治体はそのゴミを集めそして指定された公共の、また私企業のリサイクル場へ運ぶ事を担当します。種々の産業そしてビジネス、-- 食物生産者、販売者（スーパー、コンビニ、そしてレストラン）はもとより、梱包、そして容器のメーカーを含んでですが -- は実際のリサイクルと処分の手筈を整えなければなりません。新法は埋め立て地を減らすという一対の問題解決の助けとなる事を目的としています。この新法はリサイクルの責任は等しくだれにも分担されるということを確実にしています。

語句

❑ **municipal**	形	地方自治体の	❑ **call for**		～を求める
❑ **cooperation**	名	協力	❑ **get A started**		A を始める (= start A)
❑ **category**	名	部門	❑ **burn**	動	燃える ※ +able = 可燃性のある
❑ **exclude**	動	～を除く			

❑ **PET** ポリエチレンの略で、プラスティックのこと。pet [ペット] のことではない

❑ **in charge of~**		～を担当している	❑ **designated**	形	指定された
❑ **arrange for~**		～の準備をする	❑ **disposal**	名	処分
❑ **landfill space**		埋立地	❑ **ensure**	動	保証する；確実にする。

176. 正解：(A)

Who is Marine? Marine とはだれか？

(A) A newspaper editor 新聞の編集者

(B) A consumer adviser 消費者アドバイザー

(C) A radio station host ラジオ局の司会者

(D) An environmental expert 環境専門家

ポイント 読者の方々からのお手紙、そして記事の記述ですぐ分かる ⇒ **Level 2**

177. 正解：(C)

What can we say about Patrick's article? Patrick の記事について何が言えるか？

(A) It's too long. それは長すぎる。

(B) It answers all the readers' questions about the new law.
その新法について読者のすべての質問に答えている。

(C) Marine will probably be pleased with it.
Marine は多分その記事に満足するだろう。

(D) Patrick is too busy to reply to Marine's letter.
Patrick は忙しすぎて Marine の手紙に答えられない。

ポイント 200 語以内で詳しく書いてくれているので満足すると推察できる ⇒ **Level 3**

178. 正解：(A)

Which of these is NOT covered by the new recycling law?
これらのどれが新リサイクル法によって扱われていないものか？

(A) Newspapers　　　　　新聞
(B) Metal cans　　　　　金属缶
(C) PET bottles　　　　ペットボトル
(D) Burnable garbage　　燃えるゴミ

> **ポイント** 原稿内の（ ）にある。新聞紙は古紙業者が引き取るので ⇒ **Level 1'**

179. 正解：(D)

Which of these statements does NOT answer Marine's third request?
Marine の3番目の要求の答えとなっていないものはどれか？

(A) The new law will help save natural resouces.
新法は天然資源を節約する手助けとなろう。

(B) The new system will save space.
新システムはスペースを節約する。

(C) The new law aims to be fair for everyone involved.
新法は関係のあるだれにたいしても公正であることを目的としている。

(D) The new law designates various recycling sites.
新法は種々のリサイクル場を指定している。

> **ポイント** (3) には「その目的と目標を指摘してほしい」とある。(A)(B)(C) はすべて目標・目的だが、(D) だけは目的でも目標でもない ⇒ **Level 3**

180. 正解：(A)

What is the correct order for the recycling process?
リサイクの工程で正しい順序はどれか？

(A) Separate, transport, recycle
分別、移送、リサイクル

(B) Consumer, industry, business
消費者、産業（界）、実業（界）

(C) Consumer, business, government
消費者、実業（界）、政府

(D) How it works, who it affects, what its purpose is
それ（リサイクルの工程）が如何に機能するか、だれに影響を及ぼすか、その目的は何か？

> **ポイント** (D) は正しいことだが、順序としては不適切 ⇒ **Level 3**

Questions 181-185 refer to the following document and e-mails.

Memo to All Employees

Date: May 2 2019

Roland Partners New York

Referral Bonus Policy

The current policy applies to referrals of attorneys to the firm. A current full time employee(whether attorneys or non-attorneys) with the firm will be eligible for the referral bonus as follows:

 1 If the referred candidate is hired by the firm as full time and the candidate continues with the firm for 90 days, the referring employee will receive $1,000.

 2 If the referred candidate is hired by the firm as full time and the candidate continues with the firm for 6 months, the referring employee will receive $4,000.

 3 If the referred candidate remains employed with the firm for 12 months, the referring employee will receive an additional and final bonus of $5,000.

This policy is effective immediately. For any questions on this policy, please contact Mark Steiner at m.steiner @rolandpartners.com

---

ヒント☞ referral は「紹介状」、attorney は「(会社お抱えの)弁護士」、firm はここでは law firm(法律事務所)を指す。eligible for~ は「~に資格がある」、referred candidate は「紹介(照会)を受けた候補者」

Date:	Feb 20 2020
From:	Liz Capez
To:	Mark Steiner

Mark,

My name is Liz. I work with Gregg in the Boston office I saw your referral bonus policy. I am wondering if it only applies to employees in the New York office or employees in Roland's other offices are also eligible. I am asking because I may have a candidate for your current open role.

Liz

Date:	Feb 21 2020
From:	Mark Steiner
To:	Liz Capez

Hi Liz,

Yes, I confirm that persons in our other offices in the States will be eligible for the bonus if all the conditions are met. Why don't you send over the person's résumé?

Mark

Date:	Feb 22 2020
From:	Liz Capez
To:	Mark Steiner

Mark,

Thank you for your reply. I've actually decided to drop this. Although this candidate is super good, he is with one of our clients. I discussed this with Gregg and we thought we should probably play it safe.

Liz

Chapter ❶

Part 1 写真描写

Part 2 応答

Part 3 会話

Part 4 説明文

Part 5 短文穴埋め

Part 6 長文穴埋め

Part 7 長文読解

181. Why does Liz email Mark?

    (A) To challenge the policy

    (B) To introduce a candidate

    (C) To ask for a referral

    (D) To ask for an interpretation of a policy

182. Estelle works for Roland Partners full time. If she refers a candidate who continues to work for the firm for 12 months, how much referral bonus will Estelle get?

    (A) $5,000

    (B) $6,000

    (C) $8,000

    (D) $10,000

183. What does Liz mean when she says "play it safe"?

    (A) She doesn't want to lose the client by referring client's employee to her firm.

    (B) She thinks the candidate may access confidential information.

    (C) She thinks Gregg may not be happy if she gets the referral bonus.

    (D) She thinks the candidate may not be good enough.

184. What is "Roland Partners"?

    (A) A law firm

    (B) A consulting firm

    (C) A travel agency

    (D) A human resources firm

185. Which of the following is most likely to be Mark's reply to Liz's?

    (A) Our office is safe. Don't worry.

    (B) Don't you want the referral bonus?

    (C) No problem, Liz. Great that you talked to Gregg.

    (D) You shouldn't have talked to Gregg.

解答・解説

181-185 番は次の書類とメールに関するものです。

Memo to All Employees
Date: May 2 2019
Roland Partners New York
　　　　Referral Bonus Policy
The current policy applies to / referrals of attorneys to the firm. / A
current full time employee (whether attorneys or non-attorneys) with the
firm / will be eligible for the referral bonus as follows:

1 If the referred candidate is hired by the firm as full time / and the
　candidate continues with the firm for 90 days, / the referring employee
　will receive $1,000. /

2 If the referred candidate is hired by the firm as full time / and the
　candidate continues with the firm for 6 months, / the referring
　employee will receive $4,000. /

3 If the referred candidate remains employed with the firm for 12
　months, / the referring employee will receive an additional and final
　bonus of $5,000. /

This policy is effective immediately. / For any questions on this policy, /
please contact Mark Steiner at m.steiner @rolandpartners.com

書類本文の訳

(弁護士) 紹介賞与方針

現行の方針では適用されます、事務所への弁護士の紹介が。現在の事務所常勤の所員(弁護士でも弁護士でなくても)
に、次のごとく紹介賞与の資格があります。

1 もし紹介された候補者が常勤として雇用され、その候補者が90日会社に勤務を続ければ、紹介している所員は
　1000ドル受け取ることになります。

2 もし紹介された候補者が常勤として雇用され、その候補者が6カ月会社に勤務を続ければ、紹介している所員は
　4000ドル受け取ることになります。

3 もし紹介された候補者が会社に12カ月留まれば、紹介している所員は追加と最終の賞与5000ドルを受け取ること
　になります。

この方針は即、効力を発します。この方針に何か質問があれば Mark Steiner へ連絡ください。

 語句

❑ **apply to~**　～へ適用される　　❑ **be eligible for~**　～の資格がある
❑ **as follows**　のごとく　　　　　❑ **remain**　　　～のままである
❑ **firm**　　（会社組織でない）企業
　※通常「事務所」と訳すことが多い。経理事務所、コンサルティング事務所など。なお、firm (堅い;
　堅くする) の意味もあるので注意。

187

Date:	Feb 20 2020
From:	Liz Capez
To:	Mark Steiner

Mark,

My name is Liz. / I work with Gregg / in the Boston office / I saw your referral bonus policy. / I am wondering if it only applies to employees in the New York office or employees in Roland's other offices are also eligible. / I am asking / because I may have a candidate / for your current open role. /

Liz

Date:	Feb 21 2020
From:	Mark Steiner
To:	Liz Capez

Hi Liz,

Yes, I confirm / that persons in our other offices in the States / will be eligible for the bonus / if all the conditions are met. / Why don't you send over the person's résumé? /

Mark

Date:	Feb 22 2020
From:	Liz Capez
To:	Mark Steiner

Mark,

Thank you for your reply. / I've actually decided to drop this. / Although this candidate is super good, / he is with one of our clients. / I discussed this with Gregg / and we thought we should probably play it safe.

Liz

Chapter ①

Part 1 写真描写

Part 2 応答

Part 3 会話

Part 4 説明文

Part 5 短文穴埋め

Part 6 長文穴埋め

Part 7 長文読解

メール本文の訳

Liz と申します。ボストンの事務所で働いています、Gregg の下で。紹介ボーナスの方針を目にしました。私は思っています、これはニューヨーク事務所の所員にだけに適用されるのだろうかそれとも Roland の他のオフィスの所員にもまた資格があるのだろうかと。私はお尋ねしています、候補者があるかも知れませんので、そちらの現在のオープンになっている職務に対して。

そうです。確約しますよ、合衆国における私共の他の事務所の方々も、ボーナスを得る資格はあると、もしすべての条件が適合すればですが。その方の履歴書を送られたらどうですか？

お返事感謝します。私、実はこのことを口に出そうと決めたのです。この候補者はすごく適任なのですが、私共のクライアントのところで働いているのです。私はこのことを Gregg と話し合いました、そして二人とも多分大丈夫だろうと思いました。

📝 語句

❏ **work with~**　〜の所で働く

❏ **open role**　だれにもオープンになっている仕事の役目

❏ **confirm**　動　確認［確証］する　　❏ **conditions**　名　条件

❏ **meet**　〜を満足［適合］させる　　❏ **Why don't you...?**　〜するのはいかがですか？

❏ **resume**　名　履歴書　※[レジメイ]　　❏ **actually**　副　実はですね

❏ **drop**　動　ふと漏らす　　❏ **clients**　名　顧客

❏ **should**　多分〜だろう　　❏ **play it safe**　セーフだ

181. 正解：(D)

Why does Liz email Mark?　なぜ Liz は Mark にメールするのか？

(A) To challenge the policy　　方針に意義申し立てをするため

(B) To introduce a candidate　　候補者を紹介するため

(C) To ask for a referral　　紹介状を求めるため

(D) To ask for an interpretation of a policy　　方針の解釈を求めるため

🖊ポイント　(B) に苦しむはず。「自分たちにもこの方針は適用されるのか？」と尋ねているので (D) が正解　⇒ **Level 3**

182. 正解：(D)

Estelle works for Roland Partners full time. If she refers a candidate who continues to work for the firm for 12 months, how much referral bonus will Estelle get?

Estelle は Roland Partners の常勤だ。もし彼女が事務所に12カ月ずっと勤務する候補者を紹介するとしたら、Estelle はどのくらいの紹介ボーナスを手にするだろうか？

(A) $5,000

(B) $6,000

(C) $8,000

(D) $10,000

🖊ポイント　文書1の最後 (3) に「追加分＋最終5000ドル」とあるので、まず90日クリアで1000ドル、次に6カ月クリアで4000ドル追加、これに最終の5000ドルなので10,000ドルになる　⇒ **Level2**

183. 正解：(A)

What does Liz mean when she says "play it safe"?
Liz が 'play it safe' と言うのはどんな意味か？

(A) She doesn't want to lose the client by referring client's employee to her firm.
　　顧客の従業員を自分の事務所に紹介することでその顧客を失いたくない。

(B) She thinks the candidate may access confidential information.
　　彼女はその候補者が機密情報にアクセスするかもしれないと思っている。

(C) She thinks Gregg may not be happy if she gets the referral bonus.
　　彼女はもし、自分が紹介ボーナスをもらえば Gregg はうれしくないだろうと思っている。

(D) She thinks the candidate may not be good enough.
　　彼女はその候補者が十分に適任ではないかもしれないと思っている。

ポイント 引き抜きになるので顧客を怒らせることになるのではと心配して Gregg に相談したが、セーフと言われたので安心している　⇒ **Level 3**

184. 正解：(A)

What is "Roland Partners"?　Roland Partners とは何か？

(A) A law firm　　　　　　　　　　法律事務所
(B) A consulting firm　　　　　　　コンサルティング事務所
(C) A travel agency　　　　　　　　旅行代理店
(D) A human resources firm　　人材（派遣）会社

ポイント attorney は「弁護士」。firm は何人かで一緒にやっている (partners) 企業のこと。

185. 正解：(C)

Which of the following is most likely to be Mark's reply to Liz's?
つぎのどれが Liz の対する Mark のもっともありそうな返答だろうか？

(A) Our office is safe. Don't worry.
　　うちの事務所は大丈夫だよ。心配ない。

(B) Don't you want the referral bonus?
　　君は紹介ボーナスがほしくないのかい？

(C) No problem, Liz. Great that you talked to Gregg.
　　問題ないさ、Liz。Gregg に話したのはすばらしかったよ。

(D) You shouldn't have talked to Gregg.
　　Gregg に話すべきではなかったな。

ポイント 全体のメールの流れからプラスイメージをつかめば簡単　⇒ **Level 3**

練習問題 めやすは「1問1分」です！

Chapter 1
Part 1 写真描写
Part 2 応答
Part 3 会話
Part 4 説明文
Part 5 短文穴埋め
Part 6 長文穴埋め
Part 7 長文読解

Questions 186-190 refer to the following advertisement, e-mail and price list.

§ LEASE YOUR CAR, AND BE FREE! §

Buying cars for your business costs a lot of money. You have to pay for maintenance, repairs and tune-up. It is so much trouble.

With a monthly leasing plan from Masuda Lease, you don't have to worry about any of that. Just tell us what kind of cars you need and how many. We will keep all of your cars in great shape, all at a reasonable price. Our service team is ready 24 hours a day to help you, wherever you are, to fix any problem quickly.

Send us an email at leasing@masuda.auto.com

To:	leasing@masuda.auto.com
From:	aki.hadson@happy.com
Subject:	Re: Leasing plan

To whom it may concern,

I saw your ad in Daily Proud and would like to get a rough estimate of how much it would cost for me to lease three vehicles from you.

I run a small custom-furniture shop in Mechelen, Belgium. Our custom-cabinets are very popular now. We need to be able to deliver them anywhere within Mechelen.

We need one pick-up and two vans, one of which should be able to hold a 1.5m tall cabinet. We currently use our old pick-up when we need to deliver tall cabinets, but we cannot do this on rainy days. So we really need a tall box-type van. Moreover, our old vehicles use a lot of gas, which costs a lot. We need reliable vehicles that are not too expensive.

You can get in touch with me at this email address, or call me at 036-235-0564.

Aki Hadson
Aki's Furniture

type	Fee	Space in the back
Pick-up	$350/month	W100×D150
Mini-Van	$450/month	W100×D100×H100
Box-type Van	a)$550/month	W110×D160×H150
	b)$600/month	W120×D180×H180

*The monthly fee includes 24H call service

186. What is the main point of the advertisement from Masuda Lease?

(A) You don't have to lease a pick-up.

(B) It is better to lease cars than to buy them.

(C) Buying cars costs less than leasing them.

(D) It is a must to take care of your own vehicles.

187. In the advertisement, the word "shape" in paragraph 2,line 3,is closest in meaning to:

(A) Tune-up   (B) Style

(C) Condition   (D) Design

188. Why is Aki Hadson interested in the advertisement?

(A) He needs to buy a bigger van.

(B) He is interested in selling his vans.

(C) He wants to start a car lease business.

(D) He needs some new vans for his business.

189. What does Masuda Lease promise to do if a vehicle breakdown?

(A) Quickly fix the problem

(B) Discuss new lease terms

(C) Consider replacing the vehicle

(D) Send a mechanic within a week

190. If Aki decides to use Masuda Lease, how much will he likely pay each month?

(A) $1,350   (B) $1,400   (C) $1,500   (D) $1,680

解答・解説

DL音声 **53**

Chapter ①

Part 1 写真描写

Part 2 応答

Part 3 会話

Part 4 説明文

Part 5 短文穴埋め

Part 6 長文穴埋め

Part 7 長文読解

186-190 番は次の広告、メール、価格表に関するものです。

---

§ Lease your car, and be free! §

Buying cars for your business / costs a lot of money. / You have to pay for maintenance, repairs and tune-up. / It is so much trouble. /

With a monthly leasing plan from Masuda Lease, / you don't have to worry about any of that. Just tell us / what kind of cars you need / and how many. / We will keep all of your cars in great shape, / all at a reasonable price. /

Our service team is ready 24 hours a day to help you, / wherever you are, / to fix any problem quickly. /

Send us an email at leasing@masuda.auto.com

訳

あなたの車はリースで、そして自由に！

お仕事に車を買うことは多くのお金がかかります。保守、修理、調整への支払いをしなければなりません。大変やっかいなことです。Masuda Lease の月極めリースプランをお使いになれば、そのようなこと何も悩むことはありません。ただ私共におっしゃってください、どんな種類の車が必要か、そして何台必要かを。私共はあなたのお車すべてを良い状態に保ちます、すべてお手頃価格で。私共のサービスはあなたをお助けするため1日24時間いつでも準備できています、あなたがどこへおられようとも、問題をすばやく解決するために。

leasing@masuda.auto.com へメールを下さい。

語句

❏ **lease** 　動 　賃貸借契約をする 　　❏ **keep A in shape** 　A を良い状態に保つ

❏ **reasonable** 　形 　納得できる；お手頃な 　❏ **fix** 　　　動 　解決する；修理する

To:	leasing@masuda.auto.com
From:	aki.hadson@happy.com
Subject:	Re: Leasing plan

To whom it may concern,

I saw your ad in Daily Proud / and would like to get a rough estimate / of how much it would cost for me / to lease three vehicles from you. /

I run a small custom-furniture shop / in Mechelen, Belgium. / Our custom- cabinets are very popular now. / We need to be able to deliver them anywhere within Mechelen. /

We need one pick-up and two vans, / one of which should be able to hold a 1.5m tall cabinet. / We currently use our old pick-up when we need to deliver tall cabinets, / but we cannot do this on rainy days. / So we really need a tall box-type van. / Moreover, /our old vehicles use a lot of gas, / which costs a lot. / We need reliable vehicles / that are not too expensive. / You can get in touch with me at this email address, / or call me at 036-235-0564.

Aki Hadson, Aki's Furniture

関係者の方へ

Daily Proud 紙で御社の広告を見て、大体の見積もりをいただきたいと思ってます、おたくから3台の車輌をリースしたらいくら費用かかるかについて。わたしは小さな注文仕上げ家具店を営んでいます、Belgium（ベルギー）の Mechelen で。当方の注文あつらえの戸棚は今、とても人気があります。当方は Mechelen 市内のどこへでもそれらを配達することができる必要があるのです。当方は1台の小型トラックと2台のバンを必要としています－その中の1台は高さ1.5mの戸棚を収容できないといけません。当方は現在背の高い戸棚を配達するのに古い小型トラックを使用していますが、雨の日にはこれができません。そこで本当に背の高い箱型バンが必要なのです。さらに、当方の古い車輌は多くのガソリンを使い、それは高くつきます。当方は、信頼できる車を必要としています、あまり高価過ぎない。このメールのアドレスで連絡がとれます、または 036-235-0564 へお電話下さい。

語句

❏ **ad** 〔名〕 広告
❏ **rough** 〔形〕 あらましの；およその
※ advertisement の略。頻出！
❏ **estimate** 〔名〕 見積（書）
❏ **run** 〔動〕 経営する
❏ **custom** 〔動〕 注文で作る
❏ **pick-up** 運転席の後ろがオープンに荷台になっている小型トラック
❏ **reliable** 〔形〕 信頼できる
❏ **get in touch with~** ～と連絡を取る
❏ **van** 〔名〕 箱型トラック

訳

型	料金	後ろのスペース
小型トラック	$350/1ヵ月	W100×D150
ミニバン	$450/1ヵ月	W100×D100×H100
ワンボックス	a)$550/1ヵ月	W110×D160×H150
	b)$600/1ヵ月	W120×D180×H180

月ごとの料金は24時間電話サービスを含んでいます。W:width 幅、D:depth 奥行き、H:height 高さ

186. 正解：(B)

What is the main point of the advertisement from Masuda Lease?
Masuda Lease からの広告の主な要点は何か？

(A) You don't have to lease a pick-up.
　　ピックアップトラックをリースする必要はない。

(B) It is better to lease cars than to buy them.　車を買うよりリースするほうが良い。

(C) Buying cars costs less than leasing them.
　　車を買う方がリースするより費用がかからない。

(D) It is a must to take care of your own vehicles.
　　自分の車を面倒みることは必須だ。

ポイント 簡単な問題。リース会社の宣伝だ！ ⇒ Level 2

Chapter ❶

Part 1 写真描写

Part 2 応答

Part 3 会話

Part 4 説明文

Part 5 短文穴埋め

Part 6 長文穴埋め

Part 7 長文読解

187. 正解：(C)

In the advertisement, the word 'shape' in paragraph 2, line 3, is closest in meaning to:

広告の2段落、3行目の 'shape' という語は次のどれと意味が一番近いか？

(A) Tune-up　　調整

(B) Style　　　形

(C) Condition　状態

(D) Design　　デザイン

📝ポイント (A) と (C) で迷うかも知れない。身体が良い状態にあることを in shape, 悪い状態にあることを out of shape ということで覚えておこう　⇒ **Level2**

188. 正解：(D)

Why is Aki Hadson interested in the advertisement?

なぜ Aki Hadson は広告に興味を持っているのか？

(A) He needs to buy a bigger van.　　　　彼はより大きなバンを買う必要がある。

(B) He is interested in selling his vans.　彼は自分のバンを売りたがっている。

(C) He wants to start a car lease business.
　　彼は車をリースする仕事を始めたがっている。

(D) He needs some new vans for his business.
　　彼は仕事にいくらか新しいバンを必要としている。

📝ポイント あわてると (A) にしてしまう。buy でなく lease の話なので注意のこと　⇒ **Level2**

189. 正解：(A)

What does Masuda Lease promise to do if a vehicle breakdown?

もし、車が故障したら Masuda Lease は何をすると約束しているか？

(A) Quickly fix the problem　　　　　素早く問題を解決する

(B) Discuss new lease terms　　　　　新しいリース（契約）条件を話し合う

(C) Consider replacing the vehicle　　その車輌を交換することを検討する

(D) Send a mechanic within a week　　1週間以内に整備士を派遣する

📝ポイント 宣伝文の最後にベタで出ている　⇒ **Level 1**

190　正解：(B)

If Aki decides to use Masuda Lease, how much will he likely pay each month?

もし、Aki が Masuda Lease を利用しようと決めたら、各月いくら支払うだろうか？

(A) $1,350　　　(B) $1,400

(C) $1,500　　　(D) $1,680

📝ポイント 小型トラック $350、小型バン $450、箱型大型バンの (b)$600 なので 1400 ドル。バンの高さが問題だから (1.5m より高くないと戸棚が運べない)

Questions 191-195 refer to the following flyer, webpage and e-mail.

Greek National Park
Trail Notes
April 1

Bear-Resistant Storage

All trail users must use a container certified by the National Bear
Association to store food and scented items.
Bears are most often seen in June and July.
Avoid hiking alone in those months if possible.
Do not let your small chidren run ahead or wander without supervision.

  http://www.greeknationalpark.com/notice

Trail conditions today

Trail	Difficulty	Miles	Condition
Maple Creek Trail	**	4.2	Open
Sifford Trail	**	3.9	Open
Laroh Trail	*	2.8	Windy
King's Ridge	**	4.5	Open
Cold Creek Trail	*	3.5	Snow-covered
Inspiration Rock	***	7	Open
Horseshoe Trail	**	8.2	Snow-covered

Notice
The Horsehoe Trail will be closed from April 1 due to the pavement of the main
road. Users of this trail could alternatively take the Laroh trail to reach Devil's Rock
on the Horseshoe Trail. The Sifford Trail will be partially closed from now until
further notice due to the storm damage last month. Repair work is in progress and
we will update the bulletin when the repair is completed (currently we estimate the
repair to be completed by April 20,but we are not sure). During this period, users of
this trail can take the King's Ridge to get to the Sifford Waterfall on the Sifford Trail
In connection with this repair work, The west entrance of the park will be temporarily
closed for visitors.

Chapter ❶

Part 1
写真描写

Part 2
応答

Part 3
会話

Part 4
説明文

Part 5
短文穴埋め

Part 6
長文穴埋め

Part 7
長文読解

To:	National Park
From:	Susan Vocoski:
Subject:	Sifford Trail
Date:	April 25

Hi, I saw the notice on your website that the Sifford Trail is partially closed to repair until further notice. I am wondering if the repair is completed now? Also, is there a vehicle camping ground on this trail and if so, could you send me its location?

Susan

191. Which of the following is closest in meaning to "wander" in the Trail Notes?
(A) fall
(B) feed beans
(C) walk around
(D) take pictures

192. Which trail should hikers visiting the park in May take to get to Devil's Rock?
(A) Horseshoe Trail
(B) Sifford Trail
(C) Laroh Trail
(D) King's Ridge

193. When will the west entrance be open to the customers?
(A) On June 3
(B) On April 21
(C) When the repair of the Sifford Trail is completed
(D) When the pavement is completed

194. If visitors want to choose the shortest trail and avoid strong wind and snow, which trail should they choose?

(A) Sifford Trail

(B) King's Ridge

(C) Cold Creek Trail

(D) Inspiration Rock

195. What is NOT inferred in these documents?

(A) A storm hit the park last month.

(B) Visitors can store food for bears.

(C) Susan drives a car.

(D) Children should be with their parents.

解答・解説

191-195 番は次のチラシ、webサイト、メールに関するものです。

> **Greek National Park**
> **Trail Notes** April 1
> Bear-Resistant Storage
> All trail users must use a container / certified by the National Bear Association / to store food and scented items. Bears are most often seen in June and July. / Avoid hiking alone in those months if possible. / Do not let your small children run ahead / or wander without supervision. /

訳

Greek 国立公園　ハイキング道 短信　4月1日
対熊用の保管方法
すべてのハイキング道を利用する人は容器を使わなければならない、国立熊協会の認可を受けた、食べ物や匂いのするものを入れておくのに。熊は6〜7月にもっとも頻繁に見かけられる。これらの月にはできれば一人歩きは避けてください。幼いお子様を先に走らせたり、監督なしにぶらぶら歩かせることさせないように。

語句

❑ **container** 　名　コンテナ（容器）　※発音は［カンテイナー］
❑ **certify** 　動　認可する　❑ **store** 　動　蓄える　❑ **scented** 　形　匂いのする
❑ **scent** 　名　匂い　※ sent（「送る」の過去）、cent（セント）と同じ発音なので Part1,2 で注意！
❑ **supervision** 　名　監督（すること）

 http://www.greeknationalpark.com/notice

Trail conditions today

Trail	Difficulty	Miles	Condition
Maple Creek Trail	**	4.2	Open
Sifford Trail	**	3.9	Open
Laroh Trail	*	2.8	Windy
King's Ridge	**	4.5	Open
Cold Creek Trail	*	3.5	Snow-covered
Inspiration Rock	***	7	Open
Horseshoe Trail	**	8.2	Snow-covered

Notice
The Horseshoe Trail will be closed from April 1 / due to the pavement of the main road. / Users of this trail could alternatively take the Laroh trail / to reach Devil's Rock on the Horseshoe Trail. / The Sifford Trail will be partially closed from now / until further notice / due to the storm damage last month. / Repair work is in progress / and we will update the bulletin / when the repair is completed / (currently we estimate the repair to be completed by April 20, / but we are not sure). / During this period, / users of this trail can take the King's Ridge / to get to the Sifford Waterfall on the Sifford Trail. / In connection with this repair work, / The west entrance of the park will be temporarily closed for visitors. /

告知

Horseshoe 道は4月1日から閉鎖となります、幹道舗装のため。この道の利用者は代わりに Laroh 道を利用できます、Horseshoe 道にある Devil's Rock へ行くには。Sifford 道は今から部分的に閉鎖となります、さらなる告知があるまで先月の嵐被害のために。修復作業はただ今進行中で、掲示を更新します、修理が終わったら（現在4月20日までに終了すると推測していますが、はっきりとは分かりません）。この期間中、この道の利用者は King's Ridge を利用するように、Sifford 道にある Sifford 滝に行くには。この修復作業に関連して、公園の西入口は来園者には一時的に閉鎖されます。

語句

- **pavement** 名 舗装
- **alternatively** 副 交替に ※発音は[オールターナティブリー]
- **in progress** 進行中 　　**update** 動 更新する
- **bulletin** 名 掲示；告知 　　**in connection with~** ~に関連して
- **temporarily** 副 一時的に ※頻出！

To:	National Park
From:	Susan Vocoski:
Subject:	Sifford Trail
Date:	April 25

Hi, / I saw the notice on your website / that the Sifford Trail is partially closed to repair / until further notice. / I am wondering if the repair is completed now? / Also, / is there a vehicle camping ground on this trail / and if so, / could you send me its location?

Susan

訳（本文のみ）

コンニチハ、おたくのホームページの告知を見ました、Sifford 道が修理のために部分的に閉鎖だということですねさらに通知があるまで。その修理はいまでは終了していますか？　また、この道にはキャンピングカー用地がありますか、また、もしあるのであれば、その場所を送付いただけますか？

191. 正解：(C)

Which of the following is closest in meaning to "wander" in the Trail Notes?
Trail Notes の中で "wander" に意味の上でもっとも近いものは次のどれか？

(A) fall　　　　　落ちる；倒れる
(B) feed beans　　豆をやる（餌として）
(C) walk around　歩き回る
(D) take pictures　写真をとる

ポイント wander を知らなくても前後の文から推測すること。wander [ウォンダー] は「さまよい歩く」で、wonder [ワンダー] は「~かしらと思う」との違いを明確に。

192. 正解：(C)

Which trail should hikers visiting the park in May take to get to Devil's Rock?
5月に公園を訪れるハイカーは Devil's Rock に行くにはどの道を通ったらよいだろうか？

(A) Horseshoe Trail
(B) Sifford Trail
(C) Laroh trail
(D) King's Ridge

> **ポイント** 当然 Devel's Rock がキーワード。Notice の2段落目にベタで出ている　⇒ **Level 1**

193. 正解：(C)

When will the west entrance be open to the customers?
西入口はいつ客に開放されるだろうか？

(A) On June 3　6月3日に
(B) On April 21　4月21日に
(C) When the repair of the Sifford Trail is completed
　　Sifford Trail の修復が終わったら
(D) When the pavement is completed　歩道が完成したら

> **ポイント** Sifford Trail の修復は「4月20日に終了するだろうが、はっきりしない」とあるので西口もその工事に関連しているので (B) はだめ　⇒ **Level 2**

194. 正解：(B)

If visitors want to choose the shortest trail and avoid strong wind and snow, which trail should they choose?
もし訪れる人が一番短い道を選び、強風と雪を避けたければ、どの道を選ぶか？

(A) Sifford Trail
(B) King's Ridge
(C) Cold Creek Trail
(D) Inspiration Rock

> **ポイント** まず、windy と snow-covered を外し、あとは距離を見るだけ。Inspiration Rock は7マイルある。Sifford Trail は3.5マイルだが、部分的にではあるが修復中。従って4.5マイルの King's Ridge が答え　⇒ **Level 2**

195. 正解：(B)

What is NOT inferred in these documents?
これらの資料で推察できないものはどれか？

(A) A storm hit the park last month.　先月嵐がこの公園を襲った。
(B) Visitors can store food for bears.
　　訪れる人達は熊のために食べ物を蓄えておくことができる。
(C) Susan drives a car.　Susan は車を運転する。
(D) Children should be with their parents.　子供たちは親と一緒にいるべきだ。

> **ポイント** (A) は2つ目の資料の Notice にある。(B) は1つ目の資料に「熊に襲われないために、食べ物や匂いのするものを入れる容器が必要」とあるので、これが×なので正解。(C) は3つ目の資料で Susan はキャンピングカーで行くと匂わせている。(D) は5月でも熊の心配はあるだろうから、子供たちは単独では行動しない方がよいはず　⇒ **Level 3**

Chapter ❶

Part 1 写真描写

Part 2 応答

Part 3 会話

Part 4 説明文

Part 5 短文穴埋め

Part 6 長文穴埋め

Part 7 長文読解

Questions 196-200 refer to the following textbook excerpt, class bulettin and e-mail.

A 'Repairs Notice' is an effective tool for alerting the tenant of its contractual obligations to repair the premise it leases. The notice will often serve as important evidence in lease disputes. A repair notice should:
  (a) refer to the lease agreement;
  (b) list out the place(s) to be repaired
  (c) set forth the standards and requirements of the repair
  (d) specify a deadline for completing the repair; and
  (e) include a warning that the landlord can and may enter the property at reasonable hours to carry out the works at the tenant's cost if the tenant fails to complete the repair when the deadline passes away.

ヒント☞ alert は「警告する」、contractural obligations は「契約上の義務」。disputes は「論争」、set forth は「述べる」、evidence は「証拠」。specify は「明らかにする」

Messages from Professor Holmes:
Landlord and tenant signed a lease on Feb. 1, 2020. Please review the repair notice section in the textbook, draft a repair notice on behalf of the landlord (notifying the tenant to fix the water pipe damaged due to tenant's fault) and submit your draft to me no later than Mar. 20.

Grading criteria:

All points covered:	**A**	**75% - 80% covered**	**B**
90% -100% covered	**A-**	**65% - 75% covered**	**B-**
80% - 90% covered	**B+**	**55% - 65% covered**	**C+**

Late submissions will be scored no higher than B.

ヒント☞ Grading criteria は「採点基準」、landlord は「大家」、draft は「起草する;作成する」、on behalf of~ は「~に代わって」、submit は「提出する」

Chapter ①

Part 1
写真描写

Part 2
応答

Part 3
会話

Part 4
説明文

Part 5
短文穴埋め

Part 6
長文穴埋め

Part 7
長文読解

Date:	Mar. 13
To:	Prof. Holmes
From:	David
Subject:	Questions

Professor Holmes, I have a question about the repair deadline.
Is there any reasonable standard for this deadline in California?
For example, can a landlord require its tenant to repair a water pipe within one day?

Thanks
David

196. Which of the following is closest in meaning to "carry out" as used in the textbook at (e)?

(A) extend

(B) hold

(C) transport

(D) accomplish

197 Which of the followings is true in the text book?

(A) Tenants should ask for a 'Repairs Notice' from their landlords.

(B) Landlords should make it clear that there are standards of the repair.

(C) Landlords are able to enter the tenants' property at any time.

(D) Tenants have no duties to their landlords when they contract with each other.

198. Ben submitted his assignment on Mar. 22 and covered 85% of the points, what grade will he get?

(A) A

(B) A-

(C) B+

(D) B

199. Why does David email Professor Holmes?

(A) To submit his assignment

(B) To ask for an extension of the deadline

(C) To ask for a clarification

(D) To offer an opinion

200. In which class is this topic most likely being discussed?

(A) Estate Planning

(B) Property

(C) History

(D) Communication

解答・解説

196-200 番は次の教科書抜粋、クラス速報、メールに関するものです。

> A 'Repairs Notice' is an effective tool / for alerting the tenant of its contractual obligations to repair the premise it leases. / The notice will often serve as important evidence in lease disputes. / A repair notice should:
> - (a) refer to the lease agreement;
> - (b) list out the place(s) to be repaired
> - (c) set forth the standards and requirements of the repair
> - (d) specify a deadline for completing the repair; and
> - (e) include a warning / that the landlord can and may enter the property at reasonable hours / to carry out the works at the tenant's cost / if the tenant fails to complete the repair when the deadline passes away.

「修理の通知」は効果的な手段です、借家人にそれが賃借している土地建物の修理をするその契約上の義務について警告するのに。この通知はしばしば賃貸借論争において重要な証拠に役立つ。「修理の通知」は：

(a) 賃貸借契約書に照会すべき
(b) 修理されるべき箇所をリストから取り出すべき
(c) 修理の基準と要件を説明すべき
(d) 修理を仕上げるための期限を明確にすべき、そして
(e) 警告を含むべきである、借家人の費用でその作業を行う為に、大家が理に適った時間にその土地建物に入れるという、もし借家人が期限を過ぎても修理を完成させられないなら。

❏ tool	名	ここでは「手段」　※「道具」ではない
❏ serve	動	～に役立つ
❏ dispute	名	論争
❏ refer to～		～を参考[参照]する
❏ set forth～		～を述べる　※「出発する」という意味もある）
❏ specify	動	明確にする；具体的に述べる
❏ carry out		遂行する
❏ fail to～		～しそびれる

205

Messages from Professor Holmes:

Landlord and tenant signed a lease on Feb. 1, 2020. / Please review the repair notice section in the textbook, / draft a repair notice on behalf of the landlord (notifying the tenant to fix the water pipe damaged due to tenant's fault) and submit your draft to me no later than Mar. 20.

Grading criteria:

All points covered:	A
90%-100% covered	A-
80%- 90% covered	B+
75%- 80% covered	B
65%- 75% covered	B-
55%- 65% covered	C+

Late submissions will be scored no higher than B.

 訳

Homes 教授からの伝言

大家と借家人が2020年2月1日に賃貸借契約に調印した。教科書の修理通知の項を吟味し、その大家に代わって修理通告書を草案して下さい（借家人に借家人の過失で損傷した水道管を修理するよう知らせることで）、そしてあなたの起草したものを3月20日までに私へと提出して下さい。

採点基準

すべての要点が網羅されていれば：	A
90%-100% covered	A-
80%- 90% covered	B+
75%- 80% covered	B
65%- 75% covered	B-
55%- 65% covered	C+

提出遅れは B 以上には採点されない。

 語句

❏ **review** 動 再検討 [吟味] する　❏ **section** 名 項
❏ **draft** 名 草稿　❏ **due to~** ～のせいで

Date:	Mar. 13
To:	Prof. Holmes
From:	David
Subject:	Questions

Professor Holmes, / I have a question about the repair deadline. /

Is there any reasonable standard for this deadline in California? /

For example, / can a landlord require its tenant / to repair a water pipe within one day?

Thanks

David

本文の訳

件名：質問

Holmes 先生、修理の期限に関して質問があります。カリフォルニアにはこの期限に対しての何か合理的な基準がありますか。例えば、大家は借家人に要求できるとか、1日以内に水道管の修理を。

196. 正解：(D)

Which of the following is closest in meaning to "carry out" as used in the textbook at (e)?

教科書の (e) で使われている 'carry out' に意味の上でもっとも近いものは次のうちどれか？

(A) extend　　　延長する

(B) hold　　　つかむ

(C) transport　　輸送［移送］する

(D) accomplish　成し遂げる

ポイント carry out は文字通り「運び出す」だが、転じて「成し遂げる；実行する」の意味も

Go on to the next page!

197. 正解：(B)

Which of the followings is true in the text book?
教科書において当てはまるのは次のうちどれか？

(A) Tenants should request a 'Repairs Notice' from their landloads.
借家人はその大家に「修理通告」を求めるべきだ。

(B) Landlords should make it clear that there are standards of the repair.
大家は修理には基準があることを明確にすべきだ。

(C) Landlords are able to enter the tenants' property at any time.
大家はどんな時でも借家人の所に入ることができる。

(D) Tenants have no duties to their landlords when they contract with each other.
互いに契約を交わす時借家人はその大家には何の義務もない。

ポイント 大体でも読めればすぐに分かる問題　⇒ **Level 2**

198. 正解：(D)

Ben submitted his assignment on Mar. 22 and covered 85% of the points, what grade will he get?
Ben は課題を3月22日に提出し、要点の85%を入れた、彼はどの級（成績）を得るだろうか？

(A) A　　　　　(B) A-
(C) B+　　　　(D) B

ポイント 実際なら B+ だが、提出期限を過ぎている場合は B よりも上はないから　⇒ **Level 1'**

199　正解：(C)

Why does David email Professor Holmes?
David はなぜ Holmes 教授にメールしたのか？

(A) To submit his assignment　　　　課題を提出するため
(B) To ask for an extension of the deadline　締め切りの延長を求めるため
(C) To ask for a clarification　　　　明確説明を求めるため
(D) To offer an opinion　　　　　　意見を申し出るため

ポイント (A) にしてはだめ。質問しているメールだ。clarify=make it clear　⇒ **Level 2**

200. 正解：(B)

In which class is this topic most likely being discussed?
この話題は多分、どのクラスで討論されているだろうか？

(A) Estate Planning　不動産計画
(B) Property　　　　所有財産；物件
(C) History　　　　　歴史
(D) Communication　意志疎通

ポイント 大家と借家人の話なので「不動産・動産の貸した・借りた」の問題だから　⇒ **Level 3**

Chapter 2

· · · · · · · · · · ·

完全模試にチャレンジ!
問題（別冊）　解答・解説（本冊）

模試チャレンジ+本冊+
聴く勉 TOEIC 講座フル活用で 600 点取る!

　Chapter1 を終えたらもはやあなたも立派な TOEIC 通（!?）。

　ここからはさらにステップアップ!　本番と同様の問題数と制限時間で、試験本番をイメージしながら完全模試にチャレンジしましょう。

　それではさっそく別冊の問題冊子を本体から外し、ストップウォッチを用意して、これまで勉強してきた攻略法を駆使して問題に取り組んでみてください!（見開き状態でB4用紙に拡大コピーすると、より本番の気分が味わえるのでオススメです）

　終わったら本冊に戻って「解答・解説」ページを見ながら [聴く勉! TOEIC 講座] をしっかり聞いて復習し、600点超への階段を、最短で駆け上りましょう !!

1. 正解：(C)

 W

(A) They're **talking** to **each** other.
彼らは互いに話し合っている。

(B) They're **using personal computers**.
彼らは PC を使っている。

(C) They're **seated** around the **table**.
彼らはテーブルの回りに座っている。

(D) They're **wiping** off the **table**.
彼らはテーブルを拭いている。

山根ポ seat は「席につける、座らせる」という他動詞なので be seated で「座る」となる。

 語句 ❑ **wipe** 動 拭う；拭く　※車の wiper で覚える！

2. 正解：(B)

W

(A) A **woman** is **shopping** at a **boutique**.
女性がブティックで買い物をしている。

(B) A **woman** is **looking back** with a **smile**.
女性がにっこりと振り返っている。

(C) A **woman** is **carrying** a **bag** on her **back**.
女性が背にバッグを背負っている。

(D) A **woman** is **looking** for a **tote** bag.
女性がトートバッグ（丈夫な布製の袋）を探している。

山根ポ 「振り返る」の look back が聞き取れれば OK！

3. 正解：(D)

 M

(A) They're **enjoying meals** at a **table**.
彼女たちは食卓について食事を楽しんでいる。

(B) They're **leaving** a **restaurant**.
彼女たちはレストランを出ようとしている。

(C) They're **lying** on the **floor**.
彼女たちは床に横になっている。

(D) **Both** of them are **holding cups** in their **hands**.
2人とも手にカップを持っている。

山根ポ 「横になる」の lie-lay-lain と 「横たえる」の lay-laid-laid を間違わないこと。

4. 正解：(C)

(A) An **air conditioning** unit is **being cleaned**.
エアコンが清掃されている。

(B) They're **putting** on **working clothes**.
彼らは作業着を着ようとしている。

(C) They've been **inspecting** some **equipment** above them.
彼らは頭上の機器を検査している。

(D) **One man** is **reaching** for a **tool** on a **rack**.
1人の男の人がラックの道具に手を伸ばしている。

> 山根ヅバ is being...ed という受け身の進行形に注意。have been～（ずっと～だ）は現在形に訳す。

5. 正解：(A)

(A) There's a **lamp** in a **corner** of the **study**.
書斎の片隅に（電気）スタンドがある。

(B) A lot of **books** are being **piled** up on the **shelves**.
沢山の本が棚に積み上げられているところだ。

(C) Some **cabinet doors** have been **left open**.
幾つかの戸棚のドアが開けられたままである。

(D) There's been a **big collection** of **books** on **sale**.
一大蔵書本が売り出されている。

> 山根ヅバ study に「書斎」の意味があることに注意！ library に「書庫」の意味もあることも。

6. 正解：(D)

(A) A **man** is **crossing** the **street** in front of a **vehicle**.
1人の男の人が車の前で通りを横断している。

(B) A **tall street light** is being **turned on**.
背の高い街灯が明かりを点けられている。

(C) There're some **trees** on one **side of** the **street**.
通りの一方側に幾本か木がある。

(D) **Several tall buildings stand** against the **sky**.
数棟の高いビルが空を背景に立っている。

> 山根ヅバ 動かない物は stand, sit, lie と、現在形のままで進行形にしない（状態動詞になる）。

Part 2 応答

Part 3 会話

Part 4 説明文

Part 5 短文穴埋め

Part 6 長文穴埋め

Part 7 長文読解

7. 正解：(C) ⋯⋯⋯⋯⋯⋯⋯⋯⋯⋯⋯⋯⋯⋯⋯⋯⋯⋯⋯⋯⋯⋯⋯ 🇺🇸 W ⇒ 🇬🇧 M

How long are you going to stay here? ここにはどの位滞在するのですか？ ➡ 5W1H

(A) Yes, I'd like to. 　はい、そうしたいです。
(B) Since 2015. 　2015年からです。
(C) For a week or so. 　1週間かそこら。

（山根ポイント）期間を尋ねている。

8. 正解：(B) ⋯⋯⋯⋯⋯⋯⋯⋯⋯⋯⋯⋯⋯⋯⋯⋯⋯⋯⋯⋯⋯⋯⋯ 🇬🇧 W ⇒ 🇨🇦 W

Where did you park your car? 　車はどこへ駐車しましたか？ ➡ 5W1H

(A) I didn't go to the park. 　私はその公園へ行かなかった。
(B) Behind the library. 　図書館の裏にです。
(C) For a couple of hours. 　2〜3時間の間です。

（山根ポイント）場所を尋ねている。park は「駐車する」。

9. 正解：(B) ⋯⋯⋯⋯⋯⋯⋯⋯⋯⋯⋯⋯⋯⋯⋯⋯⋯⋯⋯⋯⋯⋯⋯ 🌏 M ⇒ 🇺🇸 W

Do you have time to lunch with us? 　昼食ご一緒する時間はありますか？ ➡ 単純疑問

(A) We'll have lunch at 12:30. 　私たちは12時30分に昼食を取ります。
(B) I'll be out of town this afternoon. 　今日の午後、町を出るんですよ。
(C) It's about 11:00. 　今、大体11時です。

（山根ポイント）(B) は「町を出るので昼食は一緒にはできない」ということ。Do you have the time? だと「今何時ですか？」という意味。

10. 正解：(A) ⋯⋯⋯⋯⋯⋯⋯⋯⋯⋯⋯⋯⋯⋯⋯⋯⋯⋯⋯⋯⋯⋯⋯ 🇬🇧 M ⇒ 🇬🇧 W

When will Dr. Quinn be here? 　Dr. Quinn はいつここへ来られますか？ ➡ 5W1H

(A) He'll soon be with you. 　まもなく参りますよ。
(B) He was away this morning. 　今朝は不在でした。
(C) In his clinic. 　彼の診療所に。

（山根ポイント）He'll soon be here. のこと。before long=soon もあり得る。

11. 正解：(B) ······················· 🇨🇦 M ⇒ 🇦🇺 M

This is your smart phone, isn't it? これ君のスマホだよね？ ➡ だよね構文

(A) Yes, my number is this. そう、僕の番号はこれです。

(B) Oh, I must have left it. アァ、置き忘れたに違いないな。

(C) Sorry, I don't remember the number. 申し訳ない、番号を覚えていないんだ。

> 山根ポイント 「〜ではないの?」でなく「〜だよね」と反応すると簡単に答えが出る。

12. 正解：(C) ······················· 🇺🇸 M ⇒ 🇦🇺 M

When will you be available to see Mr. Johnson?

Mr. Johnson に会うのにあなたはいつ都合がいいですか？ ➡ 5W1H

(A) I haven't seen him before. 以前彼に会ったことがない。

(B) I'll be there on time. 私は時間通りにそこへ行きます。

(C) I think 10 o'clock is convenient for me. 10時が都合いいと思います。

> 山根ポイント 時を尋ねている。I'm convenient... とは言えない。I'm available... という。

13. 正解：(B) ······················· 🇨🇦 M ⇒ 🇺🇸 W

Would you like me to pick you up at the airport?

空港にお迎えに行きましょうか？ ➡ 特殊疑問

(A) Yes, I will if you don't mind. えぇ、そうしましょう、もし差し支えなければ。

(B) That won't be necessary. その必要はないでしょう。

(C) At the arrival gate. 到着ゲートで。

> 山根ポイント Would you like me to〜? =Shall I 〜? のことで、米語ではよく耳にする。頻出！

14 正解：(A) ······················· 🇬🇧 W ⇒ 🇬🇧 M

Do you know who is going to assist us with the next project?

次のプロジェクトはだれが手伝ってくれるのか分かりますか？ ➡ 5W1H

(A) I have no idea. 皆目分かりません。（全然分かりません）

(B) Yes, Ms. Okazaki is a good assistant. はい、岡崎氏はよい補佐です。

(C) I used to be a project manager. 私がかつてはプロジェクト責任者でした。

> 山根ポイント Do you know の後にはこのように疑問詞が来る文になることが多いので、5W1H をしっかり聞き取る。たいていはそれが答えの中心になるから。しかしここでは「わかりません」という"無責任アンサー"となっている。

Chapter ②

Part 1 写真描写

Part 2 応答

Part 3 会話

Part 4 説明文

Part 5 短文穴埋め

Part 6 長文穴埋め

Part 7 長文読解

15. 正解：(C) ···························· 🇺🇸 W ⇒ 🇸🇬 M

Didn't Ms. Kou apply for the job? Ms. Kou はその仕事に応募したんだよね？ ➡️ だよね

(A) She needs some job information. 彼女は就職情報を必要としています。

(B) I saw her at an employment agency. 彼女を職業紹介所で見かけました。

(C) Perhaps she did. 多分、（彼女は）しましたね。

> 山根ポイント 「～だったんだよね?」と反応すればすぐに (C) と分かる。

16. 正解：(C) ···························· 🇬🇧 M ⇒ 🇨🇦 M

Why was the production manager looking for today's paper?
製造部長はなぜ今日の新聞を探していたのですか？ ➡️ 5W1H

(A) Because he was on vacation. なぜなら、彼は休暇だったから。

(B) To produce new products. 新製品を出すために。

(C) He didn't say. 彼は言いませんでした［教えてくれませんでした］。

> 山根ポイント これは注意を要します。なぜなら、Why...? の質問には Because... か To ～ で答えることが普通だからです。

17. 正解：(A) ···························· 🇬🇧 W ⇒ 🇺🇸 M

Didn't you get my e-mail about the merger?
合併についての e-mail を受けたんだよね？ ➡️ だよね

(A) No, I've been away. いや、不在だったので。

(B) No problem. お安い御用です。

(C) Between Novak company and Heinz company.
Novak 社と Heinz 社との間でね。

> 山根ポイント (A) は No, I didn't. I've been away. のこと。merger（合併）は頻出!

18. 正解：(B) ···························· 🇬🇧 M ⇒ 🇦🇺 M

How about ordering new uniforms for the players?
選手に新しいユニフォームを注文するのはどうかな？ ➡️ 特殊疑問

(A) Blue and red will be great. 青と赤がすてきだね。

(B) I wish the budget could allow it. 予算が許せばなあ。

(C) By choosing at a famous sports shop. 有名なスポーツ店で選ぶことで。

> 山根ポイント 「いかが ?」という提案に対する答えを選ぶ。(B) は「予算が許せばなあ」という願望（仮定法）

Chapter ❷

Part 1 写真描写

Part 2 応答

Part 3 会話

Part 4 説明文

Part 5 短文穴埋め

Part 6 長文穴埋め

Part 7 長文読解

聴く勉 TOEIC 講座！ DL音声 116

19. 正解：(B) ········· 🇺🇸 M ⇒ 🇬🇧 W

When are you starting your online class tomorrow?

明日はいつオンライン授業を始めるのですか？ ➡ 5W1H

(A) From my study at home. 自宅の書斎からね。

(B) Not until 10:20. 10時20分になってからね。

(C) Yes, I'm ready. はい、準備はできてますよ。

> 山根釈 時で答える。not until~（～までではない＝～になって初めて）は at 10:20 を強調する表現。

20. 正解：(C) ········· 🇬🇧 W ⇒ 🇬🇧 M

You've used up all the ink cartridges already, haven't you?

あなたはもうインクカートリッジを全部使ったのね？ ➡ だよね

(A) Yes, at a famous stationery store in town. はい、町の有名な文具店で。

(B) No, I didn't know that. いいえ、それは知りませんでした。

(C) Yes, so I need more refills. はい、もっと詰め替えが必要です。

> 山根釈 「～だよね?」と解釈すれば、消去法ですぐに分かるはず。

21. 正解：(C) ········· 🇬🇧 W ⇒ 🇨🇦 M

Are you planning to visit the Diet building next week?

あなたは来週国会議事堂を訪れる計画ですか？ ➡ 単疑（ひねり）

(A) Yes, I'll go on a diet. ええ、私はダイエットします。

(B) I'll skip breakfast. 私は、朝食は抜かします。

(C) If the weather permits. もし、天候が許せば

> 山根釈 Diet は大文字で「議会」、日本では「国会」。

22. 正解：(B) ········· 🇦🇺 M ⇒ 🇺🇸 M

We really need to find a competent lawyer.

私たちは本当に有能な弁護士を見つける必要があります。 ➡ 意見・感想

(A) Do you remember where the lawyer is from?

その弁護士の出身地を覚えていますか？

(B) I know a good one. Shall I contact him?

いい人を知っています。連絡しましょうか？

(C) I'm sure Mx-10 is a marvelous computer.

Mx-10 は素晴らしいコンピュータだと確信しています。

> 山根釈 competent は「有能な」、lawyer は「弁護士」、contact は「連絡を取る」。

23. 正解：(A) ····· 🇬🇧 M ⇒ 🇺🇸 W

Do you need to change the flight's departure date or return date?

フライトの出発日または帰国日を変更する必要がありますか？ ➡ **A or B**

(A) Actually, I'm cancelling the trip.　実は旅行をキャンセルするんですよ。

(B) Yes, the departure gate is No.34.　ええ、出発ゲートは34番です。

(C) My returning date is May 3.　私の帰国日は5月3日です。

> **山根ポイント** 「tea or coffee? の答え方は6通りある」の例えを覚えていますか？ tea, coffee. both, either, neither, milk などでしたね。本問は neither にあたります。

24. 正解：(B) ····· 🇬🇧 W ⇒ 🇨🇦 M

Do you want me to book a single room for you?

君のためにシングルの部屋を予約しようか？ ➡ **特殊疑問**

(A) I prefer comic books.　漫画の本が好きです。

(B) I'd appreciate it a lot.　大変ありがたいです。

(C) Yes, let me sing an English song.　はい、英語の歌を歌います。

> **山根ポイント** book（予約する）が出ると book（本）が出るという定番。appreciate は普通は「感謝する」だが、「正しく評価する」が原義。その他に「鑑賞する」「(食べ物を)味わう」という意味が大切。また、Do you want me to~? は Would you like me to~? のくだけた表現で、頻出!

25. 正解：(C) ····· 🇦🇺 M ⇒ 🇺🇸 M

When does this article need to go out?

この記事はいつ世に出る必要がありますか？ ➡ **5W1H**

(A) He'll soon be there.　彼はまもなくそちらに参ります。

(B) Don't go out after dark.　暗くなってから外出してはいけません。

(C) Let me ask our boss.　上司に尋ねてみましょう。

> **山根ポイント** いわゆる「無責任パターン」だ。要するに「自分は知らない」と責任を逃れていると考える。go out = be published（出版される）の意味もある。

聴く勉 TOEIC講座！ DL音声 118

Chapter❷

Part 1 写真描写

Part 2 応答

Part 3 会話

Part 4 説明文

Part 5 短文穴埋め

Part 6 長文穴埋め

Part 7 長文読解

26. 正解：(A) ⇒ 🇺🇸 W ⇒ 🇬🇧 M

Why don't we purchase a PC with translation apps installed?

翻訳アプリがインストールされたパソコンを買うのはいかがでしょうか？ → 5W1H

(A) How much will that cost? それはどのくらい費用がかかるの？

(B) Because it's easy to use. なぜなら、使い易いからです。

(C) It's kind of difficult to install such software.
そんなソフトを組み込むのはちょっと難しいです。

> 山根ザク Why don't...? は「なぜ〜ではないのですか？」という意味ではなく、「〜するのはどうでしょうか?」と提言する言い方（What do you say to + 名詞? / How about + 名詞又は文?）でも同じ。purchase は「購入する」だが、普通高価なものに使う。安いものを含め一般的には buy でよい。kind of (= a little) の発音は [カインダ]。

27. 正解：(C) ⇒ 🇨🇦 M ⇒ 🇬🇧 W

Didn't you get reimbursed for the last hospital charges by your insurance company?

この前の病院費用、保険会社から払い戻ししてもらったんだよね。 → だよね

(A) Yes, I was in hospital for a month. はい、私は 1 カ月入院していました。

(B) No, it's free of charge. いいえ、それは無料です。

(C) No, I'm still waiting. いいえ、まだ待っているんです。

> 山根ザク 「だよね構文」はその性質上、Yes / No に類するものが必要なので、(A)(B)(C) の全部が当てはまるが、(A) は「入院していたの?」に対する答え。(B) は「費用がかかったの?」への答えなので不適。(C) の「いや、まだ待っているんだ」は、「払い戻しをまだ受けていない」ということなので正解。

28. 正解：(B) ⇒ 🇦🇺 M ⇒ 🇺🇸 W

Would you ask the local government to speed up the procedure of issuing passports?

地方自治体にパスポート発行の手続きを速めてくれるよう頼んでいただけますか？ → 特殊疑問

(A) All right. It usually takes two weeks. いいですよ。大体2週間かかりますね。

(B) OK. I'll do it as soon as possible. 分かった。できるだけ迅速にやりましょう。

(C) Sorry, my passport is due to expire in 2021.
申し訳ない、私のパスポートは2021年に失効します。

> 山根ザク ていねいにお願いしているのでそれなりに返答しないといけないが、ここでは上から目線の答えになっている。Yes なら Sure 、No なら Sorry が頻出！

29. 正解：(C)) ⋯⋯⋯⋯⋯⋯⋯⋯⋯⋯⋯⋯⋯⋯⋯⋯⋯⋯ 🇺🇸 M ⇒ 🇬🇧 M

Your client Mr. Weaver called you while you were out.

あなたの不在中にお客様の Mr. Weaver から電話がありました。 ➡️ 意見・感想

(A) Where were you?　あなたはどこにいましたか？

(B) I want to see if he will call me back.　彼が折り返し電話をかけてくるか確かめたい。

(C) Any message for me ?　何かメッセージ（伝言）ありましたか？

〔山根ポイ〕これは質問になっていないので、聞き取れない人には難しい。

30. 正解：(B) ⋯⋯⋯⋯⋯⋯⋯⋯⋯⋯⋯⋯⋯⋯⋯⋯⋯⋯ 🇬🇧 W ⇒ 🇨🇦 M

Which production team accomplished its original goal?

どの製造チームが当初の目標を達成しましたか？ ➡️ 5W1H

(A) They accomplished a world record.
彼らは世界記録を打ち立てた。

(B) The announcement of the results will soon be made.
その結果の発表はもうすぐなされます。

(C) No, it was among sales teams.
いいえ、それは営業チームの１つでした。

〔山根ポイ〕質問に答えられない場合⇒逃れる⇒無責任アンサーだ！

31. 正解：(C) ⋯⋯⋯⋯⋯⋯⋯⋯⋯⋯⋯⋯⋯⋯⋯⋯⋯⋯ 🇺🇸 M ⇒ 🇦🇺 M

Hi, I need to book a hotel room and a rental car including a Shinkansen ticket.

コンニチハ、ホテルの部屋とレンタカーを予約する必要があるんだ、新幹線の切符を入れてね。 ➡️ 意見・感想

(A) You can read as many books as you can at the lobby.
ロビーで好きなだけ多くの本が読めますよ。

(B) Yes, there's a good one close to the station.
えぇ、駅そばにいいのがありますよ。

(C) All right. I have a great package deal for you.
かしこまりました。貴方様にすばらしいパック（セット）がございますよ。

〔山根ポイ〕(A) は book を「本」ととっている。(B) は「レンタカーショップは確かに駅のそばにはあるけど…」、(C) は「パック（セット）になってお得になっています」ということ。a good deal は「良い取引」⇒「お買い得；おいしい話」ということ。

Chapter❷

Part 1 写真描写

Part 2 応答

Part 3 会話

Part 4 説明文

Part 5 短文穴埋め

Part 6 長文穴埋め

Part 7 長文読解

COLUMN

短期留学ならフィリピンがベストです!

　春や夏、多くの大学生が短期留学に行きますが、どうしても憧れの国に行きたいという気持ちから、欧米を選択する人が大変多いですね。それも判らないでもありませんが、1〜2カ月程度の語学留学なら私は断然フィリピンを推薦します。これまで8年間、毎年50〜60人を英語特訓留学としてフィリピンへ送り出してきた私が自信を持って申し上げます!

　欧米の場合「あそこへ行きたい、これがしたい」と、憧れが強すぎてどうしても観光や遊びが中心になってしまいます。指導する講師の方もそれを心得ていて、宿題を課すような厳しい授業はしません。ひたすら楽しい思い出になるよう、優しく指導してくれます。しかもグループ授業のみなので、サボっていても見逃がされる…という、易きに流れやすいという事もあり得ます。

　フィリピンの場合、ただひたすら勉強のみ。土日の観光はあるが、地元大学との交流やボランティア活動への参加といった有益な活動が中心で、歓楽街での遊びは皆無です。加えて語学学校同士の競争が激しいので、とにかく先生方が熱心なのです。そして一番の良い点は、個人指導が中心なので、逃げ場がないことです。ほとんどが若い先生なので、やがて心が通じ合い、恥ずかしさを感じずに質疑応答ができるようになります。つまりこの"逃げ場がないこと"が逆によい環境となるわけです。「ハードだけど楽しい!」というのが参加者全員の感想です。この楽しさが、"間違うことを恐れて話せなくなっている日本人"にわずか1カ月で「話すことが怖くなくなってきた!」という効果をもたらす要因なのです。加えて夕食後にはオプションでギター、エアロビなどを英語で学べる講座も用意されていて、実践で楽しみながら英語力をつけられる環境になっています。

　最後にフィリピン留学は費用が1カ月25〜30万円なので、欧米の半額で済みます(それなのに効果は2倍以上!)。マニラやセブ、ボロカイが有名ですが、観光地だけに遊びの誘惑が多いので、1カ月という短くて貴重な時間を有効に使うことを考えて、私はバコロドのサン・アガスティン大学の語学センターを選びます(バギオにも良心的な語学学校が多いです)。ご質問があればご遠慮なく yamane@yamaguchi-u.ac.jp まで!!

Questions 32 through 34 refer to the following conversation with three speakers.

W1: Sir, thank you for your forms. Your account opening procedure / has been completed. You will receive your cash card / in about two weeks.

M: Thank you. Do you charge any account management fee? And if so, / is there a way to have it waived?

W1: Please wait a moment. Our Account service Manager will be with you shortly.

W2: Hi, my name is Cindy Thomton. I am your banking service manager. Yes, we do charge an account management fee / of $10 per month, / but this fee will be waived / if you become a premium member. Let me explain it to you / in detail.

M: Actually, / my wife is waiting outside. Is there a brochure / that I can take back?

W2: Sure sir. Here you are. You can refer to page 19 / for the requirements for the the premium membership.

訳

女1: お客様、お申し込み書をありがとうございます。貴方様の口座開設手続きが終了致しました。2週間ほど致しましたらキャッシュカードお受け取りになれます。

男： ありがとう。何か口座管理費用が掛かるのかね？　もしそうなら、それが回避できる方法があるかね？

女1: 少しお待ちください。当店の経理業務部長がすぐに参りますので。

女2: コンニチハ、Cindy Thomton と申します。私がお客様の銀行業務責任者です。はい、月に合計10ドルになりますと口座管理費をいただくことになります、しかし、この料金はもしお客様がプレミアム会員になられますと回避できます。詳しく説明させていただきましょう。

男： 実はね、妻が外で待ってるんだ。持ち帰れるような何かパンフレットあるかな？

女2: もちろんでございます。はい、どうぞ。プレミアム会員資格につきましては19ページを参照ください。

語句

❑ **procedure** 名 手続き　❑ **have A ..ed** Aを... してもらう　❑ **evade** 動 回避する
❑ **in details** 詳細に　❑ **refer to~** ～を参照する　❑ **qualification** 名 資格

Chapter ❷

Part 1
写真描写

Part 2
応答

Part 3
会話

Part 4
説明文

Part 5
短文穴埋め

Part 6
長文穴埋め

Part 7
長文読解

32. 正解：(D)

Where does the conversation most likely take place?
会話は多分どこで行われるだろうか？

(A) In a gym ジム

(B) In a car store 自動車販売店

(C) In a management company 管理会社

(D) In a bank 銀行

> 山根爽 最初の女性のせりふで「口座…キャッシュカード…」ですぐに「銀行だ!」と反応できる ⇒ **Level 2**

33. 正解：(B)

What does the man inquire about? 男性は何を尋ねているか？

(A) A location 場所

(B) A fee 料金

(C) Business hours 営業時間

(D) A credit card クレジットカード

> 山根爽 男性の疑問文を待つ。Do you charge ... fee? とすぐに出てくる ⇒ **Level 1**

34. 正解：(C)

What will the man probably do later? 男性は後で多分何をするだろうか？

(A) Charge a fee 料金を請求する

(B) Return a membership card 会員カードを返す

(C) Read a brochure パンフレットを読む

(D) Fill out forms 申し込み書に書き込む

> 山根爽 next（次に）何をするか？ なら Go back to his wife. が答えだが、later なので (C) を選ぶ ⇒ **Level 2**

Questions 35 through 37 refer to the following conversation.

W: Hi, I am planning to add some plants / to my balcony garden. But I don't know / what to choose / as I see / that you have a lot of varieties.

M: Do you want to take a look / at our succulent plants? They are really popular these days / and good for balcony gardens. They do not require constant care. Just a bit sunshine would keep them happy.

W: Sounds good. I also want some pots. Do you have them?

M: Yes, / go down this aisle, / and you'll find them. We actually have a pot sale today. Shall I take you there?

訳

女：コンニチハ。うちのバルコニー菜園に少し植物を加えようと計画してるの。でも、何を選んで良いか分からないわ、おたくにはたくさんの種類があるのでね。

男：うちの多汁性植物ご覧になりませんか？この頃とても人気があるんですよ、そしてバルコニー菜園に適してますよ。手入れに手がかかりません。ただ、ちょっと日光があればそれで満足なのですよ。

女：いいわね。私、鉢も少しいただきたいのよね。あるかしら？

男：はい、この通路をお進みくだされば、見つかりますよ。実は、うちでは今日、鉢のセールをやっております。そちらへお連れしましょうか？

語句

❏ **add A to B**　　A を B に加える　　　　　　❏ **as I see that...**　　～が分かるので
❏ **succulent plant**　多肉 [多汁] 性植物　※サボテンなど　❏ **constant**　　一定の；不変の
❏ **aisle** 通路　　　　※両側に棚とか座席がある通路のこと。発音は [アイル]

Chapter ❷

Part 1 写真描写

Part 2 応答

Part 3 会話

Part 4 説明文

Part 5 短文穴埋め

Part 6 長文穴埋め

Part 7 長文読解

35. 正解：(B)

What does the woman want to do with the plant?
女性はその植物をどうしたいのか？

(A) Put it in her kitchen　　台所に入れる

(B) Put it on her balcony　　バルコニーに置く

(C) Give it to her daughter　娘にあげる

(D) Use it in a recipe　　　レシピで使う

> 山根ポイ 最初の女性のせりふを待ち伏せすれば、すぐに「バルコニー」とベタで聞こえる
> ⇒ Level 1

36. 正解：(C)

Why does the man recommend a particular type of plant?
男性はなぜ特定の植物を勧めるのか？

(A) It is on sale.　　　　　　　売り出し中である。

(B) It does not need sunshine.　日光を必要としない。

(C) It is easy to take care of.　世話が簡単である。

(D) It repels insects.　　　　　昆虫を寄せつけない。

> 山根ポイ succulent（水分の多い）を知らなくても OK。男性のせりふから、「コンスタン
> トな care がいらない。日光だけ…」と分かる　⇒ Level 2

37. 正解：(C)

What does the man offer to do?　男性は何を申し出ているか？

(A) Give the woman a discount　　　　　　女性に割引をしてあげる

(B) Show the woman around the garden　　女性を庭を案内して回る

(C) Take the woman to the pot section　　鉢のコーナーへ連れて行く

(D) Give the woman a brochure on gardening　女性に園芸のパンフレットをあげる

> 山根ポイ 当然、男性の最後のせりふを待つ。Shall I take you there?（そちらへお連れ
> しましょうか？）と言っている。aisle（通路）が聞きとれるか？　ここでの there と
> は「鉢売り場」のこと　⇒ Level 2

223

Questions 38 through 40 refer to the following conversation.

W: Hi, / we are both here / for the new book seminar. The event leaflet says / that it starts at 2 pm.

M: We're very sorry Ma'am. The event has just been postponed to 3 pm today / due to the late arrival of our speaker.

W: Well, this may not be bad actually. My friend Sara really wanted to come / but she can't get off work/ until 2:30 today. Now she may be able to join.

M: That sounds good. If your friend wants to join, / do you mind registering for her / as our registration closes 30 minutes before the event.

W: Sure, no problem. By the way, I understand that the speaker does not speak English. Do you provide any translation headsets?

M: Yes, you can request them at the entrance. Remember to return them when you are done.

訳

女：コンニチハ、私たち二人新刊書セミナーに来ました。イベントのチラシには午後2時に始まるって書いてあります。

男：大変申し訳ございません、お客様。イベントは今日の午後3時に延ばされたところなのです、講演される方の到着が遅れているので。

女：そう、でも実際のところ悪くもないかも。友人のサラがすごく来たがったのよね、でも今日は彼女2時半まで仕事を離れられないのよ。これだと彼女参加できるかも。

男：それはよろしいですね。もし、お友達が参加されたいのでしたら、彼女に代わって登録なさいませんか、イベント30分前には登録を終了いたしますので。

女：もちろん、問題ないわ。ところで、講演の人は英語を話されないと思うわ。翻訳のヘッドフォンを用意してくださるの？

男：はい、入り口でご請求ください。お済みになったらご返却をお忘れなく。

語句

❏ **leaflet**　　　　　　　　　　[名] 印刷物；チラシ　※「小さな葉っぱ」の意味から

❏ **postpone=put off~**　　　延期する；先延ばしする

❏ **due to~**　　　　　　　　　　〜のせいで；〜のために　※ =because of~, on account of ~

❏ **do you mind...?**　　　〜してかまいませんか？　※答えるときに「構わない」と言いたかったら普通は No, not at all. や Of course not. などが来るが、会話では Sure, no problem. なども来るので注意

Chapter❷

Part 1
写真描写

Part 2
応答

Part 3
会話

Part 4
説明文

Part 5
短文穴埋め

Part 6
長文穴埋め

Part 7
長文読解

❏ **register** 　動　登録 [記帳] する
❏ **understand** 　動　理解する　※「推測してそうだと思う」という意味もあるので注意
❏ **provide** 　動　用意 [準備] する
❏ **translation** 　名　翻訳
❏ **remember to~** 　~することを覚えている　※ remember...ing (~したことを覚えている) との違いに注意

38. 正解：(B)

What type of event is being held?　どのようなイベントが開催されているか？

(A) A training session 　　(訓練の) 研修会
(B) A book workshop 　　本の講習会
(C) A sale 　　売り出し
(D) A speaking contest 　弁論大会

> 山根ポイント　最初の女性のせりふで book seminar と言っている　⇒ **Level 1'**

39. 正解：(D)

Why is the event postponed?　イベントはなぜ先延ばしになっているか？

(A) There are not enough participants.　　十分な参加者がいない。
(B) The speaker needs more time to prepare.　講演者に準備にもっと時間が必要。
(C) The speaker does not speak English.　講演者は英語を話さない。
(D) The speaker cannot arrive on time.　講演者が時間通りに到着できない。

> 山根ポイント　設問からマイナスイメージのせりふを待ち伏せる。We're very sorry... と聞こえるので、この次に答えがあると読む　⇒ **Level 1'**

40. 正解：(D)

What does the man ask the woman to return at the end of the event?
男性は女性にイベント終了時に何を返すように頼んでいるか？

(A) A registration form 　登録申し込み用紙
(B) An event leaflet 　　イベントのチラシ
(C) A sample book 　　試供品の本
(D) A headset 　　　ヘッドフォン

> 山根ポイント　最後の男性のせりふで Please が入った命令形風の内容が聞こえるのを待ち伏せる！　⇒ **Level 1**

Questions 41 through 43 refer to the following conversation.

W: Thanks for giving me a discount / on the ad making.

M: No problem. What do you want your audience to remember most / about your new model of camera?

W: Our new model is super/in a lot of aspects, / but its most amazing feature is / that it is waterproof / and therefore a great choice for divers.

M: Cool. I'll make sure / this feature goes into the ad. Is there anything else / that is great about this model?

W: Well, / this model can upload the photos as they are taken / to any devices / that are connected to Wi-Fi.

M: OK, I'll include this as well. By the way, / could you fax me your signed advertisement contract / so that I can start the work?

訳

女：広告作成を割引いただきありがとうございます。

男：おやすい御用ですよ。視聴者に何を一番覚えておいてほしいですか、御社の新型カメラについて？

女：うちの新型は多くの点で超すごいのよ、でも最も驚く特徴はそれが防水であること、だからダイバー（潜水者）にとってすごい選択になるってことなの。

男：素敵ですね。この特徴はかならず広告に入れますよ。何か他にこのモデルについてすごいことはありませんか？

女：そうね、このモデルは、写真が撮れたら Wi-Fi に接続しているどんな装置にも送信できるのよ。

男：分かりました、これも入れましょう。ところで、あなたの署名入りの広告契約書をファクスしていただけますか、私が仕事に取り掛かれますようにと。

語句

❏ **ad**	名	広告　※ =advertisement	❏ **audience**	名	視聴者　※本来は「聴衆」
❏ **amazing**	形	驚嘆するような　※よい意味	❏ **feature**	名	特徴
❏ **waterproof**	名	防水　※ fireproof は「防火」	❏ **therefore**		だから；それゆえに
❏ **cool**	形	素敵な；カッコイイ　※本来は「涼しい；冷静な」			
❏ **transmit**	動	送る；送信する　※ transmission は「伝導装置」			
❏ **as they are taken**		それらが撮られると同時に　※ as は when の意味だが「同時に」の意味がある			
❏ **as well**		～もまた；同様に			
❏ **so that... can**		構文　～できるようにと　※「その結果～」とも訳せる			

41. 正解：(B)

Chapter ❷

Part 1 写真描写

Part 2 応答

Part 3 会話

Part 4 説明文

Part 5 短文穴埋め

Part 6 長文穴埋め

Part 7 長文読解

What type of business does the woman own? 女性はどんなビジネスを持っているか？

(A) Water sports　　水上スポーツ

(B) Optical instruments　光学機器

(C) Furniture　　家具

(D) Information Technology　IT（情報科学技術）

> **山根ズバ** 最初の女性のせりふを待ち伏せる。カメラの広告を出したい人のビジネスは？ optical が分からなくても他の選択肢に「×」を出して行けばすぐ。optical は「光学の；視覚上の」という意味だが、もともとは「目」の意味があったので、眼鏡店を optical shop とか optician と言う（時折テストに出る!）　⇒ **Level 2**

42. 正解：(D)

According to the woman, what is the best feature of the product?
女性によれば、この製品のもっとも優れた特徴は？

(A) It has high cost performance.　コスパ（費用対効果）が高い。

(B) It resists extreme cold.　対極寒性がある。

(C) It has a large storage.　記憶量が豊富である。

(D) It is waterproof.　防水である。

> **山根ズバ** best に反応して、プラスイメージ一杯の女性のせりふを待ち伏せればすぐに答えが出る　⇒ **Level 1**

43. 正解：(C)

What does the man ask the woman to do? 男性は女性に何をするように頼んでいるか？

(A) Send him a picture　　写真を送るように

(B) Send him a sample　　サンプルを送るように

(C) Send him an agreement　（同意）契約書を送るように

(D) Send him a deposit　　頭金を送るように

> **山根ズバ** 当然最後の男性のせりふを待ち伏せる。依頼だから、Please が入った命令形風のものや Will you 〜?や Could you 〜?などの表現を待ち伏せる。契約書（contract = agreement）のパラフレーズに気づくこと（頻出!）。deposit は「前受け金；内金」　⇒ **Level 2**

Questions 44 through 46 refer to the following conversation.

M: Josh, / Marsha will take sick leave this Wednesday. Could you help by taking her shift? We hope you can do the presentation / that Marsha has prepared.

W: Sure, I can help. Actually, / Marsha wanted me to review the presentation, / and we discussed it a lot. So I am quite familiar with the presentation materials. Who will be the audience?

M: It will be Kathy from our client side. She is very interested in our new medicine. I had asked Marsha / to add the market share of our new medicine / to the presentation materials. Could you check to make sure / that this is included?

訳

男：Josh、Marsha がこの水曜日に病気休暇を取るんだ。彼女のシフトを引き受ける手助けをしてもらえるかな？ Marsha が準備してきたプレゼン、君ができるといいんだけど。

女：もちろん、お手伝いできるわ。実はね、Marsha が 私にそのプレゼン検討して欲しいと望んだのよ、それで私たちそれについて多く話し合ったの。それで私はそのプレゼンの資料よく知っているのよ。聴衆はだれ？

男：うちの顧客側サイドの Kathy だよ。Kathy はうちの新薬にとても興味を持っているんだ。僕は Marsha にうちの新薬の市場占有率をプレゼンの資料に加えるように頼んでいたんだ。これがちゃんと入っていることを確かめてもらえるかな？

語句

❑ take ...leave	休暇を取る　※ leave は許可してもらう休暇		
❑ help (to)	to take の to が省略されることに注意！	❑ shift 名	交替制勤務
❑ be familiar with~	~を熟知している	❑ add A to B	A を B に加える
❑ check to~	~するのを確認する	❑ make sure that...	~を確かめる
❑ include	動 含む；入れる		

Chapter ②

Part 1
写真描写

Part 2
応答

Part 3
会話

Part 4
説明文

Part 5
短文穴埋め

Part 6
長文穴埋め

Part 7
長文読解

44. 正解：(B)

What will happen this Wednesday? この水曜日に何が起ころうとしているのか？

(A) A client meeting will be cancelled. 顧客との会議が中止になる。

(B) A presentation will be given. プレゼンがなされる。

(C) New employees will join. 新しい従業員が加わる。

(D) New medicine will be prescribed. 新しい薬が処方される。

山根ポイント 未来形の文を待ち伏せる。一つは Marsha が病気休暇を取る事、もう一つは Marsha が準備してきたプレゼンを代わりにやることだ。選択肢には presentation が見えるはず ⇒ **Level 1**

45. 正解：(D)

What does the woman ask about? 女性は何について尋ねているか？

(A) Marsha's reason of absence Marsha の欠勤の理由

(B) The effects of new medicine 新薬の効果

(C) The length of the presentation プレゼンの長さ

(D) The listeners 聞き手

山根ポイント 例によって女性のせりふで疑問文風のものを待ち伏せると、ずばり Who will be the audience?（聴衆はだれ?）と尋ねている。「聴衆」とは「聞く人」なので (D) の listeners が正解とわかる ⇒ **Level 2**

46. 正解：(D)

What does the man ask the woman to check?
男性は女性に何を確かめるよう求めているか？

(A) What the price of the new medicine will be
新薬の値段はどのくらいになるのか

(B) When the next meeting will be scheduled
次の会合の予定はいつになるのか

(C) What clients' preference will be
顧客の好みはどんなものになるのか

(D) How well the new medicine has gained market share
どのくらいその新薬が市場占有率を得ているか

山根ポイント 後半の男性のセリフで check を待ち伏せれば、market share が聞き取れるはず ⇒ **Level 2**

Questions 47 through 49 refer to the following conversation.

M: Hi, this is Richard Lee from Vermont Industries. I missed your call earlier today / and I am calling back.

W: Hi, this is Anna Suzuki from Bronze Car. We have developed a new type of car / which uses the special engine of GX01. I understand / that you are one of the best producers of GX01. Would you be able to supply it to us?

M: Absolutely. We have actually added a new feature / to our GX01.It has greatly improved the burning efficiency, / meaning that your car will need less fuel.

W: Sounds great. I also want to know / if we could get any discount if we order in bulk.

M: Sure. / Why don't we meet and discuss the details?

訳

M: もしもし、Vermont Industries の Richard Lee と申します。今朝貴方様のお電話をお取りできませんでしたので、折り返させていただいています。

W: はい、こちら Bronze Car の Anna 鈴木でございます。GX01 という特別なエンジンを使う新しいタイプの車を開発致しました。御社が GX01 の最良メーカーのお一つだと理解しております。当社にそれを供給していただけますでしょうか?

M: もちろんですとも。実はですね、我が社の GX01 には新しい性能を加えたところなんです。燃焼効率が大幅に改善されました、というのはですね、御社のお車は燃料がより少なくて済むということなんです。

W: すごいですね。もし大量注文すればいくらか割引していただけるかどうかも知りたいのですが。

M: もちろんです。お会いして詳しいことをお話しするというのはいかがでしょう?

語句

❏ miss	動	(何かを)しそこなう
❏ absolutely	副	(Yesを強調して)絶対に
❏ feature	名	性能;機能 ※原義は「特徴」
❏ efficiency	名	効率 ※efficient 形 効率のよい
❏ fuel	名	燃料

❏ supply	動	供給する
❏ less	形	より少ない
❏ order in bulk		大量注文

Chapter ❷

Part 1 写真描写

Part 2 応答

Part 3 会話

Part 4 説明文

Part 5 短文穴埋め

Part 6 長文穴埋め

Part 7 長文読解

47. 正解：(B)

What product does the woman's company manufacture?
女性の会社はどんな製品を製造しているか？

(A) Gasoline　　　ガソリン

(B) Automobiles　自動車

(C) Engines　　　エンジン

(D) Furniture　　　家具

> 山根ポイント car, vehicle, automobile などのパラフレーズは基本中の基本。女性 (鈴木さん) のセリフを待ち伏せすれば、すぐに Bronze Car と聞こえる　⇒ **Level 2**

48. 正解：(D)

Why did the woman call the man?　女性はなぜ男性に電話をしたのか？

(A) To negotiate a contract　契約の交渉をするため

(B) To schedule a meeting　会合を予定するため

(C) To offer a service　サービスを提供するため

(D) To order certain parts　なんらかの部品を注文するため。

> 山根ポイント certain は「確かな」という意味が一般的だが、「名前は言わないが、ある…」という意味があるので注意。会話では some ＋ 単数形の場合でも同じ意味。つまり some man = a certain man。女性のセリフから、新型エンジンを一括大量注文したいことが分かれば Good!　⇒ **Level 2**

49. 正解：(D)

What is the new feature that the man mentioned?
男性が触れた新しい特徴とは何か？

(A) It reduces the noise.　騒音を減らす。

(B) It reduces the cost of production.　製造費を減らす。

(C) It uses environmentally friendly materials.　環境に優しい材料を使っている。

(D) It saves fuel.　燃料を節約する。

> 山根ポイント feature（特徴；性能）とはプラスイメージだ！　2つ目の男性のせりふを待ち伏せると、ずばり less fuel と言っている　⇒ **Level 1'**

Questions 50 through 52 refer to the following conversation.

W: Thank you for coming so quickly. Please come in. I will show you my balcony. The cigarette butts are still there.

M: That's unusual. We haven't had similar complaints so far. When did the problem start?

W: About two weeks ago. I think / some new guy just moved in on the 3rd floor / at that time. Since then, / cigarette butts fall onto my balcony everyday. At first, / I tried to clean them up / but now I have given up. I went upstairs yesterday / to try to talk to the guy in 303 / but he wasn't there.

M: Well, there is a single man living in Apartment 303, / but the wind might have brought these things in / from other tenants on the third floor.

訳

女：こんなにすぐに来ていただいてありがとうございます。どうぞお入りになって。バルコニーをお見せしましょう。タバコの吸い殻が依然としてそこにあるでしょう。

男：変ですね。これまでのところ同様な苦情はなかったのですがね。問題はいつ始まりましたか？

女：2週間くらい前です。その頃、だれか新しい男性が3階に丁度引っ越して来たと思います。その時から、タバコの吸い殻が毎日私のバルコニーに落ちるんです。はじめは、それらを片付けようとしましたが、今はあきらめています。私は昨日上の階に行きました、303号室の男性に話をしようとね、でも彼はいませんでした。

男：えーと、303号室には中年の独身の人が住んでいますが、風が3階の他の居住者からこれらのものを運んで来たのかもしれませんねえ。

語句

❏ **butt**	名	吸い殻
❏ **simila**	形	似ている；同様な
❏ **complaint**	名	不平；クレーム　※ **complain** 動 不平を言う
❏ **so far**		これまでのところ
❏ **some**		なにか；ある　※はっきり言わない時に使う表現　例：some guy = a certain guy
❏ **give up**		放棄する；やめる
❏ **might have** 　＋過去分詞		〜したであろう；〜したかもしれない
❏ **tenant**	名	住人（借家人）

Chapter ②

Part 1 写真描写

Part 2 応答

Part 3 会話

Part 4 説明文

Part 5 短文穴埋め

Part 6 長文穴埋め

Part 7 長文読解

50. 正解：(B)

Who most likely is the man? 男性はだれであろうか?

(A) A cigarette vendor　　　　　　　　　タバコを売る人

(B) A building manager　　　　　　　　　建物管理人

(C) A customer service representative　顧客サービス担当者

(D) A salesperson　　　　　　　　　　　営業担当者

> 山根ポイント 最初の男性のせりふを待ち伏せる。女性の苦情に対処していることを掴む
> ⇒ Level 2

51. 正解：(C)

What does the man mean when he says "That's unusual"?
男性は "That's unusual' と言う時に何を言いたいのか?

(A) He thinks this problem could cost his job.
この問題は自分の仕事に響くだろうと思っている。

(B) He thinks the woman should be complaining to a different person.
女性が違う人に文句を言っているだろうと思っている。

(C) He thinks it is a rare problem.
それはまれな問題だと思っている。

(D) He thinks he needs to check with an expert.
専門家に確認する必要があると思っている。

> 山根ポイント unusual とは usual でないこと。女性の不平に対しての言葉なので、「そんな事は普通あり得ないのですがね…」と言っている　⇒ Level 3

52. 正解：(D)

Why does the woman think that happened two weeks ago?
女性はなぜそれが2週間前に起こったと考えているのか?

(A) It started to get windy.　　　　　　風が強くなり始めた。

(B) Her neighbor started to smoke.　　隣人がタバコを吸い始めた。

(C) Her neighbor cleaned her balcony.　隣人が彼女のバルコニーを清掃した。

(D) Someone moved into her building.　だれかが彼女のビルに引っ越して来た。

> 山根ポイント ヒントは two weeks ago。これが最初の男性のせりふの When...? の質問と
> 同じだとピンとくれば Good!　⇒ Level 1

Questions 53 through 55 refer to the following conversation.

M: Hi, I am Clint Osborn from the City's Tourism Board. We are designing a tourist map for our city. We want pictures of the various tourist spots/ such as buildings and towers on the map / so that people can know what they are heading to. I saw your website about your illustrations, / which are really wonderful. I am wondering / if you could illustrate for us.

W: That sounds cool. Yes, I am happy to. I do two types of illustrations: / sketch and cartoon. Which style do you prefer?

M: I think sketch would be good / but I am not sure. Could you send me both samples / so that we can compare / and let you know? We'd also like to know your quotations.

W: The samples of both styles / are actually on my website, / if you click "styles". For quotations, / sure I will send it to you after this call.

訳

M: もしもし、私は市の観光委員会の Clint Osborn と申します。私共は当市の観光者用地図を企画しています。地図上に建物や塔のような種々の観光スポットの写真が欲しいのです、人々が何を目指して行こうか分かるようにね。私はおたくのホームページでおたくのイラストを拝見しました、そしてそれらは本当にすばらしいですね。できれば私共にイラスト（挿絵）を描いていただけないかと思っているのですが。

W: 素敵だわ。ええ、喜んで。私は2つのタイプのイラストを描きますよ。スケッチ（素描）とマンガです。どちらのスタイル（やり方）がお好みですか?

M: スケッチの方がよいと思いますが、はっきりはしていません。両方のサンプルをお送りいただけますか、そうすれば比較できて、お知らせできますが。また、おたくのお値段（相場価格）を知りたいのですが。

W: 両方のスタイルのサンプルは実は私のホームページに出ています、もし「スタイル」をクリックされればね。見積もり価格につきましては、このお電話の後で確かに御社にお送り致します。

語句

☐ **design**	動 意図する；企画する	☐ **head to/for~** ~を目指す [向かう]
☐ **wonder if~**	~かなと思う　※人を誘うときに使う。I'm wondering if you could...	
☐ **cartoon**	名 主に新聞などのコマ漫画	
☐ **compare A with B**	A と B を比較する	
☐ **quotation**	見積もり価格（相場価格）　※ quote = estimate（見積もる；引用する）	
☐ **sure**	=I'm sure のこと	

Chapter ❷

Part 1 写真描写

Part 2 応答

Part 3 会話

Part 4 説明文

Part 5 短文穴埋め

Part 6 長文穴埋め

Part 7 長文読解

53. 正解：(B)

Who most likely is the woman?　女性はだれであろうか？

(A) A photographer　写真家

(B) An illustrator　イラストレーター

(C) A tourist　旅行者

(D) A designer　デザイナー

> 山根ポイント 始めに picture と聞こえるので写真と間違えるかもしれないが、すぐに illustration がすばらしいと男性が言っているので　⇒ Level 1'

54. 正解：(B)

What does the woman ask the man about?　女性は男性に何を尋ねているか？

(A) His browsing history　彼のブラウザ履歴

(B) His drawing style　絵を描く彼のやり方

(C) The purpose of the map　地図の目的

(D) The timeline for the work　仕事の予定表

> 山根ポイント 当然女性の質問文を待つ。「どちらのスタイルがお好みですか？」と聞いている。style は「やり方；流儀；型；文体」が主な意味で、日本語の「スタイル（体つき）が良い」という意味はない。その場合は She has a good figure. と言うが、現在ではセクハラになる可能性があるので注意　⇒ Level 2

55. 正解：(D)

What does the woman say she will do?　女性は何をしましょうと言っているか？

(A) Send "sketch" samples
　スケッチのサンプルを送る

(B) Send "cartoon" samples
　コママンガのサンプルを送る

(C) Send both the "sketch" and the "cartoon" samples
　スケッチ、コママンガ双方のサンプルを送る

(D) Send prices for her work
　彼女の作品に対しての価格（表）を送る

> 山根ポイント 女性の最後のせりふに集中する。スケッチ、コママンガはウェブを見て欲しい、quotation は後で送ると言っている。quotation（estimation）の単語の意味が分からなければ消去法で行く　⇒ Level 2

Questions 56 through 58 refer to the following conversation.

W: David, / I have some concerns about your recent performance. Last Monday / you were late for our annual performance review. Yesterday / you didn't show up at our weekly meeting. You also submitted our sales report / well past the deadline.

M: I'm really sorry, Susan. You know / that we just had a new baby / and my mom was hospitalized last week. I have been trying to hire a babysitter / but I have not found one yet.

W: That's no excuse. You are in a position of great responsibility / and you should arrange your family matters properly / and not let them affect your work. Why don't you set up a meeting with HR? They can probably recommend some babysitter companies / or sign you up for some work-life balance seminars.

訳

女：David、貴方の最近の働きにすこし懸念があるの。先週の月曜日、うちの年次の業績検討会に貴方は遅刻したわね。昨日は週間ミーティングにも現れなかったわ。貴方は締め切りをゆうに過ぎてから営業報告書を提出したわ。

男：Susan、本当に申し訳ありません。あのですね、新しい赤ちゃんが生まれたばかりで、また母が先週入院したのです。ベビーシッターを雇おうとしてるんですが、まだみつからないんです。

女：それは言い訳にはなりません。あなたは大きな責任ある立場にいるのよ、そして家族の諸事はちゃんと片付けて、それを仕事に影響させてはだめでしょう。人事部とのミーティングを申し立てたらどうかしら？　多分ベビーシッターの会社を推奨してくれるか、「仕事と家庭生活のバランスを取るセミナー」に貴方が参加できるように申し込んでくれると思うわ。

語句

concern(s)	名 懸念；心配		performance	名 働き；業績；遂行；性能
annual～	形 毎年恒例の		show up	姿を現す ＝appear
submit	～を提出する ＝ hand in		well	副 十分に；ゆうに
hospitalize	動 病院に入れる			
lame	形 おそまつな ＝ poor, inefficient　※もともとは「足が不具な」という意味			
excuse	名 言い訳　※ No excuse!（言い訳するな！）			
huge	形 巨大な			
arrange	動 取り計らう；片付ける；手配する			
matters	名 事柄		properly	副 適切に；きちんと
affect	動 （悪い）影響を及ぼす		Why don't you...?	～したらどうなの？
set up	～を始める；申し立てる		sign up for～	～へ申し込む

Chapter ❷

Part 1 写真描写

Part 2 応答

Part 3 会話

Part 4 説明文

Part 5 短文穴埋め

Part 6 長文穴埋め

Part 7 長文読解

56. 正解：(B)

What meeting did David fail to attend? David は何の会合に出られなかったのか？

(A) The annual performance review meeting　年次業績検討会

(B) The weekly meeting　週間会議

(C) The project meeting　企画会議

(D) The HR meeting　人事部会議

> 山根究 マイナスイメージの雰囲気を、即聞き取れるように。fail to~ は「～しそびれる；～できない」、attend は「出席する」。あわてると遅刻した方の会議と間違う　⇒ Level 1'

57. 正解：(C)

What does the woman mean when she says "That's no excuse"?
女性は "That's no excuse" と言うときに何をいいたいのか？

(A) She thinks the man is lying.　彼女は男性がウソをついていると思っている。

(B) She thinks the man is finding fault with her.
彼女は男性が彼女のあら探しをしていると思っている。

(C) She thinks the reasons offered by the man are not persuasive.
彼女は男性が申し出た理由は説得力がないと思っている。

(D) She thinks the man lacks strategy.
彼女は男性が戦略に欠けると思っている。

> 山根究 言い訳をたしなめていることがわかれば良い。excuse [イクスキュース] は「言い訳」。なお、このような長い選択肢は読みながら聞いたらだめ！ lying, finding fault, not persuasive, lacks strategy に焦点を合わせて聞くと良い。lie は「ウソをつく」、find fault with~ は「～の欠点を探す」。persuasive は「説得力のある（⇒ persuade　動　説得する）」　⇒ Level 2

58. 正解：(B)

What does the woman suggest the man do?
女性は男性に何をするよう提案しているか？

(A) Change a babysitter　子守りを代えるように

(B) Meet with HR　人事部と会合を持つように

(C) Take some days off　数日休暇を取るように

(D) Organize a seminar　セミナーを準備するように

> 山根究 女性の後半のせりふで「～したら；なさいよ（Why don't you..?, How about...?, You should....)」などの提案型の文を待つ　⇒ Level 1

Questions 59 through 61 refer to the following conversation.

■ W: Hi, Mr. Douglas, / I am thrilled / that you are considering buying photos from me. I hope/ this could be a long-term supply arrangement.

◆ M: Yes, we are very impressed / by the portfolio you have. We want to have photos of Asian countries / in our in-flight magazines, / so that we can attract more people / to fly with us to those destinations.

■ W: This is wonderful. Speaking from my own experience, / I do find / that photos people see on planes / influence their travel decisions. So which countries do you prefer?

◆ M: Countries where we have flights, / of course. My secretary will send you a list of those countries / so that you can send us the right pictures.

訳

女：Douglas 様、私はわくわくしています、貴方様が私からの写真購入をお考えになっておられることに。これが長いお付き合いに（長期の供給取り決めに）なればと希望致します。

男：その通りです、当方は貴女のポートフォリオに大変感銘を受けております。アジア諸国の写真を機内雑誌に載せたいと思っています、そうすればそれらの目的地までご一緒に飛ぶ、より多くの人々を引き付けることができると思います。

女：素晴らしいですわ。私自身の経験から申しますと、人々が飛行機の中で見る写真は旅の決定に影響を与えると、分かりますとも。で、どちらの国々がお好みでしょうか？

男：もちろん当社の飛行便のある国々ですね。私の秘書が貴女にそれらの国々のリストを送ります、貴女が当方にふさわしい写真を送れるようにとね。

語句

❏ **thrill**　　　動　わくわくさせる　❏ **consider**　動　検討する；考慮する
❏ **impress**　　動　印象を与える　　❏ **portfolio**　名　自社製品品揃えリスト；作品集
❏ **attract**　　動　引き付ける；魅了する　❏ **destination**　名　目的地；行く先
❏ **do find that...**　　that 以下が分かりますとも（強調の do）

Chapter ❷

Part 1 写真描写

Part 2 応答

Part 3 会話

Part 4 説明文

Part 5 短文穴埋め

Part 6 長文穴埋め

Part 7 長文読解

59. 正解：(B)

What are the speakers mainly discussing? 話し手たちは主に何を話し合っているか？

(A) A tour package　　1セットのツアー

(B) A supply agreement　供給の取り決め

(C) A project deadline　企画の締め切り日

(D) A travel article　　旅行記事

> **山根ポイント** 待ち伏せていればズバリ、写真を購入してくれる機会を持てて喜んでいるので (B) が正解。商談だと気づくことが必要　⇒ Level 2〜3

60. 正解：(A)

What type of business is the man's company?
男性の会社は、どのようなビジネスか？

(A) Airline　　　　航空会社

(B) Entertainment　娯楽

(C) Travel agency　旅行代理店

(D) Media　　　　メディア

> **山根ポイント** 男性のせりふを待ち伏せすれば、in-flight... と聞こえるので簡単。(C) が落とし穴!　⇒ Level2

61. 正解：(C)

What does the woman mean when she says "speaking from my own experience"?
女性が "Speaking from my own experience" と言うとき、何を言いたいのか？

(A) She is offering her opinion.
彼女は自身の意見を述べている。

(B) She is being polite.
彼女は礼儀正しくしている。

(C) She is remembering the same feelings on a plane.
彼女は飛行機で感じた同じ気持ちを思い出している。

(D) She is an expert on travel.
彼女は旅行の専門家だ。

> **山根ポイント** 難問。(A) と (C) で迷うはずだが、(A) だと「私の経験から言えば」とはならない　⇒ Level 3

Questions 62 through 64 refer to the following telephone conversation and graphics.

🇺🇸 M: Hi, I'm calling for some information on the summer courses / that you offer for primary school students. We want some of our 5th grade students / to take a summer course this year.

🇬🇧 W: Sure, / how many students are we talking about / and what is your budget?

🇺🇸 M: We have a total of 5 students. They are the award winners of our school contests. We hope to keep the total cost per person / under $250.

🇬🇧 W: OK, / we have courses in both July and August. Which month do you prefer?

🇺🇸 M: July would be good because we'll have a regional contest in August. Do we need to pay in advance?

🇬🇧 W: You'll need to pay 30% / as a non-refundable deposit in advance, / and the remaining 70% is due within 10 days / after the completion of the course. I will send you our course brochures shortly.

訳

男：もしもし、夏期講習に関しての情報を求めて電話しているんだ、おたくが小学生のために提供しているコースの。5年生の何人かを今年の夏期講習に参加させたいのだが。

女：承知いたしました。何名の学生についてのお話しでしょうか、そしてご予算は？

男：合計で5名だ。みんな当校の競技会での受賞者たちなんだ。一人当たり250ドル以内での総費用を希望するよ。

女：了承しました、7月と8月両方にコースがございます。どちらの月をお好みでしょうか？

男：7月が良いだろう、8月に地区大会があるのでね。あらかじめ、支払いする必要があるかな？

女：あらかじめ、返金不可の頭金として30%お支払いいただく必要がございます、そして残りの70%はコース終了後の10日以内が期限となっております。すぐに、当方の講習のパンフレットをお送り致します。

語句

❏ **course**	名	講習；課程 ※普通は「コース；進路」
❏ **in advance**		前もって；あらかじめ　= beforehand
❏ **refundable**	形	返金できる
❏ **completion**	名	完了　※発音は [カンプリージャン]
❏ **shortly**	副	すぐに　= at once, soon

❏ **award**	名	賞　※発音は [アウォード]
❏ **deposit**	名	保証金；頭金；前受け金

Chapter ❷

Part 1 写真描写

Part 2 応答

Part 3 会話

Part 4 説明文

Part 5 短文穴埋め

Part 6 長文穴埋め

Part 7 長文読解

62. 正解：(B)

What type of the event is the man trying to apply for?
男性はどんなイベントに申し込もうとしているか？

(A) An internship　　　　　　　　　　　　　実習生研修

(B) A training program　　　　　　　　　　訓練プログラム

(C) A preparation course for an entrance exam　入試対策コース

(D) A concert　　　　　　　　　　　　　　コンサート

> **山根ポイント** 最初の男性のせりふで「夏期講習」ということがすぐに分かるが、勉強の講習会ではないと早く気づくこと。中盤に地区大会がある…とある　⇒ **Level 2**

63. 正解：(A)

Look at the graphic. What option will the man most likely select?

(A) Swimming　水泳

(B) Tennis　　テニス

(C) Study Aid　学習の手助け

(D) Violin　　バイオリン

> **山根ポイント** graphics の問題は解答の選択肢を見て、表ではそれ以外の部分に注目（ここでは月と予算）。7月が良くて予算は250ドル以内なら tennis ではなくて swimming となる。

価格表

選択肢	時期	1人あたりの価格
水泳	7月か8月	$240
テニス	7月か8月	$260
補習	7月か8月	$250
バイオリン	7月	$180

64. 正解：(D)

What will the woman probably do next? 女性は次に何をするだろうか？

(A) Schedule a meeting　　会合を予定に組む

(B) Issue an invoice　　　請求書を発行する

(C) Make a deposit　　　頭金を出す

(D) Send course information　講習の情報を送る

> **山根ポイント** この What will A do next? のパターンは100%最後の A の未来形のせりふに正解があるので、それを待ち伏せる。I will send you... の次に答えが来ている。もっとも前の人のせりふをうけて、A の最後のせりふが Yes, I will do 等となっているいじわるな問題もあるが…　⇒ **Level 2**

Questions 65 through 67 refer to the following conversation and graphic.

M: Linda, I'd like to ask you / to book a hotel for our new CEO Gary. I just got his itinerary. He will attend a client meeting in the Huntington Hotel / on his first day. So could you book that hotel?

W: Just a moment, / let me check... I am sorry / Huntington is full on the day Gary arrives / due to an opening ceremony of a nearby mall. But Vermont Hotel is still available, / and it is just a 5-minute walk from the Huntington.

M: OK, Vermont should work. We also need Jim / to pick Gary up from his hotel at noon. Can you make sure / you give the hotel address to Jim?

W: No problem. I will call Jim right away.

男：Linda、我が社の新しい CEO の Gary の為にホテルを予約してもらいたいんだ。彼の日程表が入ったところなんだ。彼は最初の日に Huntington Hotel で顧客とのミーティングに出席するよ。そこでそのホテルの予約してもらえるかな？

女：ちょっとお待ちください。確認いたします…。申し訳ありませんが、Hunthigton は Gary が到着する日には満杯です、近くのショッピングモールの開店式典のために。でも Vermont Hotel はまだ空がございますし、Huntington からわずか歩いて5分です。

男：いいよ、Vermont でいいだろう。また Jim に正午に Gary をホテルに迎えに行ってもらう必要があるんだ。ホテルの住所を Jim にちゃんと伝えてもらえるかな？

女：問題ございません。すぐに Jim に電話致します。

語句

❑ **itinerary**	名	旅程；日程表　※発音は［アイテネラリー］
❑ **Just a moment.**		ちょっとお待ちください。
❑ **on the day (when)...**		会話では when が省略されることが多い
❑ **available**	形	空いている　※通常は「役立つ；都合がつく；有効である」など
❑ **work**	動	機能する；役立つ
❑ **should**	助	～であるはずだ

Chapter ❷

Part 1
写真描写

Part 2
応答

Part 3
会話

Part 4
説明文

Part 5
短文穴埋め

Part 6
長文穴埋め

Part 7
長文読解

65. 正解：(A)

Look at the graphic. What street address will Linda give Jim?

図表を見なさい。Linda はどの通りの住所を Jim に渡すだろうか？

(A) Dane

(B) Jones

(C) Market

(D) Chandelier

> 山根ポイント ホテルはハンティントンかバーモントしかないので、これを良く聞くことが大切。Gary は結局バーモントに宿泊するので Jim はそこへ迎えにいくはず ⇒ **Level 2** 余談だが、Huntington Beach はサーフィンのメッカで素晴らしい風景のビーチだ！ 若いころ学生たちを連れて行ったことがある …。

```
Chandelier 株式会社
コーポレートホテルリスト
Huntington ホテル          36市場通り
Vermont ホテル             213 Dane 通り
Huntington ビーチホテル      120 海岸通り
Gary モールホテル           210 Chandelier 通り
```

66. 正解：(C)

What will Gary do on the first day of his visit?

Gary は訪問第1日に何をするだろうか？

(A) Attend an opening ceremony　開店式典に出席する

(B) Change his itinerary　日程を変更する

(C) Meet with a client　顧客と会合を持つ

(D) Cancel an order　注文を取りやめる

> 山根ポイント first day がキーワード。これをしっかり待ち伏せれば client meeting と聞こえる ⇒ **Level 1'**

67. 正解：(A)

What does the woman say she will do?　女性は何をすると言っているか？

(A) Make a phone cal l　電話をする

(B) Pick up a person　人を車で迎える

(C) Cancel a reservation　予約を取り消す

(D) Change an itinerary　日程を変える

> 山根ポイント 定番問題。この本で学んでいる人は必ず出来なければいけない問題 ⇒ **Level 1'**

Questions 68 through 70 refer to the following conversation and graphic.

🇦🇺 M: Hi, Jean, / how are you? We have 2 ballet instructors / joining us this month / and so we have updated our class schedule. Have you received the latest schedule?

🇬🇧 W: Yes I got it yesterday. Actually, / I want to talk to you / about the new assigned time for my classes. My aerobics class used to be on Thursday mornings / and now it has been changed to Thursday afternoons. I cannot do afternoons / as I have school work.

🇦🇺 M: Got it. I'll change your shifts / from next week. But for this week, / because the schedule is already out, / I think we'll have to find a substitute aerobics instructor.

🇬🇧 W: That will be great. Thank you.

男：やあ、Jean、調子はどうだい？　今月2人のバレエ講師に加わってもらうんだ、それで教室の予定を更新したんだ。一番新しい予定表を受け取ったかい？

女：ええ、昨日受け取ったわ。実は、わたしのクラスの新しい割り当て時間について、あなたにお話ししたいのよ。私のエアロビクスのクラスは木曜の午前だったの、それが今度は木曜の午後に変更になっているの。私、午後は学業があるからできないのよ。

男：分かったよ。来週から君のシフトを変えよう。でも今週は予定表がすでに出ちゃったので、代わりのエアロビクスの講師を見つけなければならないだろうね。

女：それはすごくありがたいわ。ありがとう。

語句

❏ **ballet**	名	バレエ
❏ **update**	動	更新する
❏ **assigned**	形	割り当てられている
❏ **used to~**		かつて~だった
❏ **Got it.**		分かった。
❏ **substitute**	形	代わりの；代理の；補欠の

Chapter ❷

Part 1 写真描写

Part 2 応答

Part 3 会話

Part 4 説明文

Part 5 短文穴埋め

Part 6 長文穴埋め

Part 7 長文読解

68. 正解：(C)

What does the woman want to talk about with the man? 女性は男性と何を話したいのか？

(A) Her class requirements　彼女のクラスの必要要件

(B) Her performance　　　彼女の公演

(C) Her availability　　　彼女の（勤務の）可能性

(D) He compensation　　　彼女の報酬

> 山根ポイント 女性のせりふを待てば、I want to... と、ベタで答えが聞こえる。ただし、paraphrase に注意。available は「(人の) 都合がつく」という意味がここでは良い。(A) の class が落とし穴　⇒ **Level 2**

69. 正解：(C)

Why has the schedule been updated?　なぜ予定が更新されたのか？

(A) The gym is being renovated.　　　　　　　ジムが改装されている。

(B) The gym users requested the change.　　ジムの利用者が変更を要求した。

(C) The gym has added new instructors.　　ジムが新しい講師を加えた。

(D) The gym has lost several instructors.　ジムが数名の講師を失った。

> 山根ポイント 当然 updated（更新した）がキーワード。これを待ち伏せれば、バレーの講師を 2 人入れたので…と聞こえてくるはず　⇒ **Level 1'**

70. 正解：(B)

Look at the graphic. Who will most likely be asked to take Jean's class as a substitute instructor? 図表を見なさい。代わりの講師としてだれが Jean のクラスを受け持つだろうか？

(A) Leo

(B) Mandy

(C) James

(D) Daisy

時間割

インストラクター	クラス	時間
Leo	バレエ　上級	10:30-11:15 （木）
Mandy	エアロビクス 1	9:30-10:15 （木）
Jean	エアロビクス 2	13:00-13:45 （木）
James	エアロビクス 3	14:00-14:45 （木）
Daisy	バレエ　基礎	15:30-16:15 （木）

> 山根ポイント まずエアロビクスのクラス担当者でないといけない。後は午後を受け持てる人。James はすでに午後の別のエアロビクラスを受け持っているので、頼めるのは Mandy になる。もちろん James が無理して2講座続けることも可能だが、Jean が木曜の午前に戻るのならその代わりに Mandy がその午後に回されるのが自然だろう　⇒ **Level 3**

説明文問題　解答・解説

Questions 71 through 73 refer to the following campaign talk.

🇺🇸 Ⓦ

Thank you for coming to our New Era Kitchen Workshop! We want to show you / our latest model of built-in dishwasher Romeo X01.This dishwasher has used the latest noise reduction technology. When it operates / you can hardly hear its noise. But its most amazing feature is / that it sanitizes the dishes / when it dries them. You'll no longer have to worry about bacteria or germs. If you install this dishwasher, / I am sure you can have a good rest after every meal / rather than standing in front of the sink. Fill out the order forms now / or call us at 400-295-3827 / to place the order. The first 100 customers will enjoy a 10% discount.

訳

New Era Kitchen 講習会へようこそ！　当社のはめ込み型皿洗い機 RoemeX01 の最新モデルを皆様にご披露したいと思います。この皿洗い機には最新の騒音削減技術を使用いたしました。これが稼働する時その音はほとんど聞けません。しかし、最も驚嘆すべき特徴は乾燥させる時にお皿を消毒することなのです。皆様はもはや、細菌や病原菌を心配されることはないのです。もしこの皿洗い機を組み込まれれば、きっと毎食後に十分休息ができるのです、流しの前に立つよりもむしろ。さあ、注文表に書き込んでください、注文するために、または 400-295-3827 にお電話ください、。最初の100名のお客様は10%割引がございます。

語句

❏ era	名	時代	❏ latest	形 最新の	❏ noise	名 音；騒音
❏ built-in	組み込み一体型の					
❏ reduction	名	削減 ※ reduce 動 削減する [させる]				
❏ operate	動	稼働する [させる]；操作する			❏ can hardly	ほとんどできない
❏ sanitize	動	消毒する ※ sanitation 名 消毒			❏ no longer	もはや～ない
❏ bacteria	名	菌	❏ germ	名 病原菌	❏ I am sure...	きっと～だと思う
❏ rather than	むしろ～		❏ sink	名 流し	❏ place an order	注文をする

71. 正解：(A)

What is the workshop trying to promote? この講習会は何を販売促進しているか？

(A) A home appliance　家庭家電製品

(B) A health food　　　健康食品

(C) A detergent　　　　洗剤

(D) A noise reducer　　騒音削減機

> 山根ポイント appliance は「電化製品」。これは絶対覚えておかないといけない。apply は「応用する」すなわち「電気を応用したもの」という意味で、元は electric appliance だった　⇒ **Level 2**

72. 正解：(D)

What is the most amazing feature of the product?
この製品のもっとも驚くべき特徴は何か？

(A) It is mobile.　　　　動いて移動できる。

(B) It improves health.　健康を増進する。

(C) It recycles water.　　水をリサイクルする。

(D) It removes bacteria.　細菌を除去する。

> 山根ポイント これは簡単。amazing feature がベタで聞こえるので、そこに答えがある　⇒ **Level 1'**

73. 正解：(A)

What will the first 100 customers get? 先着100名の客は何を得るだろうか？

(A) A reduction in price　　値引き

(B) A coupon　　　　　　　クーポン券

(C) A 30-day free trial　　　30日間無料試供

(D) An extended warranty　延長保証

> 山根ポイント これも簡単。100 customers を待ち伏せれば、「10%割引」が聞こえる。これにあたる paraphrase は (A) だ。とにかく同じ内容を見抜こう!という気持ちを持つこと!　⇒ **Level 2**

Questions 74 through 76 refer to the following talk.

🇬🇧 M

I just finished my meeting / with our client Jessica. She is not quite happy / about our new packaging design / for their latest shampoo. She thinks / that the color we use / does not match the features of their latest shampoo. Jessica said / that their latest shampoo uses a combination of herbs / and aims to restore damaged hair / and make hair smooth. She wants us to use colors / that feel like forests / or fresh mornings. In her mind, / customers are not rational; / they tend to choose / whatever their eyes like. Anyway, / she wants us to rethink the color scheme. I have scheduled a call / with our design team tomorrow. I'll update you / after the call.

訳

お得意先の Jessica とのミーティングを終えたところだよ。彼女はあまり満足してないんだよ、彼らの新しいシャンプーに対してうちの新しいパッケージデザインをね。彼女はうちが使っている色が彼らの最新のシャンプーの特徴にマッチしないと思っているんだ。Jessica は彼らの最新のシャンプーは薬草を組み合わせ、損傷した髪を元に戻し、髪をなめらかにすると言ったんだ。彼女は森またはさわやかな朝を感じられるような色を使ってもらいたいと思っているんだ。彼女の考えでは、お客さんは理性的ではないんだ、すなわち見て気に入るものなら何でも選ぶ傾向があるということなんだ。まあ、ともかくも、色について考え直してほしいのさ。明日デザインチームと電話するよう予定を入れたよ。その電話の後に君に最新情報を伝えるよ。

語句

❏ match	動	～にマッチする；合う
❏ combination	名	組み合わせ
❏ herb	名	薬草
❏ aim to~		～することを狙っている
❏ restore	動	修復する
❏ smooth	形	なめらかな ※発音は [スムーズ]。スムースではない
❏ feel like~		～に感じられる
❏ mind	名	心；考え
❏ rational	形	理性的な ※要するに理屈ではなく見た目でということ
❏ whatever their eye like		彼らが見て気に入るもの何でも
❏ anyway		とにかく

Chapter②

Part 1 写真描写

Part 2 応答

Part 3 会話

Part 4 説明文

Part 5 短文穴埋め

Part 6 長文穴埋め

Part 7 長文読解

74. 正解：(C)

What is Jessica not happy about? Jessica は何に不満なのか？

(A) The shampoo's quality シャンプーの品質

(B) The shampoo's texture シャンプーの感触（肌への触れ方）

(C) The shampoo's package color シャンプーの包装の色

(D) The shampoo's price シャンプーの価格

> 山根攻 not happy とはマイナスイメージの部分を待ち伏せよ!ということ。ここではそのものずばり聞こえる　⇒ **Level 1'**

75. 正解：(D)

Why dose Jessica think "customers are not rational"?
Jessica が "Customers are not rational." と言う時、何を言いたいのか？

(A) Customers are shrewd.
顧客は抜け目ない。

(B) Customers do not know which to choose.
顧客はどちらを選んでいいのか分からない。

(C) Customers need to be coached.
顧客には指導を受けることが必要だ。

(D) Customers like products which look nice.
客は見た目がよい製品が好きだ。

> 山根攻 難問。rational が難しい単語だが、常識で分かるレベルだ　⇒ **Level 3**

76. 正解：(A)

What will the speaker do tomorrow? 話し手は明日何をするだろうか？

(A) Discuss with the design team デザインチームと話し合う

(B) Schedule another meeting with the client 顧客と別の会合を予定している

(C) Suggest a new design 新しいデザインを提案する

(D) Change the shampoo color シャンプーの色を変える

> 山根攻 例によって最後の言葉を待ち伏せる。call が聞こえれば電話すると分かる。それは「話をすること…」　⇒ **Level 2**

Questions 77 through 79 refer to the following announcement.

🇬🇧 w

We are happy to announce / the opening of our community college / for senior citizens. With support from our city council / and after three years of effort, / we've finally had a modern learning center / for our parents and all rehired people / who want to learn anything / ranging from calligraphy to handcrafts. We will have a celebration and class sign-up event / at our city hall this Tuesday morning. We have invited Cathy Holmes, / the first woman professor in our town / who is now aged 88, / to make a speech then. We will also be distributing leaflets / about the classes / available at the community college.

訳

ご年配の皆様のためのコミュニティカレッジ開校の発表をうれしく思います。当市の市議会のご支援を持ちまして、3年間の取り組みの後、ついにモダンな学習センターを持つことができました、書道から手工芸品に至るあらゆるものを学びたい私共の親たち、そしてすべてのご年配の皆様のためのね。今週火曜日の午前に市役所で祝典と申し込み行事を行います。その時スピーチをいただくために、私共はこの町で最初の女性の教授で現在88歳の Cathy Holmes さんをお招きしております。また、このコミュニティカレッジにおいて利用できる授業についてのチラシもお配り致します。

語句

❏ **community college** 地域の成人住民へ学識、教養、職業教育などを施す短大のような学校
❏ **citizen** 名 市民 ❏ **council** 名 議会
❏ **effort** 名 努力 ❏ **range from A to B** A から B へわたる
❏ **calligraphy** 名 書道 ❏ **handcrafts** 名 手工芸品
❏ **distribute** 動 配布する ❏ **available** 形 利用可能な

Chapter ❷

Part 1 写真描写

Part 2 応答

Part 3 会話

Part 4 説明文

Part 5 短文穴埋め

Part 6 長文穴埋め

Part 7 長文読解

77. 正解：(C)

What is the topic of the announcement?　発表の話題は何か？

(A) Opening of city council　　　市議会の開会

(B) Opening of a seniors' home　老人ホームの開館

(C) Opening of a school　　　　学校の開校

(D) Opening of a handcrafts shop　工芸品の店の開店

> **山根流** topic は一番大切なこと、つまり最初に来るはずなので、college の開校だとつかむ　⇒ **Level 1'**

78. 正解：(D)

Who is Cathy Holmes?　Cathy Holmes とはだれか？

(A) The best calligrapher in the community　その地域一番の書道家

(B) A woman who works as a public speaker　講演者として働く女性

(C) A woman city council member　女性市議会会員

(D) A woman who used to teach at a university　大学で教えていた女性

> **山根流** もちろん、最後の Cathy Holmes を待ち伏せするだけ。大学の教授、先生　⇒ **Level 2**

79. 正解：(A)

What will happen on Tuesday?　火曜日には何があるか／起こるか？

(A) Handouts will be passed out.　　　配布物が配られる。

(B) Souvenirs will be handed out.　　お土産品が配られる。

(C) Calligraphy classes will be held.　書道のクラスが開催される。

(D) The city mayor will give a speech.　市長がスピーチをする。

> **山根流** 当然、最後の 2 〜 3 行で出て来ると読む。Tuesday がキーワード。leaflet は handout や flyer などで言い換えられる。distribute = pass out　⇒ **Level 2**

Questions 80 through 82 refer to the following talk.

Let me walk you through all the options. We have 4 types of membership: / Standard, Pool, Lux and Eco. For Standard, / you'll have access to all the areas / except the pool. The Pool membership allows you to use the pool / but its access on Saturday / is limited to the morning only. Lux includes both Standard and Pool / and it also allows you to use our sauna. I strongly recommend Lux / as it is only 10% more expensive / than the Standard membership. The Eco option works like this: / you pay for every hour / you use our facility at an hourly rate / but there is no pool access. I will send you the membership forms. Please indicate on the forms / which membership you'd like.

訳

すべての選択肢について詳しく説明させていただきます。4タイプの会員資格がございます、すなわち、Standard, Pool, Lux そして Eco でございます。Standard ですが、これはプール以外のすべてのエリアを利用できます。Pool 会員はプールを利用することはできますが、その土曜日の利用は午前のみに限定されています。Lux（会員資格）は Standard と Pool 両方（の資格）を含んでおり、サウナもご利用できます。私は Lux を特に推奨致します、Standard よりほんの10%ほどお高いだけですので。Eco（会員資格）を選ばれれば次のようになります、すなわち、私共の施設をお使いになる毎時間ごとに1時間単位の料金で払うわけです、でもプールは利用できません。会員申込書をお送り致しましょう。どうぞ、どの会員資格を好まれるか申込書にお示しください。

語句

☐ **walk A through B**	A に B について詳しく説明する
☐ **have access to...**	～を利用できる
☐ **allow A to~**	A に～させる［許容する］
☐ **work**	動 うまく運ぶ；機能する；作用する
☐ **facility**	名 施設
☐ **indicate**	動 示す；指示する

Chapter❷

Part 1 写真描写

Part 2 応答

Part 3 会話

Part 4 説明文

Part 5 短文穴埋め

Part 6 長文穴埋め

Part 7 長文読解

80. 正解：(B)

Why does the speaker recommend the Lux membership?
話し手はなぜ Lux 会員資格を勧めるのか?

(A) It allows sauna use for the elderly.
　　年配者にサウナが使えるから。

(B) It is only a little more expensive than the Standard membership.
　　Standard 会員資格よりちょっと高いだけだから。

(C) It is the most popular membership among sports fanatics.
　　スポーツ愛好家の間では最も人気がある会員資格だから。

(D) It allows 24 hour access all year round.
　　1年中24時間利用できるから。

> 山根ポイント Lux がキーワード。これが聞こえたら待ち伏せると expensive が聞き取れるはず。allow は「容認する」、freak は「熱狂する人」　⇒ **Level 1'**

81. 正解：(D)

When is a Pool member NOT able to use the pool?
Pool 会員はいつプールをつかうことができないか?

(A) Wednesday morning　　水曜の午前

(B) Wednesday afternoon　　水曜の午後

(C) Saturday morning　　土曜の午前

(D) Saturday afternoon　　土曜の午後

> 山根ポイント NOTなのでマイナスイメージ。Pool member を待ち伏せる。すぐに土曜のプール使用について聞こえてくるはず　⇒ **Level 2**

82. 正解：(D)

What will the speaker do next? 話し手は次に何をするだろうか?

(A) Change the membership fee　　会員料金を変える

(B) Choose a membership　　会員資格を選ぶ

(C) Fill out the membership forms　　会員資格申込書に書き込む

(D) Send out the membership forms　　会員資格申込書を発送する

> 山根ポイント 例によって、最後の 2 〜 3 行に答えは必ずあると読む。I will send you the membership forms. と、I will 文が聞こえる。これが答え　⇒ **Level 1**

Questions 83 through 85 refer to the following excerpt from a meeting.

M

I want to introduce our flexible working hour policy / at today's meeting. As you know, /most of our competitors have started allowing employees / to work from home. Our board has decided to do the same. From next Monday / all full-time employees / can work from home five days a week, / provided that one must come to the office / if there is a client meeting. Before you start to work from home, / you must first install our VPN software on you laptop / for safety reasons. Also, /don't forget to log into our online attendance system / to record your working hours every day.

訳

本日の会合で当社のフレックスタイム制を紹介したいと思う。ご承知のごとく競合社のほとんどが従業員に自宅で仕事をすることを容認し始めている。我が役員会も同様なことをしようと決定した。来週の月曜日からすべての常勤職員は週に5日、自宅から仕事することができる、もし顧客との会合がある場合は出社しなければならないという条件はあるが。自宅から仕事をしようとする前に、まず安全性の理由で当社の VPN ソフトウエアをノートブックパソコンにインストールしなければならない。また、当社のオンライン出席（確認）システムにログインすることを忘れてはならない、毎日労働時間を記録するためにだ。

語句

❏ excerpt	名	抜粋
❏ flexible	形	柔軟性のある；融通の効く
❏ flexible working hour policy		可変的労働時間制 (= 勤務時間自由選択制)
❏ competitor	名	競争相手
❏ board	名	委員会；役員会
❏ provided that...		〜という条件で；もし〜なら
❏ install	動	組み込む

83. 正解：(B)

What is the purpose of the meeting? 会合の目的は何か？

(A) To provide training for the new employees
新入社員に対しての研修を提供するため

(B) To explain a new way of doing things
新しいやり方を説明するため

(C) To check attendance at the board meeting
役員会の出欠を確認するため

(D) To discuss a plan proposed by a shareholder
株主から提言された計画を話し合うため

> **山根ポイ** 話の主題だから冒頭に来るはず。新しい policy の導入だから (B)　⇒ **Level 2**

84. 正解：(D)

Why will the company start this policy? 会社はなぜこの方針を始めるのか？

(A) To increase work efficency in this IT-orientated society
この IT 志向の社会において仕事の効率を上げるため

(B) To promote work-life balance among all the employees
すべての従業員の間で仕事と家庭生活のバランスが取れるよう促進するため

(C) To save office rent in case of an emergency
緊急事態に備えて社屋賃料を節約するため

(D) To keep up with other companies in the same industry
同業の他社に後れを取らないようにするため

> **山根ポイ** 重要なことだからやはり冒頭に来る。この場合は2〜3行目に述べられている。「同業他社が皆やっているのでうちも同じことをやろうと決めた」とある。(A)(B) は常識。keep up with〜 は「〜に遅れずについていく」　⇒ **Level 2**

85. 正解：(A)

What must an employee do if he or she wants to work from home?
従業員は自宅から仕事をしたい場合、何をしなければならないか？

(A) Install software　　　　　　　　　　ソフトウエアをインストールする

(B) Download an attendance form　　　出席表をダウンロードする

(C) Change his/her laptop　　　　　　　自分のノートブックパソコンを変える

(D) Obtain approval from a supervisor　上司からの承認を得る

> **山根ポイ** work from home がキーワード。これを待ち伏せる。must とあるので「義務」を待つ。大切なことなので必ず大きく発音される　⇒ **Level 1**

Chapter ❷

Part 1 写真描写

Part 2 応答

Part 3 会話

Part 4 説明文

Part 5 短文穴埋め

Part 6 長文穴埋め

Part 7 長文読解

Questions 86 through 88 refer to the following broadcast.

 W

Here comes the local news. There will be a renovation of the city's art museum / starting from this September. The renovation is expected to take 18 months / and deliver a modernized facility with Virtual Reality rooms. This project of approximately 12 million dollars / is partly funded by Mr. Horenz, / billionaire and private painting collector. Currrently / the museum already houses several paintings / donated by Mr. Horenz. During the renovation construction, / all traffic going through the Central Square / will be closed. More information on the renovation / can be found on the website of the Buffalo City Museum.

訳

はい、地元のニュースです。市の美術館の修復がこの9月から始まります。修復は18カ月かかると予測されており、バーチャルリアリティルーム付きのモダンになった施設が誕生します。およそ1200万ドルのこのプロジェクトは一部に億万長者で私的な絵画収集家であるHorenz氏に資金を出していただいております。現在、美術館はすでにHorenz氏寄贈による数点の絵画を収蔵しております。修復工事の間はセントラル広場へ通じるすべての交通は閉鎖となります。修復に関するさらなる情報はBuffalo City Museumのウエブサイトでご覧になれます。

語句

❑ **broadcast**	名	放送
❑ **Here comes the local news.**	(倒置で強調) The local news come here. のこと	
❑ **renovation**	名	修繕；修復；改修
❑ **deliver**	動	生む
❑ **virtual reality**	仮想現実 (コンピュータにより映像化された架空の空間)	
❑ **approximately**	副	およそ
❑ **fund**	動	資金 [基金] を出す
❑ **billionaire**	名	億万長者　※ **billion**　10億
❑ **house**	動	収容する；入れる　※発音は [ハウズ]
❑ **donate**	動	寄付する

Chapter❷

Part 1 写真描写

Part 2 応答

Part 3 会話

Part 4 説明文

Part 5 短文穴埋め

Part 6 長文穴埋め

Part 7 長文読解

86. 正解：(B)

What is the radio news about? ラジオのニュースは何についてか？

(A) A museum exhibition　美術館の展覧会

(B) A construction project　工事計画

(C) An art dealer　美術商

(D) A public initiative　公的な構想

> 山根ポイント public は「公に知られている（または公共の為の）」、initiative は「構想」発音は[イニシャティヴ]。もちろん冒頭の Here come the local news. に集中。(A) にだまされないこと!　⇒ **Level 2**

87. 正解：(D)

According to the news, what is true about Mr. Horenz?
ニュースによれば、Horenz 氏にあてはまるものは？

(A) He is an architect.　彼は建築家である。

(B) He is a museum owner.　彼は美術館の所有者である。

(C) He collects sculptures.　彼は彫刻を収集している。

(D) He donated paintings.　彼は絵画を寄贈した。

> 山根ポイント もちろんキーワードは Mr. Horenz だ。これを待ち伏せすれば、億万長者で、絵の収集家と聞こえてくる　⇒ **Level 1'**

88. 正解：(C)

What will happen to the museum after 18 months?
18 カ月後美術館に何が生ずるか？

(A) New paintings will arrive in the museum.
新しい絵画が美術館に届く。

(B) It will increase its ticket price.
そのチケット価格が上がる。

(C) It will have virtual reality facilities.
バーチャルリアリティの施設が持たれる。

(D) It will be moved to Central Square.
セントラル広場に移転する。

> 山根ポイント 待ち伏せるキーワードは「18カ月」。そして、未来形（ここでは be expected to..）を待てば簡単　⇒ **Level 1**

Questions 89 through 91 refer to the following speech.

Thank you for coming to our opening ceremony. You are witnessing today / the birth of a modern research institute / dedicated to the research of cancer. For the past 20 years, / we have been in a battlefield against various cancers. I am happy / that now we can have an elite group / working in the best labs / to focus on cancer research. Only when we know the cancer better, / can we understand and manage it better. We will begin the celebration dinner in 30 minutes. But before that / Dr. Newman will give us a speech / on the latest findings on breast cancer. I hope you enjoy this / as well as dinner.

訳

開館式典へお越し下さり、ありがとうございます。皆様は癌研究に専心するモダンな研究所の誕生に今、臨席されております。私共はこの過去20年間、種々の癌との戦いの場におりました。癌研究へ集中できる最高の研究所で働くえり抜きの集団をかかえることができてうれしく思います。 癌というものを知って初めて、それを理解し、よりうまく扱うことができるのです。30分いたしましたら祝宴を始めさせていただきます。しかし、その前に Newman 博士が乳癌に関しての最新の調査結果についてスピーチをして下さいます。ディナーはもちろんのこと、このお話もご享受下さい。

語句

❏ witness	動 目撃する；臨席する；証人となる		❏ birth	名 誕生
❏ institute	名 研究施設；大学		❏ dedicated to	～に専念する
❏ lab	名 研究室[所]；実験室 =laboratory		❏ focus on~	～に焦点を合わす
❏ can we understand...	強調のため倒置になっている			
❏ manage	副 うまく扱う		❏ findings	名 調査結果；発見
❏ breast	名 胸；乳房			
❏ as well as~	～はもちろんのこと；～同様			

Chapter ❷

Part 1 写真描写

Part 2 応答

Part 3 会話

Part 4 説明文

Part 5 短文穴埋め

Part 6 長文穴埋め

Part 7 長文読解

89. 正解：(C)

What event is the speaker at? 話し手はどんなイベントに出ているのか？

(A) A memorial service　　　　　　　　追悼式典

(B) A cancer seminar　　　　　　　　　癌研修会

(C) An inauguration of some facility　　ある施設の開会式

(D) A press release　　　　　　　　　　報道発表

> 山根ポイント 冒頭に opening ceremony と述べているので開会式だと気づくが (C) の inauguration（開会式；就任式）は当然知らないので、消去法で行く！ ⇒ **Level 2**

90. 正解：(A)

What does the speaker mean when she mentions "battlefield"?
話し手は "battlefield" と言うときに何を意味しているのか？

(A) It means the fight against cancer.
　　癌との戦いを意味している。

(B) It means a newly discovered cancer.
　　新しく発見した癌を意味している。

(C) It means the resources devoted to cancer research.
　　癌研に捧げられた資源を意味している。

(D) It means a new cancer medicine.
　　新しい癌の薬を意味している。

> 山根ポイント battle は戦い、field は場で、文字どおり「戦場」を表す　⇒ **Level 2**

91. 正解：(C)

Which of the following will immediately happen after the speaker finishes talking?
話し手が話し終えたら次のどれがすぐに生じるか？

(A) There will be a dinner.　　　　　　　　夕食会がある。

(B) There will be an award ceremony.　　授賞式がある。

(C) There will be a speech.　　　　　　　　スピーチがある。

(D) There will be a lab tour.　　　　　　　研究所見学がある。

> 山根ポイント 当然最後の問題なのでトークが終わる直前の文が大事だと思って聞く。but before that の後に答えがある。テストではこの but や however そして unfortunately などの後が問いになることが非常に多いので日頃から注意しておくと良い　⇒ **Level 1**

Questions 92 through 94 refer to the following telephone conversation.

Hi, my name is Susan. I am calling about the diving courses / advertised on your website. I sent my application form / to the email address shown on your website a week ago, / but I have not yet got any response. I am wondering / if I should send my application / to a different email address / or can I apply for your courses on this call? Next month / I am moving to a country / where it is difficult to learn diving. I really want to complete my diving course / before next month. I want to apply for your "fast track" course. Please let me know / how I can submit my application. Thanks.

訳

もしもし、Susan と申します。おたくのウエブサイト（ホームページ）に広告されているダイビングコース（潜水教程）についてお電話しております。1週間前おたくのウエブサイトに出ていた E- メールのアドレスに申込書を送りましたが、まだ何もお返事いただいておりません。私の申込書は別の E- メールアドレスに送るべきなのかしら、それともこの電話でおたくのコースに申し込めるのでしょうか？というのは来月には私はダイビングを習うのが難しい田舎に引っ越すんです。来月までに、本当にダイビングコースを終了したいのです。私は速修コースに申し込みたいのです。どうやって申込書を送付したらよいのか教えてくださいな。ありがとう。

❏ **advertise** 　動　宣伝[広告]をする　　❏ **response** 　名　反応；返事
❏ **I am wondering if...** 　〜かどうかなと思っている　　❏ **track** 　名　やり方（←軌道、跡）

92. 正解：(A)

What type of business is the speaker calling?
話し手はどのようなタイプのビジネスに電話しているか?

(A) A diving school ダイビングスクール

(B) A travel agency 旅行代理店

(C) An advertisement agency 広告代理店

(D) a training center 研修センター

> 山根ポイント 冒頭にすぐ出てくる。本番でこのような簡単な問題は必ず出る　⇒ **Level 1**

93. 正解：(C)

Why is the speaker calling? 話し手はどうして電話しているのか?

(A) To make a deposit 内金を入れるため

(B) To request for a refund 返金の請求をするため

(C) To apply for a course コースに申し込むため

(D) To inqure about a course コースについて尋ねるため

> 山根ポイント ザッと聞いて「diving に申し込みたい…」という要旨がつかめるようにリスニング力を鍛えよう。(C) と (D) で悩む人がいるかも　⇒ **Level 1'**

94. 正解：(A)

Why is the speaker in a hurry? 話し手はなぜ急いでいるのか?

(A) She will leave for the country soon.
彼女はまもなく田舎へ発ちます。

(B) She has received no responses.
彼女は何の返答も得てない。

(C) She is afraid of a price increase.
彼女は価格の上昇を心配している。

(D) She needs to pass a test as soon as possible.
彼女はできるだけ早く試験に合格する必要があり。

> 山根ポイント in a hurry「急いで」とわかれば待ち伏せは簡単　⇒ **Level 2**

Questions 95 through 97 refer to the following talk and pie chart.

🇨🇦 M

We did an employee survey last week / and I am going to give you the results. The survey was anonymous / so I believe / the results are credible. As you can see, / our employees' top concern is / the lack of career paths. Employees complain / that we rarely promote from within the company. We need to address this / and let our employees feel / that they have fair opportunities to be promoted. However, / our top priority at the moment / would be to address gender discrimination. Although this is not the top employee concern, / it could bring lawsuits against the company / so it should be dealt with immediately. I have scheduled a meeting with our legal department this afternoon / to find out what actions we need to take.

訳

私共は先週従業員調査を行いました、それで私はその結果を皆様にご報告致します。調査は匿名でしたので結果は信頼できると思っています。お判りのごとく、従業員の最高の関心事は昇進への道の欠如です。従業員は社内から昇進させることがめったにないことに不満をいだいています。このことに対処し従業員に昇進できる公正な機会があると感じてもらうことが必要なのです。しかしながら、目下の最大の優先事項は性差別に対処することでしょう。これは最大の関心事ではありませんが、会社が告訴をうけることもあり得ることでしょうから、それで 即座に対処されるべきなのです。私は本日の午後、我が社の法制部との会合を予定致しました、どのような行動を起こすことが必要なのかを知るために。

語句

survey	名	調査	anonymous	形	匿名の　※発音は [アナニマス]
credible	形	信用できる	lack	名	欠如
career	名	出世；昇進　※普通は「生涯の仕事」「職歴」			
path	名	道；小道	complain	動	不平[不満]を言う
rarely	副	めったに〜ない	address	動	対処する　=deal with〜
fair	形	公正な；フェアな	opportunity	名	機会
priority	名	優先事項	gender	名	性
discrimination	名	差別	bring lawsuits to〜		〜へ告訴をもたらす
immediately	副	すぐに	legal	形	法的な
find out		(調べて)知る			

262

Chapter ②

Part 1 写真描写

Part 2 応答

Part 3 会話

Part 4 説明文

Part 5 短文穴埋め

Part 6 長文穴埋め

Part 7 長文読解

95. 正解：(A)

Why does the speaker think the results are credible?
話し手は何故結果が信用できると思っているのか？

(A) There is no way to know who voted for what.
だれが何に投票したか知る方法はない。

(B) They had similar survey results the year before.
彼らはその前の年に同じような調査結果を出した。

(C) The results were confirmed by employee interviews.
結果が従業員面接により確認された。

(D) The survey was analyzed by an expert. 結果は専門家によって分析された。

> **山根ポイント** 難問。これは anonymous が判らなければできない。ただ credible が credit(信用) からの派生語だと気が付けば (B)(C)(D) でないことは判るはず ⇒ **Level 3**

96. 正解：(D)

Look at the pie chart. What is the voting percent of the concern that the speaker wants to address immediately?
円グラフを見なさい。話し手がすぐに対処したい関心事の投票率はいくらですか？

(A) 20%

(B) 60%

(C) 15%

(D) 5%

性差別 5%
休暇を取るのが難しい 15%
研修の欠如 20%
昇進の道の欠如 60%

> **山根ポイント** immediately がキーワード。すぐに対処すべきは性差別だ。ただ gender ＝ sex と判らないと厳しい問題だが、gender discrimination は聞こえるはずだ ⇒ **Level 1'**

97. 正解：(A)

What will the speaker do this afternoon? 話し手は今日の午後何をするか？

(A) Have a meeting   会合を開く

(B) Redo the survey   調査を再度する

(C) Promote an employee 従業員を昇進させる

(D) Share the survey results 調査結果を共有する

> **山根ポイント** 簡単。this afternoon だけ待ち伏せすれば楽勝！ ⇒ **Level 1'**

Questions 98 through 100 refer to the following talk and graphic.

The next item I want to discuss / is our sales for last summer. In previous years, /summer has been the best season / for our sunscreen and related products. But this year / as you can see from the sales report, / the situation has changed. June was still OK, / but July sales dropped by 5%. August sales dropped by 15% / and September was the worst with a 25% drop. The key reason is / that one of our competitors launched a new series of products in July. That's why / our June sales were OK / but our sales started to drop since July. Their new products have lured a lot of our customers / despite all our marketing campaigns.

訳

私がお話し合いしたい次の事項は昨夏の我が社の売上です。これまで夏は我が社のサンスクリーン（日焼け防止剤）とその関連製品にとってはベストの季節でした。しかし今年は売上報告書からお判りのごとく状況は変化しております。6月はまだ大丈夫でしたが、7月の売上は5%落ち込み、8月の売上は15%ほど落ち込み、9月は25%の落ち込みで最悪でした。鍵となる理由はうちの競合他社の1つが7月に新しいシリーズ製品を発売したことです。それで、うちの6月の売上は大丈夫だったのですが、7月以来うちの売上は落ち始めたのです。彼らの新製品はうちの顧客の多くを取り込んでしまいました、うちのすべてのマーケティングキャンペーンにもかかわらず。

語句

❏ **item**　名 事項；議題　※普通は品目　　❏ **situation**　名 状況
❏ **capture**　動 捕らえる　　❏ **despite**　～にもかかわらず
❏ **marketing**　名 マーケティング；市場調査

Chapter ②

Part 1 写真描写

Part 2 応答

Part 3 会話

Part 4 説明文

Part 5 短文穴埋め

Part 6 長文穴埋め

Part 7 長文読解

98. 正解：(C)

What type of product does the speaker's company sell?

(A) Tea　　　　茶
(B) Clothing　　衣服
(C) Cosmetics　化粧品
(D) Car　　　　車

> 山根ズバ cosmetics を知らなくても消去法で簡単　⇒ **Level 2**

99. 正解：(D)

Look at the graphic. Which month is the sales refering to?
図表を見なさい。売上報告書はどの月へのものか?

(A) June　　　　　6月
(B) July　　　　　7月
(C) August　　　　8月
(D) September　　9月

> 山根ズバ 25%減っているので当然最悪の9月だ　⇒ **Level 2**

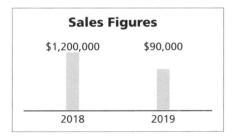

100. 正解：(C)

According to the speaker, what is the reason for the drop in sales?
話し手によれば、売上の落ち込みの理由は何か?

(A) It was extremely hot this summer.　　　　今夏は極端に暑かった。
(B) Customers complain about the quality.　　顧客が品質についてクレームをつけている。
(C) There were competing products.　　　　　競合製品があった。
(D) Marketing campaigns were insufficient.　販売促進キャンペーンが不十分だった。

> 山根ズバ マイナスイメージは何か?　competitor（競争相手）がキー　⇒ **Level 3**

---

101. 正解：(B) 中

Ms. Wada has run a small shop with ------- own savings since last year.

Ms. Wada は小さな店を経営している、自分の蓄えで、昨年以来。

(A) she　　　　　　　　　　　(B) her
(C) hers　　　　　　　　　　　(D) herself

> 山根ポイント own は「自身の (所有の)」という意味で強め。例えば my own car (マイカー)。owner と honor を混同しないように注意!

---

102. 正解：(B) 中

Construction of our new school building will ------- be completed in two months.

私たちの新しい校舎はまもなく完成します、2カ月したら。

(A) highly　副 高度に　　　　(B) soon　副 まもなく
(C) timely　形 時を得た 副 時を得て　(D) much　副 うんと

> 山根ポイント much money の much は形容詞

---

103. 正解：(D) 中

Mr. Ohara asked the publishing company ------- the deadline for his new series.

Mr. Ohara は印刷会社に頼んだ、自身の新しい連載の締め切りを延長するようにと。

(A) extend　　　名 延ばす　　(B) will extend
(C) had extended　　　　　　　(D) to extend

> 山根ポイント ask [want / tell] A to~. は「A に~するように頼む [~してほしい／~するように言う]」の意味。

---

104. 正解：(A) V

------- manufacturing costs have not significantly decreased, Takeda Co. has experienced a sharp fall in its yearly expenditure.

製造コストは目立っては減少しなかったが、タカタ社はその年間支出の急激な下落を味わった。

(A) Although　接 ~だけれども　(B) Despite　前 ~だけれども
(C) Because　接 ~なので　　　(D) Owing to　前 ~により；~に起因して

> 山根ポイント 「製造コストが目立って減少しなかったので…」とすると、後ろの文と整合性がなくなる。

聴く勉 TOEIC 講座! DL音声 144

Chapter ❷

Part 1 写真描写

Part 2 応答

Part 3 会話

Part 4 説明文

Part 5 短文穴埋め

Part 6 長文穴埋め

Part 7 長文読解

105. 正解：(A) Ⓥ

When this afternoon's business seminar ends, Dr. Hewitt will have his staff -------.

今日午後のビジネスセミナーが終われば、Dr. Hewitt は部下に会議室を清掃させるでしょう。

(A) clean 動 きれいにする ※もちろん「きれいな」という形容詞の意味もある

(B) cleaning

(C) to clean

(D) cleaned

> 山根ポ 使役動詞の make（〜に…させる）や have（〜に…してもらう）や let（〜に…させてやる）の使い方をどうしても知っておかないといけない。help も同様に help her to cook の to が無くなって help her cook となるので注意!

106. 正解：(C) Ⓥ

Hilltop Hospital used to get a lot of referrals from general practitioners, but it hasn't any -------.

Hilltop 病院は、かつては多くの紹介状を得ていた、開業医から、しかし最近では1通も得ていない。

(A) nearly 副 ほとんど　　(B) primarily 副 主に

(C) lately 副 最近　　　　(D) constantly 副 一定に

> 山根ポ any の後は referrals（紹介状）が省略されているだけ。

✎語句　❏ used to~　〜したものだった

107. 正解：(B) 中

Despite a ------- rise in oil prices, demand has stayed the same.

見た目に石油価格は上昇しているにもかかわらず、需要は同じままだ。

(A) seem 動 〜のように見える

(B) seeming 形 外観上の；もっともらしい

(C) seemed 動 （seem の過去）〜のように見えた

(D) seemingly 副 見たところ；上辺は

> 山根ポ rise は「上昇」という名詞なので、下線部には形容詞が入る。動詞は rise-rose-risen なので注意!　rise を動詞と勘違いすると「副詞だ!」と思って seemingly にしてしまう!

108. 正解：(B) Ⓥ

To make the way of paying a bonus clear, overtime work hours must be tracked -------.

ボーナスの支払い方法を明らかにするため、残業の時間は正確に追跡調査されなければならない。

(A) randomly 副 でたらめに；手当たり次第に　(B) accurately 副 正確に

(C) secretly 副 密に　(D) probably 副 多分

> 山根ポイント ボキャブラ問題なので知らなければ本番では捨てる。しかし、ここでは覚えるようにする。形容詞 accurate（正確な）も頻出!

109. 正解：(B) Ⓥ

Ms. Lawrence is ------- to apply for the managerial position at Roseville Ltd.

Ms. Lawrence は Roseville 社での管理職のポストに応募することを躊躇している。

(A) hesitate 動 hesitate to~（~に躊躇する）

(B) hesitant 形 be hesitant to~（~に躊躇している)

(C) hesitated 形 躊躇した　(D) hesitantly 副 躊躇して

> 山根ポイント 動詞と形容詞での使い方に注意!　managerial は「経営；管理の」という意味の形容詞。

110. 正解：(D) 中

Please make sure that you conclude the deal ------- next week.

必ず来週までにその取引を終えて下さいね。

(A) toward 前 ~へ向かって　(B) over 前副 ~を越えて；~にわたって

(C) at 前 ~に　(D) by 前 ~までに

> 山根ポイント by~ は「~までに」(締め切り)、till (until) ~ は「~までずっと」(継続)を表す。この2つの違いを明確に。

111. 正解：(C) 中

All AmberCreek's products, including sports gear, ------- by Priority Mail.

すべての AmberCreek 社の製品は、スポーツ用品を含んでだが、優先郵便で発送される。

(A) shipped　(B) being shipped

(C) are shipped　(D) shipping

> 山根ポイント ship は「発送 [荷送] する」という他動詞なので、主語が製品 (products) なら、「荷送りされる」となるはず。

112. 正解：(C) 中 ⋯⋯⋯⋯⋯⋯⋯⋯⋯⋯⋯⋯⋯⋯⋯⋯⋯⋯

According to the survey results, most people are ------- that the government plans to impose a higher tax on gasoline.

調査結果によると、ほとんどの人々は失望している、政府がガソリンにより高い税金を課すことに。

(A) disappoint 　動　がっかりさせる（他動詞）

(B) disappointing 　形　がっかりさせるような

(C) disappointed 　形　がっかりさせられている（がっかりしている）

(D) disappointment 　名　失望

> 山根ズバ 主語が人なので何かで「がっかりさせられている」はず。The news is disappointing.（そのニュースはがっかりさせるものだ）、など、ものや事が主語なら -ing なので注意！ interesting と interested、exciting と excited、surprising と surprised なども同じ考え方。

113. 正解：(D) 中 ⋯⋯⋯⋯⋯⋯⋯⋯⋯⋯⋯⋯⋯⋯⋯⋯⋯⋯

------- caterers charge an extra fee for cups and napkins.

ほとんどの仕出し業者は追加の料金を請求する、カップとナプキンに。

(A) Most of 　の大部分　　　　　　(B) The most 　もっとも多くの

(C) Almost 　副　ほとんど　　　　　(D) Most 　形　ほとんどの

> 山根ズバ (A) の most は名詞。「～のほとんど」であれば most of the caterers のように the が必要。almost も「ほとんど」と訳すので、間違う人が多い。注意！

114. 正解：(B) Ⅴ ⋯⋯⋯⋯⋯⋯⋯⋯⋯⋯⋯⋯⋯⋯⋯⋯⋯⋯

It will be no easy task to bend that ------- CEO to our will by Friday.

簡単な仕事じゃないだろう、あの頑固な CEO を金曜日までに僕らの望みに屈服させるのはね。

(A) elegant 　形　上品な　　　　　 (B) stubborn 　形　頑固な

(C) apologetic 　形　謝罪の；弁解の　(D) accessible 　形　近づきやすい

> 山根ズバ ボキャブラ力なので本番では知らなければパス。 will は「意志；望み；願い」。

115. 正解：(B) 中 ⋯⋯⋯⋯⋯⋯⋯⋯⋯⋯⋯⋯⋯⋯⋯⋯⋯⋯

Consumers may not even have ------- likes or dislikes at the time of purchase.

消費者は気づくほどの好き嫌いすら無いのかもしれない、購入に際しては。

(A) notice 　動　気づく　　　　　 (B) noticeable 　形　気づけるほどの；人目を引く；目立つ

(C) noticeably 　副　目立って　　　(D) noticing 　notice の -ing 形

> 山根ズバ likes, dislikes が名詞だと気づけば簡単。consumer と purchase も大事な単語なのでこの機会に覚えよう。

116. 正解：(A) 中

Both the dollar and the euro have fallen ------- the yen this past week because of the coronavirus outbreak.

ドルとユーロは両方とも先週円に対して落ちている、コロナウイルスの発生のために。

(A) against 前 ～に対して
(B) for 前 ～に対して；～の為に
(C) into 前 ～の中に
(D) to 前 ～へ

> 山根ポイント for~ は「～に対して」で、よい意味で使う。ここは「～対［対決］」の意味なので against が正解。

117. 正解：(B) 中

Save 15% on every delivery order from Aruku ------- by registering online and entering a coupon code.

アルクへの毎回の配達注文に15%節約しなさい、ただ単にオンライン登録しクーポンのコードを入力することでね。

(A) simplify 動 簡単にする
(B) simply 副 簡単に
(C) simplicity 名 簡単；簡素
(D) simplified simplify の過去・過去分詞形

> 山根ポイント by~ にひっかかってはいけない。これは受け身ではない！ by~ を修飾する副詞。

118. 正解：(C) 中

Mr. Pak, the new CEO., is ------- to improving his staff's morale to get over this crisis.

新CEO の Mr. Pak は部下の士気向上に専念している、この危機を乗り越えるために。

(A) commit 動 委ねる；専念させる
(B) commitment 名 言質；誓約；献身
(C) committed
(D) committing

> 山根ポイント commit は曲者動詞だ。一番簡単な覚え方は committee（委員会）＝「コミットされているもの＝信任を委ねられているもの」、なので「commit ＝委ねる」と覚える。本問では「～へ委ねられている＝専心している」となるので受け身になることが重要。受け身にしないで Mr. Pak commits himself to~ としても良い。

119. 正解：(A) V

Few members of staff ------- in the company retreat, so it has been cancelled.

社員のほとんどの者が会社の慰安旅行に登録しなかった、そこで、それは中止された。

(A) enrolled 形 enroll（登録［入会］する）の過去形
(B) defeated 形 defeat（打ち負かす）の過去形
(C) relieved 形 relieve（和らげる）の過去形
(D) excepted 形 except（除く）の過去形

> 山根ポイント ボキャブラだから知らなければパス！ en + roll（巻物）の中に入れるから。

Chapter❷

Part 1 写真描写

Part 2 応答

Part 3 会話

Part 4 説明文

Part 5 短文穴埋め

Part 6 長文穴埋め

Part 7 長文読解

120. 正解：(A) 中

The government announced that the ------- adjusted unemployment rate reached 6% in June.

政府は発表した、季節調整済みの失業率が6月には6% に達したと。

(A) seasonally　副　季節的に；季節毎に　　(B) seasoned　season (味付けする) の過去形

(C) seasonal　形　季節的な；季節毎の　　(D) season　名　季節　動　味付けする

> 山根ポイント　形容詞の seasonal にしたくなるが、副詞でないとだめ。なぜなら adjusted（調整されている）という形容詞にのみかかっているから。

121. 正解：(C) Ⅴ

In the recession, consumers are always ------- closer attention to their spending.

不景気なおりには、消費者はいつもその支出により細かい注意を払っている。

(A) making　　　　　　　　　(B) asking

(C) paying　　　　　　　　　(D) holding

> 山根ポイント　pay attention to... （〜に注意を払う；留意する）を知らなければできない。always + 進行形は癖や習慣を表す表現。

122. 正解：(D) Ⅴ

------- a bad thing, filing for bankruptcy is a way for the insurance company to survive.

悪いことというよりは (むしろ)、破産申請はその保険会社が生き残るには一つの方法だ。

(A) Due to　前　〜のせいで　　(B) Because　接　〜なので

(C) Except　前　〜を除いて　　(D) Rather than　副　〜というよりはむしろ

> 山根ポイント　これも知らなければパスだがこれを機会に覚えよう。file は「綴じ込む；ファイルする」だが、転じてファイルしたものを提出することから file for〜（〜を申請をする）という意味になる。

123. 正解：(A) 中

According to today's news, Henry Auto has made significant ------- in developing on all-electric vehicles.

本日のニュースによれば、Henry Auto 社は目覚ましい進歩をした、オール電化（全電動）の車の開発に。

(A) progress　　　名　進歩　動　進歩する　※ただし動詞は progress と e にアクセントあり

(B) progression　名　「進歩」の意味もあるが、「進行；行列」の意味で多く使われる

(C) progressive　形　進歩的な　　(D) progressed

> 山根ポイント　make progress in 〜 は「〜において進歩する」。これを make progression in〜 とは言わない。

124. 正解：(B) Ⅴ

Every one of you can purchase any car of your own company in six equal ------- payments.

皆さんのだれもが自身の会社のどんな車でも購入できます、6カ月均等月賦で。

(A) initiative　　名　構想　　　　**(B)** installment　名　割賦
(C) appreciation　名　感謝　　　　**(D)** acquisition　名　取得

> 山根ポイント ボキャブラ問題だが、いずれも大事な単語。install は「設置する」という動詞だがその名詞は2つあり installation（設置）と installment（分割払い）なので注意。ここでは six equal installment payments の代わりに six equal installments とも言える。

125. 正解：(D) 中

We've selected ten people for interviews ------- those who've applied for this position.

私共は面接に10名を選びました、このポストに応募している人達の中で。

(A) as to　　〜に関して　　　　**(B)** of　　　　〜の
(C) such as　〜のような　　　　**(D)** among　　〜の中 [間] に　※ from among... としても正しい

> 山根ポイント (from) among〜（〜の中から）。those が people の意味で使われることが多いので注意!

126. 正解：(B) Ⅴ

Alvinson Group has made a ------- investment in the company, but they think it's time to get out.

Alvinson Group はその会社に相当な投資をした、しかしもう脱ける時だと考えている。

(A) skillful　　形　熟練した　　　　**(B)** substantial　形　相当な
(C) conditional　形　条件付きの　　　**(D)** numerous　形　数多くの

> 山根ポイント substance は「物質；実質」という意味。形容詞 substantial にも「実質的な」という意味があるので注意。

127. 正解：(D) 中

Recent research has suggested that the government should be a little more ------- on the new consumption tax.

最近の調査は示唆している、政府は新しい消費税に対してもう少し明確にすべきだと。

(A) specifically　副　はっきりと；特に　　**(B)** specify　動　明確に述べる
(C) specification　名　詳説；仕様（スペックのこと）　**(D)** specific　形　はっきりとした；明確な

> 山根ポイント a little more（もう少し；もっと）に気をとられて名詞を選んではだめ。

128. 正解：(C) Ⅴ

The latest survey shows that consumer prices have been ------- stable in the last few months.

最新の調査は示している、消費者物価はこの2、3カ月比較的安定していると。

(A) diligently　副　勤勉に；入念に　　(B) productively　副　生産的に

(C) relatively　副　比較的；相対的　　(D) carefully　副　注意深く

> 山根ポイント　ボキャブラ問題だが、(C) と (D) は知っていて当然。

129. 正解：(A) 中

The question is ------- will be the next to go as downsizing continues.

問題はだれが次に辞めて行くかだ、企業縮小が続くにつれて。

(A) who　　　　　　　　　　　(B) those

(C) that　　　　　　　　　　　(D) which

> 山根ポイント　これは難問。who（だれ）または which（どれ）という疑問詞が来ることが分からないといけない。go には「無くなる」「消える」「辞める」などの意味がある。

130. 正解：(D) Ⅴ

Entering a recession phase, some companies tend to intentionally ------- for bankruptcy.

景気後退の段階に入ると、幾らかの会社は意図的に倒産申請をする傾向がある。

(A) apply　　動　(~for) 応募する；(~to) 適用する

(B) suit　　　動　~に似合う；~に適合する

(C) search　動　探す

(D) file　　　動　申請する　※普通は「ファイルする；綴じる；整理する」の意味

> 山根ポイント　前半に出題しているが…覚えているだろうか？ some companies... の訳し方は「~する会社もある」と習ったと思うが、そのまま頭から意味を取っていき、速読力を養おう!

長文穴埋め問題　解答・解説

Questions 131-134 refer to the following article.

TRAVEL TIPS

One area in which all nationalities seem **131.(B)** alike is in liking privacy when travelling. Business executives from Hong Kong particularly dislike getting into conversation with **132.(C)** fellow passengers, followed by the British, Americans, Germans and Singaporeans. **133.(C)** The exception seems to be the French. They are most **134.(D)** likely of all to chat to their neighbors on a flight.

 訳

旅のヒント

あらゆる国籍の人々において似たりよったりのように見える一つの領域は、旅をする際にプライバシーを好むということにある。香港の大物ビジネスパーソンたちは特に一緒に乗り合わせている乗客と会話することを嫌う、次いでイギリス人、アメリカ人、ドイツ人、そしてシンガポール人と続く。例外はフランス人になりそうである。彼らは全ての国籍の人の中でもっともお隣さんとおしゃべりしそうである、機上で。

Chapter❷

Part 1
写真描写

Part 2
応答

Part 3
会話

Part 4
説明文

Part 5
短文穴埋め

Part 6
長文穴埋め

Part 7
長文読解

131. 正解：(B) Ⓥ

(A) awake 形 目覚めて
(B) alike 形 〜に似ている
(C) afraid 形 怖い；心配である
(D) aware 形 気づいている

山根ポイント alike と同様に like も形容詞だが A＝B の形では使えない。

132. 正解：(C) Ⓥ

(A) peer 名 同等の者；同僚
(B) foreign 形 外国の
(C) fellow 形 仲間[同士]の 名 仲間；同士
(D) elderly 形 年配の

山根ポイント fellow〜 を使うと「一緒の仲間の」

133. 正解：(C)

(A) Next come the French. 次にはフランス人だ。
(B) The best example is the French. もっともよい例はフランス人だ。
(C) The exception seems to be the French. 例外はフランス人でありそうだ。
(D) Of course, the French are among them. もちろん、フランス人が彼らの中にある。

山根ポイント 直前の文で会話嫌いの国の人種を述べているが、「フランス人は話し好きそうだ」と後の文で述べているので。

134. 正解：(D)

(A) likeness 名 類似、見せかけ
(B) liking 名 好み
(C) like 形 似ている ※もちろん「好き」という動詞の意味もある
(D) likely 形 〜しそうだ；〜らしい

山根ポイント これは難問。of all を「全ての」と考えてしまうとどうしても名詞にしたくなるが、この of all は最上級があることを見抜いて「全ての中で」と解釈すると be likely to〜（〜しそうである）が見えてくる。

Questions 135-138 refer to the following letter.

Dear Joan,

Thank you very much for your inquiry and the interest you 135.(A) showed in our firm the other day. 136.(D) If you are still interested in joining us, please contact us. If you do not do so by June 30, we will assume you no longer wish to 137.(A) be considered for possible employment opportunities. Please do not call, 138.(C) because at present we are not in a position to discuss details of possible employment opportunities.

Again, thank you for your interest in William Royce Associates.

Sincerely,

Keith Mackenzie

H. R. Director

訳（手紙本文のみ）

先日は、お尋ねと私共の会社に興味を示してくださったこと感謝致します。もし、まだ私共へのご参加にご興味がおありでしたら、どうぞご連絡下さい。もし、6月30日までのご連絡がなければ、もはや雇用機会の可能性への考慮はお望みではないと推測させていただきます。お電話はなさらないで下さい。と申しますのは、私共は現在雇用機会可能性の詳細を検討する立場におりませんので。
再度、貴方様が William Royce Associates にご興味を持ってくださったことに感謝致します。

Chapter ②

Part 1 写真描写

Part 2 応答

Part 3 会話

Part 4 説明文

Part 5 短文穴埋め

Part 6 長文穴埋め

Part 7 長文読解

135. 正解：(A)

(A) showed　　過去形　　　　　　(B) show　　動　示す

(C) have shown　現在完了形　　　　(D) showing　show の ing 形

> 山根ポイント このように、時制を問う問題は必ず1〜2問出る。the other day（先日）が決め手。

136. 正解：(D)

(A) Last year you expressed you were interested in joining us.
昨年、貴方は当方に加わられることに興味があるとおっしゃいました。

(B) Continued growth of our business may create a number of new openings.
私共のビジネスのたゆまぬ成長が数多くの新しい機会を生み出すかも知れない。

(C) I very much look forward to hearing from you as soon as possible.
できるだけ早くご連絡があることをとても楽しみにしています。

(D) If you are still interested in joining us, please contact us.
もし、まだ私共へのご参加にご興味がおありでしたら、どうぞご連絡下さい。

> 山根ポイント 直後の文 If you do not do so... これが決め手!

137. 正解：(A) 中

(A) be considered

(B) consider　　　　　　　動　考慮する

(C) consideration　　　　　名　考慮

(D) be considerable　　considerable は　形　考慮すべき；相当な

> 山根ポイント you から見れば「考慮される」方だから。

138. 正解：(C) 中

(A) though　　接　〜だけれども

(B) when　　　接　〜の時に

(C) because　　接　〜なので

(D) while　　　接　〜の間；〜の一方

> 山根ポイント 「電話をしないで!」と言って、その後にその理由を述べているので。

Questions 139-142 refer to the following advice.

Research has shown that 139.(D) following a healthy eating plan can reduce the risk of 140.(A) developing high blood pressure. Study results indicated that high blood pressure levels were reduced by an eating plan that focuses 141.(C) on fruits, vegetables, and low-fat dairy foods.

Diet alone, however, is not enough. 142.(D) It must be accompanied by regular exercise. The best thing is probably to start gently by walking for 30 minutes at least twice a week.

調査によれば（⇒調査が〜を示した）健康的な食事計画が高血圧を発症するリスクを減らすということだ。研究結果によれば（⇒研究結果が〜を示した）高血圧のレベルは食事計画により減じた、果物、野菜、そして低脂肪の乳製品に焦点を合わす食事計画にだ。
しかしながら、食事療法（ダイエット）だけでは十分ではない。それには規則的な運動が伴わなければならない。ベストなのは多分徐々に始めることだ、少なくとも週に2回、30分間歩くことによって。

139. 正解：(D)

(A) follows 動 ～に従う (B) followed

(C) being followed (D) following 名 従うこと

> **山根ポイ** follow（他動詞）の使い方に注意。ここでは「～に従うこと」と動名詞になっている。他動詞での例文は、Please follow me.（私についていらっしゃい）やSpring follows winter.（春は冬のあとに来る）やFollow the rule.（ルールに従え）、Do you follow me?（私の言うことが分かりますか?）など。自動詞ならI followed after him.（彼の後について行った）など。分詞構文でのfollowing～ と (being) followed by～ の違いに注意! Following Jiro, Ken went into the room.（ジローの後について、ケンは部屋に入っていった）は、following は前置詞になっているとも考えられる。また Ken went into the room, followed by other students.（ケンが部屋に入っていった、そして他の学生たちがあとに続いた）なども Part5 と 6 で頻出!

140. 正解：(A)

(A) developing 動 develop（発達［発症］する）の -ing 形

(B) avoiding 動 avoid（避ける）の -ing 形

(C) improving 動 improve（改善する）の -ing 形

(D) obtaining 動 obtain（努力して得る (=get)）の -ing 形

> **山根ポイ** develop が「発達［発展］する」であることはだれでも知っている。「発症する」という意味があることに注意。

141. 正解：(C)

(A) to (B) in

(C) on (D) for

> **山根ポイ** focus on ～で「焦点を～に合わせる」の意味を表す。

142. 正解：(D)

(A) It costs a lot to maintain the family budget.
家庭の予算を維持するには費用が多くかかる。

(B) How about looking for other nutritious food?
他の栄養のある食べ物を探すのはどうですか?

(C) How about joining a gym or a health club?
ジムとかヘルスクラブに入るのはどうですか?

(D) It must be accompanied by regular exercise.
それには規則的な運動が伴われなければならない。

> **山根ポイ** 直前に「ダイエットだけでは十分ではない」とあるので、「運動が伴わないと…」と続くと整合性がある。

Questions 143-146 refer to the following e-mail message.

Dear Sir/Madam,

My father will **143.(C)** turn 70 on August 29 this year, and I would like to buy him a special gift for the **144.(A)** occasion. He loves reading novels. One book that I know he loves is "Snow Country" by Y. Kawabata. **145.(B)** I was wondering if you could find a first edition of this for me. I have no idea how much a first edition of this book would cost, and so I would be very **146.(C)** grateful if you could send me an estimate.

Look forward to hearing from you soon.

Best regards,
Sally Nakamura

訳 （手紙本文のみ）

父は今年8月29日で70歳になります、それで私は彼にこの特別な日に贈り物を買いたいのです。彼は小説を読むのがとても好きなのです。私が知っている、彼の愛する1冊の本は川端康成の「雪国」です。この本の（私に代わって）初版本を見つけていただけるかなと思っているのですが。この本の初版本がいくらするのか全く見当がつきません、それで、もし見積書を送っていただければありがたいのですが。
迅速なお返事をお待ちしています。
敬具

Chapter❷

Part 1 写真描写

Part 2 応答

Part 3 会話

Part 4 説明文

Part 5 短文穴埋め

Part 6 長文穴埋め

Part 7 長文読解

143. 正解：(C)

(A) be 動 ～になる　　　　　　　(B) come 動 来る

(C) turn 動 ～になる　　　　　　(D) become 動 ～になる

> 山根流 年齢はそれで終わるのではなくそこは単なる通過点（曲がり角）だと考えられるので、be や become でなく turn を使うのが正しい。

144. 正解：(A)

(A) occasion 名 特別な機会　　　(B) opportunity 名 機会

(C) incident 名 出来事　　　　　(D) moment 名 瞬間

> 山根流 occasion は、普通は「機会；場合」だが、「特別な日＝祝日［祝典］」の意味もあるので注意。

145. 正解：(B)

(A) I came across an advertisement for your book service on the Internet.
私はネットでお宅の本のサービスへの広告を偶然見つけました。

(B) I was wondering if you could find a first edition of this for me.
（私に代わって）この本の初版本を見つけていただけるかなと思っているのですが。

(C) I would be happy to know the cost will be within my budget.
費用が予算以内だとうれしいのですが。

(D) I'm afraid that it will take a long time to find a good one.
よい本を探すのに長い時間がかかるのではと思います。

> 山根流 直後の文に「初版本がいくらするのか分かりませんが…」とあるので。

146. 正解：(C)

(A) thanks 名 感謝　　　　　　　(B) appreciate 動 感謝する

(C) grateful 形 感謝して　　　　(D) favorable 形 有利な

> 山根流 be grateful to～ なら「～に感謝する」。I appreciate it if... ならこれも正解。

Questions 147-148 refer to the following advertisement.

New Store Open !

312 Hogan Avenue

June 2

We feature second-hand books / on literary classics, novels, religion, poetry, painting, photography, architecture, philosophy and critical theory. We carry books / in English, / French, / Italian, / German / and Spanish.

Opening ceremony and seminar on June 2:
Harold Winston, author of World Without Maps, will facilitate discussions / on the latest trend in contemporary novels.

Coffee, refreshments and book coupons / will be provided.
The event is free. We hope to see you there.

訳

新店オープン!　Hogan 通り312番地　6月2日

当店では古典文学、小説、宗教、詩歌、絵画、写真、建築、哲学そして批判理論に関する中古本を目玉商品にしております。当店では英語、フランス語、イタリア語、ドイツ語そしてスペイン語の本を扱っております。

開店式典とセミナーは6月2日です。

World Without Maps の著者、Harold Winston は現代小説の最新の傾向に関する討論を盛り上げてくれます。

コーヒー、軽食、そして本のクーポン券が提供されます。

イベントは無料です。会場（そちら）でお会いできることを楽しみにしています。

語句

❏ **feature** 動　〜を特徴とする；〜を目玉にする　　❏ **carry** 動　（商いとして）扱う
❏ **author** 名　著者　　❏ **facilitate** 動　助長する；促進する

Chapter ❷

Part 1
写真描写

Part 2
応答

Part 3
会話

Part 4
説明文

Part 5
短文穴埋め

Part 6
長文穴埋め

Part 7
長文読解

147. 正解：(D)

What most likely is World Without Maps?　World Without Maps は何だろう？

(A) A book on geography　　　地理の本

(B) A book on baking　　　パン焼きの本

(C) A book on architecture　　建築の本

(D) A novel　　　　　　　　小説

> 山根爽　contemporary novel とずばりある　⇒ **Level 1**

148. 正解：(C)

What will happen on June 2?　6月2日に何が起こるか？

(A) There will be a book signing ceremony.　　本のサイン会がある。

(B) A new book will be released.　　　　　　新しい本が発売される。

(C) Coupons will be available.　　　　　　　クーポン券が手に入る。

(D) Discounts will be available.　　　　　　割引が利用できる。

> 山根爽　コーヒー、軽食のあとにクーポン券が出てくる　⇒ **Level 1**

Questions 149-150 refer to the following e-mail.

From: info@mayflowerresort.com
To: j.swartz@gladmail.com
Subject: Re: question re-room
Date: April 23

Mr. Swartz,

Thank you for choosing us. Your reservations of 2 king-size rooms / have been completed. Attached please find your reservation details. I am sorry / that we don't have museum tours / but we do know a travel agency / that arranges such tours. If you would like to sign up for a museum tour, / please fill out the attached form, / and we will pass that / to the travel agency.

Thanks.

Alan Douglas
Mayflower Resort

訳（件名とメール本文のみ）

件名：Re: 部屋予約についての質問

当方を選んでいただきありがとうございます。特大のお部屋2室のご予約承っております。添付しております予約の詳細をご覧ください。あいにく当方には博物館ツアーはご用意しておりませんが、そのようなツアーを手配している旅行代理店を確かに存じております。もし博物館ツアーにお申し込みなさりたいのでしたら、添付の申込書にお書き込み下さい、そうなさいましたら、当方でその旅行代理店へ回させていただきます。

ありがとうございます。

Alan Douglas
Mayflower Resort

Chapter❷

Part 1
写真描写

Part 2
応答

Part 3
会話

Part 4
説明文

Part 5
短文穴埋め

Part 6
長文穴埋め

Part 7
長文読解

 語句

❑ **complete** 　[動]　もれなく記入する　=fill out
❑ **attached** 　[形]　添付されている　※本来は You'll find.....attached. の語順になるはずだが、強調のため attached が前に出される。
❑ **do** 　〜ですとも　※強調
❑ **sign up for〜** 　〜に申し込む

149. 正解：(D) ···

What most likely is Mayflower Resort? 　Mayflower Resort は何であろうか？

(A) An aquarium 　水族館
(B) A botanic garden 　植物園
(C) A travel agency 　旅行代理店
(D) A hotel 　ホテル

> 山根ポイント 冒頭の文に king-size room の予約とある　⇒ Level 2

150. 正解：(C) ···

What should Mr. Swartz do if he wants to join a museum tour?
Mr. Swartz は博物館ツアーに参加したければ何をすべきか？

(A) Make a deposit 　保証金を払う
(B) Contact a travel agency 　旅行代理店に連絡をとる
(C) Complete a form 　申込書に書き込む
(D) Sign a contract 　契約書に署名する

> 山根ポイント museum tour がキーワード。fill out the form のパラフレーズが complete the form　⇒ Level 2

Questions 151-153 refer to the following article.

SAN FRANCISCO (May1)-Monsoon has announced today its sale / to Mustang, a NY based steakhouse, / for 13 million USD. Monsoon has been one of the most successful restaurant chains / with over 20 branches in California. Market was caught by surprise.

Monsoon started from a family bakery 60 years ago. Alan Roland, / the founder, was only 10 years / when his father asked him / to help in the family bakery. When Alan was 18, / the family bakery was so successful / that it has turned itself / into a restaurant serving steak meals. At 25, / Alan became the owner of the family restaurant / with 3 branches in San Francisco. Two years later / he changed the style of the restaurant / by making it less fancy / while sticking to the principle / that its food was unbeatable. Such a move brought the cost down / and boosted the profits by 150%. By 2014, / Monsoon has become one of the most successful steak chains in California. Alan says / he is about to retire / and wants to cash out the business. Market speculates other reasons.

訳

サンフランシスコ（5月1日）Monsoon は本日ニューヨークに本店を置くステーキハウスの Mustang へ1300万米ドルで自社売却したことを発表した。Monsoon はカリフォルニアに20以上の支店を持つもっとも成功したレストランチェーンの一つなのだ。市場は驚きに包まれた。

Monsoon は60年前家族経営のパン屋から始まったのだ。創始者の Alan Roland は父親が彼に家族のパン屋を手伝うように頼んだときほんの10歳だった。Alan が18歳だった時、この家族経営のパン屋は大変成功したのでステーキの食事を出すレストランへと店を変えたのだ。25歳のとき Alan はサンフランシスコに3つの支店を持つファミリーレストランのオーナーになった。2年後レストランのスタイルを変えたのだった、料理は他に負けないという原則に固執する一方で高級さを抑える事によって。そのような進展はコストダウンをもたらし利益を150%ほど押し上げた。2014年までに、Monsoon は カリフォルニアにおいて最も成功したステーキチェーンの一つになったのだ。Alan は言う、もうまさにリタイアしようと思っている、商売は現金化しよう、と。市場は他に理由があると推測している。

語句

❑ **be caught by surprise**	驚かされる；不意をつかれる		❑ **founder**	動	創始者
❑ **so...that** 構文	大変…なので〜		❑ **turn A into B**		AをBに変える
❑ **fancy**	形	超高級な；法外な値段の；奇抜な	❑ **stick to〜**		〜に固執する
❑ **principle**	名	原理；原則	❑ **unbeatable**	形	打ち負かされることのない
❑ **boost**	動	押し上げる；強化する	❑ **be about to〜**		まさに〜しようとしている
❑ **speculate**	動	思索 [推測] する　※「投機する」という意味もある			

Chapter②

Part 1
写真描写

Part 2
応答

Part 3
会話

Part 4
説明文

Part 5
短文穴埋め

Part 6
長文穴埋め

Part 7
長文読解

151. 正解：(B)

What does the article indicate about Monsoon?
Monsoon について記事には何と出ているか？

(A) It started from a family restrant.　ファミリーレストランから始まった。

(B) It maintains the principle that food should be delicious.
食べ物はおいしくあるべきだという原則を維持している。

(C) It succeeded in baking business and Alan became its owner.
パンを焼くことで成功して Alan がそのオーナーになった。

(D) It opended its first branch when Alan was 25.
Alan が25歳のとき最初の支店を開いた。

> 山根ズバ これは難問。最後の方まで読まないとできない。このような問題の場合、ざっと読んで×を出していくと良い　⇒ **Level 2**

152. 正解：(D)

How did Alan change the style of Monsoon after he became the owner?
Alan はオーナーになった後 Monsoon のスタイルをどのように変えたか？

(A) He renovated the restaurant.　彼はレストランを改装した。

(B) He increased the price.　彼は値段を上げた。

(C) He changed the menu.　彼はメニューを変えた。

(D) He focused on food taste.　彼は食べ物の味に焦点を合わせた。

> 山根ズバ オーナーになったところを読む。(A)(B)(C) はざっと読んだだけですぐ×が出せるはず　⇒ **Level 3**

153. 正解：(C)

Which of these did Alan NOT do in his life?
アランが彼の人生でしなかったのはこれらのうちどれか？

(A) He became a member of the staff of his family bakery when he was very young.
幼い頃、家族のパン屋のスタッフになった。

(B) He was asked by his father to help with his business.
彼は父親から彼のビジネスを手伝うように頼まれた。

(C) Since he was satisfied with his success, Alan wanted to quit his job.
成功に満足していたので、アランは仕事を辞めたいと思った。

(D) When he was around 27, Alan decided to serve not expensive but delicious food at his restaurant.
27歳の頃、アランは自分のレストランで高価ではなく美味しい料理を提供することに決めた。

> 山根ズバ 全文をざっと読めないとできない、すなわち時間がかかる問題。成功したのでやめたかったかどうかはわからないので (C) が正解　⇒ **Level 3**

Questions 154-155 refer to the following e-mail.

To: Catherine Leeds
From: Lucy Geller
Subject: Re: new open position
Date: May 2

Dear Catherine,

My name is Lucy Geller / and I'm a lead recruiter with Talent, Inc.
I'm currently looking to fill a position / of a customer service specialist / in a real estate company based in Boston / and I am wondering / if you may be interested in this position.
In this role, / you will work as a customer service specialist / in a famous real estate company / and handle requests from customers / on daily bases.

　　　Client's requirements on the candidate:
　　　A collaborative mindset;
　　　Highly responsive in dealing with repetitive requests; and
　　　Attentive to details and highly organized.

If you are interested in the above position, / please let me know.

Thanks,
Lucy

 訳

件名 :Re: 新しい空ポスト
Catherine へ
私は Lucy Geller と申しまして、Talent 社の主席採用担当者です。
私は現在ボストンに本社を置く不動産会社の顧客サービス担当の専門家のポスト補充を検討しております、そこであなたさまにはこのポストにご興味がおありかどうかなと思っております。
この役割におきましては、有名な不動産会社の顧客サービス担当の専門家として勤務され、日々顧客から

Chapter②

Part 1 写真描写

Part 2 応答

Part 3 会話

Part 4 説明文

Part 5 短文穴埋め

Part 6 長文穴埋め

Part 7 長文読解

の要求を処理することになります。

クライアントからの候補者への要件

協力的な考え方の人

繰り返される要求に対処するのに大いに受け答えできること

そして細かいことに気を配り、非常に理路整然としていること

もし上記ポストにご興味がおありになれば、お知らせください。

Thanks,

Lucy

語句

- ❏ **look to~** 〜しようと検討 [注視] する
- ❏ **mindset** 名 考え方
- ❏ **repetitive** 形 繰り返される
- ❏ **organized** 形 きちんとしている
- ❏ **collaborative** 形 協力的な
- ❏ **responsive** 形 受け答えできる
- ❏ **attentive to...** 〜に気を配る

154. 正解：(C)

Why was the e-mail written? このメールはなぜ書かれたのか？

(A) **To sell a service**
サービスを提供するため

(B) **To respond to a customer complaint**
顧客のクレームに答えるため

(C) **To encourage the recipient to apply for a job**
メールを受け取った人に仕事へ応募することを勧めるため

(D) **To describe an employee benefit**
従業員給付金について説明するため

> 山根ポイント メール、手紙の場合は「Subject, Re（件名）」がとても大切。これだけで (C) と分かる ⇒ Level 2

155. 正解：(C)

What is suggested of Talent, Inc.? Talent 社に関して何が分かるか？

(A) **It is a real estate company.** 不動産会社である。

(B) **It is based in Boston.** ボストンに本拠を置いている。

(C) **It is a headhunter company.** ヘッドハンティングの会社である。

(D) **It is looking to hire a specialist.** 専門家の雇用を検討している。

> 山根ポイント 1行を読んですぐに派遣会社だと気づいたと思う。その中でも headhunter の文字どおり「頭を狩る人」。専門技術を持って人の指導にあたれるような有能な人材を一つの会社から引き抜き他社へ売り込む会社。最近、非常に脚光を浴びている。

Questions 156-158 refer to the following e-mail.

From: alumni@winston.edu
To: s.heathcliff@gladmail.com
Date: May12 2020
Subject: Join us in ocean talk

Dear alumni:

The Winston Environmental Society invites fellow Winston alumni for a discussion on:

    Plastics in Ocean and Our Responses
    Led by Professor Mark Cohen
    Wednesday, May 20, 2020
    12:00pm
    Boom Webinar

Professor Cohen will give remarks and take questions on issues / such as impact of plastics dumping, state (federal) orders on ocean protection, / ethical issues regarding over-fishing, latest technology on plastics disposal and many other interesting issues / that we face at this moment.

Professor Cohen is an alumni of Winston. He majored in Biotechnology & Bioethics. Since 2010, / he has been a professor at Lincoln University for 10 years.

Professor Cohen has published over 30 articles on ocean protection / and is one of the world's leading experts / on ocean environmental issues. Cohen is the author, co-author, editor, or co-editor / of more than fifteen books.

    Register for Virtual Talk
    Advanced registration required
    The event link will be included in your confirmation email.
    Questions? Please email info@winston.alumni.edu.

訳（メール本文のみ）

件名：海洋の話にご一緒ください。
同窓生の皆様へ、
Winston 環境協会は Winston 大の同窓生のみなさんを次の討論会にお誘いいたします。
　海中のプラスティック製品と我々の反応　　　　　指導：Mark Cohen 教授
　2020 年5月20日水曜日12時　　　　　　　　　Boom ウエブセミナー
Cohen 教授が以下のような問題に所見を述べ、質問を受けます――プラスティックごみ投棄の影響、海洋保護に関しての州（連邦政府）の命令、過度な漁獲に関する倫理的問題、プラスティックごみ廃棄への最新の技術、そして私たちが目下直面している多くの興味深い問題のような。
Cohen 教授は Winston 大の同窓生です。彼は生物工学と生物倫理学を専攻しました。2010年から10年リンカーン大の教授をしておられます。Cohen 教授は海洋保護に関して30以上の論文を出しておられ、

Chapter ❷

Part 1
写真描写

Part 2
応答

Part 3
会話

Part 4
説明文

Part 5
短文穴埋め

Part 6
長文穴埋め

Part 7
長文読解

海洋環境問題の世界の主要専門家の一人です。Cohen はまた15冊以上の本の著者、共著者、編集者、共同編集者です。

バーチャル・トークへの登録　　　　　　　　　　事前登録必要

イベントのリンクはあなたの確認メールに含まれます。質問ですか？ info@winston.alumni.edu へ

語句

❏ **Boom**	ネット上の架空のバーチャルミーティングシステム名			❏ **Webinar**	=Web-Seminar の造語
❏ **alumni** 名	同窓生　※読みは [アラムナイ]			❏ **remark** 名	意見
❏ **dump** 動	投棄する	❏ **federal** 形	連邦政府の	❏ **issue** 名	問題
❏ **ethical** 形	倫理的な	❏ **regarding**	～に関して	❏ **disposal** 名	処分
❏ **major in~**	～を専攻する	❏ **article** 名	論文 (記事)		

156.　正解：(A)

What is the purpose of the e-mail?　メールの目的は何？

(A) To invite people to a web seminar　　ウエブ上のセミナーに人々を誘うため

(B) To call for donation for ocean protection　海洋保護への寄付を求めるため

(C) To introduce a professor　　　　　　教授を紹介するため

(D) To reduce plastic dumping　　　　　プラスチックごみ投棄をへらすため

山根ダメ Subject を見てピンとこなくてはいけない　⇒ **Level 2**

157.　正解：(B)

What is suggested about Professor Cohen?　Cohen 教授についてなにが分かるか？

(A) He majored in ocean protection.　彼は海洋保護を専攻した。

(B) He graduated from Winston.　彼は Winston を卒業した。

(C) He is now teaching in Winston.　彼は今 Winston で教えている。

(D) He makes environmental policies.　環境政策を立てる。

山根ダメ Cohen のところを探し読みすればすぐにできる　⇒ **Level 2**

158.　正解：(A)

What is suggested about the recipient of the email?

メールの受信者について何がわかるか？

(A) He/She is a Winston alumni.　彼 [彼女] は Winston 大の同窓生。

(B) He/She is a student of Prof. Cohen.　彼 [彼女] は Cohen 教授の学生だ。

(C) He/She is co-author with Prof. Cohen.　彼 [彼女] は Cohen 教授の共著者だ。

(D) He/She provides webinar services.　彼彼女]はウエブセミナーのサービスを提供している。

山根ダメ 全体を skimming する練習によい問題　⇒ **Level 2**

Questions 159-160 refer to the following text-message chain.

Susan Craig 3:50pm

Have you got a plan on our company trip? Our board members may want to see it on next Monday's board meeting.

Jack Homes 3:53pm

Not yet. I want to discuss with Fred to get a better budget. Current budget is too tight.

Susan Craig 3:54pm

But you do not even have a destination?

Jack Homes 3:56pm

No, destination will largely depend on how much we can spend.

Susan Craig 3:57pm

Can we make a tentative plan? If you leave everything up in the air, the prices of flights and hotels will just be much higher. And it would be more difficult to negotiate a better budget.

 訳

Susan Craig 3:50pm	社員旅行の計画できた？役員たちが次の月曜の役員会で見たがるかもよ。
Jack Homes 3:53pm	まだだよ。もっと予算をもらえるようにFredと話し合いたいんだ。今の予算じゃきつすぎるよ。
Susan Craig 3:54pm	でも、行く先すらも決めてないじゃないの。
Jack Homes 3:56pm	うん。行く先は主にいくら使えるかにかかっているだろう。
Susan Craig 3:57pm	暫定的な計画ができないかしら？　もし何もかも未決定のままだと、飛行機の便やホテルの価格はさらに高くなるだけでしょう。そしてよりよい予算の交渉をするのも難しくなるでしょうよ。

Chapter ②

Part 1 写真描写

Part 2 応答

Part 3 会話

Part 4 説明文

Part 5 短文穴埋め

Part 6 長文穴埋め

Part 7 長文読解

✎ 語句

❏ **tight** 　形　きびしい；きつい　　❏ **destination** 　名　行く先；目的地
❏ **tentative** 　形　一時的な；暫定の　❏ **leave... up in the air** …を中ぶらりんにしておく
❏ **negotiate** 　動　交渉する

159. 正解：(D)

Why doesn't Jack have a destination? 　Jack はなぜ目的地を決めていないのか？

(A) He doesn't know about the board meeting.
　　彼は役員会について知らない。

(B) He doesn't have enough time to work on it.
　　彼はそれに取り組む十分な時間がない。

(C) He is split between various choices.
　　彼は種々の選択に（考えが）割れている。

(D) He thinks he can get a revised budget.
　　彼は改定された予算を得られると思っている。

> 山根ポイント 最初の Jack のメッセージを読めば「予算」だとすぐに分かる　⇒ **Level 3**

160. 正解：(B)

What does Susan most likely mean when she writes "if you leave everything up in the air"?

Susan は "if you leave everything up in the air" と書くとき何を意味しているだろうか？

(A) She means "if Jack leaves everything at high prices."
　　彼女は「もし Jack がすべてを高値のままにすれば」を意味している。

(B) She means "if Jack leaves everything undecided."
　　彼女は「もし Jack がすべてを未決定のままにすれば」を意味している。

(C) She means "if Jack leaves everything to the board meeting."
　　彼女は「もし Jack がすべてを役員会に任せれば」を意味している。

(D) She means "if Jack leaves everything behind."
　　彼女は「もし Jack がすべてを置き去りにすれば」を意味している。

> 山根ポイント leave...in the air~ を「空中に放っておく」から想像すれば…簡単かも
> 　　⇒ **Level 3**

Questions 161-164 refer to the following article.

"When I first started the business, / I never thought / we would become this big."

After Cynthia Harrow lost her factory job in 2009, / she started to think about / how she could support her family financially. -[1]- Being a single mother with two children, / she had to find a way to generate income.

She started making healthy cookies. To reduce fat, she used fruit purees instead of butter, / and egg whites / instead of yolks. -[2]- She first sold the cookies on line. When she learned / that her cookies were highly welcomed, /she rented a corner in a local supermarket / to sell her cookies. In 2011, / she opened her own cookie store.

In 2012, / one of her daughters was diagnosed / with type 1 diabetes, / a disease that requires the restriction of sugar and carb intake. Cynthia started to make sugar and carb free cookies. She knew that to do so / she needed to get rid of the flour, /the basic ingredient for almost all cookies.

After many trials, / she finally found the best ingredient. -[3]- Her daughter tasting the almond cookies, /predicted that these cookies would just sell themselves.

Cynthia's almond cookies soon became popular / among weight watchers. Sale rocketed. By 2014, / her business went from two employees / to 56. -[4]- "It was stressful, / but it was awesome" said Cynthia. Today Cynthia sells 40,000 almond cookies a day, / all based on her 8-year-old recipe, / which she refuses to change. "People kept saying / adding this or adding that to my cookies / but I don't want to change something / that was signed off by my daughter. I love her. I respect her judgement."

 訳

「私が最初にこの仕事を始めたとき、こんなにも大きくなるとは思いもしなかったわ」
2009年に工場での仕事を失った後で、Cynthia Harrow さんはどうやって家族を財政的に支えていくことができるだろうかと考え始めた。2人の子供を抱えたシングルマザーだったので、彼女は収入を産み出す方法を見いださなければならなかった。

Chapter ❷

Part 1
写真描写

Part 2
応答

Part 3
会話

Part 4
説明文

Part 5
短文穴埋め

Part 6
長文穴埋め

Part 7
長文読解

彼女はヘルシーなクッキーを作り始めた。脂肪を減らす為に、バターでなく果物のピューレを使った、そして卵黄でなく卵白を使った。彼女は最初クッキーをネットで販売した。彼女のクッキーが大変歓迎されていることを知って、彼女は自分のクッキーを売るために地元のスーパーの一角を借りた。2011年、彼女は自身の店を開いた。

2012年、彼女の娘の一人が第1種糖尿病−糖と炭水化物の摂取の抑制を必要とする病気−だと診断された。Cynthia は糖と炭水化物を含まないクッキーを作り始めた。彼女にはそうするためには小麦粉−ほとんどすべてのクッキーの基本的な材料だが−を除く必要があることを知った。

何度も試作したのちに、彼女はついに最良の材料を見つけた。[3] 彼女は小麦粉の代わりにアーモンド粉を使ったのだ。彼女の娘はこのアーモンドクッキーを味わった後で、これらのクッキーはただそれ自体が宣伝になって売れるだろうと予言した。

Cynthia のアーモンドクッキーはまもなく体重を気にする人々の間で人気が出た。売上は急上昇した。2014年までに、彼女のビジネスは従業員2人から56人へとなった。「ストレスの多いものだったけど、素晴らしいことだった。」と Cynthia は言った。今日、Cynthia は 1 日に40,000個のアーモンドクッキーを販売している、すべて彼女の8年の月日を経たレシピに基づいてだ、そして彼女はそれを変えることを拒んでいる。「人は私のクッキーにこれを加えろ、あれを加えろと言い続けたが、私は娘に認められたものを変えたくないのです。私は娘を愛しています。彼女の判断を尊重しています。」

語句

❑ support	動	支える；養う	❑ financially 副	財政的 [金銭的] に
❑ generate	動	産み出す	❑ income 名	収入
❑ purees	名	ピューレ (果物を煮詰めて裏ごしでこしたもの)		
❑ instead of~		~の代わりに；~でなく	❑ yolk 名	卵黄
❑ diagnose	動	診断する ※発音は [ダイアグノウズ]		
❑ diabetes	名	糖尿病 ※発音は [ダイアビーティーズ]		
❑ carb	名	炭水化物 ※ =carbo-hydrate の略語		
❑ intake	名	取り入れること = 摂取	❑ get rid of~	~を除く
❑ flour	名	(小麦) 粉 ※ flower (花) と同じ発音	❑ ingredient 名	材料 (主に食材)
❑ taste	動	味わう	❑ predict 動	予言する
❑ sell oneself		それ自体が宣伝となって売れる		
❑ weight watchers		体重を気にして監視する人	❑ rocket 動	急上昇する
❑ awesome	形	身震いするほど素晴らしい		
❑ sign off~		認める；認可する (口語表現) ※もともとは「署名して関係を断つ；廃する」の意味だが		

161. 正解：(C)

How did Cynthia sell her cookies at first?
Cynthia は、はじめはどうやって彼女のクッキーを売ったのか？

(A) Via her friends 友人を通じて　**(B) Via a supermarket corner** スーパーの一角を通じて

(C) Via the Internet インターネットを通じて　**(D) Via her daughter** 娘を通して

山根ポイント ざっと読んでいき、「売る = sell, sold」が出てくるのを待つ。via は「~を通じて；~によって」 ⇒ **Level 2**

162. 正解：(A)

Why did Cynthia change the basic ingredient of the cookies?

Cynthia はなぜクッキーの基本材料を変えたのか？

(A) Her daughter had a disease that restricts carb intake.

　　彼女の娘が炭水化物の摂取を制限する病気だった。

(B) She wanted to reduce fat in the cookies.　彼女はクッキーの脂肪を減らしたかった。

(C) She wanted to cater to her customers' preferences.

　　彼女は顧客の好みに合わせたかった。

(D) She wanted to follow the latest trend in healthy food.

　　彼女は健康食料の最近のトレンドに従いたかった。

> **山根ポイント** 当然 change がキーワード。ここを scanning する。当然「娘の為に…」という部分に注目する。cater to... はここでは「～を喜ばせようとする；～に迎合する」だが、「仕出しをする」という使い方の方が一般的　⇒ **Level 1'**

163. 正解：(D)

Why does Cynthia refuse to change her current recipe?

Cynthia はなぜ今の自分のレシピを変えることを拒んでいるのか？

(A) This recipe is the best-seller.　このレシピはベストセラーである。

(B) This recipe is popular with weight watchers.

　　このレシピは体重を気にする人に人気がある。

(C) This recipe is made by her daughter.　このレシピは娘が作ったものである。

(D) This recipe is liked by her daughter.　このレシピは娘に好まれている。

> **山根ポイント** 最後の段落でレシピのある部分を scanning しよう。「愛する娘のために…」という母の気持ちを読み取る　⇒ **Level 3**

164. 正解：(C)

In which of the following positions marked [1] [2] [3] and [4] does the following sentence belong?

"She used almond powder to replace the flour."

[1]，[2]，[3]，そして［4］とマークされている次のどの位置に次の文が入るか？

「彼女は小麦粉の代わりにアーモンド粉を使った。」

(A) [1]　　　(B) [2]　　　(C) [3]　　　(D) [4]

> **山根ポイント** 「アーモンド粉に代えた」がキー。the best ingredient に気が付くこと　⇒ **Level 3**

Chapter ②

Part 1 写真描写

Part 2 応答

Part 3 会話

Part 4 説明文

Part 5 短文穴埋め

Part 6 長文穴埋め

Part 7 長文読解

Questions 165-167 refer to the following email notice.

From: general affairs@abe.com
To: All employees
Subject: Notice of Fire Drill
Date: Oct. 23

We are having a fire drill on November 13. Participation of employees/ (including managers and executives) / is required.

The fire drill is conducted / in order for employees to confirm evacuation site and routes / so that they can safely evacuate, / and for a workplace disaster prevention team / to reconfirm their roles/ in case of disasters such as fire. Please find the details of the drill below:

1. Time & Date: From 16:00 to 17:00 on November 13(Tue)
2. Participants: all full-time and part-time employees, / excluding clients or guest and those / who are with them. Please have a few persons stay / at the offices on each floor / for telephone calls.
3. Flow and roles of the drill: please refer to the attached "Outline of Nov13 Fire Drill.xls" for details.
4. Registration: to ensure participation, / you will need to register your name in the building lobby / when you arrive there / at the end of the drill.

For any questions, / please contact us / by replying to this e-mail.

Thanks,
Sandy Lim
General Affairs

 訳

総務部から、すべての従業員へ、火災訓練への通告　10月23日送信
11月13日に火災訓練を行います。従業員（含む：部長、役員）の参加が求められます。
火災訓練は従業員に避難場所とルートを確認してもらうため行われます、皆が安全に避難できるようにと、また、職場の災害防止チームが火事のような災害の場合その役割を再確認してもらうために行われます。下記の訓練詳細をご覧ください。

1 日時：11月13日（火）16時～17時
2 参加者：すべての常勤、非常勤職員で、依頼人、客及びそれらと同行の人々は除きます。各階オフィスには電話応対のため少数の人を残してください。

3 訓練の流れと役割：詳細には添付の「11月13日の火災訓練」を参考にして下さい。

4 登録：参加を確実にするために、皆さんは名前を建物のロビーで登録する必要があります、訓練が終わってそこへ到着したら。

何か質問があれば、このメールに返答することで連絡を下さい。

ご協力感謝します。
Sandy Lim 総務部

165. 正解：(D)

What will most likely happen on November 13?
11月13日には何が起こるだろうか？

(A) There will be no one in the office. 　事務所にはだれもいなくなるだろう。

(B) There will be a speech on fire prevention. 　防火に関するスピーチがあるだろう。

(C) There will be a fire inspection. 　火事にそなえての検査があるだろう。

(D) There will be a name registration stand in the lobby.
　ロビーに名前登録スタンドが備えられるだろう。

> **山根ずば** 当然防火訓練があると考えて選択肢にそれを探すが…ない！　なれば×を出していくと、(A)(B)(C) が×となる。(D) は 4 の登録のところにあるので〇　⇒ **Level 2**

166. 正解：(D)

What is the purpose of the drill? 　訓練の目的は何か？

(A) To identify the cause of fire 　火事の原因を突き止めるため

(B) To eliminate the cause of fire 　火事の原因を消去していくため

(C) To confirm that fire prevention facilities are working
　防火設備が機能していることを確認するため

(D) To confirm routes to leave the building in case of fire
　火事の場合に建物を離れるルートを確認するため

> **山根ずば** 防火訓練の目的は常識でもすぐにわかる　⇒ **Level 2**

167. 正解：(A)

Who should remain in the office during the drill?
だれが訓練中に事務所に残るであろうか？

(A) Clients 　顧客たち
(B) Executives 　重役たち
(C) Managers 　部長たち
(D) Part-time employees 　パートの従業員たち

> **山根ずば** 2の「参加者」のところを読めばすぐにわかる。exclude (除く)という動詞は大事！　⇒ **Level 1**

Chapter ②

Part 1 写真描写
Part 2 応答
Part 3 会話
Part 4 説明文
Part 5 短文穴埋め
Part 6 長文穴埋め
Part 7 長文読解

Questions 168-171 refer to the following article.

The summer drink of choice in Melos Verma, Mexico is Coolsprite, /a beer-flavored soda commonly sold in glass bottles.

-[1]- Taco House, / known for its creative desserts and drinks, / is releasing a new drink / made from Coolsprite called Summer Passion. Starting from July 1, / children and adults in Melos Verna / craving for innovative cool summer drinks / can try this new creation. Summer Passion is a mixture of Coolsprite and lemonade.

It has four flavors to choose from: mint, peach, plum and green tea. -[2]- The drink is sold in limited quantities / and only during July and August. A medium size goes for 100 pesos.

-[3]- Taco House had been a local chain / offering traditional Mexican tacos / until bought by a Japanese fast food chain Moriasa in 2013.The acquisition turned the taco shop / to a full fast food store / serving burgers, sandwiches, fries, chickens, and various drinks / such as shakes and juices. "We didn't expect / the acquisition would turn the taco shop / to such a huge success, / but it did thanks to the Japanese elements brought in", / said David Demarco, / market analyst with a local food journal. -[4]- Since the acquisition / the Japanese fast food chain has introduced flavors / such as plum and green tea. Consumers were fascinated by the distinctive Japanese flavors / that they had not had a chance to savor.

訳

Melos Vermaにおける夏の飲み物選択は通常ガラス瓶で販売されるビール味のソーダCoolspriteです。[1]今、Coolspriteは新しく生まれ変わります。その独創的なデザートで知られているTaco HouseはSummer Passionと呼ばれるCoolspriteから作られる新しい飲料を発売します。7月1日に始まり、独創的な冷たい夏の飲料を熱望するMelos Vernaの子供も大人もこの新しい新製品を試すことができます。Summer PassionはCoolspriteとレモネードのミックスです。それは4つの味があり、つぎから選べます。ミント、ピーチ、プラムそして緑茶から。その飲料は限定数販売で7月と8月の期間のみです。中サイズは100ペソで売られます。

Taco Houseは2013年に日本のファストフードチェーン店モリアサに買収されるまで伝統的なメキシコのタコスを提供する地元の1チェーン店でした。その買収はタコスの店を100%ファストフード店へと変えました、バーガー、サンドイッチ、フライ、チキンそしてシェイクやジュースのような種々の飲み物を提供する店へと。「買収によってタコス店がそんな大成功を収めるとは期待していなかったが、それは確かに日本的要素がもたらされたお陰だった」と当地の食専門紙のマーケティングアナリストのDavid Demarcoは言いました。その買収以来その日本のファストフードチェーンはプラムや緑茶のような味を導入してきました。消費者はこれまで味わうチャンスのなかった特有の日本の味に魅了されました。

語句

❏ ~ flavored	~味の	❏ crave for~	~を渇望する		
❏ innovative	形 独創的 [革新的] な	❏ turn A to B	A を B に変える		
❏ fascinate	動 魅惑する	❏ distinctive	形 独特 [特有] の	❏ savor	=taste

168. 正解：(B)

What is suggested of Summer Passion? Summer Passion について何が分かるか？

(A) It is a traditional Mexico drink. メキシコの伝統的な飲み物である。

(B) It contains lemonade. レモネードが入っている。

(C) It is a popular winter drink. 人気のある冬の飲み物である。

(D) It is sold in glass bottles. ガラスビンで売られている。

> 山根ポイント Summer Passion の部分をざっと読むと、最後に「Coolsprite と lemonade（レモン水）とのミックス」と出てくる　⇒ **Level 1**

169. 正解：(A)

Which of the following is closest in meaning to "innovative" in the 2nd paragraph?
次のどれが第2段落の innovative に意味の上で一番近いか？

(A) Original 独創的な ※「本来の；最初の」という意味もある (B) Traditional 伝統的な

(C) Exotic 異国風の (D) Fresh 新鮮な

> 山根ポイント innovative は「独創的な」。語彙力の問題なのでわからなかったらとにかくどれかにマークしておく。

170. 正解：(D)

What is the most likely reason for the success of the acquisition?
買収の成功のもっともありそうな理由は何か？

(A) A traditional drink was used. 伝統的な飲み物が使われた。

(B) A variety of items were served. 多様な品目が供された。

(C) A new menu was introduced. 新しいメニューが導入された。

(D) Exotic flavors were introduced. 異国風の味が導入された。

> 山根ポイント 向こうの人には日本風は異国風だ　⇒ **Level 2**

171. 正解：(A)

In which of the following positions marked [1] [2] [3] and [4] does the following sentence belong?

"Now, Coolsprite is getting a new life."

[1]、[2]、[3]、そして [4]とマークがついている次の位置のどこに次の文が入るか？
「今、Coolsprite は新しく生まれ変わります」

(A) [1] (B) [2] (C) [3] (D) [4]

> 山根ポイント 「Coolsprite から作られる新しい飲料を発売する」と続くことから、Coolsprite が新しく生まれ変わったと考えられる　⇒ **Level 3**

Questions 172-175 refer to the following online discussion.

Customer Service   (2:34pm):
　　Hello, my name is Ada. I'm at your service today. How can I help you?
Mia Portman   (2:34pm):
　　I ordered three cans of rose tea on June 5. The packages arrived today /
　　with two of the three cans broken.
Customer Service   (2:35pm):
　　Sorry to hear that. Can I have your telephone number?
Mia Portman   (2:36pm):
　　Yes. 617-3363-9222.
Customer Service   (2:36pm):
　　OK, one moment please....OK, I've got your order now. It is 3 cans of
　　Aroma Rose Tea, right?
Mia Portman   (2:39pm):
　　Yes. Two of the cans were broken. I'm sending you a picture now. I took
　　it when I opened the package.
　　　　　　　　　　　　　　Picture loading
Customer Service   (2:40pm):
　　We are very sorry about the broken cans. When we shipped the tea, / the
　　cans were not broken. It seems / that something happened during the
　　shipment.
Mia Portman   (2:41pm):
　　Whether it's because of you or the courier company, / I didn't get what I
　　paid for. Could you re-deliver 2 new cans?
Customer Service   (2:42pm):
　　We are very sorry. Yes, we can send you two new cans of Aroma Rose
　　Tea.
Mia Portman   (2:42pm):
　　When can you deliver?
Customer Service   (2:43pm):
　　Let me check. Oh, sorry we do not have Aroma Rose Tea in stock right
　　now/ and they will not be available for another 3-4 weeks.
Mia Portman   (2:43pm):
　　That's too bad. I will be out of town in two weeks / and I need to take the
　　rose tea with me.
Customer Service   (2:45pm):
　　How about changing to our Jasmine Tea? They are of the same price /
　　and we have stock right now.
Mia Portman   (2:45pm):
　　Not left with much choice.

お客様係	2:34pm：	もしもし、Ada と申します。本日お客様の担当でございます。ご用件は？
Mia Portman	2:34pm：	私ね、6月5日にローズ茶3缶を注文したのよ。小包が届いたのよ、3缶のうち 2缶が破損した状態でね。
お客様係	2:35pm：	それは申し訳ございません。お客様の電話番号いただけますか？
Mia Portman	2:36pm：	いいですよ。617-3363-9222 です。
お客様係	2:36pm：	承知しました。ちょっとお待ちください…はい、あなた様のご注文票がただ今 手に入りました。Aroma ローズ茶3缶でございますね？
Mia Portman	2:39pm：	そう。缶の2つは破損していたの。今、写真を送るわね。小包を開けたとき写 真をとったのよ。
		[写真アップロード中]
お客様係	2:40pm：	壊れた缶に関しましては誠に申し訳ございません。お茶を発送した際には缶は 壊れていませんでした。発送中に何かが生じた様です。
Mia Portman	2:41pm：	それがおたくの原因であれ配送会社の原因であれ、私は支払いに対価する物 を受け取らなかったわ。新しく2缶再度配達してくださる？
お客様係	2:42pm：	まことに申し訳ありません。新品の Aroma のローズ茶2缶をお送りいたします。
Mia Portman	2:42pm：	いつ届けてくださる？
お客様係	2:43pm：	確認させていただきます。あぁ、申し訳ございません、ただ今 Aroma ローズ 茶は在庫がございません、もう3～4週間は手に入らないようです。
Mia Portman	2:43pm：	それはまずいわね。私2週間したら町の外に出るのよ、それでローズ茶を持っ て行く必要があるのよ。
お客様係	2:45pm：	当店のジャスミン茶に変更されてはいかがでしょう？　同じお値段で、ただ今在 庫がございます。
Mia Portman	2:45pm：	それほど選択の余地もなさそうね。

語句

❏ **account**　　　　　　名　取引　※ account number は「顧客番号」
❏ **It seems that...**　　～のように思える
❏ **whether A or B**　　A であれ B であれ　　　❏ **in stock**　　在庫あり

172. 正解：(C)

Why does Mia contact Customer Service?　Mia はなぜお客様係へ連絡したのか？

(A) To return an item　　　　　　　　　　品物を返すため

(B) To request for expedited shipment　急ぎ発送を求めるため

(C) To report a problem with an order　注文品に関しての問題を報告するため

(D) To revise an order　　　　　　　　　注文を変更するため

> 山根ポイ このような簡単な文は、さっと読めるよう練習すべき。冒頭で broken とあるの で簡単なはず。同じ内容を言い換えている　⇒ **Level 2**

Chapter❷

Part 1
写真描写

Part 2
応答

Part 3
会話

Part 4
説明文

Part 5
短文穴埋め

Part 6
長文穴埋め

Part 7
長文読解

173. 正解 : (C)

What is suggested about the package? パッケージについて何が分かるか?

(A) It was delivered to the wrong address. 間違った住所へ配達された。

(B) It was delayed. 遅延した。

(C) It contained broken items. 壊れた品目が入っていた。

(D) It contained wrong items. 間違った品目が入っていた。

> 山根先生 172と同時にわかる簡単な問題　⇒ **Level 1'**

174. 正解 : (A)

Why does Mia send the picture? Mia はなぜ写真を送るのか?

(A) To show the problem 問題を示すために

(B) To show shipment progress 発送の進捗状況を示すため

(C) To request for refund 返金を求めるため

(D) To provide order number 注文番号を用意するため

> 山根先生 壊れた品の証拠写真なので (A) が正解　⇒ **Level 2**

175. 正解 : (D)

What does Mia mean when she writes "not left with much choice"?

Mia が "not left with much choice" と言うとき何を意味しているか?

(A) **Only Jasmin Tea is the same price as Aroma Rose Tea.**
ジャスミン茶のみが Aroma ローズ茶と同じ値段だ。

(B) **Her choice of tea is limited.**
彼女のお茶の選択には限りがある。

(C) **She should have chosen another store.**
彼女は別の店を選ぶべきだった。

(D) **She has to accept the proposal given the circumstances.**
状況を考慮すればこの提案を受け入れなければならない。

> 山根先生 given... は分詞構文からの流れで、「〜が与えられれば＝〜を考慮すれば」を意味する。I'm not left with... という文の省略なので「私はそれほど多くの選択権を持って置かれてはいない」という意味から (D) が当てはまる　⇒ **Level 3**

Questions 176-180 refer to the following web page and email chain.

---

http://www.orchidfootwear.com/home/

At Orchid Footwear, / we design our shoes to bring you comfort, / so if they're not working exactly right for you, / we've got you covered. Whether you shop on orchidfootwear.com or in an Orchid Footwear Store, / you can have a 20-day "trial wear" with your purchases. This means that / you can return any item (EXCEPT items on sale) for any reason within those 20 days / if you are uncomfortable wearing them. We want you to shop with confidence.

Now through March 25, / items purchased online are "buy-one-get-one 50% off. And for items here, / you can save 5% on orders of $99 or more by entering the promotion code "ORCHIDDEAL" at your online checkout. Note that invoices for all sale items are only provided online through downloading.

Separately, / we are having a boots sale (with maximum discount up to 50%) / at our following stores until April 10:

124 Ellis Avenue, Marilyn Drive. Check it out today!

訳（ウェブページ本文のみ）

Orchid 靴店では皆様に履き心地の良さをもたらすよう靴のデザインをしています、ですからもし、皆様の足にぴったりと機能しないのであれば、私共がカバー（補填）させていただきます。皆様がネットの orchidfootwear.com で買われようが、Orchid 靴店で買われようが、ご購入に際して20日間の試着期間があります。これはどんな商品でも（売り出し品は除く）いかなる理由でもその20日以内に返品できるということを意味しています、もしそれを履いていて居心地が悪ければですが。私共は皆様に自信を持って買っていただきたいのです。

さて、3月25日まで、オンラインでの購入につきましては商品は1足お買い上げでもう1足は50％オフとなります。そしてこれらの商品に対しましては、99ドルかそれ以上のご注文品には5％の節約ができます、オンラインでのお支払い時に ORCHIDDEAL という販売促進コードを入力していただくことで。すべての販売品目の請求書はオンラインにおいてダウンロードを通してのみ提供となりますことをご留意下さい。それとは別に、次の店で4月10日までブーツのセールも行っています（最大50％オフにて）

124 Ellis Avenue, Marilyn Drive. 本日チェックください！

語句

❏ orchid	名	蘭（花の名前） ※発音は [オーキッド]		
❏ footwear	名	履き物；靴	❏ comfort	心地よさ ※発音は [カンファト]
❏ work right		正常に機能する	❏ we've got	=we have got
❏ have you covered		you がカバーされるようにする ※要するにあなたへの負担は面倒見ますということ		
❏ confidence	名	自信	❏ separately	副 別に

Chapter ❷

Part 1
写真描写

Part 2
応答

Part 3
会話

Part 4
説明文

Part 5
短文穴埋め

Part 6
長文穴埋め

Part 7
長文読解

From: r.holmes@gladmail.com
To: customerservice@orchidfootwear.com
Date: March 20
Subject return of sneakers

I'm writing to share my unpleasant experience / at your store on Ellis Avenue.
Last Friday, / I bought a pair of sneakers there. I had seen the free trial wear
on your website earlier / so I thought I could try the sneakers and have the
opportunity to return them / if they wouldn't fit.
It turned out that this pair of sneakers was indeed not comfortable. So I went
to your store yesterday with the receipt. But I was told / I could not return
the sneakers. I asked to talk to the store manager, / but was told that the
manager was not there.
Attached is a picture of my receipt. Please let me know / how I can return the
sneakers.

Thanks,
Rachel Holmes

訳（メール本文のみ）

Ellis通りのおたくの店での不快な体験をお伝えしようと書いています。先週の金曜日、私はそちらでスニーカーを1足買いました。ちょっと前におたくのウェブサイトで無料のお試し靴を見ていたので、スニーカーを試着でき、そしてもしフィットしなければ返品する機会があると思ったのです。
このスニーカーは実際履き心地がよくないことが判明しました。それで昨日領収証を持っておたくの店に行ったのです。しかし、スニーカーは返品できないと言われました。私は店長に話したいと求めましたが、店長は不在だと言われました。
添付は私の領収証の写真です。どうやったらこのスニーカーを返品できるがお教え下さい。

よろしく。
Rachel Holmes

 語句

❏ **it turned out that...** 　〜ということが判明した

From: customerservice@orchidfootwear.com
To: r.holmes@gladmail.com
Date: March 22
Subject: Re: return of sneakers

Hi, Rachel,

We are very very sorry for your experience. We checked the item on your receipt and found that it was an item on sale. Sale items do not enjoy the 20-day free trial wear. If you had taken notice of the phrase 'EXCEPT items on sale', you would have got it. We are sorry if our store staff didn't explain clearly to you. Since the sneakers do not enjoy the free trial wear, they cannot be returned unless it is due to a quality issue. But you can change to a different size of the same sneakers. Or alternatively you can return the sneakers in exchange of store credits at 80% of the price.

Once again we apologize for the inconvenience. We hope you will shop with us again.

Sincerely,

Samantha Hills
Customer Services
Orchid Footwear

訳（メール本文のみ）

Rachel 様

あなたの体験、誠にお気の毒に思います。私共は領収証での品目を確認しそれが売り出しの品だと知りました。売り出し商品は、20日無料お試しは受けられないのです。もしあなたが売り出し品は除くという語句に注意して下さっていれば、それがお分かりになったのですが。そのことをうちの店のスタッフがはっきりと説明しなかったのでしたら申し訳ございません。そのスニーカーは無料お試しを受けられませんので返品できません、もし品質の問題のせいでなければ。しかし、同じスニーカーの別のサイズのものへの変更はできます。または、代わりに値段の80％のストアクレジットとの交換で返品できます。再度ご不便おかけしたこと謝罪させていただきます。今後も当店にてお買い物くださるよう希望いたします。

敬具

Samantha Hills　お客様係　Orchid Footwear

語句

☐ **take notice of~**　～に気づく
☐ **due to ~**　～のせい；～のために
☐ **in exchange of~**　～との交換で
☐ **unless**　=if...not
☐ **quality**　名 品質

Chapter❷

Part 1 写真描写

Part 2 応答

Part 3 会話

Part 4 説明文

Part 5 短文穴埋め

Part 6 長文穴埋め

Part 7 長文読解

176. 正解：(B)

What is suggested about Orchid Footwear? Orchid 靴店について何がわかるか？

(A) It is an online shoe store. オンラインの靴屋である。

(B) It can change shoes to fit customers' needs.
顧客のニーズに合わせて靴を変えることができる。

(C) It allows sale items to be returned within 20 days.
売り出し商品は20日以内の返品を認める。

(D) It will give Rachel coupons with 20% discount.
Rachel に20%割り引きのクーポン券を与える。

> 山根ポイント 最初の段落に「もし、皆様の足にぴったりと機能しないのであれば、私共がカバー（補填）させていただきます」とある ⇒ **Level 2**

177. 正解：(D)

Why did Rachel request to speak with the store manager?
Rachel はなぜ店長と話すことを要求したのか？

(A) She wanted to return her purchase without receipt.
彼女は領収証なしで購入品を返したかった。

(B) She wanted to inquire about the return policy.
彼女は返品方針について尋ねたかった。

(C) She wanted to change the return policy. 彼女は返品方針を変えたかった。

(D) She was not convinced. 彼女は納得いかなかった。

> 山根ポイント この手の簡単な英文は、ざっと読み通して事情をつかむと×がすぐに出せる。(A) と (C) はすぐに変だと気が付くはず。(B) は迷う選択肢だが、Rachel はこの時点ではセール商品は除くという語句を読んでいないので「気に入らなかったら返品できると書いてあるのに納得いかない」と思っているだけ ⇒ **Level 3**

178. 正解：(A)

Which of the following is closest in meaning to "we've got you covered" in the first paragraph on the webpage?
次のどれがウェブの第1段落にある "we've got you covered" と意味の上で一番近いか？

(A) We will take care of your needs. あなた様のニーズを大事に致します。

(B) We will give you discounts. 割引を致します。

(C) We will show you a variety of shoes. 種々の靴をお見せ致します。

(D) We will extend footwear warranty. 靴の保証を延長致します。

> 山根ポイント have got you covered がはっきり分からなくても、よい意味で使っているとつかめることが大切 ⇒ **Level 3**

179. 正解：(C)

What is "ORCHIDDEAL"? "ORCHIDDEAL" とは何か？

(A) It is a code for online purchase. ネット購入のための番号である。

(B) It is a code for online log in. コンピューターにログインするための番号である。

(C) It is a code for discounts. 割引のための番号である。

(D) It is a code for invoices download. ダウンロードされる請求書のための番号である。

> 山根ポイント deal は「取引」という意味だが、「お得な；おいしい」話、提案、値引きサービスを意味することが多い　⇒ Level 1'

180. 正解：(C)

What is suggested of the boots sale? ブーツのセールについて何が分かるか？

(A) It is only available in March.
3月のみ有効である。

(B) Boots sale requires a minimum purchase of $99 to qualify for discounts.
ブーツのセール割引の資格を持つには最低購入額99ドルを要求している。

(C) Rachel bought the sneakers in the store where there was a boots sale.
Rachel はブーツのセールがある店でスニーカーを買った。

(D) 5% of the items in the boots sale are half price.
ブーツのセールにおいて商品の5%が半額である。

> 山根ポイント boots sale がキーワードなのでまずはそこを読む。すると (A) はすぐ×だと分かる。(B) も99という数値に注目すればブーツセールに関係ないと分かる。(D) も同様に半額に注目すれば、ブーツのセールには無関係だとわかる。結局、あまり重要でもない (C) が事実なので答えとなる。ブーツのセールは Ellis Avenue の店でのみ行われる。そして Rachel はこの店でスニーカーを買ったと言っているので　⇒ Level 2

Questions 181-185 refer to the following email and newsletter.

From: a wager@halis.fr.com
To: All Instructors
Date: November 25
Subject: Dec. class and Oct. newsletter

Dear Instructors,

Time flies! There is only a month left this year. Please find attached or class schedules of December. Thanks to new instructors on board, we are adding the following new classes in December.
--French
--Chinese
--Piano

New students:
--Sophie Kurt & Mary Kurt(twins; both 5-year-old) will join on Dec.1
--James Harris (6-year-old) will join on Dec. 2

Also attached is our October Newsletter.

In order to make our November newsletter, / could you send me the following:
-What did the students learn at your class in November?
-What are the students going to learn in December?

It would be helpful if you send them to me by Thursday 28th. Parents have really been fond of our newsletters, and they have asked for more!

By the way, / thank you for sending me your professional photos. We have completed processing them / and they will be displayed at our entrance and on our website / from Monday next week.

Thank you,
Anna

Part 1 写真描写
Part 2 応答
Part 3 会話
Part 4 説明文
Part 5 短文穴埋め
Part 6 長文穴埋め
Part 7 長文読解

訳（件名とメール本文のみ）

件名：12月の授業と10月の会報について

講師の皆様へ、

時が経つのは速いですね！ 今年はひと月しか残っていません。添付書類または12月のクラス予定をご覧ください。新しい講師が加わって下さったので、12月には次の新しいクラスを加えます。
- フランス語
- 中国語
- ピアノ

新しい受講生：
Sophie Kurt & Mary Kurt（5歳の双子）が12月1日に参加します。
James Harris（6歳）が12月2日に参加します。

また、添付書類は10月の会報です。

11月の会報を作るのに次のものをお送りいただけますか：
- 11月のあなたのクラスで生徒たちは何を学びましたか？
- 生徒たちは12月には何を学ぶことになりますか？

28日木曜日までにそれらを送付いただけると助かります。親御さんは私共の会報を大変気に入っておられ、もっと出してほしいと求められています！

ところで、皆さんからお送りいただいた職業に関するお写真ありがとうございます。それらの処理を終わらせて、入り口のところとウェブサイトに来週月曜から掲げられます。
ありがとうございます。
Anna

語句

❏ **on board**	いっしょの職場に ※元の「乗船して」「同じ船に乗り合わせて」という意味からこの意味に			
❏ **helpful**	形 助かる；役立つ	❏ **be fond of~**	~をすごく好む	
❏ **complete**	動 仕上げる；完成させる	❏ **process**	名 処理；整理	

Halis Newsletter-October

Hello Parents! Discover our exciting month at Halis!
Below is what the children learned in October / and what they are going to learn in November (marked "coming up")!

Yoga: learned Halloween poses and yoga music
Coming up: crane pose, tree pose and ball pose

Chapter ❷

Part 1 写真描写

Part 2 応答

Part 3 会話

Part 4 説明文

Part 5 短文穴埋め

Part 6 長文穴埋め

Part 7 長文読解

Spanish: learned fruit names, and body parts such as hand, eye, nose
Coming up: numbers 10-20, seasons, vegetables

Programming: learned simple games, shapes, bridge building
Coming up: chess games, programming for a shopping mall

Art: explored oil painting
Coming up: paper folding, clay shaping

Math/Science: learned clocks, counting, played floating games
Coming up: moon and earth; bubble games

訳

Halis（ハリス）の会報 - 10月

ご父母の皆様コンニチハ！ Halis の塾でわくわくする月を見つけましょう。

下記にはお子様が10月に学ばれたこと、そして11月に学ばれること（「これからは」の印がついています）が出ています。

・ ヨガ：ハロウイーンのポーズとヨガの音楽を学びました。

　これからは：鶴のポーズ、木のポーズ、そしてボールのポーズ

・ スペイン語：果物の名前、そして手、目、鼻などの身体のパーツを学びました。

　これからは：10から20までの数字、季節、野菜

・ プログラミング：簡単なゲーム、型、ブリッジ組み立てを学びました。

　これからは：チェス、ショッピング・モールのプログラミング

・ アート：油絵を探求しました。

　これからは：折り紙、粘土細工

・ 数学／科学：時計、数の数え方を学び、水に物を浮かばせるゲームをしました。

　これからは：月と地球そしてシャボン玉ゲーム

 語句

❏ **below is...** 下にあるのは～です　❏ **what** 「～のもの」という関係代名詞

181. 正解：(D)

What is Halis? Halis とは何か？

(A) A language school 語学学校　**(B) A yoga studio** ヨガのスタジオ

(C) A news agency 通信社　(D) An educational facility 教育施設

> 山根ポイント Halis がキーワード。ニュースレターの1行目を読むだけで、子供のおけいこ塾だと気づくはず　⇒ **Level 2**

182. 正解：(B)

Why are new classes added to December? なぜ12月に新しいクラスが加えられたか?

(A) Because new students have joined. なぜなら新しい学生たちが参加したから

(B) Because new teachers have joined. なぜなら新しい先生たちが参加したから

(C) Because parents are fond of new classes. なぜなら親たちが新しいクラスを好んだから。

(D) Because teachers of some existing classes have left.
なぜなら既存の教室のいくつかの先生たちがやめたから。

> 山根ポイント メールの December に注目、「新しいインストラクターが加わって下さったので…」とベタで出ている ⇒ **Level 1**

183. 正解：(D)

What does Anna ask the instructors to do in her email?
Anna はメールの中で講師たちへ何をするよう頼んでいるか?

(A) Send professional photos 職業に関する写真を送る

(B) Upload photos to website 写真をウェブサイトに載せる

(C) Send December Newsletter 12月の会報を送信する

(D) Send November activities 11月の活動を送信する

> 山根ポイント 頼む (ask) 内容を知るには本文に Could/Would/you.. や Please... を探すこと ⇒ **Level 2**

184. 正解：(A)

Which of the following did children learn in October?
子供たちは 10 月には次のどれを学んだか?

(A) Spanish words for body parts 身体のパーツを表すスペイン語の単語

(B) French words for fruits 果物を表すフランス語の単語

(C) Crane poses in Yoga ヨガでの鶴のポーズ (D)Chess games チェス

> 山根ポイント 探すだけですぐに見つかる! ⇒ **Level 1**

185. 正解：(A)

According to the newsletter, which of the following are children going to learn in November? ニュースレターによると子供たちは11月には次のどれを学ぶだろうか?

(A) Spanish words for seasons 季節を表すスペイン語の単語

(B) French words for vegetables 野菜を表すフランス語の単語

(C) Oil painting 油絵 (D) Piano classes ピアノの授業

> 山根ポイント 11月のおけいこは Coming up を見るのがポイント! ⇒ **Level1**

Questions 186-190 refer to the following webpage, brochure and email.

http://www.lacorelos.com

Welcome to La Corelos

A TROPICAL PARADISE.
A SECLUDED LUXURIOUS EXPERIENCE.

La Corelos is an exclusive beach resort / to the north of Verto Polos, Mexico.

Accessible only by boat / and nestled between the green tropical mountains, /La Corelos is truly a paradise found. It is an unexplored gem.

We have rooms / with spectacular ocean views or forest view. All rooms are decorated with local Mexican artwork / and equipped with the best of amenities / including Wi-Fi, flat screen TVs, air-conditioning, and private bath tubs. We provide daily housing / and complimentary laundry services as well.

Our recently renovated resort / has added a new spa area and a gym! Click here / for a quick view.

La Corelos is unique / in that it is one of the best wedding and honeymoon destinations in Mexico. Either a magnificent celebration / or an intimate family gathering, / we help you realize your dream wedding here. Imagine your vows to be exchanged / on a garden terrace overlooking the ocean / or surrounded by cascading waterfalls!

Click here to see galleries of our wedding celebrations.

Book your wedding package today!

Email us at info@lacorelosresort.com for any questions you may have.

訳（ウェブページ本文のみ）

La Corelos へようこそ
熱帯のパラダイス。
人里離れた贅沢な体験。
La Corelos はメキシコの Verto Polos の北にある高級ビーチリゾートです。
アクセスは船によってのみで、緑の熱帯の山々の間に抱かれており、La Corelos は真に発見されたパラダイスです。それはまさに探索されていない宝石です。
当方には壮大なオーシャンビューまたフォレストビューのお部屋がございます。すべてのお部屋は当地メキシコの芸術作品で装飾されており、最高のアメニティを備えておりまして、Wi-Fi、薄型テレビ、エアコン、そして各室浴槽付きです。日々のお部屋のお手入れと無料のお洗濯サービスも同様に提供しております。
最近改装致しました当方のリゾートには新しい温泉場とジムを加えました！ こちらをクリックいただければすぐにご覧

になれます。

La Corelos はメキシコにおいて最高の結婚式とハネムーン目的地の1つという点で珍しいものです。壮大な祝宴または親しい家族の集いでも、あなたの夢の結婚式をここで実現されるお手伝いをいたします。あなたの誓いが大海原を見晴らす、または流れ落ちる滝に囲まれたガーデンテラスで交わされることをご想像下さい！

ここをクリックして私共の結婚祝宴のギャラリーをご覧下さい。

さあ、あなた様のウェディングパックを本日ご予約下さい！

語句

❏ exclusive	形 排他的な；高級な	❏ to the north of~	～の北へ
❏ in the north of~	～の北部に	❏ unexplored	形 探索されない；未踏破の
❏ spectacular	形 壮大な	❏ be equipped with~	～の備わった
❏ housing	部屋の整理・整頓などの手入れ	❏ complimentary	形 ご優待の (＝ 無料の)
❏ in that...	～という点で	❏ magnificent	形 すばらしい；壮麗な
❏ intimate	形 親密な　※発音は [インティミット]		
❏ vow	名 誓い　※発音は [ヴァウ]	❏ cascade	動 滝のように流れる

La Corelos

Activities Brochure

- Snorkeling-Snorkeling equipment is provided(snorkes, masks and fins).
- Parasailing*-2 beaches Verto Polosa and Hosona offer parasailing.
- Kayaking-5 kayaks are available on the beach for your use.
- Scuba diving*-Scuba lessons on site(we provide certification)
- Waterfall hikes-Check out our amazing waterfalls on a hiking tour.
- Yoga lessons*-We have plenty of spaces for yoga / and instructors can be arranged.
- Yacht excursions*-We take you to explore the bay by yacht; wine on board!
- Whale watching(seasonal)*-Humpback whales can be spotted December-April.
- Sailing courses*-Learn to sail with our certified instructors / and explore the nearby beaches by sailboat.
- Fishing trips(seasonal)*-Charter a boat and bring back dinner! Available June-November.
- Wine tasting-Tasting experiences may be arranged at La Fort,/award-winning local winery.
- Day trips to Verto Polosa-About a 20-minute trip from hotel; local art village

Activities with * require advance booking.

Activities without * can be signed up for a front desk.

Chapter ❷

Part 1 写真描写

Part 2 応答

Part 3 会話

Part 4 説明文

Part 5 短文穴埋め

Part 6 長文穴埋め

Part 7 長文読解

訳

La Corelos

アクティビティのパンフレット

・シュノーケリング：シュノーケリングの装備は提供されます（シュノーケル、マスク、ヒレ）。
・パラセーリング＊：Verto Polosa と Hosona の2つのビーチがこれを提供します。
・カヤッキング：お客様用として5艘のカヤックがビーチでご利用できます。
・スキューバダイビング＊：現場にてスキューバのレッスン（証明書をご用意できます）
・滝へのハイキング：ハイキングツアーで私共の驚くほどすばらしい滝をその目で見てください。
・ヨガのレッスン＊：ヨガのための十分なスペースがございます、また、インストラクターの手配可能です。
・ヨット周遊＊：ヨットで湾内探検へお連れ致します。船上でワインを!
・鯨ウォッチング（季節限定）＊：12月から4月にかけてザトウクジラを見ることができます。
・セーリング教程＊：資格をもった講師から帆走を学び、そして近隣のビーチを帆船で探検します。
・魚釣りの小旅行（季節限定）＊：船をチャーターして夕食を持ち帰りましょう! 6月〜11月可能です。
・ワイン試飲：受賞歴のある地元のワイナリー La Fort で試飲体験ができます。
・Verto Polosa への日帰り旅行：ホテルから約20分の日帰り旅行：地元の芸術村

＊印のついている活動はあらかじめの予約要。
＊印のついていないものはフロントで申し込み可能。

語句

❏ on site　現場で［に］　❏ spot　動　見分ける　❏ sign up for...　〜に申し込む

From: info@lacorelosresort.com
To: s.doghlas@gladmail.com
Date: June 8
Subject: Re: romantic package

Hi, Sophia,

Thank you for booking our romantic package with us. We're thrilled about your upcoming wedding / at our hotel next week.

We actually have a campaign / from now to the end of June. The campaign allows you / to include three activities / into your wedding package for free. Regarding the activities, / take a look at the attached brochure. Please let me know / what three activities / you want to include in your package. Note that sailing course and any seasonal activities are / not available during the campaign period.

Thank you for sending us your flight information. Note that the boat from your arrival airport to our island / takes about 3 hours by boat. Last, could you confirm / if you require any vegetarian meal / during your stay with us?
Sincerely,
Jose Antonio

訳（メール本文のみ）

Sophia 様、

私共のロマンティック・パックにご予約下さりありがとうございます。今度の来週の当ホテルでのあなたの結婚式にわくわくしております。

実のところ今現在から6月末までキャンペーンをしております。あなたのウェディング・パックに3つのアクティビティを無料で追加していただけます。アクティビティに関しましては添付のパンフレットをご覧下さい。

あなたのパックにどの3つのアクティビティを追加されたいのかをお知らせください。セーリング教程と季節限定のアクティビティは、キャンペーン期間中には利用できませんのでご留意ください。あなたの飛行便の情報をお送り下さりありがとうございます。到着空港から私どもの島へは船で3時間くらいかかりますのでお気をつけください。最後に、当方にご滞在中、菜食主義の食事が必要かどうかお知らせいただけますか？

敬具　Jose Antonio(ホセ・アントニオ)

語句

❏ **allow A to~**　A に~することを認める [容認する]　❏ **regarding~**　~に関して
❏ **vegetarian**　[名]　菜食主義者

186. 正解：(A)

Which of the following is closest in meaning to "nestled" as appearing in the webpage?

次のどれがウエブページに出ている "nestled" と意味において一番近いか？

(A) located　位置している

(B) covered　覆われている

(C) decorated　装飾されている

(D) injected　注入されている

> 山根彩　nestled は「優しく抱かれている」。nest（巣；巣作りする）を知っていれば想像できるが…　⇒ Level 2

187. 正解：(C)

Which of the following can the newly couple join without booking?

次のどれに新しいカップルは予約なしで参加できるだろうか？

(A) Scuba diving　スキューバダイビング

(B) Yacht excursions　ヨット周遊

(C) Waterfall hikes　滝へのハイキング

(D) Sailing courses　セーリング教程

> 山根彩　予約要の印＊を見るだけ　⇒ Level 1

Chapter ❷

Part 1 写真描写

Part 2 応答

Part 3 会話

Part 4 説明文

Part 5 短文穴埋め

Part 6 長文穴埋め

Part 7 長文読解

188. 正解：(A)

What activity cannot be included into Sophia's wedding package?
ソフィアのウェディングパックに追加することができないものはどのアクティビティか？

(A) Fishing trips　　　　魚釣りの小旅行　　　(B) Parasailing　パラセーリング

(C) Day trips to Verto Polosa　Verto Polosa への日帰り旅行

(D) Yacht excursions　ヨット周遊

> 山根ポイント Jose からのメールの後半部分の条件を読むと「セーリング教程と季節ものはだめ」とある　⇒ Level 1

189. 正解：(D)

What does Jose ask Sophia to provide?
ホセはソフィアに何を用意してくれるよう頼んでいるのか？

(A) Credit card number　クレジットカードの番号

(B) Flight number　　　　航空便の番号

(C) Arrival airport　　　　到着空港

(D) Food preference　　　食べ物の好み

> 山根ポイント Jose からのメールの最後に vegetarian（菜食主義者の…）とあるぞ！　⇒ Level 2

190. 正解：(D)

Which is true of this package tour?　このパックツアーに当てはまるものは？

(A) Participants of this tour can directly fly to the resort.
このツアーの参加者は直接このリゾートへ飛行機で行ける。

(B) Guest staying at La Corelos can receive a laundry service for a small fee.
La Corelos の宿泊客は少額の料金で洗濯のサービスを受けられる。

(C) You can enjoy yacht excursions, but drinking on board is prohibited.
ヨット周遊を楽しめるが、船上では飲酒禁止である。

(D) The newly couple are visiting the resort in the middle of June.
新婚カップルは6月中旬にこのリゾートを訪れる。

> 山根ポイント 難しくはないが時間がかかる問題　⇒ Level 2

Questions 191-195 refer to the following article, notice and email.

(Boston June 12)-After more than 40 years in business, / Le Candy closed its last location in Lincoln Square last week.

The Lincoln Square Le Candy /--located at 57 Hanson Avenue /--is the flagship store of the originally Boston-based bakery-cafe, / which is now based in New York, / operating 6 stores in Massachusetts / and 8 stores in California. Le Candy serves / an array of coffee, soups, baked goods, and sandwiches.

The bakery-cafe was founded in 1985 by Mark Stevens, / a coffee and soup lover and MBA graduate from Lincoln University, / located just 3 blocks from the flagship cafe. It was acquired by Aroma Cafe, / a New York based cafe shop, in late 2007.Since the acquisition, / Le Candy has kept its name. When asked the plan for its New York stores, / Cindy Walworth, / CEO of Aroma Cafe, said / "We just want to consolidate our domestic operations / to New York. We are reforming the style of our New York stores / and we expect to bring a brand-new cafe concept / to our customers / in next year."

Customers said / they were sad to see the popular chain go. Allie Harris, a patron of the chain in Boston, said that she relied on Le Candy / for its cream pea soup.

Now she misses that every morning.

 訳

（ボストン6月12日）
40年以上もの営業の後、Le Candy は先週リンカーン広場の最後の拠点である店を閉店した。
リンカーン広場の Le Candy、ハンソン通り57番地にあるが、元来ボストンに本拠を置く、ベーカリーカフェの旗艦店なのだが、今はニューヨークに本拠を置いており、マサチューセッツに6店舗、カリフォルニアに8店舗を運営している。Le Candy はコーヒー、スープ、焼き菓子、そしてサンドイッチを出している。
このベーカリーカフェは1985年に Mark Stevens ーコーヒーとスープを愛し、旗艦店からほんの3ブロックの所にあるリンカーン大学の MBA の修士号をもつ卒業生ーによって創始された。その店は2007年の遅くにニューヨークに本拠を置くコーヒーショップの Aroma Cafe に買収された。買収後も Le Candy はその名前を保ってきている。ニューヨーク店への計画を問われた際に、Aroma Café CEO の Cindy Walworth は「我々はただ国内の事業をニューヨークに統合したいだけなんです。ニューヨーク店のスタイルを改革し、来年にはお客様に真新しいコンセプトをもたらせると期待しています。」と言った。
顧客たちは人気のあるチェーン店がなくなるのを見るのは悲しいと言った。ボストンのチェーン点のひいき客の Allie Harris さんは Le Candy のクリーム豆スープに頼っていたのに、と言った。いまでは毎朝それがないのを寂しく感じている。

Chapter ❷

Part 1 写真描写

Part 2 応答

Part 3 会話

Part 4 説明文

Part 5 短文穴埋め

Part 6 長文穴埋め

Part 7 長文読解

語句

❑ **flagship store**	旗艦店（中心となる店）	❑ **an array of~**	~の勢揃い
❑ **found**	動 創設する	❑ **acquire**	動 取得［買収］する
❑ **consolidate**	動 統合［一つに］する	❑ **brand-new**	形 真新しい；ピカピカの
❑ **rely on~**	~に頼る；あてにする	❑ **miss~**	~がないのが寂しい

NOTICE OF STORE CLOSE

Dear customers,

We are deeply sad to inform you / that Le Candy Lincoln Square is closing. For operational reasons, / we have made the most difficult decision to close this store. We sincerely apologize for any inconvenience / that you may have. We also want to thank all of our loyal and dedicated customers / for your patronage over the years. As we leave Boston, / we hope you will continue to support us. Please visit our stores in New York. We will have a sale of our stock items / (from 20% off to 60% off) / on the last Saturday of May / from 10am to 3pm. Sale items include / baking ingredients and utensils.

Again we want to thank all of our wonderful customers / who spend mornings with us in sun or in rain. It has been a pleasure to serve you.

Our last day of operation here at Lincoln Square / will be June 1 Monday.

Le Candy, Lincoln Square

訳

閉店のお知らせ
顧客の皆様へ
非常に悲しいことですが、Le Candy のリンカーン広場店の閉店をお知らせいたします。運営上の理由を持ちまして、当店を閉店するという最も困難な決定を致しました。皆様がお感じになるであろういかなるご不便に対しまして心から謝罪いたします。また、長年にわたりましての誠実な、そして献身的なすべてのお客様のご愛顧に対しまして感謝いたします。ボストンを離れますが、相変わらずのご支援を希望いたします。ニューヨークの私共のお店にいらして下さい。在庫品のセール（20%～60%オフ）を5月最終土曜日10時から午後3時までを行います。セールにはパン焼きの材料と器具も含んでおります。
あらためて、晴れの日も雨の日も当店で朝を過ごして下さるすばらしいお客様すべてに感謝を述べたいと思います。皆様にご奉仕できることは喜びでございます。
私共のリンカーン広場店の最終営業日は6月1日月曜日です。

Le Candy, リンカーン広場店

語句

❏ **deeply** 副 深く
❏ **sincerely** 副 心から；誠実に
❏ **loyal** 形 忠実な；誠実な
❏ **dedicated** 形 献身的な
❏ **patronage** 名 ひいき；愛顧 ※発音は [ペイトロニジ／パトロニジ]
❏ **ingredients** 名 食材
❏ **utensils** 名 (料理) 器具

From: l.smith@springland.com
To: m.wong@lecandy.com
Date: May 28 2019
Subject: Re: termination of lease

Hi, Mindy,

I'm sorry to hear / that you are closing your store. Your notice of lease termination on May 27 is acknowledged / and we confirm that you will vacate the premise by June 2.

Last month in our property check, / we noticed some stains on the kitchen wall. We hope you would have removed those / by the end of this week.

Also, / our property manager has indicated to us / that the premise slightly smells butter. As our next tenant is likely to go a fashion tenant, / we do hope that you could do something to remove the smell. We know a few really good cleaners / with reasonable price. Attached / please find their name cards. Hope / these would be helpful.

Thanks,
Linda

訳（メール本文のみ）

Mindy 様、
お店を閉店されると聞いて残念です。5月27日の貴方様の賃貸契約終了の御通知を承っておりまして貴方様が6月2日までに土地建物を明け渡されることを確認いたしております。
先月、我が社の物件のチェックの際に、厨房の壁に少しシミがあるのに気づきました。今週末までにそれらを除去しておかれるよう希望致します。
また、当方の不動産責任者が私共に建物がわずかにバターの匂いがすると指摘しました。当社の次のテナントは服飾ファッションのお店になりそうですので、この匂いを除去するためになんらかやっていただけますよう切に希望いたします。お手頃価格でやってくれる本当によい清掃業者を二、三知っております。彼らの名刺を添付しておきます。
お役に立てることを望んでおります。

Chapter❷

Part 1
写真描写

Part 2
応答

Part 3
会話

Part 4
説明文

Part 5
短文穴埋め

Part 6
長文穴埋め

Part 7
長文読解

語句

❏ lease	名	賃貸契約	❏ termination	名	終了；終結
❏ acknowledge	動	承認する	❏ vacate	動	立ち退く；空にする
❏ premise	名	土地建物	❏ property	名	物件；不動産；財産
❏ stain	名	シミ	❏ would have removed		除去しているであろう
❏ indicate	動	指摘する	❏ go	動	〜になる
❏ reasonable price	お手頃価格				

191. 正解：(B)

According to Le Candy, what will most likely happen to the New York stores?

Le Candy によれば、ニューヨーク店には何が起こりそうか？

(A) They will be moved. 移転されるだろう。

(B) They will be renovated. 改装されるだろう。

(C) They will be sold. 売りに出されるだろう。

(D) They will be consolidated into one store. 1つの店に統合されるだろう。

> 山根式　記事の後半にあるので難しい。未来の質問なので当然後半にあると読まないといけない。「reform する」とある。(D) で迷うだろうが、「国内事業をニューヨークに一本化する」と言っているので間違わないこと！ ⇒ **Level 2**

192. 正解：(D)

What is suggested of Mark Stevens? Mark Stevens について何が分かるか？

(A) He added the cream pea soup to the menu of Le Candy.
Le Candy のメニューにクリーム豆スープを加えた。

(B) He acquired Le Candy and expanded its business.
Le Candy を買収し、その事業を拡大した。

(C) He moved the head office of Le Candy to New York.
Le Candy の本社をニューヨークへ移した。

(D) He studied near Le Candy.
彼は Le Candy の近くで勉強した。

> 山根式　答えが意外なのでびっくりだけど、Mark に関する記述のところを読めば彼がリンカーン大学の卒業生だとわかる。そしてその大学はわずか3ブロック先だ。近い！ ⇒ **Level 2**

193. 正解：(A)

When can a person buy discounted baking powder at Le Candy?
人はいつ Le candy で割引になったベーキングパウダーを買えるだろうか？

(A) May 30　5月30日   (B) May 31　5月31日

(C) June 1　6月1日   (D) June 2　6月2日

> 山根ポイント 「5月最終土曜日」としか本文にはないが、最終営業日の6月1日が月曜日なので 5月30日（土曜）と推理できる　⇒ Level 2

194. 正解：(C)

What is the purpose of the email from Linda? Linda からのメールの目的は何か？

(A) **She feels sad to hear the cafe is gone.**
カフェがなくなると聞いて悲しい。

(B) **She hopes to make the tenant change his mind.**
テナントに心変わりしてほしいと思っている。

(C) **She wants the premise to be as clean as before.**
土地建物を以前のようにきれいにしてほしいと思っている。

(D) **She'd like to introduce another real estate agent.**
他の不動産会社を紹介したいと思っている。

> 山根ポイント 確かに (A) もあり得るかも知れないが、真意は立ち退く場合、建物の傷やシミ などは修復しておいてほしいということ。それが賃貸の常識　⇒ Level 3

195. 正解：(A)

Why does Linda send name cards to Mindy? なぜ Linda は Mindy に名刺を送るのか？

(A) **She wants to help the store remove the smell.**
彼女は店が匂いを除去する手助けをしたい。

(B) **She wants the store to remove the burn marks.**
彼女は店に焼け焦げの跡を除いてほしい。

(C) **She wants the store to find another premise.**
彼女は店に別の土地建物を見つけてほしい。

(D) **She wants to inform the store of a potential future tenant.**
彼女は店に可能性のある将来のテナントについて知らせたい。

> 山根ポイント メールの最後の文を読めばすぐにわかる。清掃業者の名刺だ！　⇒ Level 2

Chapter ②

Part 1 写真描写

Part 2 応答

Part 3 会話

Part 4 説明文

Part 5 短文穴埋め

Part 6 長文穴埋め

Part 7 長文読解

Questions 196-200 refer to the following advertisement and two letters.

> TRAINING COURSES
>
> Managing Aggression in the Workplace
>
> Course Organizer: Devere Training and Development
>
> Cost and Length: $750; two days
>
> Aimed at: Anyone who has to manage difficult or aggressive staff or / who is struggling to manage his or her own aggressive behavior.
>
> What You Learn: How to identify and deal with aggressive behavior / from colleagues in the workplace. Participants are also offered ways to deal with their own behavior / if they are finding it difficult to control aggression. The course encourages/ the exploration of alternative ways of communicating and behaving. Participants will also discuss the consequences / of not dealing with such problems.
>
> Next Course: March 5th and 6th
>
> Information:www.devere.com

研修コース
職場における攻撃行動をうまく処理するには
研修主催者：Devere 研修開発（社）
費用と期間：750ドル；2日間
対象：難しいまたは攻撃的な職員を扱わなければならない方、または自身の攻撃的言動をうまく処理するのに奮闘している方。
学ぶこと：職場における同僚からの攻撃的言動を見極め処理する方法。参加者はまた、参加者自身の言動を処理するやり方も提供される、もし参加者が攻撃性をコントロールすることが困難だと気づいているならば。このコースは意志疎通やふるまいの代替の方法の探索を奨励する。参加者はまたそのような問題を扱わない場合の結果についても話し合うことになる。
次回コース：3月5、6日
情報：www.dever.com

❏ aim at...	～を目的とする	❏ manage	動 うまく処理する
❏ aggressive	形 攻撃的な（けんか好きな）	※「意欲的な」というよい意味もある	
❏ struggle	動 奮闘する；もがく	❏ behavior	名 ふるまい；行動
❏ identify	動 見極める	❏ deal with...	～を処理する；扱う
❏ aggression	名 攻撃（性）	❏ encourage	励ます；勧める；奨励する
❏ exploration	名 探索	❏ alternative	形 代替の
❏ participant	名 参加	❏ consequences	名 結果

From: David Sinclair, ATC Travel, H.R.

To: Devere Training and Development

Re: Training course

To whom it is concerned,

I've been having a problem / with one of the staff in my department --Mr. X. He's one of the most knowledgeable people there, and he's quick and efficient. The problem is that he's also one of the most impatient people / I've ever worked with. If he thinks people on his team are working too slowly, / he gets very annoyed with them, / and often loses his temper. He's also very intolerant of colleagues/ who know less than he does. I think his co-workers are now afraid to ask him questions / because he always answers them so rudely. I've tried talking to him one-one-one on several occasions, / but I can't seem to solve the problem. So I'd like to attend this course / in order to find some solutions to this matter.

David Sinclair, ATC Travel, H.R.

訳（メール本文のみ）

私の部署の職員の一人——Mr. Xに関してずっと問題を抱えてきています。彼は職場において最も物知りの一人です、そして（仕事が）すばやく、効率的です。問題は彼が私がいままで一緒に仕事をしてきたもっとも忍耐力のない人の一人でもあるということです。もし彼が自分のチームの人々の作業があまりに遅いと思うと、彼はその人達にとてもいらつき、そしてしばしば平静心を失います。彼はまた自分ほどにものを知らない同僚にとても不寛容でもあります。

Chapter ❶

Part 1 写真描写

Part 2 応答

Part 3 会話

Part 4 説明文

Part 5 短文穴埋め

Part 6 長文穴埋め

Part 7 長文読解

彼の同僚たちはいま彼に質問することを怖がっています、彼はいつも大変無礼に答えるものですから。私は何度かの機会に彼と1対1で話してみましたが、問題を解決できないように思えます。そこで私はこの件への解決法を見いだすためにこのコースに参加したいと思っています。

✏️ **語句**

❏ **H.R.** 人事部 ※ Human Resources の略　❏ **knowledgeable** 形 物知りの
❏ **efficient** 形 効率のよい　❏ **impatient** 形 辛抱強くない (⇔ patient)
❏ **be annoyed with~** ～にイライラする；腹を立てる
❏ **lose one's temper** 平静を失う　❏ **intolerant** 形 寛容でない
❏ **rudely** 副 粗野に；無作法に　❏ **occasion** 名 機会
❏ **solution** 名 解決策　❏ **matter** 名 件

From: Linda Slove, President, Devere T.D.
To: David Sinclair, ATC Travel, H.R.
Re: Welcome to our TRAINING COURSES

Hi, David,

Thank you for your letter. I've understood your worry. Please come and join us.

If you attend this course, you'll surely learn / how to deal with that kind of problem staying calm.

Here's a Course Director's Comment:

"Participants will gain a clear understanding of / what drives the aggressive impulse / and how they can manage their own behavior, / and the behavior of others, more effectively."

See you soon,

Linda Slove

President, Devere T.D.

お手紙感謝します。貴方様のお悩み分かりました。どうぞいらしてください。

もしあなたがこのコースに参加されれば、きっとその種の問題を冷静に処理するやり方を学べますよ。

これはコースの指導者のコメントです：

「参加者の皆さんは何が攻撃的な衝動を駆り立てるのか、そしてどうやって自身の言動、また他の人々の言動をさらにもっと効果的にうまく処理できるのかについて明確な理解を得られることでしょう」

語句

❏ **attend** 動 出席する ❏ **stay calm** 冷静でいる ❏ **drive** 動 駆り立てる
❏ **impulse** 名 衝動 ❏ **effectively** 副 効果的に

196. 正解：(C)

What is NOT a feature of the training course?
そのトレーニングコースの特徴でないものは？

(A) **How to manage other people's aggressive behavior**
他の人々の攻撃的行動（喧嘩腰の態度）をうまく処理する方法

(B) **How to manage one's own aggressive behavior**
自身の攻撃的行動をうまく処理する方法

(C) How to become a more aggressive manager
もっと積極果敢な管理者になる方法（aggressive のよい意味に注意！）

(D) **How to understand what causes aggressive behavior**
何が攻撃的行動を引き起こすかの理解方法

> 山根ポ 簡単！ aggressive が分からなくてもプラスイメージかマイナスイメージかの判断ですぐにピンと来るはず ⇒ **Level 2**

197. 正解：(B)

What methods does the course teach for solving the problem of aggression?
攻撃的であるという問題を解決するためにこの教程（コース）はどんなメソッドを教えているか？

(A) **Finding aggressive people** 攻撃的な人々を見つけるやり方

(B) Using different communication methods 異なった意志疎通のやり方の利用法

(C) **Giving people a different job** 人々に違う仕事を与えるやり方

(D) **Offering psychological counseling** 心理学的なカウンセリングの提供法

> 山根ポ これは (B) と (D) で迷うはず。確かに心理学的なカウンセリングは必要かもしれないが、広告でそのことには一切触れられていない ⇒ **Level 1'**

198. 正解：(C) ···

What dose Mr. Sinclair want to do?　Mr. Sinclair (David) は何をしたがっているか?

(A) He wants to organize a course in his company　自分の会社でコースを計画したい

(B) He wants to ask Mr. X to attend the course　Mr. X にこのコースに出席してほしい

(C) He wants to attend the course himself　自分がこのコースに参加したい

(D) He wants to contact the Director　ディレクターに連絡を取りたい

> **山根ポイント** Mr. Sinclair とは David のこと。よくこのようにひねった出題がされるので注意
> ⇒ **Level 1**

199. 正解：(D) ···

What's Mr. X's problem?　Mr. X の問題は何か?

(A) He doesn't want to attend the course.
　　彼はこのコースに参加したくないと思っている。

(B) He didn't read the Director's comment beforehand.
　　彼は事前に Director のコメントを読まなかった。

(C) He's not a competent worker.
　　彼は有能な働き手ではない。

(D) He doesn't work well with colleagues.
　　彼は同僚とうまく働けない。

> **山根ポイント** Mr. X が問題の人であることを読み取ればすぐに分かる問題　⇒ **Level 2**

200. 正解：(C) ···

Which word is closest in meaning to "consequences" in the advertisement, "What You Learn"?

広告の 「What You Learn」の中での consequences の意味に最も近いものは?

(A) Reactions 反応　　　　　　　(B) Causes　　原因

(C) Results　　結果　　　　　　(D) Decisions　決定

> **山根ポイント** con (= together) + sequence (= follow) とともに続いて起こる事
> ⇒ 成り行き；結果。通常 "よくないこと" の結果として使われる。serious
> consequences は 「深刻な結果」

☐ **adjust** [ədʒʌ́st] 合わせる；適応させる；調節する	You should **adjust** yourself to this environment. 貴方は自身をこの環境に adjust させるべきだ。 ◆ adjustment（n）⇒ make an adjustment
☐ **advertise** [ǽdvərtàiz] ～を広告［宣伝］する	Let's **advertise** this product in a newspaper. この製品を新聞で advertise しよう。 ◆ advertisement（n）⇒長いので通常は ad や ads と省略形を使う。［例］run［place］an ad（広告を出す）
☐ **agree** [əgríː] ～ に 同意［賛成］する（to, with）	We all **agree** to your plan. 僕らは皆君のプランに agree だ。 ◆ agreement（n）⇒ make an agreement with～ ◆ agree ⇔ disagree
☐ **appear** [əpíər] 現れる；出る	My mother will **appear** on TV tomorrow. 私の母が明日テレビに appear します。 ◆ appearance（n）⇒ make an appearance appear ⇔ disappear
☐ **approach** [əpróutʃ] 近づく；(問題に) 取り掛かる	The train is **approaching** the station. 列車は駅に approach しています。 We need to **approach** hacking problems. 我々はハッキングの問題に approach する必要がある。 ◆ approach（n）⇒ make an approach to～
☐ **arrive** [əráiv] ～に着く（at, in）	I'm soon **arriving** at Tokyo. 私はもうすぐ東京（駅）に arrive します。 📖 in Tokyo ならもっと広いニュアンス ◆ arrival（n）
☐ **ban** [bǽn] 禁止する	Our school **banned** long hair. うちの学校は長髪を ban した。 ◆ ban（n）⇒ put the ban on～
☐ **bear** [béər] ① 生じる；産する（=produce, yield） ② 耐える；忍ぶ（=endure, stand） ③ 運ぶ（=carry） ④ 持つ（=have）	① This bond **bears** 5% interest. この債権には5%の利息がつく。 ② I can't **bear** this pain. この痛みには耐えられない。 ③ **Bear** it to him. それを彼に持って行って。 ④ He **bears** the title of Doctor. 彼は博士の称号を持っている。 📖 すべて born（生まれて）の原形 bear（生む）に源がある。
☐ **believe** [bilíːv] 信じる；思う（that...）	I **believe** you. 私は君を believe するよ。 ◆ belief（n）

❑ **break** [bréik] 壊す；破る；壊れる；敗れる	Glass **breaks** easily. ガラスは簡単に break する。 Ken **broke** the window. ケンは窓を break した。 ◆ break （n）休憩　⇒ Let's have a break.（一休みしよう）
❑ **bring** [bríŋ] 持って来る（⇔ take）	Please **bring** me a cup of tea. 私に紅茶を一杯 bring 願います。
❑ **build** [bíld] 建てる；組み立てる	They are **building** a hotel. 彼らはホテルを build しています。
❑ **carry** [kǽri] 運ぶ	Let's **carry** goods to the warehouse. 商品を倉庫に carry しよう。
❑ **cause** [kɔ́:z] 引き起こす	What **caused** the accident? 何がその事故を cause したのかな？ ◆ cause （n）原因　⇔ effect（結果）
❑ **change** [tʃéindʒ] 変える；変わる	Please **change** trains at Shibuya. 渋谷で change trains して下さい。 📝 trains と複数形になることに注意 ◆ change （n）　⇒ make a change
❑ **check** [tʃék] 預ける；正誤を確かめる（check A with B)	**Check** your coat at the cloakroom コートはクロークに check 下さい。 ◆ check （n）阻止；抑制；検査照合；小切手；預かり証
❑ **choose** [tʃú:z] 選ぶ	She'll **choose** you only for money. 彼女は金だけのために君を choose するだろう。 ◆ choice （n）　⇒ make a （one's) choice
❑ **clean** [klí:n] きれいにする	Always **clean** your room. いつも窓をクリーンに！ 📝 形容詞の clean で Always keep your room clean. ◆ cleanse [klénz] (v)
❑ **close** [klóuz] 閉じる；締結する	We finally **closed** the contract. 私たちはついに契約を close した。 ◆ closure （n）
❑ **collect** [kəlékt] 集める	I **collected** some money from them. 私は彼らから少しのお金を collect した。 ◆ collection （n） 📝 correct （v）訂正する　形容詞の「正しい」と混同しないこと。

❑ **compare** [kəmpéər] 比較する	Why don't you **compare** English with French? 英語とフランス語を compare してみたら? ◆ comparative (a) comparison (n)
❑ **confuse** [kənfjú:z] 混同する；混乱する；乱す	Don't **confuse** 'fold' with 'hold'. fold（たたむ）と hold（つかむ）を confuse するな。 ◆ confusion (n) ⇒ throw~ into confusion
❑ **continue** [kəntínju:] 続く；続ける	He **continued** working for 10 years. 彼は10時間仕事を continue した。 ◆ continuity (n) continual (a) 📖 continue と last は両方「続く」という意味だが、前者は期限を言わないが、後者はその期限中にしっかり続くという意味。
❑ **correspond** [kɔ̀:respánd] 相応する；一致する（with）	These rules **correspond** to each other. これらの規則は互いに correspond している。 ◆ correspondence (n) 一致；通信 correspondent (n)駐在員
❑ **claim** [kléim] （当然の権利として）要求する； 主張する	Anybody can **claim** his right. だれもが自分の権利を claim できる。 ◆ claim (n) ⇒ put in a claim to~
❑ **decide** [disáid] 決める；決心する（to do, on [upon]）	Let's **decide** on what to do. 何をするかについて decide しよう。 ◆ decision (n) ⇒ make a decision
❑ **depend** [dipénd] ～に頼る；～次第である（on [upon]）	That **depends** on [upon] you. それは君に depend するね。（= それは君次第だ） 📖 That depends.（それは時と場合による） ◆ dependant (a) ◆ dependence (n) ⇒ put dependence on~
❑ **describe** [diskráib] 述べる；評する；（様子を）描写 する。	Can you **describe** the scene? その場面を describe してくれますか? ◆ description (n) ⇒ give a description of~
❑ **design** [dizáin] デザインする；する意図である (to)	He **designs** to study law. 彼は法律を勉強しようと design している。 ◆ design (n) = plan や project の意味もあることに注意!
❑ **disappear** [dìsəpíər] 見えなくなる	The cat **disappeared** behind the door. 猫はドアの後ろに disappear した。 ◆ disappearance (n)
❑ **discover** [diskʌ́vər] ～に気づく；発見する	I **discovered** that I was very late. 僕は自分がとても遅れていることを discover した。 ◆ discovery (n) ⇒ make a discovery

☐ **drive** [dráiv] 追いやる	The tweet **drove** him to despair. そのツイートが彼を絶望へ drive した。 ◆ drive（n）大掛かりな運動（= campaign）の意味があることに 　注意！
☐ **encourage** [inkə́:ridʒ] 励ます；元気づける	I **encouraged** him to try again. 私は彼にもう一度トライするよう encourage した。 ◆ encouragement（n）⇒ give an encouragement to~
☐ **enroll** [inróul] 登録する；入れる；名簿に載せ る	I **enrolled** my child in an elementary school. 私は子供を小学校に enroll した。 ◆ enrollment（n）
☐ **enter** [éntər] 入力する；入学する；入る	**Enter** your account number. あなたの顧客番号を enter（入力）してください。 He **entered** a drama school. 彼は演劇学校に enter した。 📖 enter into~　~に加わる；~を始める。 ◆ entrance（n）
☐ **establish** [istǽbliʃ] 設立；創設する；定着させる	Mr. Oka **established** his company here. Mr. Oka はここに会社を establish した。 ◆ establishment（n）は、設立；創設の他に①会社；営業所；②既 　成の上流社会階層 ＝ エスタブリッシュメントの意味もあるので注意！
☐ **estimate** [éstimèit] 見積もる；評価する	I **estimate** my loss at one million yen. 私は損失を100万円と estimate している。 ◆ estimate（n）　estimation（n）⇒ make an estimation 　of~
☐ **explain** [ikspléin] 説明する	Please **explain** the rule to me. そのルールを私に explain して下さい。 ◆ explanation（n）⇒ give an explanation of~
☐ **express** [iksprés] 表現する；示す	Can you **express** your feeling? あなたの気持ちを express してくれますか？ 📖 他に「速達便；急行」という意味の名詞・形容詞あり！ ◆ expression（n）⇒ give expression to~
☐ **face** [féis] ~方を向く；面する；直面する	We're **facing** danger now. 私たちは今、危険に face している。
☐ **fade** [féid] 消えていく；色あせていく；衰え る	The outline has **faded** (away). 輪郭が fade してしまった。
☐ **fill in (out)** （書類に）書き込む	Please **fill out** this application form. この申込書を fill out して下さい。（fill in も可）

❑ **fold** [fóuld] 折る；折りたたむ	Please **fold** a sheet of paper in two. 1 枚の紙を二つに fold して下さい。 📖 hold（つかむ；催す）との違いに注意!
❑ **follow** [fálou] 従う；ついて行く；〜に続く	O.K. I'll **follow** you. O.K. あなたに follow しましょう。 📖 前置詞 following（〜に引き続いて；〜の後で）に注意!
❑ **host** [hóust] 主催する；主人役をつとめる	Mr. Abe **hosted** a dinner yesterday. Mr. Abe は昨日晩餐会を host した。 📖 a host of~, hosts of~= a lot of~, lots of~（語源が違うので注意）
❑ **hurt** [hə́ːrt] 痛む；痛める（=injure）	My fingers still **hurt**. 僕の指まだ hurt だ（痛い）。 📖 発音注意! ◆ hurt（n）⇒ do hurt to+ 人（人を傷つける）
❑ **impress** [imprés] 印象づける	Mr. Obama's last speech **impressed** us a lot. = We were **impressed** a lot by Mr. Obama's last speech. オバマ氏の最後のスピーチが私たちをとても impress した。 ◆ impression（n）⇒ make an impression on~
❑ **improve** [imprúːv] 良くなる；良くする	You should **improve** your pronunciation first. 君はまず発音を improve すべきだね。 ◆ improvement（n）⇒ make an improvement on~
❑ **injure** [índʒər] 傷つける（=hurt）	A lot of people were **injured** in the accident. 多くの人々がその事故で injure した。 ◆ injury（n）⇒ do injury to+ 人（人を傷つける）
❑ **last** [lǽst] 続く；持続する	How long will this cold weather **last**? この寒い天候はいつまで last するだろうか？ 📖 continue とのニュアンスの違いを思い出して!
❑ **lead** [líːd] 導く	The road **leads** me to your door. その道が私を貴方の戸口へと lead する。 ◆ leading（a）一流の；すぐれた ⇒ a leading company 📖 lead to ~（ある結果）に至る Hard work leads to success.（勤勉は成功に至る。）

leave [líːv]

① 〜から離れる；去る
② 〜へ向けて出発する
③ 〜を残す；置き忘れる
④ A を B のままにしておく
⑤ A を B に任せる。

① I'm **leaving** Tokyo.
私は東京を発ちます。
② I'm **leaving** for Tokyo.
私は東京へ発ちます。
③ I **left** my bag in the locker.
ロッカーにバッグを忘れてきた［置いてきた］。
④ Don't **leave** the door open.
ドアを開けたままにしておくな。
⑤ **Leave** everything to him.
すべてを彼に任せなさい。
◆ 語源の違う leave（n）許可；休暇

miss [mís]

〜しそこなう；乗りそこなう；会いそこなう

I **missed** the 8:00 train.
8時の列車を miss した。
◆ miss（v）〜がいないのを寂しく思う ⇒ I miss you tonight.

notice [nóutis]

気づく；告知する

I didn't **notice** her in the room.
私は部屋の中の彼女に notice しなかった。
◆ notice（n）注意；通知 ⇒ give notice of〜, have notice of〜

organize [ɔ́ːrɡənàiz]

計画準備する；組織編制する

Thank you for **organizing** the meeting.
会議の organizing ありがとう。
◆ organization（n） organizer（n）主催者；まとめ役

oversee [òuvərsíː]

監督；統括する

Mr. Oka will **oversee** the project.
Mr. Oka がこのプロジェクトを oversee する。
📖 overseas（海外に）と混同しないこと

participate [pɑːrtísəpèit]

〜に参加する（in）（=take part in）

Did you **participate** in yesterday's meeting?
君は昨日の会議に participate したかい？
◆ participation（n） participant（n）参加者

pay [péi]

払う（お金・敬意・訪問など）

We get **paid** every month.
私たちは毎月 pay されている。
◆ pay（n） ⇒ provide pay
◆ payment（n） ⇒ make a payment

perform [pərfɔ́ːrm]

成す；成し遂げる；行う

Our company is **performing** well.
うちの会社はよく performing してるよ。
◆ performance（n）公演；演技の他に成績；履行；業績；性能など多義

pick up

（景気などが）回復する；良くなる；車にのせる

I hope the economy is **picking up** soon.
景気［経済］がやがて pick up するぞ。
I'll **pick** you **up** at the airport.
私が貴方を空港で pick up します。

☐ **praise** [préiz] ほめる；賞賛する	He **praised** me for my ability to speak Spanish. 彼は私のスペイン語を話せる能力を praise した。 ◆ praise（n） ▧ prize（賞）と混同しないこと!
☐ **retire** [ritáiər] 退職［引退］する（from）	Mr. Oka is **retiring** from the company next month. Mr. Oka は来月会社を retire します。 ◆ retirement（n） ▧ quit は「放棄する；断念する」意味での「辞める」。resign は「（公式に）辞任する」
☐ **return** [ritə́ːrn] 戻る；戻す	I will **return** your call as soon as I return. return しましたらすぐにお電話 return します。 ▧ 「戻り次第折り返し連絡する」という意味 ◆ return（n）見返り；返品の意味もあるので注意!
☐ **ride** [ráid] 乗る；乗って行く	I want to **ride** a bicycle. 私は自転車を ride したい。 ▧ ride on a bicycle も可 ◆ ride（n） ⇒ give a person a ride（人を車に乗せてやる）go for a ride（ドライブに出掛ける）
☐ **rise** [ráiz] 上がる；昇る	Sugar will **rise** in its price. 砂糖は値が rise するだろう。 ◆ rise（n） ◆ raise（他動詞）〜を上げる；（賃金などを）引き上げる
☐ **run** [rʌ́n] ① 計画などが）行われる ②（契約などが）効力を維持している ③ 経営［運営］する	① The program is **running** on time. 計画は予定通り run しています。 ② The contract **runs** for 2 years. 契約は2年 run します。 ③ He **runs** three companies. 彼は3つ会社を run している。 ▧ いずれも「走る」イメージで! ◆ run into〜（〜に出くわす） run out of〜（〜がなくなる） run through〜（ざっと〜に目を通す）などが TOEIC テスト頻出!
☐ **save** [séiv] 節約［倹約］する；取っておく；救う	You can **save** some money by using a bicycle. 自転車を使えば少しお金を save できるよ。 ◆ savings（n）貯金；貯蓄；蓄え ⇒常に複数で!
☐ **share** [ʃéər] 分かち合う；共有する；分担する（with）	I'd like to **share** the latest news with you. 最新のニュースを皆さんと share したいと思います。 ◆ share（n）分け前（シェア）；株；株式
☐ **ship** [ʃíp] 出荷；発送する	We've **shipped** the following items. 次の品目を ship 致しました。 ◆ shipment（n） ⇒ make a shipment of〜

❏ **solve** [sálv] 解く；解決する	It's easy to **solve** this problem. この問題を solve するのは簡単だ。 ◆ solution（n）⇒ work out a solution（解決する）
❏ **spend** [spénd] （金；時間を）使う；費やす	I **spent** a lot of money playing video games. 僕はゲームをするのに多くのお金を spend した。 ◆ spending（n）
❏ **stick** [stík] くっつく；固執する（to）	We should **stick** to the first plan. 我々は最初のプランに stick すべきだ。 ◆ stuck（過去分詞）⇒ be stuck in~（~で身動きできない）
❏ **stock** [sták] 仕入れる；在庫として蓄える	This store is well **stocked** with excellent goods. この店はすばらしい商品が stock されていますね。 ◆ stock（n）⇒ in stock（在庫あり）⇔ out of stock
❏ **store** [stɔ́:r] 蓄える；保管する；供給する	Let's **store** up food for winter. 冬に備えて食料を store しましょう。 ◆ storage（n）　storehouse（倉庫）
❏ **subscribe** [səbskráib] 購読する(to)；(署名して)寄付(を約束)する	I **subscribe** to the Yomiuri. 私はヨミウリを subscribe している。 He subscribed a large sum to charities. 彼は慈善事業に多額の金を subscribe した。 ◆ subscription（n）　subscriber（n）購読者；寄付[出資]者
❏ **tie** [tái] 結ぶ；縛る	Friendship will **tie** us together. 友情が私たちを tie するだろう。 ◆ tie（n）結び；紐；ネクタイ；絆；同点など多義
❏ **visit** [vízit] 訪れる	I'd like to **visit** my aunt. 伯母を visit したい。 🔖 他動詞なので to は不要 ◆ visit（n）⇒ pay a visit to~（~を訪問する）
❏ **wonder** [wándər] ~かしらと思う；~を知りたいと思う	I **wonder** where to spend the holidays. 休暇をどこで過ごそうかしら。 ◆ wonder（n）驚き；奇跡；不思議
❏ **worry** [wá:ri] 心配する[させる]；悩む[悩ませる]（about, over）	There's nothing to **worry** about. 何も worry することはないよ ◆ worry（n）
❏ **wrap** [rǽp] 包む；くるむ	Shall I **wrap** this toy for you? このおもちゃを wrap 致しましょうか？ ◆ wrap（n） 🔖 wrap up（包み込む⇒終える）　wrap up the meeting（会議を終える）

●著者

山根和明　Yamane Kazuaki

山口大学経済学部観光政策学科特命教授。ラサール高－山口大学経済学部卒業。英国語学留学の後、母校にて講師、準教授として教鞭をとり、平成18年に「山口大学ベストティーチャー賞」を授賞。大阪の私大にて教授として5年勤務の後、再び母校に戻って今日に至る。TOEIC990点。大学入試、TOEIC関係の著作は多く、中には40万冊を超えるロングセラー書もある。音声講義を中心にした独特の指導法は多くの受験生の共感を呼んでいる。趣味は音楽、スポーツに幅広い。健康維持のため、妻との毎日のウォーキングは欠かさない。

●問題作成協力者

Anna Zhang

サンフランシスコや上海の米国企業オフィスで通訳・翻訳業務を経験したのち、2014年3月から東京にある米国企業で、日本人従業員のビジネス英語を指導する語学トレーナーおよび契約書の翻訳者として活躍中。一方、イングリッシュブートキャンプで日本人学生にビジネス英語を教えるファシリテーター・インストラクターとしても活動している。日本語能力検定試験N1。

カバーデザイン	滝デザイン事務所	ナレーション
本文デザイン・DTP	アレピエ	Howard Colefield ［米］
イラスト	田中斉	Jennifer Okano ［米］
模試校正	文字工房燦光	Alexander Stylianou ［英］
		Nadia McKechnie ［英］
		Neil DeMaere ［加］
		Stuart O ［豪］

本書へのご意見・ご感想は下記URLまでお寄せください。
https://www.jresearch.co.jp/contact/

はじめて受ける人のための
TOEIC® L&R TEST 全パート対策スピードマスター

令和3年（2021年）4月10日　初版第1刷発行
令和4年（2022年）2月10日　　第2刷発行

著　者	山根和明
発行人	福田富与
発行所	有限会社　Jリサーチ出版
	〒166-0002　東京都杉並区高円寺北2-29-14-705
	電話 03（6808）8801（代）　FAX 03（5364）5310（代）
	編集部 03（6808）8806
	URL https://www.jresearch.co.jp
印刷所	㈱シナノパブリッシングプレス

ISBN978-4-86392-511-3 禁無断転載。なお、乱丁・落丁はお取り替えいたします。

©2021 Kazuaki Yamane, All rights reserved.

はじめて受ける人のための
TOEIC® L&R テスト
全パート対策
スピードマスター

完全模試　問題

この別冊は、強く引っぱると本体から取り外せます

Jリサーチ出版

TOEIC is a registered trademark of Educational Testing Service (ETS).
This publication is not endorsed or approved by ETS.
*L&R means LISTENING and READING.

●リスニングテスト：2回に分けて学習効果 UP !!

音声ファイルを再生し、本番のつもりで取り組みましょう！

①音声（DL 音声 56 ～ 85）を再生し、まずは Part1 & 2 に取り組みます。終わったら本冊（P210 ～）と聴く勉 TOEIC 講座！（DL 音声 111 ～ 119）を使って、答え合わせと復習をしてください。初級者でも 6 割確保できるといいですね。

②続いて Part3 & 4（DL 音声 86 ～ 110）を「24 秒ルール＆待ち伏せ攻撃法」を駆使して一気にやりましょう。終わったら本冊（P220 ～）と聴く勉 TOEIC 講座！（120 ～ 142）を使って答え合わせと復習をします。初級者は 69 問中 40 問程度正解できればいいですね。この流れで学習することで、急速に力がつきますよ！

●リーディングテスト：自分に厳しく、時間管理を徹底！

Stage1 （= Part5 & 6）を、タイマーを設定して20分で通過！

📖 Part5 & 6 の Ⅴ 問題は、知らない語彙ならすべて捨てる。Part6 で時間をかけ過ぎないこと。分からないものはすべて捨てて、適当にマークして割り切ること！

Stage2 （= Q147-175）を25分で飛ばして解こう！

Stage3 （= Q176-200）を30分で走り切ろう！

📖 Part7 は全てキーワードが見抜ける問題だけ。特に資料が複数の Q176 以降は数値、人、場所などのヒントが最初の資料にあることが多いのでそのつもりで！

終わったらすぐに本冊を開いて、**[聴く勉　TOEIC 講座！]** を聴いてしっかり復習です！これを怠ると本書の効果は半減します！

LISTENING TEST

In the Listening test, you will be asked to demonstrate how well you understand spoken English. The entire Listening test will last approximately 45 minutes. There are four parts, and directions are given for each part. You must mark your answers on the separate answer sheet. Do not write your answers in your test book.

PART 1

Directions: For each question in this part, you will hear four statements about a picture in your test book. When you hear the statements, you must select the one statement that best describes what you see in the picture. Then find the number of the question on your answer sheet and mark your answer. The statements will not be printed in your test book and will be spoken only one time.

Statement (C), "They're sitting at a table," is the best description of the picture, so you should select answer (C) and mark it on your answer sheet.

Listening

1.

2.

GO ON TO THE NEXT PAGE →

3.

4.

5.

6.

GO ON TO THE NEXT PAGE

PART 2

Directions: You will hear a question or statement and three responses spoken in English. They will not be printed in your test book and will be spoken only one time. Select the best response to the question or statement and mark the letter (A), (B), or (C) on your answer sheet.

7. Mark your answer on your answer sheet.

8. Mark your answer on your answer sheet.

9. Mark your answer on your answer sheet.

10. Mark your answer on your answer sheet.

11. Mark your answer on your answer sheet.

12. Mark your answer on your answer sheet.

13. Mark your answer on your answer sheet.

14. Mark your answer on your answer sheet.

15. Mark your answer on your answer sheet.

16. Mark your answer on your answer sheet.

17. Mark your answer on your answer sheet.

18. Mark your answer on your answer sheet.

19. Mark your answer on your answer sheet.

20. Mark your answer on your answer sheet.

21. Mark your answer on your answer sheet.

22. Mark your answer on your answer sheet.

23. Mark your answer on your answer sheet.

24. Mark your answer on your answer sheet.

25. Mark your answer on your answer sheet.

26. Mark your answer on your answer sheet.

27. Mark your answer on your answer sheet.

28. Mark your answer on your answer sheet.

29. Mark your answer on your answer sheet.

30. Mark your answer on your answer sheet.

31. Mark your answer on your answer sheet.

PART 3

Directions: You will hear some conversations between two or more people. You will be asked to answer three questions about what the speakers say in each conversation. Select the best response to each question and mark the letter (A), (B), (C), or (D) on your answer sheet. The conversations will not be printed in your test book and will be spoken only one time.

32. Where does the conversation most likely take place?

(A) In a gym
(B) In a car store
(C) In a management company
(D) In a bank

33. What does the man inquire about?

(A) A location
(B) A fee
(C) Business hours
(D) A credit card

34. What will the man probably do later?

(A) Charge a fee
(B) Return a membership card
(C) Read a brochure
(D) Fill out forms

35. What does the woman want to do with the plant?

(A) Put it in her kitchen
(B) Put it on her balcony
(C) Give it to her daughter
(D) Use it in a recipe

36. Why does the man recommend a particular type of plant?

(A) It is on sale.
(B) It does not need sunshine.
(C) It is easy to take care of.
(D) It repels insects.

37. What does the man offer to do?

(A) Give the woman a discount
(B) Show the woman around the garden
(C) Take the woman to the pot section
(D) Give the woman a brochure on gardening

GO ON TO THE NEXT PAGE

7

38. What type of event is being held?

(A) A training session
(B) A book workshop
(C) A sale
(D) A speaking contest

39. Why is the event postponed?

(A) There are not enough participants.
(B) The speaker needs more time to prepare.
(C) The speaker does not speak English.
(D) The speaker cannot arrive on time.

40. What does the man ask the woman to return at the end of the event?

(A) A registration form
(B) An event leaflet
(C) A sample book
(D) A headset

41. What type of business does the woman own?

(A) Water sports
(B) Optical instruments
(C) Furniture
(D) Information Technology

42. According to the woman, what is the best feature of the product?

(A) It has high cost performance.
(B) It resists extreme cold.
(C) It has a large storage.
(D) It is waterproof.

43. What does the man ask the woman to do?

(A) Send him a picture
(B) Send him a sample
(C) Send him an agreement
(D) Send him a deposit

8

44. What will happen this Wednesday?

(A) A client meeting will be cancelled.
(B) A presentation will be given.
(C) New employees will join.
(D) New medicine will be prescribed.

45. What does the woman ask about?

(A) Marsha's reason of absence
(B) The effects of new medicine
(C) The length of the presentation
(D) The listener

46. What does the man ask the woman to check?

(A) What the price of the new medicine will be
(B) When the next meeting will be scheduled
(C) What clients' preference will be
(D) How well the new medicine has gained market share

47. What product does the woman's company manufacture?

(A) Gasoline
(B) Automobiles
(C) Engines
(D) Furniture

48. Why did the woman call the man?

(A) To negotiate a contract
(B) To schedule a meeting
(C) To offer a service
(D) To order certain parts

49. What is the new feature that the man mentioned?

(A) It reduces the noise.
(B) It reduces the cost of production.
(C) It uses environmentally friendly materials.
(D) It saves fuel.

GO ON TO THE NEXT PAGE

50. Who most likely is the man?

(A) A cigarette vendor
(B) A building manager
(C) A customer service representative
(D) A salesman

51. What does the man mean when he says "That's unusual"?

(A) He thinks this problem could cost his job.
(B) He thinks the woman should be complaining to a different person.
(C) He thinks it is a rare problem.
(D) He thinks he needs to check with an expert.

52. Why does the woman think that happened two weeks ago?

(A) It started to get windy.
(B) Her neighbor started to smoke.
(C) Her neighbor cleaned her balcony.
(D) Someone moved into her building.

53. Who most likely is the woman?

(A) A photographer
(B) An illustrator
(C) A tourist
(D) A designer

54. What does the woman ask the man about?

(A) His browsing history
(B) His drawing style
(C) The purpose of the map
(D) The timeline for the work

55. What does the woman say she will do?

(A) Send "sketch" samples
(B) Send "cartoon" samples
(C) Send both the "sketch" and the "cartoon" samples
(D) Send prices for her work

Listening

56. What meeting did David fail to attend?

(A) The annual performance review meeting
(B) The weekly meeting
(C) The project meeting
(D) The HR meeting

57. What does the woman mean when she says "That's no excuse."?

(A) She thinks the man is lying.
(B) She thinks the man is finding fault with her.
(C) She thinks the reasons offered by the man are not persuasive.
(D) She thinks the man lacks strategy.

58. What does the woman suggest the man do?

(A) Change a babysitter
(B) Meet with HR
(C) Take some days off
(D) Organize a seminar

59. What are the speakers mainly discussing?

(A) A tour package
(B) A supply arrangement
(C) A project deadline
(D) A travel article

60. What type of business is the man's company?

(A) Airline
(B) Entertainment
(C) Travel Agency
(D) Media

61. What does the woman mean when she says "Speaking from my own experience"?

(A) She is offering her opinion.
(B) She is being polite.
(C) She is remembering the same feelings on a plane.
(D) She is an expert on travel.

GO ON TO THE NEXT PAGE

11

62. What type of the event is the man trying to apply for?

(A) An internship
(B) A training program
(C) A preparation course for an entrance exam
(D) A concert

63. Look at the graphic. What option will the man most likely select?

(A) Swimming
(B) Tennis
(C) Study Aid
(D) Violin

Options	Time	Fees per person
Swimming	July or August	$240
Tennis	July or August	$260
Study Aid	July or August	$250
Violin	July	$180

64. What will the woman probably do next?

(A) Schedule a meeting
(B) Issue an invoice
(C) Make a deposit
(D) Send course information

65. Look at the graphic. What street address will Linda give Jim?

(A) Dane
(B) Jones
(C) Market
(D) Chandelier

Chandelier, Inc.
Corporate Hotels List

Huntington Hotel	36 Market Street
Vermont Hotel	213 Dane Street
Huntington Beach Hotel	120 Beach Street
Gary Mall Hotel	210 Chandelier Street

66. What will Gary do on the first day of his visit?

(A) Attend an opening ceremony
(B) Change his itinerary
(C) Meet with a client
(D) Cancel an order

67. What does the woman say she will do?

(A) Make a phone call
(B) Pick up a person
(C) Cancel a reservation
(D) Change an itinerary

68. What does the woman want to talk
with the man?

(A) Her class requirements
(B) Her performance
(C) Her availability
(D) Her compensation

69. Why has the schedule been updated?

(A) The gym is being renovated.
(B) The gym users requested the
change.
(C) The gym has added new instructors
(D) The gym has lost several instructors.

70. Look at the graphic. Who will most
likely be asked to take Jean's class as
a substitute instructor?

(A) Leo
(B) Mandy
(C) James
(D) Daisy

Instructor	Class	Time
Leo	Ballet advanced	10:30-11:15 (Thu)
Mandy	Aerobics 1	9:30-10:15 (Thu)
Jean	Aerobics 2	13:00-13:45 (Thu)
James	Aerobics 3	14:00-14:45 (Thu)
Daisy	Ballet basics	15:30-16:15 (Thu)

GO ON TO THE NEXT PAGE

PART 4

Directions: You will hear some talks given by a single speaker. You will be asked to answer three questions about what the speaker says in each talk. Select the best response to each question and mark the letter (A), (B), (C), or (D) on your answer sheet. The talks will not be printed in your test book and will be spoken only one time.

71. What is the workshop trying to promote?

(A) A home appliance
(B) A health food
(C) A detergent
(D) A noise reducer

72. What is the most amazing feature of the product?

(A) It is mobile.
(B) It improves health.
(C) It recycles water.
(D) It removes bacteria.

73. What will the first 100 customers get?

(A) A reduction in price
(B) A coupon
(C) A 30-day free trial
(D) An extended warranty

74. What is Jessica not happy about?

(A) The shampoo's quality
(B) The shampoo's texture
(C) The shampoo's package color
(D) The shampoo's price

75. What did Jessica mean when she said "customers are not rational"?

(A) Customers are shrewd.
(B) Customers do not know which to choose.
(C) Customers need to be coached.
(D) Customers like products which look nice.

76. What will the speaker do tomorrow?

(A) Discuss with the design team
(B) Schedule another meeting with the client
(C) Suggest a new design
(D) Change the shampoo color

77. What is the topic of the announcement?

(A) Opening of the city council
(B) Opening of a seniors' home
(C) Opening of a school
(D) Opening of a handcrafts shop

78. Who is Cathy Holmes?

(A) The best calligrapher in the community
(B) A woman who works as a public speaker
(C) A woman city council member
(D) A woman who used to teach at a university

79. What will happen on Tuesday?

(A) Handouts will be passed out.
(B) Souvenirs will be handed out.
(C) Calligraphy classes will be held.
(D) The city mayor will give a speech.

80. Why does the speaker recommend the Lux membership?

(A) It allows sauna use for the elderly.
(B) It is only a little more expensive than the Standard membership.
(C) It is the most popular membership among sports fanatics.
(D) It allows 24 hour access all year round.

81. When is a Pool member NOT able to use the pool?

(A) Wednesday morning
(B) Wednesday afternoon
(C) Saturday morning
(D) Saturday afternoon

82. What will the speaker do next?

(A) Change the membership fee
(B) Choose a membership
(C) Fill out the membership forms
(D) Send out the membership forms

GO ON TO THE NEXT PAGE

83. What is the purpose of the meeting?

(A) To provide training for the new employees

(B) To explain a new way of doing things

(C) To check attendance at the board meeting

(D) To discuss a plan proposed by a shareholder

84. Why will the company start this policy?

(A) To increase work efficiency in this IT-orientated society

(B) To promote work-life balance among all the employees

(C) To save office rent in case of an emergency

(D) To keep up with other companies in the same industry

85. What must an employee do if he or she wants to work from home?

(A) Install software

(B) Download an attendance form

(C) Change his/her laptop

(D) Obtain approval from a supervisor

86. What is the radio news about?

(A) A museum exhibition

(B) A construction project

(C) An art dealer

(D) A public initiative

87. According to the news, what is true about Mr. Horenz?

(A) He is an architect.

(B) He is a museum owner.

(C) He collects sculptures.

(D) He donated paintings.

88. What will happen to the museum after 18 months?

(A) New paintings will arrive in the museum.

(B) It will increase its ticket price.

(C) It will have virtual Reality facilities.

(D) It will be moved to Central Square.

89. What event is the speaker at?

(A) A memorial service
(B) A cancer seminar
(C) An inauguration of some facility
(D) A press release

90. What does the speaker mean when she mentions "battlefield"?

(A) It means the fight against cancer.
(B) It means a newly discovered cancer.
(C) It means the resources devoted to cancer research.
(D) It means a new cancer medicine.

91. Which of the following will immediately happen after the speaker finishes talking?

(A) There will be a dinner.
(B) There will be an award ceremony.
(C) There will be a speech.
(D) There will be a lab tour.

92. What type of business is the speaker calling?

(A) A diving school
(B) A travel agency
(C) An advertisement agency
(D) A training center

93. Why is the speaker calling?

(A) To make a deposit
(B) To request for a refund
(C) To apply for a course
(D) To inquire about a course

94. Why is the speaker in a hurry?

(A) She will leave the country soon.
(B) She has received no responses.
(C) She is afraid of a price increase.
(D) She needs to pass a test as soon as possible.

GO ON TO THE NEXT PAGE

95. Why does the speaker think the results are credible?

(A) There is no way to know who voted for what.

(B) They had similar survey results the year before.

(C) The results were confirmed by employee interviews.

(D) The survey was analyzed by an expert.

96. Look at the graphic. What is the voting percent of the concern that the speaker wants to address immediately?

(A) 20%

(B) 60%

(C) 15%

(D) 5%

•Employee concerns ·Percent of employees voting yes

Gender discrimination 5%

Difficulty of taking leave 15%

Lack of training 20% 60%

Lack of career path

97. What will the speaker do this afternoon?

(A) Have a meeting

(B) Redo the survey

(C) Promote an employee

(D) Share the survey results

98. What type of product does the speaker's company sell?

(A) Tea

(B) Clothing

(C) Cosmetics

(D) Car

99. Look at the graphic. Which month is the sales refering to?

(A) June

(B) July

(C) August

(D) September

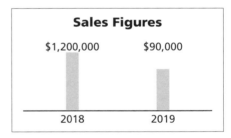

Sales Figures

$1,200,000 $90,000

2018   2019

100. According to the speaker, what is the reason for the drop in sales?

(A) It was extremely hot this summer.

(B) Customers complain about the quality.

(C) There were competing products.

(D) Marketing campaigns were insufficient.

This is the end of the Listening test. Turn to Part 5 in your test book.

GO ON TO THE NEXT PAGE

READING TEST

In the Reading test, you will read a variety of texts and answer several different types of reading comprehension questions. The entire Reading test will last 75 minutes. There are three parts, and directions are given for each part. You are encouraged to answer as many questions as possible within the time allowed.

You must mark your answers on the separate answer sheet. Do not write your answers in your test book.

PART 5

Directions: A word or phrase is missing in each of the sentences below. Four answer choices are given below each sentence. Select the best answer to complete the sentence. Then mark the letter (A), (B), (C), or (D) on your answer sheet.

101. Ms. Wada has run a small shop with ------- own savings since last year.

(A) she
(B) her
(C) hers
(D) herself

102. Construction of our new school building will ------- be completed in two months.

(A) highly
(B) soon
(C) timely
(D) much

103. Mr. Ohara asked the publishing company ------- the deadline for his new series.

(A) extend
(B) will extend
(C) had extended
(D) to extend

104. ------- manufacturing costs have not significantly decreased, Takeda Co. has experienced a sharp fall in its yearly expenditure.

(A) Although
(B) Despite
(C) Because
(D) Owing to

105. When this afternoon's business seminar ends, Dr. Hewitt will have his staff -------.

(A) clean
(B) cleaning
(C) to clean
(D) cleaned

106. Hilltop Hospital used to get a lot of referrals from general practitioners, but it hasn't any -------.

(A) nearly
(B) primarily
(C) lately
(D) constantly

107. Despite a ------- rise in oil prices, demand has stayed the same.

(A) seem
(B) seeming
(C) seemed
(D) seemingly

108. To make the way of paying a bonus clear, overtime work hours must be tracked -------.

(A) randomly
(B) accurately
(C) secretly
(D) probably

109. Ms. Lawrence is ------- to apply for the managerial position at Roseville Ltd.

(A) hesitate
(B) hesitant
(C) hesitated
(D) hesitantly

110. Please make sure that you conclude the deal ------- next week.

(A) toward
(B) over
(C) at
(D) by

111. All AmberCreek's products, including sports gear, ------- by Priority Mail.

(A) shipped
(B) being shipped
(C) are shipped
(D) shipping

112. According to the survey results, most people are ------- that the government plans to impose a higher tax on gasoline.

(A) disappoint
(B) disappointing
(C) disappointed
(D) disappointment

113. ------- caterers charge an extra fee for cups and napkins.

(A) Most of
(B) The most
(C) Almost
(D) Most

114. It will be no easy task to bend that ------- CEO to our will by Friday.

(A) elegant
(B) stubborn
(C) apologetic
(D) accessible

115. Consumers may not even have ------- likes or dislikes at the time of purchase.

(A) notice
(B) noticeable
(C) noticeably
(D) noticing

116. Both the dollar and the euro have fallen ------- the yen this past week because of the coronavirus outbreak.

(A) against
(B) for
(C) into
(D) to

117. Save 15% on every delivery order from Aruku ------- by registering online and entering a coupon code.

(A) simplify
(B) simply
(C) simplicity
(D) simplified

118. Mr. Pak, the new CEO, is ------- to improving his staff's morale to get over this crisis.

(A) commit
(B) commitment
(C) committed
(D) committing

GO ON TO THE NEXT PAGE

Reading

119. Few members of staff ------- in the company retreat, so it has been cancelled.

(A) enrolled
(B) defeated
(C) relieved
(D) excepted

120. The government announced that the ------- adjusted unemployment rate reached 6% in June.

(A) seasonally
(B) seasoned
(C) seasonal
(D) season

121. In the recession, consumers are always ------- closer attention to their spending.

(A) making
(B) asking
(C) paying
(D) holding

122. ------- a bad thing, filing for bankruptcy is a way for the insurance company to survive.

(A) due to
(B) because
(C) except
(D) rather than

123. According to today's news, Henry Auto has made significant ------- in developing on all-electric vehicles.

(A) progress
(B) progression
(C) progressive
(D) progressed

124. Every one of you can purchase any car of your own company in six equal ------- payments.

(A) initiative
(B) installment
(C) appreciation
(D) acquisition

125. We've selected ten people for interviews ------- those who've applied for this position.

(A) as to
(B) of
(C) such as
(D) among

126. Alvinson Group has made a ------- investment in the company, but they think it's time to get out.

(A) skillful
(B) substantial
(C) conditional
(D) numerous

127. Recent research has suggested that the government should be a little more ------- on the new consumption tax.

(A) specifically
(B) specify
(C) specification
(D) specific

128. The latest survey shows that consumer prices have been ------- stable in the last few months.

(A) diligently
(B) productively
(C) relatively
(D) carefully

129. The question is ------- will be the next to go as downsizing continues.

(A) who
(B) those
(C) that
(D) which

130. Entering a recession phase, some companies tend to intentionally ------- for bankruptcy.

(A) apply
(B) suit
(C) search
(D) file

PART 6

Directions: Read the texts that follow. A word, phrase, or sentence is missing in parts of each text. Four answer choices for each question are given below the text. Select the best answer to complete the text. Then mark the letter (A), (B), (C), or (D) on your answer sheet.

Questions 131-134 refer to the following article.

TRAVEL TIPS

One area in which all nationalities seem ------- is in liking privacy when
131.
travelling. Business executives from Hong Kong particularly dislike getting
into conversation with ------- passengers, followed by the British, Americans,
132.
Germans and Singaporeans. ------- They are most ------- of all to chat to their
133.   **134.**
neighbors on a flight.

131. (A) awake
(B) alike
(C) afraid
(D) aware

132. (A) peer
(B) foreign
(C) fellow
(D) elderly

133. (A) Next come the French.
(B) The best example is the French.
(C) The exception seems to be the French.
(D) Of course, the French are among them.

134. (A) likeness
(B) liking
(C) like
(D) likely

GO ON TO THE NEXT PAGE

Reading

Dear Joan,

Thank you very much for your inquiry and the interest you ------- in our firm the
135.
other day. ------- If you do not do so by June 30, we will assume you no longer
136.
wish to ------- for possible employment opportunities. Please do not call,
137.
------- at present we are not in a position to discuss details of possible employment
138.
opportunities.

Again, thank you for your interest in William Royce Associates.

Sincerely,
Keith Mackenzie
H. R. Director

---

135. (A) showed
(B) show
(C) have shown
(D) showing

136. (A) Last year you expressed you were
interested in joining us.
(B) Continued growth of our business
may create a number of new
openings.
(C) I very much look forward to hearing
from you as soon as possible.
(D) If you are still interested in joining
us, please contact us.

137. (A) be considered
(B) consider
(C) consideration
(D) be considerable

138. (A) though
(B) when
(C) because
(D) while

Research has shown that ------- a healthy eating plan can reduce the risk of
139.
------- high blood pressure. Study results indicated that high blood pressure
140.
levels were reduced by an eating plan that focuses ------- fruits, vegetables,
141.
and low-fat dairy foods.

Diet alone, however, is not enough. -------. The best thing is probably to
142.
start gently by walking for 30 minutes at least twice a week.

139. (A) follows
(B) followed
(C) being followed
(D) following

140. (A) developing
(B) avoiding
(C) improving
(D) obtaining

141. (A) to
(B) in
(C) on
(D) for

142. (A) It costs a lot to maintain the family budget.
(B) How about looking for other nutritious food?
(C) How about joining a gym or a health club?
(D) It must be accompanied by regular exercise.

Reading

GO ON TO THE NEXT PAGE

To:	bookbum@info.ne.un
From:	Joanna@b-able.co.jp
Re:	Book request

Dear Sir/Madam,

My father will ------- 70 on August 29 this year, and I would like to buy
143.
him a special gift for the -------. He loves reading novels.
144.
One book that I know he loves is "Snow Country" by Y. Kawabata.

-------. I have no idea how much a first edition of this book would cost,
145.
and so I would be very ------- if you could send me an estimate.
146.
Look forward to hearing from you soon.

Best regards,
Sally Nakamura

143. (A) be
(B) come
(C) turn
(D) become

144. (A) occasion
(B) opportunity
(C) incident
(D) moment

145. (A) I came across an advertisement for your book service on the Internet.
(B) I was wondering if you could find a first edition of this for me.
(C) I would be happy to know the cost will be within my budget.
(D) I'm afraid that it will take a long time to find a good one.

146. (A) thanks
(B) appreciate
(C) grateful
(D) favorable

PART 7

Directions: In this part you will read a selection of texts, such as magazine and newspaper articles, e-mails, and instant messages. Each text or set of texts is followed by several questions. Select the best answer for each question and mark the letter (A), (B), (C), or (D) on your answer sheet.

Questions 147-148 refer to the following advertisement.

NEW STORE OPEN !
312 Hogan Avenue
June 2

We feature second-hand books on literary classics, novels, religion, poetry, painting, photography, architecture, philosophy and critical theory.

We carry books in English, French, Italian, German and Spanish.

Opening ceremony and seminar on June 2:

Harold Winston, author of World Without Maps, will facilitate discussions on the latest trend in contemporary novels.

Coffee, refreshments and book coupons will be provided.

The event is free. We hope to see you there.

---

147. What most likely is World Without Maps?

(A) A book on geography
(B) A book on baking
(C) A book on architecture
(D) A novel

148. What will happen on June 2?

(A) There will be a book signing ceremony.
(B) A new book will be released.
(C) Coupons will be available.
(D) Discounts will be available.

GO ON TO THE NEXT PAGE

Questions 149-150 refer to the following e-mail.

From:	info@mayflowerresort.com
To:	j.swartz@gladmail.com
Subject:	Re: question re-room
Date:	April 23

Mr. Swartz,

Thank you for choosing us. Your reservations of 2 king-size rooms have been completed. Attached please find your reservation details. I am sorry that we don't have museum tours but we do know a travel agency that arranges such tours. If you would like to sign up for a museum tour, please fill out the attached form, and we will pass that to the travel agency.

Thanks,

Alan Douglas
Mayflower Resort

149. What most likely is Mayflower Resort?

(A) An aquarium
(B) A botanic garden
(C) A travel agency
(D) A hotel

150. What should Mr. Swartz do if he wants to join a museum tour?

(A) Make a deposit
(B) Contact a travel agency
(C) Complete a form
(D) Sign a contract

SAN FRANCISCO(May1) — Monsoon has announced today its sale to Mustang, a NY based steakhouse, for 13 million USD. Monsoon has been one of the most successful restaurant chains with over 20 branches in California. Market was caught by surprise.

Monsoon started from a family bakery 60 years ago. Alan Roland, the founder, was only 10 years when his father asked him to help in the family bakery. When Alan was 18, the family bakery was so successful that it has turned itself into a restaurant serving steak meals.

At 25, Alan became the owner of the family restaurant with 3 branches in San Francisco. Two years later he changed the style of the restaurant by making it less fancy while sticking to the principle that its food was unbeatable. Such a move brought the cost down and boosted the profits by 150%. By 2014, Monsoon has become one of the most successful steak chains in California. Alan says he is about to retire and wants to cash out the business. Market speculates other reasons.

151. What does the article indicate about Monsoon?

(A) It started from a family restaurant.
(B) It maintains the principle that food should be delicious.
(C) It succeeded in baking business and Alan became its owner.
(D) It opened its first branch when Alan was 25.

152. How did Alan change the style of Monsoon after he became the owner?

(A) He renovated the restaurant.
(B) He increased the price.
(C) He changed the menu.
(D) He focused on food taste.

153. Which of these did Alan NOT do in his life?

(A) He became a member of the staff of his family bakery when he was very young.
(B) He was asked by his father to help with his business.
(C) Since he was satisfied with his success, Alan wanted to quit his job.
(D) When he was around 27, Alan decided to serve not expensive but delicious food at his restaurant.

Reading

GO ON TO THE NEXT PAGE

To:	Catherine Leeds
From:	Lucy Geller
Subject:	Re: new open position
Date:	May 2

Dear Catherine,

My name is Lucy Geller and I'm a lead recruiter with Talent, Inc.
I'm currently looking to fill a position of a customer service specialist in a real estate company based in Boston and I am wondering if you may be interested in this position.
In this role, you will work as a customer service specialist in a famous real estate company and handle requests from customers on daily bases.

Client's requirements on the candidate:
A collaborative mindset;
Highly responsive in dealing with repetitive requests; and
Attentive to details and highly organized.

If you are interested in the above position, please let me know.

Thanks,
Lucy

154. Why was the e-mail written?

(A) To sell a service
(B) To respond to a customer complaint
(C) To encourage the recipient to apply for a job
(D) To describe an employee benefit

155. What is suggested of Talent, Inc.?

(A) It is a real estate company.
(B) It is based in Boston.
(C) It is a headhunter company.
(D) It is looking to hire a specialist.

From:	alumni@winston.edu
To:	s.heathcliff@gladmail.com
Date:	May12 2020
Subject:	Join us in ocean talk

Dear alumni:

The Winston Environmental Society invites fellow Winston alumni for a discussion on:

Plastics in Ocean and Our Responses
Led by Professor Mark Cohen
Wednesday, May 20, 2020
12:00pm
Boom Webinar

Professor Cohen will give remarks and take questions on issues such as impact of plastics dumping, state(federal) orders on ocean protection, ethical issues regarding over-fishing, latest technology on plastics disposal and many other interesting issues that we face at this moment. Professor Cohen is an alumni of Winston. He majored in Biotechnology & Bioethics. Since 2010, he has been a professor at Lincoln University for 10 years.
Professor Cohen has published over 30 articles on ocean protection and is one of the world's leading experts on ocean environmental issues.
Cohen is the author, co-author, editor, or co-editor of more than fifteen books.

Register for Virtual Talk
Advanced registration required
The event link will be included in your confirmation email.
Questions? Please email info@winston.alumni.edu.

---

156. What is the purpose of the e-mail?

(A) To invite people to a web seminar
(B) To call for donation for ocean protection
(C) To introduce a professor
(D) To reduce plastic dumping

157. What is suggested about Professor Cohen?

(A) He majored in ocean protection.
(B) He graduated from Winston.
(C) He is now teaching in Winston.
(D) He makes environmental policies.

158. What is suggested about the recipient of the e-mail?

(A) He/She is a Winston alumni.
(B) He/She is a student of Prof. Cohen.
(C) He/She is co-author with Prof. Cohen.
(D) He/She provides webinar services.

Reading

GO ON TO THE NEXT PAGE

Questions 159-160 refer to the following text-message chain.

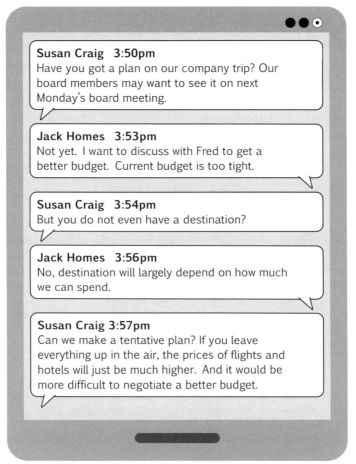

Susan Craig   3:50pm
Have you got a plan on our company trip? Our board members may want to see it on next Monday's board meeting.

Jack Homes   3:53pm
Not yet. I want to discuss with Fred to get a better budget. Current budget is too tight.

Susan Craig   3:54pm
But you do not even have a destination?

Jack Homes   3:56pm
No, destination will largely depend on how much we can spend.

Susan Craig 3:57pm
Can we make a tentative plan? If you leave everything up in the air, the prices of flights and hotels will just be much higher. And it would be more difficult to negotiate a better budget.

159. Why doesn't Jack have a destination?

(A) He doesn't know about the board meeting.
(B) He doesn't have enough time to work on it.
(C) He is split between various choices.
(D) He thinks he can get a revised budget.

160. What does Susan most likely mean when she writes "if you leave everything up in the air"?

(A) She means "if Jack leaves everything at high prices".
(B) She means "if Jack leaves everything undecided".
(C) She means "if Jack leaves everything to the board meeting".
(D) She means "if Jack leaves everything behind".

"When I first started the business, I never thought we would become this big."

After Cynthia Harrow lost her factory job in 2009, she started to think about how she could support her family financially. —[1]— Being a single mother with two children, she had to find a way to generate income.

She started making healthy cookies. To reduce fat, she used fruit purees instead of butter, and egg whites instead of yolks. —[2]— She first sold the cookies online. When she learned that her cookies were highly welcomed, she rented a corner in a local supermarket to sell her cookies. In 2011, she opened her own cookie store.

In 2012, one of her daughters was diagnosed with type 1 diabetes, a disease that requires the restriction of sugar and carb intake. Cynthia started to make sugar and carb free cookies.

She knew that to do so she needed to get rid of the flour, the basic ingredient for almost all cookies.

After many trials, she finally found the best ingredient. —[3]— Her daughter tasting the almond cookies, predicted that these cookies would just sell themselves.

Cynthia's almond cookies soon became popular among weight watchers. Sale rocketed. By 2014, her business went from two employees to 56. —[4]— "It was stressful, but it was awesome" said Cynthia. Today Cynthia sells 40,000 almond cookies a day, all based on her 8-year-old recipe, which she refuses to change. "People kept saying adding this or adding that to my cookies but I don't want to change something that was signed off by my daughter. I love her. I respect her judgement."

161. How did Cynthia sell her cookies at first?

(A) Via her friends
(B) Via a supermarket corner
(C) Via the Internet
(D) Via her daughter

162. Why did Cynthia change the basic ingredient of the cookies?

(A) Her daughter had a disease that restricts carb intake.
(B) She wanted to reduce fat in the cookies.
(C) She wanted to cater to her customers' preferences.
(D) She wanted to follow the latest trend in healthy food.

163. Why does Cynthia refuse to change her current recipe?

(A) This recipe is the best-seller.
(B) This recipe is popular with weight watchers.
(C) This recipe is made by her daughter.
(D) This recipe is liked by her daughter.

164. In which of the following positions marked [1],[2],[3], and [4] does the following sentence belong?

"She used almond powder to replace the flour."

(A) [1]
(B) [2]
(C) [3]
(D) [4]

GO ON TO THE NEXT PAGE

Reading

Questions 165-167 refer to the following email notice.

From:	general affairs@abe.com
To:	All employees
Subject:	Notice of Fire Drill
Date:	Oct.23

We are having a fire drill on November 13. Participation of employees (including managers and executives) is required.

The fire drill is conducted in order for employees to confirm evacuation site and routes so that they can safely evacuate, and for a workplace disaster prevention team to reconfirm their roles in case of disasters such as fire.
Please find the details of the drill below:

1. Time & Date: From 16:00 to 17:00 on November 13(Tue)
2. Participants: all full-time and part-time employees, excluding clients or guest and those who are with them. Please have a few persons stay at the offices on each floor for telephone calls.
3. Flow and roles of the drill: please refer to the attached "Outline of Nov13 Fire Drill.xls" for details.
4. Registration: to ensure participation, you will need to register your name in the building lobby when you arrive there at the end of the drill.

For any questions, please contact us by replying to this e-mail.

Thanks,
Sandy Lim
General Affairs

---

165. What will most likely happen on November 13?

(A) There will be no one in the office.
(B) There will be a speech on fire prevention.
(C) There will be a fire inspection.
(D) There will be a name registration stand in the lobby.

166. What is the purpose of the drill?

(A) To identify the cause of fire
(B) To eliminate the cause of fire
(C) To confirm that fire prevention facilities are working
(D) To confirm routes to leave the bulding in case of fire

167. Who should remain in the office during the drill?

(A) Clients
(B) Executives
(C) Managers
(D) Part-time employees

The summer drink of choice in Melos Verma, Mexico is Coolsprite, a beer-flavored soda commonly sold in glass bottles.

—[1]— Taco House, known for its creative desserts and drinks, is releasing a new drink made from Coolsprite called Summer Passion. Starting from July 1, children and adults in Melos Verna craving for innovative cool summer drinks can try this new creation. Summer Passion is a mixture of Coolsprite and lemonade.

It has four flavors to choose from: mint, peach, plum and green tea. —[2]— The drink is sold in limited quantities and only during July and August. A medium size goes for 100 pesos.

—[3]— Taco House had been a local chain offering traditional Mexican tacos until bought by a Japanese fast food chain Moriasa in 2013. The acquisition turned the taco shop to a full fast food store serving burgers, sandwiches, fries, chickens, and various drinks such as shakes and juices. "We didn't expect the acquisition would turn the taco shop to such a huge success, but it did thanks to the Japanese elements brought in", said David Demarco, market analyst with a local food journal. —[4] — Since the acquisition the Japanese fast food chain has introduced flavors such as plum and green tea. Consumers were fascinated by the distinctive Japanese flavors that they had not had a chance to savor.

168. What is suggested of Summer Passion?

(A) It is a traditional Mexico drink.
(B) It contains lemonade.
(C) It is a popular winter drink.
(D) It is sold in glass bottles.

169. Which of the following is closest in meaning to "innovative" in the 2nd paragraph?

(A) Original
(B) Traditional
(C) Exotic
(D) Fresh

170. What is the most likely reason for the success of the acquisition?

(A) A traditional drink was used.
(B) A variety of items were served.
(C) A new menu was introduced.
(D) Exotic flavors were introduced.

171. In which of the following positions marked [1], [2], [3], and [4] does the following sentence belong?

"Now, Coolsprite is getting a new life."
(A) [1]
(B) [2]
(C) [3]
(D) [4]

GO ON TO THE NEXT PAGE

Reading

Questions 172-175 refer to the following online discussion.

Online Chat

Customer Service (2:34pm): Hello, my name is Ada. I'm at your service today. How can I help you?

Mia Portman (2:34pm): I ordered three cans of rose tea on June 5. The packaged arrived today with two of the three cans broken.

Customer Service (2:35pm): Sorry to hear that. Can I have your telephone number?

Mia Portman (2:36pm): Yes. 617-3363-9222.

Customer Service (2:36pm): OK, one moment please.......OK, I've got your order now. It is 3 cans of Aroma Rose Tea, right?

Mia Portman (2:39pm): Yes. Two of the cans were broken. I'm sending you a picture now. I took it when I opened the package.

[Picture loading]

Customer Service (2:40pm): We are very sorry about the broken cans. When we shipped the tea, the cans were not broken. It seems that something happened during the shipment.

Mia Portman (2:41pm): Whether it's because of you or the courier company, I didn't get what I paid for. Could you re-deliver 2 new cans?

Customer Service (2:42pm): We are very sorry. Yes, we can send you two new cans of Aroma Rose Tea.

Mia Portman (2:42pm): When can you deliver?

Customer Service (2:43pm): Let me check. Oh, sorry we do not have Aroma Rose Tea in stock right now and they will not available for another 3-4 weeks.

Mia Portman (2:43pm): That's too bad. I will be out of town in two weeks and I need to take the rose tea with me.

Customer Service (2:45pm): How about changing to our Jasmine Tea? They are of the same price and we have stock right now.

Mia Portman (2:45pm): Not left with much choice.

---

172. Why does Mia contact Customer Service?

(A) To return an item
(B) To request for expedited shipment
(C) To report a problem with an order
(D) To revise an order

173. What is suggested about the package?

(A) It was delivered to the wrong address.
(B) It was delayed.
(C) It contained broken items.
(D) It contained wrong items.

174. Why does Mia send the picture?

(A) To show the problem
(B) To show shipment progress
(C) To request for refund
(D) To provide order number

175. What does Mia mean when she writes "not left with much choice"?

(A) Only Jasmin Tea is the same price as Rose Tea.
(B) Her choice of tea is limited.
(C) She should have chosen another store.
(D) She has to accept the proposal given the circumstances.

http://www.orchidfootwear.com/home/

At Orchid Footwear, we design our shoes to bring you comfort, so if they're not working exactly right for you, we've got you covered. Whether you shop on orchidfootwear.com or in an Orchid Footwear Store, you can have a 20-day "trial wear" with your purchases. This means that you can return any item (EXCEPT items on sale) for any reason within those 20 days if you are uncomfortable wearing them. We want you to shop with confidence.

Now through March 25, items purchased online are "buy-one-get-one 50% off. And for items here, you can save 5% on orders of $99 or more by entering the promotion code "ORCHIDDEAL" at your online checkout. Note that invoices for all sale items are only provided online through downloading.

Separately, we are having a boots sale (with maximum discount up to 50%) at our following stores until April 10:

124 Ellis Avenue, Marilyn Drive Check it out today!

Reading

GO ON TO THE NEXT PAGE

From:	r.holmes@gladmail.com
To:	customerservice@orchidfootwear.com
Date:	March 20
Subject:	return of sneakers

I'm writing to share my unpleasant experience at your store on Ellis Avenue. Last Friday, I bought a pair of sneakers there. I had seen the free trial wear on your website earlier so I thought I could try the sneakers and have the opportunity to return them if they wouldn't fit.

It turned out that this pair of sneakers was indeed not comfortable. So I went to your store yesterday with the receipt. But I was told I could not return the sneakers. I asked to talk to the store manager, but was told that the manager was not there.

Attached is a picture of my receipt. Please let me know how I can return the sneakers.

Thanks,
Rachel Holmes

From:	customerservice@orchidfootwear.com
To:	r.holmes@gladmail.com
Date:	March 22
Subject:	Re: return of sneakers

Hi, Rachel,

We are very very sorry for your experience. We checked the item on your receipt and found that it was an item on sale. Sale items do not enjoy the 20-day free trial wear. If you had taken notice of the phrase 'EXCEPT items on sale', you would have got it. We are sorry if our store staff didn't explain clearly to you. Since the sneakers do not enjoy the free trial wear, they cannot be returned unless it is due to a quality issue. But you can change to a different size of the same sneakers. Or alternatively you can return the sneakers in exchange of store credits at 80% of the price.

Once again we apologize for the inconvenience. We hope you will shop with us again.

Sincerely,

Samantha Hills
Customer Services
Orchid Footwear

176. What is suggested about Orchid Footwear?

(A) It is an online shoe store.
(B) It can change shoes to fit customers' needs.
(C) It allows sale items to be returned within 20 days.
(D) It will give Rachel coupons with 20% discount.

177. Why did Rachel request to speak with the store manager?

(A) She wanted to return her purchase without receipt.
(B) She wanted to inquire about the return policy.
(C) She wanted to change the return policy.
(D) She was not convinced.

178. Which of the following is closest in meaning to "we've got you covered" in the first paragraph on the webpage?

(A) We will take care of your needs.
(B) We will give you discounts.
(C) We will show you a variety of shoes.
(D) We will extend footwear warranty.

179. What is "ORCHIDDEAL"?

(A) It is a code for online purchase.
(B) It is a code for online log in.
(C) It is a code for discounts.
(D) It is a code for invoices download.

180. What is suggested of the boots sale?

(A) It is only available in March.
(B) Boots sale requires a minimum purchase of $99 to qualify for discounts.
(C) Rachel bought the sneakers in the store where there was a boots sale.
(D) 5% of the items in the boots sale are half price.

GO ON TO THE NEXT PAGE

From:	a wager@halis.fr.com
To:	All Instructors
Date:	November 25
Subject:	Dec. class and Oct. newsletter

Dear Instructors,

Time flies! There is only a month left this year. Please find attached or class schedules of December. Thanks to new instructors on board, we are adding the following new classes in December.

— French
— Chinese
— Piano

New students:

— Sophie Kurt & Mary Kurt (twins; both 5-year-old) will join on Dec.1
— James Harris (6-year-old) will join on Dec. 2

Also attached is our October Newsletter.

In order to make our November newsletter, could you send me the following?:

— What did the students learn at your class in November?
— What are the students going to learn in December?

It would be helpful if you send them to me by Thursday 28th. Parents have really been fond of our newsletters, and they have asked for more!

By the way, thank you for sending me your professional photos. We have completed processing them and they will be displayed at our entrance and on our website from Monday next week.

Thank you,
Anna

Halis Newsletter-October

Hello Parents! Discover our exciting month at Halis!
Below is what the children learned in October and what they are going to learn in November (marked "coming up")!

Yoga: learned Halloween poses and yoga music
Coming up: crane pose, tree pose and ball pose

Spanish: learned fruit names, and body parts such as hand, eye, nose
Coming up: numbers 10-20, seasons, vegetables

Programming: learned simple games, shapes, bridge building
Coming up: chess games, programming for a shopping mall

Art: explored oil painting
Coming up: paper folding, clay shaping

Math/Science: learned clocks, counting, played floating games
Coming up: moon and earth; bubble games

181. What is Halis?

(A) A language school
(B) A yoga studio
(C) A news agency
(D) An educational facility

182. Why are new classes added to December?

(A) Because new students have joined.
(B) Because new teachers have joined.
(C) Because parents are fond of new classes.
(D) Because teachers of some existing classes have left.

183. What does Anna ask the instructors to do in her email?

(A) Send professional photos
(B) Upload photos to website
(C) Send December Newsletter
(D) Send November activities

184. Which of the following did children learn in October?

(A) Spanish words for body parts
(B) French words for fruits
(C) Crane poses in Yoga
(D) Chess games

185. According to the newsletter, which of the following are children going to learn in November?

(A) Spanish words for seasons
(B) French words for vegetables
(C) Oil painting
(D) Piano classes

GO ON TO THE NEXT PAGE

Reading

http://www.lacorelos.com

Welcome to La Corelos

A TROPICAL PARADISE.
A SECLUDED LUXURIOUS EXPERIENCE.

La Corelos is an exclusive beach resort to the north of Verto Polos, Mexico.

Accessible only by boat and nestled between the green tropical mountains, La Corelos is truly a paradise found. It is an unexplored gem.

We have rooms with spectacular ocean views or forest view. All rooms are decorated with local Mexican artwork and equipped with the best of amenities including Wi-Fi, flat screen TVs, air-conditioning, and private bath tubs. We provide daily housing and complementary laundry services as well.

Our recently renovated resort has added a new spa area and a gym! Click here for a quick view.

La Corelos is unique in that it is one of the best wedding and honeymoon destinations in Mexico. Either a magnificent celebration or an intimate family gathering, we help you realize your dream wedding here. Imagine your vows to be exchanged on a garden terrace overlooking the ocean or surrounded by cascading waterfalls!

Click here to see galleries of our wedding celebrations.

Book your wedding package today!

Email us at info@lacorelosresort.com for any questions you may have.

La Corelos
Activities Brochure

- **Snorkeling**—Snorkeling equipment is provided(snorkes, masks and fins).
- **Parasailing***—2 beaches Verto Polosa and Hosona offer parasailing.
- **Kayaking**—5 kayaks are available on the beach for your use.
- **Scuba diving***—Scuba lessons on site(we provide certification)
- **Waterfall hikes**—Check out our amazing waterfalls on a hiking tour.
- **Yoga lessons***—We have plenty of spaces for yoga and instructors can be arranged.
- **Yacht excursions***—We take you to explore the bay by yacht; wine on board!
- **Whale watching(seasonal)***—Humpback whales can be spotted December-April.
- **Sailing courses***—Learn to sail with our certified instructors and explore the nearby beaches by sailboat.
- **Fishing trips(seasonal)***—Charter a boat and bring back dinner! Available June-November.
- **Wine tasting**—Tasting experiences may be arranged at La Fort, award-winning local winery
- **Day trips to Verto Polosa**—About a 20-minute trip from hotel; local art village

Activities with * require advance booking.
Activities without * can be signed up for a front desk.

GO ON TO THE NEXT PAGE ➡

From:	info@lacorelosresort.com
To:	s.doghlas@gladmail.com
Date:	June 8
Subject:	Re: romantic package

Hi, Sophia,

Thank you for booking our romantic package with us. We're thrilled about your upcoming wedding at our hotel next week.

We actually have a campaign from now to the end of June. The campaign allows you to include three activities into your wedding package for free. Regarding the activities, take a look at the attached brochure. Please let me know what three activities you want to include in your package. Note that sailing course and any seasonal activities are not available during the campaign period.

Thank you for sending us your flight information. Note that the boat from your arrival airport to our island takes about 3 hours by boat. Last, could you confirm if you require any vegetarian meal during your stay with us?

Sincerely,
Jose Antonio

---

186. Which of the following is closest in meaning to "nestled" as appearing in the webpage?

(A) located
(B) covered
(C) decorated
(D) injected

187. Which of the following can the newly couple join without booking?

(A) Scuba diving
(B) Yacht excursions
(C) Waterfall hikes
(D) Sailing courses

188. What activity cannot be included into Sophia's wedding package?

(A) Fishing trips
(B) Parasailing
(C) Day trips to Verto polosa
(D) Yacht excursions

189. What does Jose ask Sophia to provide?

(A) Credit card number
(B) Flight number
(C) Arrival airport
(D) Food preference

190. Which is true of this package tour?

(A) Participants of this tour can directly fly to the resort.
(B) Guest staying at La Corelos can receive a laundry service for a small fee.
(C) You can enjoy yacht excursions, but drinking on board is prohibited.
(D) The newly couple are visiting the resort in the middle of June.

(Boston June 12)—After more than 40 years in business, Le Candy closed its last location in Lincoln Square last week.

The Lincoln Square Le Candy — located at 57 Hanson Avenue — is the flagship store of the originally Boston-based bakery-cafe, which is now based in New York, operating 6 stores in Massachusetts and 8 stores in California. Le Candy serves an array of coffee, soups, baked goods, and sandwiches.

The bakery-cafe was founded in 1985 by Mark Stevens, a coffee and soup lover and MBA graduate from Lincoln University, located just 3 blocks from the flagship cafe. It was acquired by Aroma Cafe, a New York based cafe shop, in late 2007. Since the acquisition, Le Candy has kept its name When asked the plan for its New York stores, Cindy Walworth, CEO of Aroma Cafe, said "We just want to consolidate our domestic operations to New York. We are reforming the style of our New York stores and we expect to bring a brand-new cafe concept to our customers in next year."

Customers said they were sad to see the popular chain go. Allie Harris, a patron of the chain in Boston, said that she relied on Le Candy for its cream pea soup.

Now she misses that every morning.

NOTICE OF STORE CLOSE

Dear customers,

We are deeply sad to inform you that Le Candy Lincoln Square is closing. For operational reasons, we have made the most difficult decision to close this store. We sincerely apologize for any inconvenience that you may have. We also want to thank all of our loyal and dedicated customers for your patronage over the years. As we leave Boston, we hope you will continue to support us. Please visit our stores in New York. We will have a sale of our stock items (from 20% off to 60% off) on the last Saturday of May from 10am to 3pm. Sale items include baking ingredients and utensils. Again we want to thank all of our wonderful customers who spend mornings with us in sun or in rain. It has been a pleasure to serve you. Our last day of operation here at Lincoln Square will be June 1 Monday.

Le Candy, Lincoln Square

GO ON TO THE NEXT PAGE

Reading

From:	l.smith@springland.com
To:	m.wong@lecandy.com
Date:	May 28 2019
Subject:	Re: termination of lease

Hi, Mindy,

I'm sorry to hear that you are closing your store. Your notice of lease termination on May 27 is acknowledged and we confirm that you will vacate the premise by June 2.

Last month in our property check, we noticed some stains on the kitchen wall. We hope you would have removed those by the end of this week.

Also, our property manager has indicated to us that the premise slightly smell butter. As our next tenant is likely to go a fashion tenant, we do hope that you could do something to remove the smell. We know a few really good cleaners with reasonable price. Attached, please find their name cards. Hope these would be helpful.

Thanks,
Linda

191. According to Le Candy, what will most likely happen to the New York store?

(A) They will be moved.
(B) They will be renovated.
(C) They will be sold.
(D) They will be consolidated into one store.

192. What is suggested of Mark Stevens?

(A) He added the cream pea soup to the menu of Le Candy.
(B) He acquired Le Candy and expanded its business.
(C) He moved the head office of Le Candy to New York.
(D) He studied near Le Candy.

193. When can a person buy discounted baking powder at Le Candy?

(A) May 30
(B) May 31
(C) June 1
(D) June 2

194. What is the purpose of the email from Linda?

(A) She feels sad to hear the cafe is gone.
(B) She hopes to make the tenant change his mind.
(C) She wants the premise to be as clean as before.
(D) She'd like to introduce another real estate agent.

195. Why does Linda send name cards to Mindy?

(A) She wants to help the store remove the smell.
(B) She wants the store to remove the burn marks.
(C) She wants the store to find another premise.
(D) She wants to inform the store of a potential future tenant.

TRAINING COURSES
Managing Aggression in the Workplace

Course Organizer: Devere Training and Development

Cost and Length: $750;two days

Aimed at: Anyone who has to manage difficult or aggressive staff or who is struggling to manage his or her own aggressive behavior.

What You Learn: How to identify and deal with aggressive behavior from colleagues in the workplace. Participants are also offered ways to deal with their own behavior if they are finding it difficult to control aggression. The course encourages the exploration of alternative ways of communicating and behaving. Participants will also discuss the consequences of not dealing with such problems.

Next Course: March 5th and 6th

Information: www.devere.com

Reading

GO ON TO THE NEXT PAGE

From: David Sinclair, ATC Travel H.R.
To: Devere Training and Development
Re: Training course

To whom it is concerned,

I've been having a problem with one of the staff in my department—Mr. X. He's
one of the most knowledgeable people there, and he's quick and efficient. The
problem is that he's also one of the most impatient people I've ever worked with.
If he thinks people on his team are working too slowly, he gets very annoyed
with them, and often loses his temper. He's also very intolerant of colleagues
who know less than he does. I think his co-workers are now afraid to ask him
questions because he always answers them so rudely. I've tried talking to him
one-one-one on several occasions, but I can't seem to solve the problem. So I'd
like to attend this course in order to find some solutions to this matter.

David Sinclair, ATC Travel H.R.

From: Linda Slove, President, Devere T.D.
To: David Sinclair, ATC Travel H.R.
Re: Welcome to our TRAINING COURSES

Hi, David,

Thank you for your letter. I've understood your worry. Please come and join us.
If you attend this course, you'll surely learn how to deal with that kind of problem
staying calm.
Here's a Course Director's Comment:
"Participants will gain a clear understanding of what drives the aggressive
impulse and how they can manage their own behavior, and the behavior of others,
more effectively."

See you soon,

Linda Slove
President, Devere T.D.

196. What is NOT a feature of the training course?

(A) How to manage other people's aggressive behavior
(B) How to manage one's own aggressive behavior
(C) How to become a more aggressive manager
(D) How to understand what causes aggressive behavior

197. What methods does the course teach for solving the problem of aggression?

(A) Finding aggressive people
(B) Using different communication methods
(C) Giving people a different job
(D) Offering psychological counseling

198. What dose Mr. Sinclair want to do?

(A) He wants to organize a course in his company.
(B) He wants to ask Mr. X to attend the course.
(C) He wants to attend the course himself.
(D) He wants to contact the Director.

199. What's Mr. X's problem?

(A) He doesn't want to attend the course.
(B) He didn't read the Director's comment beforehand.
(C) He's not a competent worker.
(D) He doesn't work well with colleagues.

200. Which word is closest in meaning to "consequences" in the advertisement, "What You Learn"?

(A) Reactions
(B) Causes
(C) Results
(D) Decisions

Stop! This is the end of the test. If you finish before time is called, you may go back to Parts 5, 6, and 7 and check your work.

Reading

リーディングテスト全体は75分ですが、900点レベルの人以外、全部は絶対に手が出せないということを理解していないといけません。あなたのねらいは4割ですか、5割ですか、それとも6割ですか？しっかり自分に言い聞かせてから試験に入るべきです。

　本書を使って［聴く勉］をしてから本番に臨むだけで、今までのあなたの点を50〜100点は上回るはずです。また、時間があれば、公式問題集をどれか1つ"山根メソッド"でやっておくと、かなり楽しく受験できるはずです！　皆さんの感想メールを待っています。

yamane@yamaguchi-u.ac.jp
山口大学経済学部教授（特命）山根和明

Answer Sheet

TOEIC® L&R テスト全パート対策スピードマスター

Chapter2 完全模試解答用紙

フリガナ

NAME 氏名

LISTENING SECTION

Part 1

No.	ANSWER (A B C D)
1	Ⓐ Ⓑ Ⓒ Ⓓ
2	Ⓐ Ⓑ Ⓒ Ⓓ
3	Ⓐ Ⓑ Ⓒ Ⓓ
4	Ⓐ Ⓑ Ⓒ Ⓓ
5	Ⓐ Ⓑ Ⓒ Ⓓ
6	Ⓐ Ⓑ Ⓒ Ⓓ
7	Ⓐ Ⓑ Ⓒ
8	Ⓐ Ⓑ Ⓒ
9	Ⓐ Ⓑ Ⓒ
10	Ⓐ Ⓑ Ⓒ

Part 2

No.	ANSWER (A B C)
11	Ⓐ Ⓑ Ⓒ
12	Ⓐ Ⓑ Ⓒ
13	Ⓐ Ⓑ Ⓒ
14	Ⓐ Ⓑ Ⓒ
15	Ⓐ Ⓑ Ⓒ
16	Ⓐ Ⓑ Ⓒ
17	Ⓐ Ⓑ Ⓒ
18	Ⓐ Ⓑ Ⓒ
19	Ⓐ Ⓑ Ⓒ
20	Ⓐ Ⓑ Ⓒ

No.	ANSWER (A B C)
21	Ⓐ Ⓑ Ⓒ
22	Ⓐ Ⓑ Ⓒ
23	Ⓐ Ⓑ Ⓒ
24	Ⓐ Ⓑ Ⓒ
25	Ⓐ Ⓑ Ⓒ
26	Ⓐ Ⓑ Ⓒ
27	Ⓐ Ⓑ Ⓒ
28	Ⓐ Ⓑ Ⓒ
29	Ⓐ Ⓑ Ⓒ
30	Ⓐ Ⓑ Ⓒ

No.	ANSWER (A B C)
31	Ⓐ Ⓑ Ⓒ
32	Ⓐ Ⓑ Ⓒ Ⓓ
33	Ⓐ Ⓑ Ⓒ Ⓓ
34	Ⓐ Ⓑ Ⓒ Ⓓ
35	Ⓐ Ⓑ Ⓒ Ⓓ
36	Ⓐ Ⓑ Ⓒ Ⓓ
37	Ⓐ Ⓑ Ⓒ Ⓓ
38	Ⓐ Ⓑ Ⓒ Ⓓ
39	Ⓐ Ⓑ Ⓒ Ⓓ
40	Ⓐ Ⓑ Ⓒ Ⓓ

Part 3

No.	ANSWER (A B C D)
41	Ⓐ Ⓑ Ⓒ Ⓓ
42	Ⓐ Ⓑ Ⓒ Ⓓ
43	Ⓐ Ⓑ Ⓒ Ⓓ
44	Ⓐ Ⓑ Ⓒ Ⓓ
45	Ⓐ Ⓑ Ⓒ Ⓓ
46	Ⓐ Ⓑ Ⓒ Ⓓ
47	Ⓐ Ⓑ Ⓒ Ⓓ
48	Ⓐ Ⓑ Ⓒ Ⓓ
49	Ⓐ Ⓑ Ⓒ Ⓓ
50	Ⓐ Ⓑ Ⓒ Ⓓ

No.	ANSWER (A B C D)
51	Ⓐ Ⓑ Ⓒ Ⓓ
52	Ⓐ Ⓑ Ⓒ Ⓓ
53	Ⓐ Ⓑ Ⓒ Ⓓ
54	Ⓐ Ⓑ Ⓒ Ⓓ
55	Ⓐ Ⓑ Ⓒ Ⓓ
56	Ⓐ Ⓑ Ⓒ Ⓓ
57	Ⓐ Ⓑ Ⓒ Ⓓ
58	Ⓐ Ⓑ Ⓒ Ⓓ
59	Ⓐ Ⓑ Ⓒ Ⓓ
60	Ⓐ Ⓑ Ⓒ Ⓓ

No.	ANSWER (A B C D)
61	Ⓐ Ⓑ Ⓒ Ⓓ
62	Ⓐ Ⓑ Ⓒ Ⓓ
63	Ⓐ Ⓑ Ⓒ Ⓓ
64	Ⓐ Ⓑ Ⓒ Ⓓ
65	Ⓐ Ⓑ Ⓒ Ⓓ
66	Ⓐ Ⓑ Ⓒ Ⓓ
67	Ⓐ Ⓑ Ⓒ Ⓓ
68	Ⓐ Ⓑ Ⓒ Ⓓ
69	Ⓐ Ⓑ Ⓒ Ⓓ
70	Ⓐ Ⓑ Ⓒ Ⓓ

Part 4

No.	ANSWER (A B C D)
71	Ⓐ Ⓑ Ⓒ Ⓓ
72	Ⓐ Ⓑ Ⓒ Ⓓ
73	Ⓐ Ⓑ Ⓒ Ⓓ
74	Ⓐ Ⓑ Ⓒ Ⓓ
75	Ⓐ Ⓑ Ⓒ Ⓓ
76	Ⓐ Ⓑ Ⓒ Ⓓ
77	Ⓐ Ⓑ Ⓒ Ⓓ
78	Ⓐ Ⓑ Ⓒ Ⓓ
79	Ⓐ Ⓑ Ⓒ Ⓓ
80	Ⓐ Ⓑ Ⓒ Ⓓ

No.	ANSWER (A B C D)
81	Ⓐ Ⓑ Ⓒ Ⓓ
82	Ⓐ Ⓑ Ⓒ Ⓓ
83	Ⓐ Ⓑ Ⓒ Ⓓ
84	Ⓐ Ⓑ Ⓒ Ⓓ
85	Ⓐ Ⓑ Ⓒ Ⓓ
86	Ⓐ Ⓑ Ⓒ Ⓓ
87	Ⓐ Ⓑ Ⓒ Ⓓ
88	Ⓐ Ⓑ Ⓒ Ⓓ
89	Ⓐ Ⓑ Ⓒ Ⓓ
90	Ⓐ Ⓑ Ⓒ Ⓓ

No.	ANSWER (A B C D)
91	Ⓐ Ⓑ Ⓒ Ⓓ
92	Ⓐ Ⓑ Ⓒ Ⓓ
93	Ⓐ Ⓑ Ⓒ Ⓓ
94	Ⓐ Ⓑ Ⓒ Ⓓ
95	Ⓐ Ⓑ Ⓒ Ⓓ
96	Ⓐ Ⓑ Ⓒ Ⓓ
97	Ⓐ Ⓑ Ⓒ Ⓓ
98	Ⓐ Ⓑ Ⓒ Ⓓ
99	Ⓐ Ⓑ Ⓒ Ⓓ
100	Ⓐ Ⓑ Ⓒ Ⓓ

READING SECTION

Part 5

No.	ANSWER (A B C D)
101	Ⓐ Ⓑ Ⓒ Ⓓ
102	Ⓐ Ⓑ Ⓒ Ⓓ
103	Ⓐ Ⓑ Ⓒ Ⓓ
104	Ⓐ Ⓑ Ⓒ Ⓓ
105	Ⓐ Ⓑ Ⓒ Ⓓ
106	Ⓐ Ⓑ Ⓒ Ⓓ
107	Ⓐ Ⓑ Ⓒ Ⓓ
108	Ⓐ Ⓑ Ⓒ Ⓓ
109	Ⓐ Ⓑ Ⓒ Ⓓ
110	Ⓐ Ⓑ Ⓒ Ⓓ

No.	ANSWER (A B C D)
111	Ⓐ Ⓑ Ⓒ Ⓓ
112	Ⓐ Ⓑ Ⓒ Ⓓ
113	Ⓐ Ⓑ Ⓒ Ⓓ
114	Ⓐ Ⓑ Ⓒ Ⓓ
115	Ⓐ Ⓑ Ⓒ Ⓓ
116	Ⓐ Ⓑ Ⓒ Ⓓ
117	Ⓐ Ⓑ Ⓒ Ⓓ
118	Ⓐ Ⓑ Ⓒ Ⓓ
119	Ⓐ Ⓑ Ⓒ Ⓓ
120	Ⓐ Ⓑ Ⓒ Ⓓ

No.	ANSWER (A B C D)
121	Ⓐ Ⓑ Ⓒ Ⓓ
122	Ⓐ Ⓑ Ⓒ Ⓓ
123	Ⓐ Ⓑ Ⓒ Ⓓ
124	Ⓐ Ⓑ Ⓒ Ⓓ
125	Ⓐ Ⓑ Ⓒ Ⓓ
126	Ⓐ Ⓑ Ⓒ Ⓓ
127	Ⓐ Ⓑ Ⓒ Ⓓ
128	Ⓐ Ⓑ Ⓒ Ⓓ
129	Ⓐ Ⓑ Ⓒ Ⓓ
130	Ⓐ Ⓑ Ⓒ Ⓓ

Part 6

No.	ANSWER (A B C D)
131	Ⓐ Ⓑ Ⓒ Ⓓ
132	Ⓐ Ⓑ Ⓒ Ⓓ
133	Ⓐ Ⓑ Ⓒ Ⓓ
134	Ⓐ Ⓑ Ⓒ Ⓓ
135	Ⓐ Ⓑ Ⓒ Ⓓ
136	Ⓐ Ⓑ Ⓒ Ⓓ
137	Ⓐ Ⓑ Ⓒ Ⓓ
138	Ⓐ Ⓑ Ⓒ Ⓓ
139	Ⓐ Ⓑ Ⓒ Ⓓ
140	Ⓐ Ⓑ Ⓒ Ⓓ

Part 7

No.	ANSWER (A B C D)
141	Ⓐ Ⓑ Ⓒ Ⓓ
142	Ⓐ Ⓑ Ⓒ Ⓓ
143	Ⓐ Ⓑ Ⓒ Ⓓ
144	Ⓐ Ⓑ Ⓒ Ⓓ
145	Ⓐ Ⓑ Ⓒ Ⓓ
146	Ⓐ Ⓑ Ⓒ Ⓓ
147	Ⓐ Ⓑ Ⓒ Ⓓ
148	Ⓐ Ⓑ Ⓒ Ⓓ
149	Ⓐ Ⓑ Ⓒ Ⓓ
150	Ⓐ Ⓑ Ⓒ Ⓓ

No.	ANSWER (A B C D)
151	Ⓐ Ⓑ Ⓒ Ⓓ
152	Ⓐ Ⓑ Ⓒ Ⓓ
153	Ⓐ Ⓑ Ⓒ Ⓓ
154	Ⓐ Ⓑ Ⓒ Ⓓ
155	Ⓐ Ⓑ Ⓒ Ⓓ
156	Ⓐ Ⓑ Ⓒ Ⓓ
157	Ⓐ Ⓑ Ⓒ Ⓓ
158	Ⓐ Ⓑ Ⓒ Ⓓ
159	Ⓐ Ⓑ Ⓒ Ⓓ
160	Ⓐ Ⓑ Ⓒ Ⓓ

No.	ANSWER (A B C D)
161	Ⓐ Ⓑ Ⓒ Ⓓ
162	Ⓐ Ⓑ Ⓒ Ⓓ
163	Ⓐ Ⓑ Ⓒ Ⓓ
164	Ⓐ Ⓑ Ⓒ Ⓓ
165	Ⓐ Ⓑ Ⓒ Ⓓ
166	Ⓐ Ⓑ Ⓒ Ⓓ
167	Ⓐ Ⓑ Ⓒ Ⓓ
168	Ⓐ Ⓑ Ⓒ Ⓓ
169	Ⓐ Ⓑ Ⓒ Ⓓ
170	Ⓐ Ⓑ Ⓒ Ⓓ

No.	ANSWER (A B C D)
171	Ⓐ Ⓑ Ⓒ Ⓓ
172	Ⓐ Ⓑ Ⓒ Ⓓ
173	Ⓐ Ⓑ Ⓒ Ⓓ
174	Ⓐ Ⓑ Ⓒ Ⓓ
175	Ⓐ Ⓑ Ⓒ Ⓓ
176	Ⓐ Ⓑ Ⓒ Ⓓ
177	Ⓐ Ⓑ Ⓒ Ⓓ
178	Ⓐ Ⓑ Ⓒ Ⓓ
179	Ⓐ Ⓑ Ⓒ Ⓓ
180	Ⓐ Ⓑ Ⓒ Ⓓ

No.	ANSWER (A B C D)
181	Ⓐ Ⓑ Ⓒ Ⓓ
182	Ⓐ Ⓑ Ⓒ Ⓓ
183	Ⓐ Ⓑ Ⓒ Ⓓ
184	Ⓐ Ⓑ Ⓒ Ⓓ
185	Ⓐ Ⓑ Ⓒ Ⓓ
186	Ⓐ Ⓑ Ⓒ Ⓓ
187	Ⓐ Ⓑ Ⓒ Ⓓ
188	Ⓐ Ⓑ Ⓒ Ⓓ
189	Ⓐ Ⓑ Ⓒ Ⓓ
190	Ⓐ Ⓑ Ⓒ Ⓓ

No.	ANSWER (A B C D)
191	Ⓐ Ⓑ Ⓒ Ⓓ
192	Ⓐ Ⓑ Ⓒ Ⓓ
193	Ⓐ Ⓑ Ⓒ Ⓓ
194	Ⓐ Ⓑ Ⓒ Ⓓ
195	Ⓐ Ⓑ Ⓒ Ⓓ
196	Ⓐ Ⓑ Ⓒ Ⓓ
197	Ⓐ Ⓑ Ⓒ Ⓓ
198	Ⓐ Ⓑ Ⓒ Ⓓ
199	Ⓐ Ⓑ Ⓒ Ⓓ
200	Ⓐ Ⓑ Ⓒ Ⓓ